ROUTLEDGE LIBR
POLITICAL SCIENCE

THE POLITICAL SCIENCES

THE POLITICAL SCIENCES

General Principles of Selection in Social Science and History

By

HUGH STRETTON

Volume 46

Routledge
Taylor & Francis Group

LONDON AND NEW YORK

First published 1969

This edition first published in 2010
by Routledge
2 Park Square, Milton Park, Abingdon, Oxon, OX14 4RN

Simultaneously published in the USA and Canada
by Routledge
711 Third Avenue, New York, NY 10017

First issued in paperback 2012
Routledge is an imprint of the Taylor & Francis Group, an informa business

© 1969 Hugh Stretton

British Library Cataloguing in Publication Data
A catalogue record for this book is available from the British Library

ISBN 13: 978-0-415-49111-2 (Set)

Publisher's Note
The publisher has gone to great lengths to ensure the quality of
this reprint but points out that some imperfections in the original
copies may be apparent.

Disclaimer
The publisher has made every effort to trace copyright holders and
would welcome correspondence from those they have been unable
to trace.

ISBN13: 978-0-415-65257-5 (PBK)
ISBN13: 978-0-415-55587-6 (HBK)

The
Political Sciences

*General principles of selection in
social science and history*

HUGH STRETTON

LONDON

Routledge & Kegan Paul

First published 1969
by Routledge & Kegan Paul Ltd
Broadway House, 68-74 Carter Lane
London EC4

First Published as a Paperback 1972

Printed in Great Britain
by W & J Mackay & Co Ltd
Chatham Kent

ISBN 0 7100 7480 8

Preface

This book is about the mixtures of knowledge, imagination and persuasion to be found in the work of historians and social scientists. They are influential people these days. They advise and staff governments and other institutions and in rich countries they help to educate almost everybody. Most of them teach more than they discover. Their work wants watching, for its increasing social effect.

Obviously, their values affect their work. Facts are facts, but theories order them and explanations select them. The political and professional values of the scientists affect these selections, which also get political direction from technical choices of method. Some nevertheless try to purge the values from the work, and attempt other irrational imitations of the forms of physical science. These efforts are called by their critics 'scientistic'. 'Scientism' flourishes in sociology like cargo cult in Melanesia, invoking magical plenty wherever conventional production is scantiest.

Strict social scientists like to search for the regular, measurable, general and objective facts of social life. Will those principles of selection net much useful understanding of a life which is complex, changing, and sometimes perhaps freely chosen? Softer social scientists think not. What is the difference between the strict scientific methods and their softer rivals? Most of the rivals would allow practical aims and social valuations to guide the detail of the research. Some such intrusion of values is inevitable, but strict scientists keep trying to exclude them, by increasingly curious principles of selection. The worst offenders when misused, sometimes with devastating effect, are various rules of objectivity. These were meant to make observation accurate. They are misapplied to the different business of selecting concepts and identities and classes, and causes and effects.

Value-judgments seem so unscientific that even 'soft' authors are often content to confess them, and critics to detect them, so that readers can discount them. It is worth going further to see just what the valuations do and how they do it, and what the scientistic rules would do instead. It is a conclusion of this study that valuations contribute rationally and indispensably to a wide range of scientific selections and constructions, from the most 'applied' to the most 'pure'. They should be improved, not replaced. Those who teach their students otherwise, corrupt them.

Part 1 looks at the old science before the new rules troubled it much – at history, and other disciplines when they were as hospitable to ideologies and engineering interests as history is still. Part 2 introduces the rival rules of science, and Part 3 examines the rivalry in various examples of history, sociology, political science and elementary economics. 'Social' in the book's subtitle records its neglect of psychology. It adds nothing to the philosophy of history or science, though gratefully borrowing from them and taking sides in their disputes. Its method includes similar questioning of examples from book after book, with some tedious repetition of themes, but that seemed the best way to observe scientific practice and to support the theory which appeared to fit it. The examples may still interest readers who resist the theory. Even if you persist in believing that science usually corrupts values, or that values always corrupt science, it is fascinating to see in detail how they do it.

Readers who know them will see how indebted I am to theoretical works by Paul Streeten, Peter Winch, William Dray, Gunnar Myrdal, C. Wright Mills and E. H. Carr. Most of any theoretical originality is theirs and any misapplications of it are mine. I thank W. G. K. Duncan, Richard Franklin, Israel Getzler, Richard Hare, John LaNauze, Richard Southern and Donald Whitehead for very helpful criticism of passages which strayed into their fields; William Dray, Jean Martin and Jerzy Zubrzycki for advice about books to read; and the Australian National University for its hospitality. I also thank some persuaders, simultaneously clever and good as all social scientists should be, who must long ago have forgotten the occasions for this gratitude – Stephen Yarnold and Arthur Burns, Kathleen Fitzpatrick and Max Crawford, Christopher Hill, Eric Goldman and Joe Kraft.

Speaking of clever and good, my wife Pat enabled this book to be written. I thank her, most of all.

H.S.

Contents

Contents

Contents

References

Footnotes* are with the text. Where a section of text discusses a book at length, the book's title is in the text and quotations from it are followed by bracketed pages numbers (123). The remaining references are numbered thus [1] in the text, and appear at the back of the book.

Acknowledgments

Passages are quoted from the works listed below by kind permission of the publishers, editors and authors whose names are distinguished by asterisks:

Sir Isaiah Berlin*, 'History and Theory', *History and Theory*, I.

Bernhard Prince von Bülow, *Imperial Germany*, Cassell & Co.*

Edward Hallett Carr*, *What is History?*, Macmillan & Co.*, and Alfred Knopf*.

Lewis Coser, *The Functions of Social Conflict*, The Free Press*, and Routledge & Kegan Paul*.

Ralf Dahrendorf, *Class and Class Conflict in Industrial Society*, Stanford University Press*, and Routledge & Kegan Paul*.

David Easton, *A Systems Analysis of Political Life*, John Wiley & Sons*.

D. K. Fieldhouse, "Imperialism': an historiographical revision', *Economic History Review*, 2 ser., XIV, 2.

J. L. Garvin and Julian Amery*, *The Life of Joseph Chamberlain*, Macmillan & Co.*

Murray Groves*, 'Dancing in Poreporena', *Journal of the Royal Anthropological Institute*, 84.

Elie Halévy, *England in 1815* (vol. 1 of *A History of the English People in the Nineteenth Century*), Ernest Benn*, and Barnes & Noble*.

John Maynard Keynes, *The General Theory of Employment, Interest and Money*, Macmillan & Co.* and the Trustees* of the late Lord Keynes.

V. I. Lenin, *Collected Works*, vol. 22, Lawrence & Wishart*, and International Publishers, Inc.*

Acknowledgments

William L. Langer, *The Diplomacy of Imperialism*, Alfred Knopf*.

Gunnar Myrdal, *An American Dilemma, The Negro Problem and Modern Democracy*, Harper & Row*.

Paul Samuelson, *Economics, An Introductory Analysis*, McGraw-Hill*.

Peter Winch*, *The Idea of a Social Science and Its Relation to Philosophy*, Routledge & Kegan Paul*.

E. M. Winslow, *The Pattern of Imperialism*, Columbia University Press*.

Part 1 - Use

This is a study of relations between the logical forms of explanations and their social uses. Plenty has been written about their forms, but their uses have to be studied by observation of cases.

Examples for comparison are sometimes hard to find. The same scientific question is seldom approached by enough different investigators, sufficiently various in their methods and politics. So to begin with, and to sketch some models, I resort to fiction. How (otherwise than by psychologists) are the social acts of individuals explained? Chapter 1 outlines some common methods of explaining them, and in Chapter 2, besides some genuine accounts of one politician's act, other explanations of it are made up to fit the purposes of a variety of imaginary investigators, each looking for a different illumination of the same act.

The first chapter should therefore expound theory, but even that is done easier by example, so the example is introduced immediately. To keep things realistic it is a question posed by a real historian about an act of a real politician, but to keep things simple it is a minor act. The (dead) French historian's view of the (forgotten) English event has little interest now, least perhaps for any American reader. It deserves the dozen lines some general histories spare it, and a dozen pages in the politician's five-volume biography. But for his own comfort the reader is implored to raise more interest in it than that, because for the sake of science, here begin two whole chapters about it.

I

Why Men Act

1. A question

In December 1899 Joseph Chamberlain, the best known protagonist of social reform then in the British cabinet, apparently changed his mind about old age pensions. Every historian of that act has thought that it required explanation. Why?

When the Unionists came into power in 1895, two or three years had passed since the attention of the working class had been drawn to the question [of pensions for aged workmen] by Charles Booth, the philanthropist, famous for his inquiries into social conditions. The scheme proposed by Booth was, it is true, completely different from Bismarck's solution. He asserted the right of every man without exception to a pension in old age. Neither workmen nor employers were to contribute. He did not speak of insurance, but of relief. And Chamberlain had obtained the support of a group of Members of Parliament, belonging to both parties, for a carefully studied scheme, far more moderate than Booth's proposal, or even Bismarck's law – a system of optional insurance to be assisted by the State – and had again developed his proposals before a Royal Commission, appointed in 1893 to inquire into the question. The Commission, however, had in 1895 reached a purely negative conclusion. It was the same with a Parliamentary Committee appointed in 1896 which reported in 1898. But Booth's proposal suddenly acquired an unexpected importance when the Government of one of the self-governing Colonies passed legislation, based on a principle similar to that which he had enunciated. . . . The New Zealand legislation was immediately explained to the British public by the agent-general of the colony in London, the Fabian, W. P. Reeves; and Booth made use of it to push his own scheme. He launched an extensive campaign throughout Great Britain, for which he obtained the support of the trade unions, the co-operative societies, the Nonconformist bodies, twenty-seven Anglican Bishops, and Cardinal Vaughan. Three months had not passed, and his National Committee of

Organized Labour for Promoting Old Age Pensions for all had scarcely been formed, before Parliament was roused to action. A committee of seventeen members appointed by the House of Commons reported, after a rapid inquiry, in favour of the New Zealand system. . . . The movement had been well launched in the traditional English fashion. It enjoyed the support of the working classes. If in any party a statesman, inspired by Fabian principles, was prepared to adopt either Booth's scheme, or the system which had been set up in New Zealand, he would have the country behind him. What was Chamberlain going to do?

He did nothing. At first sight his inaction is surprising. He was universally understood to have given an explicit pledge before the election of 1895 to provide the workers with old age pensions. From the zeal he had displayed in defending the Compensation Bill, when it was debated in 1897, one might expect that he would continue to advocate a bold policy of social reform. And surely his imperialism could not fail to be attracted by a reform which had originated in one of those self-governing Colonies whose bonds with the mother country it was his constant endeavour to draw closer. Nevertheless, he did nothing.[1]

In the first of those two paragraphs, Halévy's story may not be complete but it is not puzzling. It does not tell why Booth chose relief instead of insurance, or why the New Zealand government did what it did. There are such gaps in any narrative. No narrative is 'complete', in that it explains all its own parts. It must keep moving and a judgment to be explored later chooses which parts to take for granted. But when in 1900 Chamberlain 'did nothing' about pensions, Halévy will not permit a suspension of curiosity; here is not an omission, but a puzzle. Art helps life to make the puzzle: Halévy establishes explanations that would be satisfactory if they accounted for what Chamberlain did. The trouble is that they explain, instead, something which he did not do. Their form illustrates a conventional classification of explanations for individual acts.

First, Halévy gives Chamberlain the habits of a social reformer and an imperialist, just such habits as would dispose him to import a pension scheme from New Zealand. To have done so would have repeated a pattern of his past, would have been an act which his record shows him to have been disposed to do; and for the act, we would then have a dispositional explanation.

Second, Halévy confronts Chamberlain with a political opportunity, and we know how politicians usually respond to political opportunities. Chamberlain was a politician, and if he had behaved more like one on this occasion we would be satisfied; we would recognize a case of what experience has taught us to be a law of political behavior.*

Third, Halévy might offer a more prevalent type of explanation – one that followed the working of Chamberlain's mind, 'empathized' or 're-thought' his thoughts, so that we might understand the passions or calculations which led him to act as he did. Explanations of this sort vary in the methods and evidence they use in penetrating other minds; they may cite intentions or reasons or emotions; we may lump them together as 'understanding' explanations, noticing that they appear to have few equivalents in the natural sciences.

But dispositional and law-based explanations do not explain Chamberlain's change of mind in 1899, and the contents of his mind remain a mystery. More information is needed. Perhaps Halévy's dispositional arguments were untrue, or incomplete, or irrelevant.

2. Disposition

Acts may be known more certainly than thoughts; what can be learned of his disposition from the outward and visible facts of Chamberlain's career?

Chamberlain's imperialist and reformist proclivities can scarcely be questioned. As Colonial Secretary he did more for the office, and for the good government of colonies, than any before him. He spoke incessantly of his own and his country's imperial mission. He tried to join the self-governing colonies into various political, military and economic reunions. He was currently fighting to annex the Boer republics.

His radical record is just as consistent, and longer. He reformed his family's fortunes and Mr. Nettlefold's hardware business and several Sunday Schools. He worked for the reform of education first in Birmingham and then throughout the nation. His radical accomplishments in city government were famous. In national politics, his 'unauthorised programmes' were decades ahead of legislation. He reformed the structure of the Liberal party and, as far as he could, the social conscience of the Conservative party. He helped the reform of shipping safety, commercial law, local government, accident compensation, and the franchise itself. Three

---

*It is hard to understand why such sharp distinctions are sometimes drawn between the 'dispositional' and 'law-based' explanations—one makes Chamberlain's act a case of a local law about Chamberlain's regular behavior, the other makes it a case of a more general law about other politicians' behavior.

years after this change of mind about pensions, he was to attack the traditional foundations of public financial policy and private commercial liberty. At different times in earlier decades, he had menaced the House of Lords, the Established Church, and the institution of Monarchy.*

But if these were causes he was disposed to advance, what were his habitual methods of advancing them? Did some trait of cowardice or incapacity betray his promise of pensions? We should look at another of his dispositions – what were his customary methods of getting what he wanted?

He spent his youth exploiting the British rights to an American screw-making patent. The patent would have enabled anyone to starve out the hand-ironmongers, but Chamberlain did more than that. He built one of the first and fastest of the great industrial monopolies; he beat imports out of the British market, and he beat competitors out of a wide foreign territory as well. He paid well when he bought out competitors, often hired them on good terms afterwards, and was himself a model employer. He fought competition itself as hard as he fought competitors, and he won a famous victory for consolidation, monopoly, high prices, and his famous 'ransom' to labour.

As in private so in public business. He set out to reform Birmingham's schools. Beaten at first in the Birmingham School Board, he then established a control of the Town Council which enabled him to use its powers, illegally and successfully, to frustrate both the School Board and the Court of Queen's Bench. Then he recaptured the School Board, giving Birmingham a lesson in caucus organization which he soon applied on a national scale. His personal control of the national liberal caucus and his personal following of midland, nonconformist and radical voters were wielded like weapons to win his seat in the Liberal cabinet and his share in its legislative programme. And when he finally split the liberal party, it remained ineffective for twenty years.

The same temper stiffened his foreign policies. He used rebellion, and South African and British arms, against the Boer republics. When the frontiers of British and Russian influence approached each other in southern and eastern Asia, it was the instinct of the Prime Minister, Lord Salisbury, to reach agreement with the Russians in order to avoid conflict, divide the spoils and exclude weaker contenders. It was Chamberlain's instinct to acquire an army – any army – capable of beating the Russians, if we may so interpret his approaches within a single month of 1898 to Japanese, Americans and Germans.

*This and subsequent passages without numbered references are composed for the occasion, unless the text indicates otherwise.

So there is a pattern in his response to opposition. The thing to do with a competitor is not in the end to surrender, or compete, or compromise, or join, or split the spoils. The thing to do is to acquire him, or kill him. The method is to establish control of an organization capable of beating him, then to fight him – as the Boers and the Liberal party and the Birmingham School Board and dozens of bankrupt ironmongers had discovered.

This selection of traits omits an important one: what was Chamberlain's way when personal ambition came into conflict with habitual policy or principle? Authorities disagree. Paul Cambon thought that

it would not do to forget that M. Chamberlain has no political principles whatsoever: he is a man of the moment, able to change his opinions with incredible ease, entirely untroubled by any earlier statements he may have made; a man who has never for a moment hesitated to contradict himself. He also has a very exact appreciation of the exigencies of public opinion, and excels in following all its fluctuations, while appearing to direct them. This is the secret of his popularity.[2]

But R. C. K. Ensor concluded that

an air of frustration clings round his record. . . . He was in politics for constructive aims – to 'get things done'; yet outside the colonial office work it was little that he actually achieved. In all human relations his instincts were intensely loyal; yet he helped to wreck each of the great parties in succession. Both episodes were charged to his personal ambition; yet it is obvious that in both he was acting conscientiously, against and not for his own interest.[3]

These traits cannot explain why Chamberlain should betray his favorite causes. Even Cambon's suspicion would have him sticking to those causes, if Halévy is right in thinking that in doing so 'he would have the country behind him'. Before his dispositions can be related to the obstinate fact that he did change his mind, both the circumstances and the intention of that change of mind will have to be better understood.

'Dispositional analysis is a kind of *spectatorism*'.[4] It relates an act to habits of action, rather than to motives or calculations. These distinctions, logically dubious, are common in the practice of historians. It may be true that the very notion of an act has to include something of its significance, and therefore of its context; but the fact that Chamberlain opposed various pension schemes in 1900 can

7

be separated from a lot of knowledge about the circumstances in which he did so. To that extent it is possible to think separately about the act and about its context. In the same way, though it be some idea of its reason and intention that allows us to call it a political act at all, it may be well enough or badly enough understood to allow a working distinction between the act, and the thought that went with it. The dispositional explanation relates an act to a record of action, with minimal understanding of either. What use is such a device?

Historians have various uses for it. The commonest purpose is to calm curiosity or keep it at bay, rather than to satisfy it; this is a quick way to clear the narrative of interruptions, as if quite different facts had allowed Halévy to write

In 1900, Chamberlain repeated his customary annual evasion of the pension question

or

in that year pensions made no progress, because Booth's political inexperience led him to concentrate his persuasions upon that impenetrable Tory, the Lord Chancellor.

'Customary annual', 'political inexperience' and 'impenetrable Tory' will give perfunctory satisfaction if the narrative has bigger business to be getting on with.

When such explanations are made to do more important duty, it is usually because no better ones can be constructed. A man's reasons have such familiar relation to the world around him, and such familiar expression in speech, that they are often easier to reconstruct than are his passions or inconsistencies. When action is wild or irrational, the historian can seldom replace the detail of calculation with the equivalent detail of passionate feeling or impulse; he retreats instead to a general pattern of passionate or irrational conduct. Calculation is usually easier to follow than miscalculation.[5]

Wild action is only one case of the resort to dispositions whenever there is a lack of evidence about thought or intention. Historians must sometimes write of unrevealing acts, secretive persons, inscrutable systems. Less respectably, they may want to make plain acts obscure, or obscure acts unduly plain. Mistakes, sacrifices of persons to necessity, sacrifices of principle to personal loyalty, can

8

be discredited by isolating acts from their intentions. A bald enough
record of his actions, divorced even from the thread of reason that
Cambon allowed them, could give Chamberlain the disposition of a
chronic turncoat, and make his treachery to pensions an unsurprising
instance of an invariable habit. A German Chancellor wrote of him:

There was hardly a British statesman who had changed so often in his
political career, who had altered his standpoint so frequently and so
suddenly, or with whom one must be so much prepared for surprises, for
some unexpected divagation, as with Joseph Chamberlain. From a Radical
democrat he changed to a Conservative Tory, from a republican to a loyal
monarchist, from a pacifist to an imperialist, from an enthusiastic free-
trader and follower of Bright and Cobden to a passionate protectionist. . . .
There was hardly a political question in which he had not, like the
Sicambrian king, burned what he had previously worshipped and
worshipped what he had previously burned.[6]

This is dispositional explanation, pure in form if not in purpose. Its
purpose is not always to smear – the German Chancellor was using
it to predict. But whatever their uses, dispositions are very blunt
instruments of explanation. Why did Chamberlain's 'disposition to
change his mind frequently' overcome, on *this* occasion, his dispositions to clever political calculation, to imperialism, to social
reform, to popular *rapport*? How do we know whether he changed
his mind (according to one disposition) or merely his tactics (according to some other disposition)? An act can seldom be identified as an
instance of a habit, of a class of acts, without some understanding of
its thought and its context; and even if it could, habits would still
mislead. Except for Ensor's, the foregoing notes of Chamberlain's
disposition stuck to the facts: to habits of action. From that behaviorist form they drew one deceiving bias. He was a skilful man, who
generally tried only what he could accomplish; but from his record
we all too easily infer that what he tried for was all he wanted, and
that what he wanted, he usually got. His *habitual* acceptance of
frustration, noticed by Ensor, is an equally important part of his
history; but it cannot even be known, without an understanding of
his thoughts. Perhaps, for the dispositional explanation which sets
acts into patterns of habit, we should try to substitute an understanding explanation which sets understood acts into character:
into patterns of thought and feeling and personality, as well as
patterns of action.

9

3. Character

The delineation of character must depend on a selective interest, in history as in art. Chamberlain's change of mind could be related to a dozen aspects of his personality, all in some way illuminating. Chamberlain is as human as Lear, though unlikely to be as well understood: there is an inconvenient difference between historical and poetic truth. It is only when exceptional evidence reveals character, or when exceptional power allows it to reveal itself, that historians can usually do it human or artistic justice. Like the requirement of truth, other requirements of science may also limit what can be said of it.

Some people think that historians should share one of Shakespeare's aims – the precise understanding of individuals – while sociologists should have Shakespeare's other aim: to discern in individuals what is common to humanity. But evidence and method and professional ritual inhibit them both; compare Shakespeare's efforts with

King Lear divided his kingdom foolishly; which may be sufficiently understood by noting that he was (a) old, (b) kind, (c) insensitive, and (d) credulous;

or

disequilibrium between structured goals and life-chances conditioned Thane Macbeth's deviation from peer-reference-group norms to mate-membership-group norms. Crosscutting status-sets did not minimise tension here, but produced intra-contradictory role-sets tending to tension issuing in non-revolutionary rebelliousness (Goals +, Means —, on R. K. Merton's scale).

It would not be irrelevant to Chamberlain's change of mind if we could know how that mind privately resolved its dilemmas of public and private fidelity, or confronted the conscience of the rich with the politics of the possible.

Chamberlain's ambition has a special fascination. It seems to have been, not the prizes, but something in the process of the fight and the finish, that excited him most. He loved reorganizing, constructing, getting things done. In politics, such an appetite has to be fed by radical policies and changes of course. His enjoyment of power did not arise from the eminence it gave him, nor did it arise from any cruel interest in the sufferings of the defeated; it seems to have been more like the thrill with which some contractors can watch their earth-moving machinery as it moves mountains.

If we had any reliable knowledge of it, this private nature might help to explain his great political mistakes. It is a suspicion of this nature that prompts some of the explanations offered later in this chapter: such a man could not have so quietly borne *that* frustration, at *those* hands, unless he had already in mind some inkling of how he might in the end retaliate.

If such human curiosity ended with the setting of action fully and subtly into character, we might call its owner biographer rather than historian. But it serves other interests; and on those other interests will depend the choice of the traits of personality to which acts or thoughts are related, in explanations of acts or thoughts. Whoever expects these relations to be few, or simple, or of the same type, need only remember what a flood of literary criticism has still failed to exhaust the relation of action to character in fiction. Of their various relations in history, one contrast will serve as an example.

If I want to learn more about the effects of different political systems in promoting people of different types, my historical explanations will often relate acts to the personalities of actors; but in ways that may still vary widely, according to the ways in which I choose to classify types.

If I classify psychological types, if for example I want to know what arrangements offer power to sado-masochists or authoritarian personalities or love-oriented popularity-seekers, I shall explain Chamberlain's change of mind in terms of its intimate stimulants, motives and emotional accompaniments. There were hints in Halévy's explanation:

Chamberlain . . . no longer felt the need to justify his conversion to Toryism by a programme of social reform. Defy Russia, humiliate France, crush the Boers—that was the way to win a brilliant reputation at home and abroad! This terrible fellow had now something else to think of than old age pensions.[7]

Halévy had some marginal interest in the fortunes of psychological types. He saw, with misgiving, that democracy would be led by enthusiasts, and feared that enthusiasm was usually accompanied by other characteristics which might be too easily tempted to pervert democracy. He liked peaceful progress and thought that the peace depended on the progress, and the progress on increasing political attention to the working class. But he saw what opportunities the working class offered to the salesmen of socialist and imperialist excitements, both of which he feared. This led him to a delicate definition of political good: popularity without imperialism, reform without socialism. Unhappily his history of England was begun soon after Gladstone's death had concluded the historical life of the latter combination. Halévy lived and worked on through two British Labour governments into the age of the New Deal and the Popular Front. He came to see a degree of collectivism as inevitable, and resigned himself to it with the reluctance of one to whom history reveals both a dangerous trend, and a contradiction in his own morality. But if some socialism was inevitable, imperialism was not, and he never forgave those who led it; least of all, social reformers who led it. He had both to discredit Chamberlain and to explain him; he explained him as a man prone to the illicit excitements of war and imperialism, and as a careerist willing to profit by exciting such feelings in others. So Halévy's explanation of this particular change of mind, though it mentions financial difficulties briefly, seems at first sight (but see below, p. 27) to concentrate on personal psychology and the calculation of personal political advantage.

But it requires a very small shift of interest to prompt a very large amendment of this explanation. If my interest is not in psychological but in *political* types, I may want to know what systems promote, say, public orators rather than parliamentary orators, administrators rather than demagogues, parliamentary managers rather than party managers. If this is my interest, it will lead me to relate Chamberlain's acts to his public capacities rather than his private character (though the two are not entirely unrelated and Halévy's explanation referred to both). I may neglect the private understanding for the public image; whether sincere or hypocritical, it is that image which attracts votes and must, if its owner would survive, be expressed in action. Perhaps

he was an exact judge of public mood and conservative psychology, and that skill told him that he had to defer pensions. The heat of wartime feeling left in the public mind neither the boredom nor the decent sensibility that he would need to work on, to whip up the popular pressure which alone could move Lord Salisbury to social reform. His only use to

Salisbury came from his command of votes; his only threat, that without reform he might lose those votes. But if his old character as reformer had got him into power, his new character as the hero of 'Chamberlain's war' was quite sufficient to keep him there. Joe the Radical divided the country in a way that recruited some otherwise-Liberal votes to Salisbury's coalition; but Joe the Imperialist recruited even more, and with less division and embarrassment to the conservative majority of the coalition. For once, it was the security of Chamberlain's popular position that enabled Salisbury to ignore Chamberlain's social policies. Chamberlain knew it, and would not start a fight on pensions which in that particular year he must have lost.

Such an explanation does treble service. It makes the change of mind intelligible by reference to reasons and situations. It improves our picture of the undemocratic Marquess and the radical manufacturer for whose joint leadership some of the first literate working-class voters were apparently voting; and it brings Chamberlain's skill to the aid of our own in understanding why they did vote for such presumptive enemies of their class. The last two are not the ostensible objects of the explanation, but a reader whom they interest will be satisfied with this explanation, as a more psychiatric investigator will not. For the explanation says nothing of Chamberlain's feeling or sincerity; except for slightly different judgments of the choice he had, it is quite consistent with Halévy's, and differs from Halévy's not in contradicting it but in satisfying a different curiosity. At the same time it has gone far beyond a consideration of Chamberlain's private or public character in isolation from his public situation; indeed, its chief value is the light it casts upon his situation. Disposition, motive, reason, skill and character can seldom be understood apart from one another, and none of them can be understood, or indeed conceived of, apart from the situations in which they are exercised. They exchange information about each other and give meaning to each other. They are analytical abstracts from 'whole actions' and it is not always helpful to discuss them as separate types or ingredients of explanations.

4. *Thought and situation*

Historical acts are done in situations which are complexes of social facts, including processes of change. If these social facts and processes are discussed now as the context of individual acts, and are then discussed again in later chapters as being themselves the subjects of larger explanations, there is bound to be some mixture of omission and repetition in both accounts. For this the writer apologizes to the reader.

An important part of any politician's thought is his understanding of his world and of the situation in which he acts. Sometimes he makes this picture public. Many of his speeches and writings are meant to define situations, in one way or another. But he may not always do this. He may often assume that because he and his public live together in the same world, each can rely on the other to see and understand it in much the same way. Likewise, for an investigator to know that world is often to know well enough how it appeared to the actors in it. But the historian must be careful. He may live in a world, and think in ways, that still resemble Chamberlain's, but such resemblances may sometimes deceive. 'Any analysis of the structure of Soviet society in the NEP period' E. H. Carr writes, 'is complicated by an incompatibility between the objective conditions of the society and the terms in which its leaders and its intellectuals, faithful to the Marxist tradition, habitually thought and wrote about it.'[8] However like or unlike the investigator's world may be to Chamberlain's or Lenin's, it will obviously be unlike the world of a Pharaoh or a medieval abbot or an African tribesman. Nor will modern research into those remote worlds necessarily yield the same picture as Pharaoh or abbot or tribesman (or Chamberlain, or Lenin) had of them, unless those people's methods of thought and observation are also understood.

We may set out to understand an act by reading the actor's own account of his situation as he saw it. This is evidence about the actor's situation, or about his impression of it, or about his methods of observation, or about all three; and in all three respects it may be unreliable. This situation, about which we and the historical actor think, is mainly composed of other people's thoughts and plans or habits or powers of action; we are not studying anything so simple as our actor's methods of observation of the material world in which he lived. In spite of these difficulties, we try to establish an independent view of the situation. From this, we may infer the actor's view of it, assuming that he saw much of what we now see, but did not think it necessary to spell it all out. If he did spell it out, we may check his observation, his understanding, his truthfulness; we may learn more

about his methods of thinking and seeing. These methods of thinking and seeing may be very general features of his world, like its
conceptual language or its economic or religious theories; or they
may be peculiar features of his individual mind, like Chamberlain's
tendency to think voters more persuadable than they really were.
Not only does our independent view of the actor's world help us to
penetrate the actor's mind; both our perception and his perception
are necessary to explanations if it is our curiosity, not his, that the
explanations have to satisfy.

It has sometimes been argued that the actor's thought, as the
'inside' of his action, affords the only and sufficient explanation of
his act, and satisfies the only curiosity properly called 'historical'.
If this view were held in simple-minded form, we would have to
explain witch-burning *only* as an effective preventer of black magic;
we could not explain any unintended or mistaken effects of action
which arose from actors' mistakes about the world; we should
never be satisfied with an explanation that related a program or plan
to a situation, without first proving that it was so related by its
author; it would be difficult to distinguish 'different roles in the
same institution' if the role-players all saw different institutions; and
so on. We could not ask those anachronistic questions whose high
interest and importance create the famous necessity for each generation to re-discover the past. We could not write

A political reality arose from an economic illusion, an illusion in which
most members of parliament had both a sincere and a vested interest.
Pensions could not be financed from direct taxation as long as most of
Chamberlain's colleagues continued to expect that the revenue from
income tax would actually decline if the rate rose above 10% of income.

R. G. Collingwood, the most insistent philosopher of a re-thinking
and understanding history, took care of this objection by asserting
that the re-enactment of experience

is not a passive surrender to the spell of another's mind; it is a labour of
active and therefore critical thinking. The historian not only re-enacts
past thought, he re-enacts it in the context of his own knowledge and therefore, in re-enacting it, criticizes it, forms his own judgement of its value,
corrects whatever errors he can discern in it.[9]

This does not always seem consistent with Collingwood's opinion
that 'A natural process is a process of events, an historical process is a

process of thoughts', and historians should attend exclusively to the process of thoughts. It is true that a great deal of the independent, critical view of an actor's thought and situation will arise from understanding the minds and acts of his contemporaries, in the manner that Collingwood recommends. But much of that thought is about events; when the re-thinking historian criticizes the thought, it must be against his independent judgment of the events. Many events, though they may arise in some fashion out of conscious human action, nevertheless do so in ways which it would be curious to describe as 'error or mistake', and impossible to explain merely by 'criticizing the mistaken thought' of the people concerned. The citizens individually may be making no mistakes at all in their economic activities, yet these may have aggregate effects of prosperity or adversity which they neither intended nor counter-intended, but which it is certainly the historian's business to explain. Other actions may be so coerced by circumstances, and the circumstances be so obvious, that the psychological accompaniments of action may be irrelevant to explanations of it – it had to be done, whatever the actor experienced in doing it. In some passages Collingwood can almost be taken as advocating a history of open choices only; but such a history would be patchy, and even its open choices often unintelligible.

More important to the present subject, which is the choice rather than the truth of explanations, is the necessity for any inquirer to select, both in everyday life and in Collingwood's scheme for historians. In daily life many other people's actions present themselves inscrutably as facts or events, as things rather than thoughts. There is a barrier across the road, a shortage of food or money, a law on the books, a painting on the wall, a school in the neighborhood. No doubt other people's actions have generated all these things, some intentionally, some by mistake, some by involuntary chains of effect that lie outside the range of conscious calculation altogether. In one mode of description, these are the culture: a residue of facts with lives and natures of their own which survive, or can be understood apart from, anybody's intentions. Explanations of acts may very well concentrate on these 'external' conditions and restraints, just as for other purposes it may suffice to explain an act by showing how it did or could fit its situation, without asserting anything about the actor's calculations. Of any reconstruction of action-in-a-situation, different parts may be emphasized for different purposes; it is not necessarily 'unhistorical' to regard the thought within the action as merely one of these parts, to be explored or not according to one's explanatory purposes.

For an example, consider Chamberlain's original commitment to pensions in the years 1893–5. At that time he explained his action by offering very different reasons to different audiences. To the working men who might expect to draw pensions themselves, he would declare that pensions are just, and well deserved, and that the economy can afford them. To philanthropists: proposals for pensions are humane and practicable, but not if they are extravagant enough to deter parliament from enacting them. To parliament and its committees: pensions are part of the price of social peace and industrial growth and, therefore, national power; the rich are well advised to pay such ransoms to forestall revolution and to preserve their privileges. To the conservative leaders of the Unionist Party: pensions are part of the price they must pay to keep Chamberlain's electoral following attached to him, and both attached to the Unionist party, and thus to give that party its chance of power. To himself, no doubt: pensions attached to his name would comfort his social conscience, and enlarge his radical following, and keep him personally indispensable to any Unionist prime minister. From all these bargains there emerged a political program with the virtues typical of political programs: to some extent it re-defined the world; it attracted voters, whether by pocket or conscience; it attached their allegiance to a leader, which gave the leader the power necessary to get the program legislated (though in this case, not quite enough of such power).

In order to succeed, this program obviously had to satisfy all the necessary conditions suggested by Chamberlain's different persuasions to different parties. I leave to another chapter the purposes that lead historians to choose some such necessary conditions as more important than others. Here, in dealing with problems of thought and motive, it is worth considering the common question: did Chamberlain *really* want to pension the poor, or did he *really* want to preserve the rich, or did he *really* want power for himself for its own sake? This question may express an interest in his motives and morality, and if that is the investigator's interest, the question will have to be answered. But in historical explanations the question more typically asks about the circumstances in which Chamberlain could be expected to desert the cause, or stand by it. It is a difficult question to answer and not always a necessary one to ask. Who can say of himself, when he is rewarded for doing some good and enjoyable job, which of the good, the joy or the reward he 'really' values? What he likes best of all is the felicitous combination of all three. When a political program cannot achieve any of its ends except by achieving them all, it may not be possible to find out which of its many effects the politician 'really' wanted. Whether or not the investigator feels compelled to probe and guess, will depend on whether he is interested in a morality of motive or a morality of consequence; in the logic of the scheme or the skill of its author; or perhaps on whether he has a humane interest in Chamberlain or a historical interest in what Chamberlain's act caused to happen.

Some follies might be avoided if this question were always seen in this way. Whether saint or sinner, the author of a program usually wants it to succeed, so he designs it to succeed. The power-getting element in programs (and in politicians) is one among the conditions of their success, one as vital to saint as to sinner, if for different reasons. But whole schools of political science and of 'conflict-model' sociology have been built upon the abstraction of the power-getting elements in programs and politicians, and of the power-distributing mechanisms of political and social systems. There is no theoretical objection to abstracting this element for study, but in practice it is seldom long before the power-getting motive, as the axiomatic principle of the investigator's model, becomes the dominant motive of the people he studies – a motive of which all other motives (unstudied) must be servants or rationalizations.

Even if they do not attempt to separate one motive from another, explanations can certainly be organized to shine a search-light on personal responsibilities, or to leave them in the dark altogether; to make heavy demands on persons or groups or classes, or to make none. In 'Some Causal Accounts of the American Civil War'[10] William Dray shows in a most lucid way how different selections and valuations of causes can impute very different responsibilities to different people – or none to anybody. The historian's idea of 'reasonable behavior in the circumstances' is a texture of moral and technical evaluation, and it often determines his choice and emphasis of causes. If people act as one historian would expect people to act in such circumstances, he may see them as mere transmitters of historical forces. If another historian expects less or more of them, that expectation may reorganize his explanation to expose their acts as independent – and therefore originative, technically causal as well as morally responsible.

A man's reasoning can seldom be reconstructed, nor his own account of it tested for truth, nor his motive, morality or skill appraised, nor any of these identified as characteristic of him, without the best possible understanding of his situation. It is time to review Chamberlain's situation in more detail. The following is some of the information available to historians of his change of mind; from it, it will be possible to see how different historians will choose their explanations, according to their different interests, purposes and values.

Chamberlain had never expected Lords and Commons to legislate pensions on their merits. He would have to force them, by threatening to break the unity and majority of the Unionist party. So rather than try to persuade the party first, he had begun his campaign by first committing himself. He was able to do this in the years 1893–5 because he and the Unionists were then out of office, he was not yet a formal ally of their party, and party platforms were in any case not yet as official and rigid as they were later to become. By 1899 he had the party as well as himself committed to pensions, though vaguely as to details or dates.

But the commitment of Salisbury, the Prime Minister, was reluctant, for party reasons as well as personal lack of interest. The alliance with Chamberlain was useful for imperial purposes, but dangerously embarrassing on most domestic issues; Salisbury never expected it to last. 'I fear these social questions are destined to break up our party; but why incur the danger before the necessity has arrived, and while the Party may still be useful to avert Home Rule?'[11] Chamberlain did have one success in extracting social reform from the reluctant Unionist party; but while that Workmen's Compensation bill was passing through parliament in 1897, Lord Londonderry was not the only conservative to deplore 'the dominating will of the Colonial Secretary whose Radical views on home politics we have always regarded with disapproval, however much we may admire him as an Imperialist.'[12]

In 1901 Salisbury was still expecting the party to disintegrate if serious social reform were proposed to it, and he still wanted to defer the proposal if he could.

The split in the party was expected to come, not about reform directly, but about ways and means of financing it. Most members thought high taxation the enemy of prosperity, growth and employment. Many thought that some natural limit of expenditure should restrict policy, rather than that policy should determine expenditure. Direct and indirect taxes were generally expected to contribute each about half of the revenue, but each was a limited resource. Indirect taxes must only fall where they would have no protective effect, and the acceptable taxes on liquor, tobacco, and a few imported staple foods grew even less popular as more working men voted. Increases in income tax would shift the incidence of direct taxes even further from land to the earnings more typical of the urban middle class, and from the poor to the rich; and this was also thought to be the suitably flexible tax to keep in reserve for war and emergency.

The most conservative of these fiscal views were held by Sir Michael Hicks Beach, Chancellor of the Exchequer in Salisbury's government. Among other things, he thought that the tax would defeat itself if it ever exceeded a rate of about 10%. Intermittently throughout the Boer War he fought to preserve some vestige of his Treasury control over the war expenditures of the War Office and Colonial Office; he fought even harder to prevent any further domestic expenditure. He was about ready to retire, and could and did threaten resignation easily, always on financial issues; one of the threats mentioned old age pensions explicitly.[13]

In this conflict, which continued for two years, Salisbury generally supported the war ministers on war expenditure (he thought the 'jingoistic gale' of public opinion left no option about that) but he often supported Hicks Beach against any wartime commitments to new peace-time expenditure. One of his letters to Hicks Beach (14 September 1901) again foreshadowed the disintegration of the government as soon as peace should make opportunity for decisions about peace-time policy and economy. But 'I think it is the duty of all of us not to do anything to bring about that catastrophe . . . *while the war lasts*.'[14] There seems to be no record of Salisbury's having impressed that same duty on Chamberlain, but he must surely have done it no later than the end of 1899. It was from that time that Chamberlain's talk of pensions became vague and procrastinating. In the end Salisbury and Hicks Beach retired together in the year in which the war ended. But while they remained, the terms of peace which Salisbury imposed on his cabinet are plain enough: Hicks Beach must stop trying to reduce war expenditure, or popular opinion would blame the slow progress of the war on government meanness; and Chamberlain must stop advertising pensions or Hicks Beach would resign, giving and getting uncomfortable quantities of sympathy from a back bench whose unity might be split on such an issue.

Some of Hicks Beach's strength, and Salisbury's support of him, must have arisen from what all parties knew about the long-established spending and reforming habits of the House of Commons. For seventy years it had from time to time reformed itself and other institutions with remarkable disregard for the privileges of its members and of the classes they represented. Parliament, the established church, the ancient universities, the courts of law, the governments of colonies, the armed and civil services, the municipal corporations and the public houses had all been stripped of one sort of privilege or another by act of parliament. Parliament gave away privilege in this way readily enough, for reasons which often included very short views of party advantage, and very short shrift for Hicks Beach's variety of classical economic theory. But what parliament scarcely ever gave away, was money. Most of the great Victorian reforms either saved public money or at least spent very little of it; the Education Act of 1870 was a comparatively rare exception. The election of 1895 returned certainly more business men, and perhaps less social conscience, than to any House of Commons of the century, yet that House still passed a Workmen's Compensation Act which interfered radically in the relation of employer to employee. Pensions would have been less offensive than Workmen's Compensation, to the economic orthodoxy of the time, because they would not concern or alter the productive process at all; but they would also have been, in almost any form, the most expensive single social reform in parliament's history. It is no surprise that Salisbury avoided proposing such a thing to a parliament whose members must already have been paying more income tax than any of their precursors.

To this collection of items one of Chamberlain's biographers adds another. This is interesting as an illustration of some of the services which act, situation and character may do for each other in the historian's mind. For what follows, Garvin offers no real evidence; indeed, some historians might think that he went too far in an inference that must have been drawn from Chamberlain's situation in 1900, his speeches and actions in 1903, and from knowledge of his character:

When he meditated the future . . . in these last weeks of 1900 what did he mean or dream concerning his future as a social reformer? The war would not last for ever; and the Treasury as he supposed would not always be in negative hands. And something unspoken recurred to him when he turned over possibilities in his mind. He had long conjectured as one possibility that a revolution in the commercial policy of the country— providing new financial resources by the revenue derived from some kind of tariff system—might advance together both the social and Imperial questions. "Free imports without free trade", introduced over half a century before, was regarded by most Unionist statesmen no less than by all Liberal statesmen as eternal law. Should a great challenge become practicable and successful after the war the same policy that knitted the Empire might provide means for Old Age Pensions.[15]

Other points above illustrate similar reciprocations: event, character and the 'logic of situations' all illuminate each other. Besides showing what a variety of evidence and inference the explainer may draw on, the long passage also exposes the location and limited interest of whoever wrote it. It could be extended in many directions without losing any of its relevance to Chamberlain's change of mind. For one thing it almost ignores his change of *mind*, to concentrate on his change of circumstances. It will not satisfy the inquirer who wants to know about Chamberlain's feelings and motives, as distinct from his 'reasons'. Except for that failing, it is probably a sufficient array of information to meet the range of interests catered for by text-book writers whose market is the English universities in the nineteen-seventies. For others it would not do at all. American students might well want explanations that included more of the ground-rules of English politics:

Chamberlain and Salisbury had to change Chamberlain's mind about pensions because they could not have the legislature do the hatchet job for them. English executives cannot survive if their proposals to the legislature fail.

French students might want such vague notions of social reform located precisely in the intellectual systems that begot them; Halévy himself did this office for the utilitarian reformers of an earlier generation. When the grand-parents of the English and French students were in college, they might have wanted to explore Chamberlain's ambivalent representation of both employed and employing classes; they might have taken his failure with pensions as being sufficiently explained by the mere attempt at such an illogical alliance. And so on – to rub in the point that several pages of information still satisfy a limited range of interests.

Text-book writers cannot spare as many pages as that for the explanation of such a minor act; how do they choose what to put into the sentence or two that they *can* spare? Monographers or biographers may have more space; how do they decide how much of it to give to Chamberlain's situation, how much to his reasoning, how much to his feelings?

2

For example: Why did Chamberlain change his Mind?

1. The variety of historians' interests

Some historians are interested – or think their readers will be interested – in politics: in political systems and in the actors themselves whose acts are to be explained. Other historians are more interested in societies: in the social opportunities for individual action and in its social and historical effects.

This classification is crossed by a second. Some are conservative, others welcome change. The terms are used here of historians' values, not their expectations: of course conservatives may expect (though they deplore) change, and revolutionaries may expect (though they deplore) that unjust systems will continue.

Both classifications are crossed by a third: some take a more determinist, others a more open view of history.

The last distinction is even less satisfactory than the first two. At one extreme are men committed by faith or induction to the opinion that human affairs are determined by God, National Spirit, climate, rules of growth, cyclic laws or the means of production. At the other extreme it is 'one of the principles of any unprejudiced view of politics that everything is possible in human affairs'. Between extremes are scattered the many historians who think that the extent to which political acts are determined is something which research must discover of each new act it investigates; societies and situations differ in the power they afford to politicians, and the same investigator may consistently take a determinist view of some decisions and an open view of others. Sometimes the facts seem to make the judgment easy. Chamberlain could not avoid deferring pensions. Hitler could easily have avoided making war on Europe or the Jewish race. But even these clear contrasts of fact can fade into problems of philosophy if we ask how inevitable were Chamberlain's circumstances or Hitler's mental states.

Nor is any of these classifications entirely technical, or entirely otherwise. A greater interest in politics or in society, a fear or a love of change, may seem to be matters of value; but they value a technically understood world. Determinism may seem to be a technical conclusion about history, but it nearly always has moral foundations as well, as Dray argued in the article mentioned earlier. If one historian says 'Hitler had a perfectly free choice between war and peace' and another says 'his whole personality made his aggressions inevitable; he no more chose them, than he chose his heredity or his headaches or his tantrums', their disagreement is largely moral: it is a disagreement about personal responsibility, or about the questions worth asking of history. Determinism presents other difficulties if we ask, not 'was it inevitable that the man should do what he did?', but 'was history inevitable, whatever the man did?' Liberty of individual action is consistent with the historical determination of effects; conversely, a man's act may be rigidly determined by his circumstances or his psychology, but its effects may still be seen as a matter of haphazard chance. If we try to limit 'determinism' to mean the opinion that social events are determined, whatever individuals try to do about them, the notion still includes very diverse thoughts about diverse facts. For example it includes the highly-placed man whose use of his power is circumscribed by his situation (an odd but common conception of power) together with the man whose very impotence to affect events may set him acting with frantic unpredictability – both of these inhabit systems in which events are thought to be determined otherwise than by the decisions of individuals.

It is necessary to show in this way how muddled and confusing these categories can be, in order that their following use shall not be misunderstood. They do not make boxes into which historians can be neatly sorted, nor exhaust the things which it is interesting to study in historians' work. At best they make a crude grid of reference, a pattern of latitudes and longitudes and altitudes by which many explanations and their organizing purposes may be roughly located. Of the three opposites – political and social, conservative and progressive, determinist and non-determinist – eight combinations are formally possible. The non-determinist combinations will be discussed together in the next section, then the four determinist combinations separately in the following one.

2. *Explaining acts that made history*

Surely there is one simple, proper form for the explanation of any free political act? It must describe in turn the actor's situation, the alternatives that he knew to be open to him, the reasoning by which he arrived at his decision, and then perhaps the psychology that led him to choose some aims rather than others. Sometimes this simple model works well enough; but sometimes, for reasons touched on already in the discussion of thought and situation, it will not work at all.

First, it supposes that the actor's own sight of his situation will match our modern interest in it, and will be the guide that sorts out for us the facts of his situation that are relevant from those that are not. But modern readers do sometimes want to know that bacteria as well as fate spread the plague in the fourteenth century, that there were errors in the economic theories prevalent in Chamberlain's England. Acts may need to be explained by ignorance or mistake, or by circumstances so familiar to the actor that he never noticed them.

Second, the simple model supposes that alternatives present themselves ready-made to politicians; whereas in life politicians are sometimes inventive. The historian need not limit himself to the alternatives that occurred to the politician. He may quite legitimately ask why the politician could think of no better ideas than those. In the politician's circumstances (such as political recruiting systems or educational systems) the historian may seek reasons why politicians were generally stupid or inventive or cautious at that time; or in individual psychology he may seek reasons for the particular occurrence of such qualities in individuals. The historian may write:

Chamberlain did nothing because he had lost the fire and political originality of his youth. He may have thought that he had no choice. It may seem to us that he had no choice. But the hindrances to action were just as strong in the next decade, when Asquith and Churchill and Lloyd George invented novel means of overcoming them. If they in their turn had merely been less able men, we should be solemnly describing their situation as hopeless, like Chamberlain's before them.

In practice the historian develops 'a sense of possibilities', mixed of his own practical wisdom and his knowledge of what contemporaries thought possible, and of what history earlier or later proved to be possible. This sense of proprieties and possibilities is usually too complex to be reduced to rules; it is seldom wholly technical; it is affected a great deal by the historian's own interests and values.

When at last the actor is established in his situation, meditating his alternatives, there are still various ways of explaining why he makes whatever choice he makes. It may be explained rationally: one was a better way than another to achieve his ends, or he thought that it was. It may be explained simply by indicating what his ends were: one course was cheaper than another, or attracted more votes, or avoided war. If his ends or means were unusual, or if we have some reason for wanting to know more about the attractions of familiar ends or means, then psycho-analysis or studies of his intelligence or experience may be called in to explain why he chose such ends, and why he pursued them by such brilliant, or stupid, or novel, or ordinary, means. There is no necessary conflict between explanations of Chamberlain's act which have him abandoning pensions because he was a strong enough man to defy the opposition, because he was a weak enough man to surrender to Hicks Beach and Salisbury, because he was too old and tired to fight, because he had a plan in mind to fight for pensions another day, or because his authoritarian personality was better pleased fighting Boers than fighting back-benchers. There is no necessary conflict, that is to say, if he had any real choice; if he had not, then most of this information, whatever other interest it may have, does not explain anything about his act. But if they are all relevant, is there no rule that will distinguish worse explanations from better? Has each writer and reader an absolute right to name his own curiosity?

One rule, though a vague one, suggests itself. There ought to be a sensible relation between the identification of an act and the explanation of it. A laconically reported act may be sufficiently explained by its obvious rational purposes. Psychological explanation of it makes no sense until the act to be explained is better identified, as a mental act of choice. If the act was a choice, we don't in any psychological sense know what the act was, until we know what the actor thought his alternatives were. To illustrate the point, Halévy's own explanation of Chamberlain's change of mind may be quoted again, this time in full:

'The time', declared the Queen's Speech, 'is not propitious for any domestic reforms which involve a large expenditure'. The explanation was that circumstances had changed since 1897. Not only had the Boer War begun and was proving a heavy financial burden, but Chamberlain, who had recovered from the effects of his initial fiasco and was once more the protagonist of a militant imperialism, no longer felt the need to justify his conversion to Toryism by a programme of social reform. Defy Russia, humiliate France, crush the Boers—that was the way to win a brilliant reputation at home and abroad! This terrible fellow had now something else to think of than old age pensions.[1]

If the cost of war left Chamberlain *no* choice, the rest of the explanation is unnecessary, insofar as it is a psychological explanation of an act that never happened, a choice that Chamberlain did not make. However, Halévy's 'not only . . . but' does not clearly measure the liberty that remained to Chamberlain, and we must suppose it to mean that *some* choice remained to him. Of the choice that he made, what explanation does Halévy's translator offer? Was it to his own conscience that Chamberlain once had to 'justify his conversion to Toryism by a programme of social reform'? Or did he justify it to others so that he need not feel ashamed in their presence? Either reading introduces a psychological explanation in terms of the guilt or shame that Chamberlain disliked to live with. But 'justify' is a bad translation of Halévy's *faire excuser* and 'his conversion to Toryism' is a bad translation of *son ralliement au parti conservateur*. Though the difference is only of shade and implication, the French suggests that Chamberlain used social reform to placate his followers when he attached himself to the conservative party (which is different from being converted to Toryism) and that he then used imperialism to replace social reform as a vote-getter, rather than as a solace to his conscience. Even if he had to drop pensions, this suggestion about the manipulation of his following and his public reputation helps to explain why he could drop pensions without much political loss. So the explanation, a very 'rational' one, is consistent with almost any reading of Halévy's imprecise estimate of the extent of choice that Chamberlain had. But the translator has Chamberlain acting because his inner feelings drove or allowed him to act; and that is not a helpful explanation of his choice, unless he really thought he had some choice. For the translator's explanation, the act to be explained should be more precisely identified.

If Chamberlain had no choice, this psychological information is not explanatory, though it may still be interesting for its own sake. In either language Halévy's words are so unkind that we may suspect him of having written them with more interest in discrediting Chamberlain than in explaining him. Halévy was usually careful to make clear a politician's range of choice. Perhaps he was vague this time, and underemphasized the first and financial half of his explanation, so that there would still be logical room for the second and polemical part. Whatever his reasons, it is not the polemics that make it a bad explanation. It is a bad explanation because the explanatory information is related too ambiguously to an act which is too vaguely defined in the first place.

But if this suggests a rule of general application, together with all the obvious rules about true facts, appropriate logic and fair comment, there is still room for legitimate difference among explanations of individual, non-determined acts. Do any of such differences arise consistently from the differences between generally political and generally social interests, or between conservative and progressive prejudices? Some; but I think not many. These categories are more useful for sorting out explanations of 'determined' acts, or of those larger social facts and events that are not called 'acts' at all. But one or two general features can be noticed.

If my interest is in the progress of societies rather than in politics for its own sake, but if I nevertheless belong in this present group because I think that the progress of society is sometimes affected by the deliberate acts of politicians, I will tend to explain an act by describing how history made an act – *some* act, a choice – necessary. I will describe the growth of the 'open' situation. I will try to judge just how open it was. What acts were possible, what would be the consequences of this one or that? The politician who made the choice is valuable to me because he offers a vantage point, a pair of eyes, a practised contemporary judgment of possibilities. At that moment his range of choice was society's, which is what I want to estimate. So I must ask, as he did, hypothetical questions, and put the answers in my book. (This may attract the scorn of English reviewers, who tend to damn all hypothetical speculation, while surprisingly continuing to praise its most famous exponents, Thucydides and Halévy, whose fictitious speeches and rhetorical questions respectively serve as devices for the very careful delimitation of fields of choice.) When the politician has made his mind up, I will try to explain his act by its public, social purposes, as long as it is credible that these weighed among his own reasons for his act, for it is the social consequences of his act that interest me enough for me to want to explain the act in the first place. I may not mind much whether he personally rose or fell in politics, or lost or saved his soul on the way. For me, he is an incident in the historical manufacture of social opportunities; his act is explained when I understand the provenance of his opportunity, what choice it gave him, and what public, social effects he tried to contrive. I can treat his act as a *Times* reporter would, and not as a muck-raker or a tabloid reporter or a psychoanalyst might. I can report:

Chamberlain thought the war more immediately pressing than reform. Though he could have beaten Hicks Beach if he had tried, he thought that war and reform might both suffer from any attempt to press both at once; and he was beginning to think that reform might be done better and more generously, in the long run, by another method altogether.

If on the other hand politics interest me more than society does, this same situation may appear not as a moment in the mutation of a society, but as a moment in the career of a politician, and as an illustration of the pressures which societies apply to politicians. My explanation may say more about the device of the political program, and the service it does for elector, press, party, and politician: about the mechanics by which social issues are got ready for political action, and by which private ambition in politics is made to serve public ends. According to my judgment of the politician's thoughts and feelings, I may show legislation as a by-product of his ambition, or I may show his power-getting activities as the disciplined servants of his desire to write his ideals into law. One way or another, I will probably connect the conditions of political life with the products of political action.

Our 'political' category had to include more than this mechanic's interest in political systems; it ambiguously included an interest in politicians as such, and also as human beings. So I may explain an act in terms of the types of people whom this or that system promotes, or the particular situation or psychology of this or that politician.

It can always be said, that a man had to be what he was in order to do what he did. To explain why he did what he did, historians may cite any of the things that he was, or any of the things that made him what he was, just as they may cite any other necessary conditions of his act. More is said in later chapters about selecting some from other necessary conditions. But perhaps nowhere more than in connecting acts with character and feeling, are historians less careful of the 'necessity' of the conditions they cite, whether these be the passions of the moment or qualities of character. Some historians resort to the actor's feelings only when his reasons seem inadequate. This is understandable, as Dray noticed in connection with dispositional explanations, but it can have queer effects – a passionate man is likely to get a name for coldness if his intelligence serves his passions efficiently, because his 'reasons' will be sufficient to make his acts intelligible without reference to his passions. To get a name for passion in a history book nowadays, you really have to be both passionate and stupid: Hitler was passionate and Stalin was not, for example, for no more apparent reason than that Stalin calculated better, won his wars and died in his bed.

In deciding how much of their explanations they should give to situations, how much to reasons and how much to emotions, plenty of historians are simply partisan. It is easy to cite the self-serving conditions for your enemies' acts, the public-serving conditions for your friends' acts, and perhaps the scientific-sounding conditions for acts to which you are so indifferent that they make occasion for a display of neutral scholarship:

Booth wanted pensions because his heart bled for the poor. Chamberlain wanted them because his heart yearned for power. Salisbury, the interest-broker for party unity, moved as any manipulator so-placed would have had to move, to exclude from the party's interior politics an issue on which there were flat, non-marketable disagreements.

It is in this crude way that the difference between conservative and progressive explainers is most obvious. It used to be possible to pick the historian's party by finding out which of his historical characters sought money and power, and which sought only truth and the public good. This was as true between other factions, as between progressive and conservative politicians. There was a time when Catholic historians had the Popes wanting to serve God and Henry VIII wanting the lead off the monastery roofs, while protestant historians knew all about Luther's religious experience and Tetzel's rake-off on indulgences. Not in all the books by white gentile protestant capitalist democrats, but still in some of them, medieval acts continue to be explained by pious superstition, communist acts by love of naked power, white South African acts by racial prejudice, black South African acts by love of liberty, white East Asian acts by love of liberty, yellow East Asian acts by racial prejudice, and so on. Macaulay was perhaps the most famous of all practitioners of this method.

The obvious iniquities of this propagandist method had one curious consequence. Instead of trying to make investigators more moral, efforts were made to make them less moral – there arose a scientific desire to clear social investigation of value-judgments. Writers strove to give their work an air of moral abstinence. That did not prove possible in practice, but the next best thing to abstinence is neutrality – all systems, persons and acts should be given the same moral color, and to avoid charges of naivete, not too rosy a color. But however the researcher might judge all motives alike, the public obtusely continued to judge some motives to be nobler than others; so neutrality could be achieved only by giving all the characters motives of the same type. So, for example, in the name of science the *issues* disappeared from political studies. The mechanics of personal political advancement had to supply everybody with the only mentionable motive for every act; or else every act had to be traced back to its affective origins, whatever they were before the actor's 'rationalizing' set in. The result was a revival, with new terminology, of some very old explanatory systems, especially 'single factor' systems. Except that they fixed on the different notion of 'power', some of the new explanations were very like the cruder and earlier versions of single-factor economic interpretation. Meanwhile the moral neutrality, often unintentionally, re-created a respectable old mood of conservative melancholy, which saw no point in fiddling with laws and systems under any of which an immutable human nature would take its same, sad, inevitable and sinful course.

It is not my intention to do the same: to suggest that all interests, and all the explanations they prompt, are as good and as bad as each other. I endorse, instead, two other conclusions. First, moral abstinence, besides being a moral act like any other, often does serious *technical* damage to explanations, by excluding many of their technically important parts. Important necessary conditions are omitted because they might excite the readers' passions, or expose the writer to the suspicion that he had passions of his own. Second, explanations must generally be judged not only by 'objective' tests, but also by the interest or aptness, the goodness or badness, of their guiding purposes – not only by agreed tests, that is to say, but also by disagreed tests; not only by technical, but also by political or artistic tests.

Explanations and their purposes do seem to vary most eccentrically when historians explain the free acts of powerful persons. Perhaps this is because those acts are less predictable than collective ones; or perhaps life and literature give to historians a wider, wilder variety of interests in individuals than in crowds. When larger, more abstract, less personal social events have to be explained, the relation between explanation and ideology is often strict and clear. Between these personal and impersonal extremes lie the explanations to be considered next – explanations of individual acts which are seen as the instruments or transmitters or effects of social forces, but not as their causes.

3. Explaining acts that history made

In determinist explanations of individual acts, more order is visible than in the non-determinist ones, but it is necessary to say again that the following method of classifying their general purposes is quite imprecise and not at all exhaustive; at best it suggests some 'ideal types' by differentiation from which the unique, cross-bench performances of real historians may sometimes be described. It is also prudent to add that for present purposes 'non-determined' means little more than unpredictable or potent, and 'determined' means either impotent or unchosen. This has, I hope, nothing to do with the philosophical problem of free-will.

(i) Political – conservative – determinist

A variety of interests may be grouped thus. Here, first, is the ideal situation for the literary biographer of a politician, more interested in the Life than the Times, who can attend to the development of his character in a society that need not be questioned much. This biographer must notice as much about society as his character notices, suffers by, or takes advantage of; but that is all. His biography is a revelation, not primarily of the defence or manipulation of social systems, but of one man's experience of politics and of the texture of political life.

Here belongs also the conservative who wants to learn political skill in order to get on in politics, or at least to indulge his imagination in that way: the reader who would imitate in his career, or re-live in his armchair, the triumphs of Metternich or Lord Salisbury.

Whoever takes this view, takes both the form and the product of the political system as fixed (unlike Metternich and Lord Salisbury themselves). If he asks 'why did this man act thus?' he cannot want to know about the man's range of choice (assumed to be narrow) of social effects (which are assumed to be inevitable, whatever politicians do). He may want, instead, to know what personal satisfaction or advancement a man expected of his act. He may want to understand how a political system is manipulated for private advantage rather than for public effect. Politics, for him, is likely to be about the achievement of office, and the use of office to affect the distribution of other offices. (If he thought that political choices had important public effects, we would remove this investigator to another classification.) He *may* examine the forces which fix this unmanipulable society, in an effort to convince us that his deterministin view of it is the right one; but his interest in the political life itself is more important, and his determinist view allows him with good enough conscience to take that short, tactical view of politics with which most working politicians are occupied in most of their waking hours.

To this, as to other positions in this classification, one may arrive unintentionally, as the haphazard result of some scientific, disciplinary or conventional choice of method. The political scientist who tries too hard to abstract the getting and exercise of power from everything else – from its social purposes and effects, for example – may drift into this position. An early example was Bertrand Russell's *Power: a new social analysis.*[2] Readers of that book may remember how hard it proved to sustain the new abstraction. By the end of the book the author was back with the Aristotelian categories from which he had sought to escape: naked power, economic power, priestly power, and so on, don't differ much from the old concepts which they re-name. They were brought back in order to relate 'pure' power to its conditions and uses and effects, perhaps because the author found that 'pure' power threatened to confine him – *him*, of all people! – to a tactical and conservative interest in politics.

L. B. Namier's analysis of English politics in the later eighteenth century affords a more successful example. The books,[3] rather than the author, are located by our classification; the author would probably have claimed that his 'determinism' was true of English eighteenth-century politics but certainly not of all politics. When Hitler (with more power over society than Lord Newcastle had) threatened to lay waste Namier's native and adopted countries, then Namier began dramatically to connect politics with policies. But to the end of his life, he was still criticized for the gap that seemed to exist between his two skills – between the perfect mechanic of political systems, and the rather intuitive generalizer about their modes of growth and their social foundations. Between these extremes, at the systematic study of the immediate social determinants and consequences of policy, he was not so good or so patient. Not because he did not see the need; but perhaps because he found it hard to bear the result. That scholarly austerity which can tolerate large generalizations as long as they make no pretense to certainty, finds it harder to tolerate the detailed relation of politics to policy, in local but uncertain statements, statements that look as if they ought to be proved, but are not. To *prove* a determinist position is difficult; to *assume* it, allows the historian to concentrate on the detailed political in-fighting whose every fact has its footnote. Conservative and determinist assumptions about society, if they are complacently held, may encourage the historian to ignore society and write only about its politics. Conservative professional assumptions about the historian's craft often reinforce conservative opinions about society, for they encourage the historian to avoid speculation about the uncertain connections of events, in favor of safe precision in the discovery of events. With the progressive determinist it is otherwise; he has all sorts of reasons for wanting to establish his determinist diagnosis, and they often lead him to neglect the detail of politics. The conservative criticism of progressive work is thus precise, quarrelling with its truth and documentation. Progressive criticism of conservative work is vague, quarrelling with its triviality, its lack of interest or relevance. Conservative criticism of progressive work can be technical, while progressive criticism of conservative work has to be unfashionably moral. The conservative exercise requires an exact discipline which some elders think good for the edification of the young. The progressive method makes more daring connections and speculations and syntheses, which the young themselves often find more attractive, and which allow examiners to test young people's imaginative and reflective faculties. Paedagogically, these approaches are in chronic conflict; but professionally, the conservative determinist has inevitable scholarly advantages over his progressive colleague. Meanwhile I must guard against confusion; this is a narrow non-interventionist conservatism. Conservatives who wish actively to preserve society (rather than merely to accept or approve of it) appear in a different light in later chapters. Also, disciplines differ. For historians, professional and social conservatism may go together, as argued here. But in other social sciences it is often the radical pioneers of new methods who insist on the socially conservative limitation of studying only what can be proved for certain, by objective quantitative methods.

Cutting across our three classifications there is always a fourth: clever and stupid. This group which includes Namier, includes also a lot of dull old text-books. These were the history texts which came too late for the heroic view that once saw great men moulding the world at will, but too soon for the radical transfer of interest from the political narrative to the forms of social development. Many worthy motives – to inform without disturbing, to convey precise fact that could be committed to memory, to waste no time and lose no customers by speculative interpretations – converged to produce pedestrian political narratives, paying their inappropriate respects to Ranke by their accuracy, and to Bury by the scientific inevitability with which act, choice and event fell into determined order.

To all these, the common interest by which we have grouped them will suggest explanations of a man's act which make it an intelligible part of the pursuit or enjoyment of power for its own sake, or for its private rewards: e.g.,

Chamberlain changed his mind because only so could he, in that situation, preserve his position with the Prime Minister, the Cabinet, the parliamentary majority and a sufficient number of electors. Even if they were not quite the same electors as had followed him before, they would serve as well as the former lot, and there were more of them.

(ii) *Social – conservative – determinist*

Theoretically, an extremist in these three views could have only one motive for explaining political acts at all. He might want to explain failures, to show the members of society that their affairs really are determined, in order to allay anxieties to which their illusions of free will might otherwise expose them. He might, for example, want to save reformers from wearing themselves out, or the rich from guilt, or the poor from hope.

This is perhaps the conservatism that is commonest in daily life: 'human nature is immutable, the growth and decay of human institutions are inexorable; history, for all its local variations, is sufficiently determined and explained by that human nature; politicians peddle trivia, impotent to affect such big matters as are governed by the laws of nature, or evolution, or the jungle, or supply and demand.'

In the text-book trade, just as heroism was earlier discounted, so presently were scissors-and-paste, and political history itself. All-facts-mentioned-in-other-texts must now be organized into causal systems, and made relevant to the social condition of the citizens; but still without offensive diagnoses or any implied encouragement of dangerous remedies. The old routines of nineteenth century politics were abbreviated and mixed with social statistics to become The Consequences of the Industrial Revolution. The old diplomatic routines, stripped of the detailed human interest they once had, were mixed with mild references to colonies and armaments and popular patriotism to become The Causes of World War One. Between profound causes and their large effects, politics became a mere link, or transmitter. Its detail did not matter and it need not be searched for critical decisions. If school boards require uncontroversial conclusions, but academic fashion requires the analysis of profound social causes, then a conservative determinism is nearly inevitable; it is wholly so if detailed political narrative is out of fashion, and doubly so if detailed political narrative has been declared pre-scientific.

But a conservative and determinist view, concentrating on society rather than on its politics, may equally be lit by high and sensitive intelligence. It is this approach more than any other which has explored the other human needs than bread and butter, and the other-than-economic determinants of social development. Men variously need religion, family ties, neighbors; symbols and illusions and allegiances; membership, community, nationality. The intelligent social-determinist-conservative devotes his time to reflection upon these needs. He may be as angry as any progressive about the commercial exploitation of humanity's non-economic needs; but he does not think the needs would disappear if the exploiters did. (Both, to introduce a term omitted from our classification, differ creditably from many liberals, who neither recognize such non-material needs, nor raise any objection to their commercial exploitation.) There is no special reason why conservatives should neglect or dislike economic determinants, and many don't; but the label often distinguishes them from liberals, because of the values which some conservatives think the world had before its capitalist liberation, or because of the need they see in present times for other forms of order and allegiance than those of a well-run market-place. Their social interest, which may be in the quality of everyman's individual experience as well as in the bonds of society, combines with their determinism to make politics matter little to them, at ordinary times.

These are brought into this classification by their conscious values. Others join it inadvertently, by choice of discipline or method. In the flesh, many structural-functional sociologists could scarcely look, talk or write less like philosophical conservatives; but they stray into the same territory in their search for disciplinary identity and scientific law. In wanting to show that social structure and function determine each other in some scientifically reliable way they are already, in the crude terms of this category, social and determinist. They are very likely not conservative by temperament or conviction. They want to break and re-make many familiar categories of study and images of society. But whatever radical feelings there may be in the functional analyst's heart, there are some very conservative tendencies in his science. He usually denies this – the point is argued below, in Chapter 6.

Even if the deliberate conservative be as determinist as either his sociological or his Marxist colleagues, he can nevertheless approach the past more flexibly than they can. Many sociologists wish to omit valuation, or else to use society's rather than their own valuations, in their study of society. Many Marxists purport to derive their values from their study of society. Conservatives more commonly feel free to believe that their morals come from outside history, but can be freely applied to history. Some distrust change itself, perhaps because of its risks, its contempt for experience, its psychological unsettlements, its danger to accumulated social or religious goods. But this attitude to change, which has supplied most of our examples so far, is only one of many kinds of conservative thought. Conservatism more often values particular qualities of societies, and where those qualities do not exist, is accordingly radical in wanting to establish or restore them. To be Marxist about the present is usually to be Marxist about the past. To be conservative about the present is often to be radical about some at least of the past. Unlike the Marxist, who must judge all steps as not necessarily pleasant but at least necessary and 'upward', the conservative can see a rake's progress, or some alternation of good, bad and indifferent for which progress, or any other linear word, would be a misnomer. The judgments and explanations of the eclectic conservative are harder to predict than the Marxist's, at least until you know the conservative much better than you need to know the Marxist.

A twentieth-century conservative who is made conservative by his dislike of change as such, or by his feeling for the bonds of society which reduce the isolation of individuals, may find in medieval times, in local power and universal religion, qualities which he admires and would wish to have conserved. But a modern conservative of the stockbroking kind, conservative because he values capitalist economy, protestant diversity and democratic government, may have a radical distaste for all preceding institutions. The affinities or antipathies which define historians' attitudes to past societies are many, subtle, and, especially among conservatives, unsystematic. Think of the different sorts of 'lack of restraint' by which different conservatives may seek to explain the buccaneering quality of many individual lives in Elizabethan England. The Augustan points to the want of civilized and refined conventions of conduct. The romantic conservative points to the common language and manners of Elizabethan society, to the lack of that segregation of classes which is necessary for the final refinement of the rich and the final degradation of the poor. The stockbroking conservative notices how little capital you needed to get started in those days, and what real rewards and opportunities there were for buccaneers. The religious conservative shows how religious schism combined with irreligious rapacity to free men from the ties that had once bound them to land, church, and each other. It is not so much their different technical understanding of history, as the different value they put on different aspects and kinds of experience, that makes their explanations differ; none of the explanations is incompatible with any other, and all are in some sense conservative, determinist, and concerned with the quality of social life rather than with its political management.

By definition, political management does not interest this group much; if they explain political acts at all, it is likely to be by reference to the general, rather than the tactical, determinants of action. Without any logical necessity, it happens in practice that many also emphasize the non-economic aspects of human nature and society. So, from stupid to intelligent, from old-fashioned to new-fangled, their contributions to Chamberlain's problem might range from

it wanted eight years more of industry and democracy, ere the currents of change would ripen the political climate for such charitable medicine for the aged working man's predicament.

to

Three centuries after his ancestor Cecil had given the English Crown the fatal notion that it might rescue the poor from the mercies of parliament, Lord Salisbury had learned better: he counted votes. Lords and Commons, respectively the ancient patrons and the new representatives of the poor, counted taxes. The poor themselves, expected any day to use their votes to plunder the rich, preferred instead to have the rich plunder the Boers, and counted corpses in the *Daily Mail*, while their aged parents died less publicly in workhouses, savouring these bitter first fruits of popular democracy.

or

'Imperial Britain' was a more attractive in-group than 'the poor' or 'the have-nots', both for the under-privileged to identify with, and for the privileged and the media to encourage. It carried dominant, as against subordinate, status. The belief that Imperialism was also a rational way to wealth, was enough to tip the scale finally against the undesirable status- and role-identification which was involved in voting for the internal re-distribution of wealth. Political programs are for maximizing the number, rather than the intensity, of affiliations; Chamberlain acted accordingly.

(iii) Political – progressive – determinist

Here is revolutionary careerism, for the lad with Lenin's baton in his knapsack – not how to contrive revolutions which would otherwise fail, but how to lead revolutions which would otherwise be led by others. But for revolutionaries and especially for Marxists, the correct diagnosis of historical situations is so central a part of individual political skill, that this interest in personal politics necessarily includes a good deal of interest in general economic and social forces also.

Lenin's books had immediate political purposes: to define situations and therefore policies, and to discredit deviations from them. He explains the acts of enemies in only three ways: as based on class interest, historical mistake, or personal careerism. Political skill consists in working with history, not against it. The Tsar does not understand history at all. The Mensheviks may understand it but they do not know the stage it has reached; they have misplaced themselves in history and consequently misconceived their role in it. Lenin understands it, and locates himself in it exactly. It is to judgments or misjudgments of this sort that Lenin ascribes men's acts in his books. Not always, perhaps, in life; but books, for Lenin, were acts too.

In this view, politicians tend to be judged by the historical correctness of their policies, rather than by the dexterity of their tactics. In a determinist understanding, Lenin must have succeeded because he was right about Russian capitalism or the stage reached by Russian agriculture, rather than because he was right about the exhaustion of Russian soldiers, or sensitive to the changing moods of peasants or soviets. Trotsky must have fallen because he was wrong about Permanent Revolution, rather than because he was wrong about Stalin. Marxist revolutionaries write this sort of history more commonly than do Marxist historians, whose conventional concern is with the historical forces themselves, rather than with the persons who obstructed or took advantage of them.

The 'political – progressive – determinist' view is as common outside Marxist writing as within it. Plenty of non-Marxists have observed that Coolidge did not foresee the forces of change, or that Hoover did not understand them. The determinist friends of the New Deal explain Roosevelt's acts by his having understood the forces of change; and since he couldn't lick 'em, joined 'em. The enemies of Roosevelt who see him keeping afloat merely by good luck and Morgenthau's devices upon a turbulent flood of change, make a different judgment of his understanding, but the same determinist judgment of his situation. The difference here between conservative and progressive explainer may not be great, in that they both tend to explain political acts by reference to the factors that left the actors no choice. But because of his special connection of political skill with historical diagnosis, the progressive more often emphasizes his actor's understanding of the forces of history, and the conservative more often emphasizes his actor's understanding and manipulation of the political machinery with which history has presented him.

In practice, no historian is rigidly determinist; certainly no historian with an interest in the detail of politics. From Lenin to Schlesinger, whatever their respect for history's immutable forces, the friends of change have allowed their politicians in some degree at least to arrest, accelerate or deflect the forces of which they were the political representatives. What tends to distinguish the progressive-political-determinist from his conservative equivalent, is his commoner interest in economic determinants; what tends to distinguish him from his progressive-social-determinist colleague, is his concern with the detailed political expression of the determining factors. Marxist and reformist might thus briefly explain Chamberlain's act, according to their different views of his historical situation:

Chamberlain was trying to buy off a non-class-conscious proletariat with a double bribe. They and the rich together could be joint parasites upon the toiling masses of the colonial empire. His 'ransom' of social reforms was meant to convince them that they could also be parasites upon the rich at home. But the rich found the former method cheaper, and in 1900 Chamberlain had to give up the pretense that a bourgeois parliament would pay any ransom at all if it had to come from local bourgeois pockets.

or (substantially repeating an explanation cited earlier for other reasons)

Though public need and public support for pensions were both adequate, their passage was still prevented by the parliamentary structure and by the configuration of parties. The conservative power of the House of Lords, though now used with caution, was unbroken. The cross-cutting of radical and imperial issues had transferred Chamberlain's vital group from the Liberal party, which was left too weak to govern, to the Conservative party, where the radical faction was swamped by greater numbers who disliked reform and owed nothing to reformist voters. Chamberlain acknowledged the logic of the new alliance when in 1896 he chose an imperial, rather than any domestic, cabinet post. Deserting pensions in 1900 was merely his final capitulation to that logic.

(iv) *Social – progressive – determinist*

Here are located many left-wing historians, including many of the Marxists who are professional historians, and those liberals who earn the label by believing that history is freeing individuals, rather than that individuals can make free with history.

These are all distinguished from their 'political' equivalents by their lesser interest in politics as such, or by a larger scale of study which allows them to ignore entirely whatever limited and local power they still allot to politicians. Like conservative social determinists, progressive social determinists may have little interest in political acts, which they will explain, if at all, as expressions of general historical forces. Thus in his studies of French politics, which told what political advantage various parties took of the historical situations in which they found themselves, Marx belongs in our previous category, as do most histories by active revolutionaries; but to this present group belongs Marx's *Manifesto*, which attends to the general growth of historical situations. Beard's *Economic Interpretation*, full of the devices by which the founding fathers inevitably wrote their class interests into their country's constitution, perhaps belongs in the 'political' category, while the impersonal social determinism of Turner's *Frontier* belongs in this.

Among those of social and determinist tendency, the progressive and conservative divisions do not differ much. The examples so far have tended to show conservatives explaining stability and progressives explaining change. It is only necessary to catch them at the opposite tasks to see how alike their explanations often are. Metternich and Salisbury were mentioned as non-determinist conservatives, and so they were in that each exercised, he thought, a deliberate delaying power; but exercised it against forces which each thought irresistible in the long run. Metternich ascribed the same vitality as any liberal would ascribe to nascent nationalism. Salisbury was a gloomy but accurate prophet of the welfare state, too gloomy and not so accurate in expecting it to destroy his party and his class. Conversely, Marxists are under compulsion to explain static societies; if their rules of growth hold only for Europe, they must save the generality of the rules by discovering what extraordinary economic factors must have arrested the civilizations of the Nile and Euphrates, of India and China. So they show that the river valleys made for monocultures and easy communications, so that whole regions came under the restraint of premature military monarchies; or that an overcrowded relation of men to land in India prevented the extraction of a surplus sufficient for development, and produced an appropriate superstructure of regimes and religions inimical to change. There are these similarities between conservative and progressive determinist explanations. But there are also some differences.

It is argued later that a good deal of explanation is guided by norms, both of value and of expectation: why did specially good, specially bad or specially surprising things happen? Conservatives often want to explain change as a deviation from stability, while progressives want to explain stability as an interruption of progress. There is a conservative tendency to explain change in terms of the appearance of novel forces, and a progressive tendency to explain the novel forces as products of the breakdown of old (and undesirable) systems. Guizot had the bourgeois class overthrowing the new monarchies, long before Marx had the new monarchies accelerating the generation of a bourgeoisie. Both were progressive determinists of sorts; but in Guizot's later, conservative and less determinist years, he was inviting all the rich to unite against all the poor, while Marx (issuing the reciprocal invitation) was explaining that the rich had themselves created the proletariat. This large scale of explanation is the business of a later chapter. It is sufficient to notice here one difference between the progressive and conservative explanation of acts to which neither, as determinist, ascribes much importance. If a progressive determinist finds that his politician understood history and was on its side, then approval is automatic, curiosity is satisfied, and Marx and Macaulay are alike in that they people the past with silhouettes, of whom it is only important to know whether they were on the right or the wrong side; and if wrong, whether from mistake or malice. The conservative, being free to deplore history however well he understands it and however inevitably it happened, may ascribe the same moral autonomy to politicians as to himself, and may sometimes want to explore or condemn the way their consciences bent before the winds of change. And if he wants to show why and how their acts were determined by their circumstances, his explanations may cite subtler and more complex and individual aspects of their psychology than Marx or Macaulay needed to bother with. Marx knew that people were complex and all different, but he thought that a few constant qualities in themselves and their situations sufficiently determined most of their public and historical roles. The conservative Namier was forced by ignorance to do the same, and depicted a system running on psychology as simple as Marx's; but with the difference, that Namier thought this was not a fact of human nature but a limitation of historical research, regretted it, and looked to the day when the science of psychology might do something about it.

When the progressive-social-determinist explains individual acts at all, therefore, he does it in a way sufficiently illustrated by the examples in the last section, with even less connection of historical forces to local political situations: Chamberlain changed his mind because the middle class made him.

4. J. L. Garvin and Julian Amery

This chapter has been illustrated by short explanations written to fit particular historical interests. Can the exercise be reversed – can an historian's general interests be discovered from his explanations of acts? Chamberlain's official biography offers two explanations, by different authors, of his suspension of interest in pensions; they will do as concluding examples. J. L. Garvin's third volume of *The Life of Joseph Chamberlain*, published in 1934, takes the story to the end of 1900 and includes an explanation of Chamberlain's first retreat in 1899–1900. In the fourth volume, published in 1951, Julian Amery explains why Chamberlain missed the opportunity to revive a pension scheme when the war ended in 1902.

Garvin shows Chamberlain persisting even after the war started in 1899; as late as November 17 he was writing a Cabinet memorandum in favor of making a moderate but immediate beginning with pensions. But when the change came, Garvin's explanation of it is short and sure:

But after that came the Black Week; war costs multiplied; and the resistance of the Treasury became impregnable for the time.[4]

This has to be read in context. Garvin has already noticed some of the conservative opposition to Chamberlain's domestic schemes, and he goes on, in a passage quoted earlier, to put into Chamberlain's head ideas of a strategic project for tariff reform by which 'the same policy that knitted the Empire might provide the means for Old Age Pensions.' But although it gets some outside help in such ways, the explanation itself is still brusque. Why did the Treasury resist? Yes, it had to pay for the war, but why was it unwilling to pay for pensions as well? What allies or political resources made it 'impregnable'? What structure of society and institutions made those allies and resources available to it? Garvin does not attend directly to such questions. The obstructions to high expenditure are represented, not as facts of society, but as conditions of politics. So Garvin seems to belong in our 'political' category. But although the explanation itself allows Chamberlain no choice, the speculation that follows it implies that in only slightly different circumstances he might have had a large power to direct the course of English economic, social and imperial development. Garvin thus distinguishes very different powers in different situations, and since he also rejoices at every radical use of such powers, we may write him down as 'political – progressive – non-determinist'. As a busy, politicking liberal editor, he would not have objected to that.

But this classification is only a crude beginning of what may be learned about him from his book. That passage of speculation, for example, imagines what radical effects Chamberlain might have accomplished by tariff reform. But however rich might have been the benefits to society, Garvin keeps his dramatic light, not on those social effects, but upon Chamberlain himself: Chamberlain in action, or contemplating action. Strangely, for a man who in his own life was busy with so many reforming causes, Garvin's three volumes are fairly represented by this passage in that they communicate little compassion, and a more passionate interest in social power than in social welfare. Though vast social changes are mooted or accomplished or celebrated in every volume, their literary function seems to have been to manufacture opportunities for Chamberlain to act, and then to be the physical measure of the magnitude of the action. This can be defended – the book is a life of Chamberlain, not of Victorian England. But Garvin seems to show less interest even than Chamberlain had, in society for its own sake: less interest than Chamberlain in the mountains to be moved, and a more dazzled obsession than even Chamberlain had, with the spectacle of Chamberlain moving them. In a style as bombastic, but with concerns more trivial, than Carlyle's, Garvin is the boasting advocate not so much of Chamberlain's good causes as of Chamberlain's greatness, measured mostly by political muscle. It is not surprising that his explanation of this much-criticized defeat should be an explanation which does not mention Chamberlain's name, nor reveal that there ever was a fight. The Treasury was impregnable; there was no choice.

In the length and care of Amery's explanation it would perhaps be impertinent to discern some intention to improve on Garvin's work, but it is not impertinent to be grateful for the result. Amery's first explanation is the same as Garvin's: there was no money. But instead of a brisk mention of the Boer War, it is an extensive social analysis which explains why there was no money:

We have reached one of those points in history, when material and ideological forces, long dammed up, suddenly find their spokesmen and break into the main stream of political life. To harness these revolutionary forces to their interest was the task which challenged Chamberlain and his colleagues.

Everybody was ready for old age pensions, and the workers were ready to support whoever gave them pensions.

Here, then, was a great opportunity for Chamberlain to secure the glitter of his Imperial achievements with the hard currency of domestic reform. Yet, on this score, he remained strangely passive.

There follows an account of various speeches and proposals on the subject during 1901 and 1902, and a note of the profound consequences of Chamberlain's surrendering, to Lloyd George and the Liberal party, the leadership of the movement for social reform.

Why did Chamberlain change his Mind?

What is the explanation of Chamberlain's strange passivity? Had the time come at last, when even he no longer had a social message to deliver?

. . . In the past, while it still reflected a predominantly landed interest, the Tory party had not been averse to measures of municipal or state socialism; especially when the burden of them fell chiefly upon the urban middle class. But with the Home Rule split and the Imperial policies of the 90's – both of them Chamberlain's work – that same middle class had become the dominant partner in Unionism. In the House, and still more in the country, business men were now the backbone of the Unionist alliance. Essentially individualists, they were stubbornly opposed to any measures which [might add] to the burden of taxation. . . At this very time, moreover, they were engaged in a general offensive against the Trades Unions. . . They were, thus, in no mood to make concessions to Labour. Yet these were the men who looked to Chamberlain. He was their foremost representative, and it was upon them that he relied for the furtherance of his Imperial policies.

The temper of Unionism was thus unfavourable to a programme of Social Reform. More immediately deterrent, perhaps, were the opinions of the Chancellor of the Exchequer and his advisers at the Treasury.

Here follows an account of the continuing conflict with Hicks Beach.

Something would have to be sacrificed to his plea for economy. The dangers of the international situation made it hard to contemplate a reduction in the Defence Estimates. The cut, therefore, would have to come in his projects for Social Reform. Here is the surest explanation of his abandonment of Old Age Pensions. It is difficult to see what else he could have done in the circumstances. . . One look . . . at the Unionist benches in the House of Commons must have been enough to convince him that there would be no support from that quarter for any taxation which involved a redistribution of wealth.[5]

For easier comparison with Garvin's, the essentials of this explanation might be condensed thus:

Partly by Chamberlain's doing, the Unionist party had acquired as its dominant component an urban middle class which was opposed to labor, to redistributive taxation, and therefore to both the ends and the means of the pension program. To the means, the Treasury was also opposed, for professional reasons.

In some ways this explanation resembles Garvin's. Both conclude that Chamberlain had no choice. But Amery's conclusion is more hesitant, even if 'it is difficult to see what else he could have done in the circumstances.' But if Garvin's immediate explanation of this particular incident is more strictly determinist, his general account of the situation (as of many others) allows Chamberlain more independent power than Amery allows him. Both, reasonably since they are writing political biography, organize social analysis to show what roles society offered to its politicians. In Garvin's account, there are often opportunities for Chamberlain to make great muscular alterations to society. To Amery, the opportunities more often appear as opportunities to profit by, to lead, and perhaps to guide, the great currents of change – not to create them, or divert their courses much. 'To harness these revolutionary forces to their interest was the task which challenged Chamberlain and his colleagues.' Though Amery's explanation leaves Chamberlain a little more choice about pensions than Garvin's allowed him (indeed, perhaps he had more in 1902 than in 1900) Amery's general view of his situation is a more determinist one than Garvin's, in that it allows to Chamberlain less independent power to affect, by choice, the development of English society. It will be argued later, that difference of this sort cannot be resolved by wholly technical reference to the facts. Here it is perhaps worth noticing that Garvin was a most successful journalist, a liberal in various senses of the word, a man whose interest in politics was, almost from professional necessity, an interest in dramatizing it and moralizing about it. Both operations go better if the dramatis personae can act with effect on more important things than the advancement of themselves and their parties. Amery, on the other hand, in his father's experience and his own, has an insider's view of politics and of the conservative party; a different interest in politics, and a more modest sense of its powers and possibilities.

Are similar differences visible between the political values of the two writers? Here it is as well worth asking what they do not explain, as what they do. Garvin generally attends to large social changes only in immediate connection with their political manifestations. He does not explain how the Treasury achieved its impregnability; though his suggestion that a change of persons might easily change its politics, implies that its 'impregnability' arose from the accident of Hicks Beach's 'negative' personality and economic faith. In a similar way, we may notice that what Amery does not question much, is the belief and conduct to be expected of the new middle class in the Unionist party. He thinks it worth explaining how and why the members of that class had begun to rally to the party, but not why they thought as they did about labor and taxation. Amery reports without surprise that they were engaged in a general offensive against the Trade Unions. They were also opposed to any shift of taxation from low rates to high, from land to business incomes, and from poor to rich incomes. This does not cause surprise either, or need explanation.

In short, Amery finds it necessary to explain the arrival of this class in the Unionist party, but quite unnecessary to explain its selfish opinions. The significance of this becomes clearer if we compare it with an opposite treatment of the same subject. One man at least has since taken it for granted, as needing no explanation at all, that the new industrial middle class would inevitably predominate in the conservative party. But he thought it by no means natural or inevitable that the new class should use the party for a war on labor and for opposition to social reform. He thought those decisions of the years 1900–1902 were the worst and the most self-destructive mistakes which the business class and the conservative party had made in the whole history of either. This was not some socialist critic; he was the first industrialist to become conservative party leader and prime minister in the twentieth century. Stanley Baldwin thought that the follies of 1902 were surprising, and wanted explaining, not because he took a harsher view than Amery of the business man, but because he took a more charitable view. It was because he thought business men capable of longer and more intelligent and less selfish views of their own interests, that he could judge the views of the business men of 1902 to have been needlessly short, stupid and selfish. In this, he was like other business men who had risen high in the party: Robert Peel, father and son, and Joseph Chamberlain and his son Neville. The Peels, Baldwin and the Chamberlains were manufacturers who had dealt directly with labor. They thought that their fellow business men could be educated to deal with labor, both in industry and in politics, as intelligently as they themselves had done. The Amery family is not particularly aristocratic, nor devoid of business interests, but its education has been more professional and aristocratic than industrial, its central interest is in public life, and its regard for both business and labor seems more detached, and perhaps less sanguine, than Baldwin's or Chamberlain's. At least, it does not appear to surprise Julian Amery when business men behave as crudely as, in England, noblemen and professional men and working men have often agreed in expecting business men to behave.

Another way of divining Amery's interests from his explanation, is to ask what that explanation implies about the alternatives which might have taken the place of the half-century of English history introduced by the decisions the Unionist party took in 1902. It is obvious that Amery could have wished Chamberlain to have persevered and succeeded. What result would he have expected of this? Not the radical changes *in society* that Garvin would have expected; but radical changes in politics. The course which in fact the party forced upon Chamberlain

meant that Chamberlain had renounced the leadership of the great movement for Social Reform. Under him, it had transcended party dissensions for thirteen years. Now it would turn once more to the Liberal party and find a new leader in [Lloyd George]. One day, Old Age Pensions would be among his victories.[6]

Here and elsewhere an alternative English history is implied. Social change proceeds in much the same way, and social legislation only a little faster. The parties compete more evenly in legislating social reform and in attracting working class votes. Neither party takes sides in the class war, and both parties, being broadly based, have an interest in conciliating the classes. A broader combination of interests in the conservative party provides both an education and (where education fails) a restraining force for that stockbroking conservatism to which the different conservatism of this more co-operative picture is opposed.

What does Amery mean by inviting Chamberlain 'to secure the glitter of his Imperial achievements with the hard currency of domestic reform'? Whether he means that it needed social reform to justify the Imperial policy, or to secure the Imperial policy, or to secure Chamberlain in office and good reputation, he certainly implies that the two policies should have continued together, and together might have kept the Unionist party in good relations with the working classes. But the new middle-class 'temper of Unionism' prohibited this alternative history from beginning; and for Amery the cause of that failure was not so much the choice the new men made (which was to be expected of men of that sort) but simply their arrival in power (which nobody could have prevented).

Though Amery has the same enthusiasm as Garvin had for Chamberlain's proposals of reform, and looks at English society with more of both urbanity and compassion than Garvin had, yet his implication of the best – but still impossible – alternative future for English society is one that locates him as 'political – conservative – determinist'. Such rough location reinforces the doubt, that those categories have served any better purpose than to give the contents of this chapter a workable order. Amery's 'political' interest, for example, does not prevent his tracing political conditions to their deep social causes. His determinism is flexible: he hints that a more inventive Chamberlain might somehow have found a way. Above all, his 'conservatism' can be located more exactly than by that general label. His hesitant determinism, his urbane, grey view of business men and working men, his thought that the party might include and restrain and conciliate both if it could stand (as in its landowning days it had once stood) apart from both, his view of parties 'harnessing interests', his use of 'glitter' and 'hard currency' – these place him as far from stockbroking conservatism as from Garvin's heroic-capricious liberalism. Except for a radical difference over military imperialism, they would place him in the philosophical, evolutionary, conciliatory tradition of Burke. That is not where most contemporary critics place Mr. Amery – they see him in the Conservative Party's right wing. But today's Conservative Party is somewhat left of Burke, and somewhat less philosophical.

Not all of this could be discovered from Amery's immediate explanation of Chamberlain's acts. Those were explained by the close facts of his political situation. It is in relating these close facts to their social and historical roots, that the explainer's philosophy has most work to do, and reveals itself by the way it does it. It is when historians turn from individual actions to larger, less personal things – to war and revolution, social stability and change – that their purposes and philosophies are plainest, and most clearly related to their explanations.

3

Why Histories Happen

1. Choices of causes

Two dear old-fashioned figures of speech used to express the complexities of social change: 'endless chains of cause and effect', and 'the seamless web of history'.

Simple historians saw simple chains:

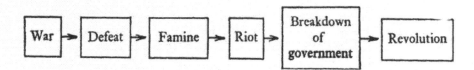

The more sophisticated might list the 'necessary conditions' which converged to combine in a 'sufficient set':

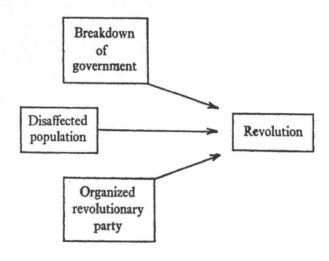

Most practitioners combined both, whether in historical detail –

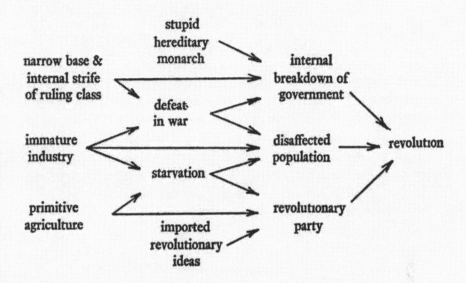

– or in more abstract or analytical terms:

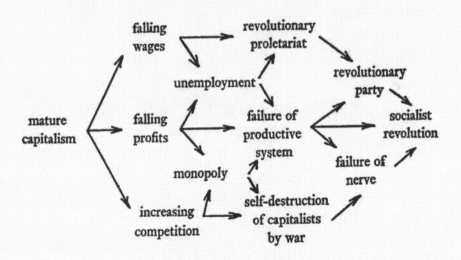

The textile metaphor, with some fancy weaving, allows us to imagine a seamless web sufficiently complicated to accommodate

any of these patterns. Similar patterns can depict the more permanent relations of continuing social facts – interrelations within
economic systems or social structures. An ingenious printer could
elaborate further. Lines of different color might represent different
strands of development: red for economic interests, blue for power,
pink for the history of ideas, yellow for indexes of integration or
anomie. He might progress from plane to solid geometry to represent
different levels of analysis in a three-dimensional web. He might
abandon textiles for other images of causal relations – double-ended
arrows to indicate reciprocal causation, vicious and virtuous and
self-equilibrating circles, spirals and other patterns of cumulative,
reciprocal or dialectical causation. The events of human history, and
the facts of social system and structure, are uncountable. So are the
relations through which they appear to affect one another. So are the
possible ways of grouping, isolating and naming all those 'facts'. But
as long as the reader keeps these complicated possibilities in mind,
the simplest diagrams will suffice to illustrate what different 'shapes'
may be seen in different explanations of the same thing-to-be-
explained. Different explainers may, for example, break a chain of
cause and consequence at different points; they may choose chains
that run in different directions; they may choose not chains but
patterns of converging causes or conditions – and the possible
patterns are innumerable.

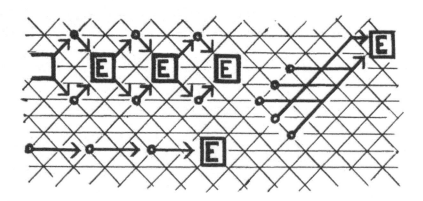

But no chain or pattern points *only* to the particular effect it was
chosen to explain. From each link in each chain, from each point

within each pattern, lines of influence spring out in other directions, pointing to other consequences.

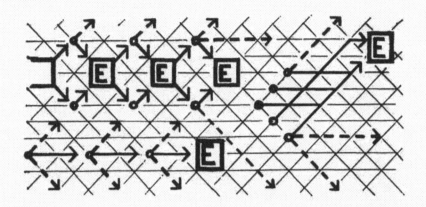

Remembering the original and ostensible purpose of the explanation – to explain the event E – we may call these other effects 'side effects' or 'by-products'. It is the theme of this chapter that such by-products are seldom irrelevant to the choice of an explanation for the original thing-to-be-explained. Indeed, very important reasons for the choice of an explanation are often to be found in the pattern of its by-products.

A scientist may choose an effect's most regular relations, hoping to build laws. If he is a system analyst he may select relations he can plot in circular patterns. For example, governments serve people, who support governments, who serve people, etc. Neither the support nor the service is the system analyst's Effect; his Effect is the self-sustaining persistence of the whole as a system. Nevertheless these circular relations *can* always be plotted in a linear way, along a one-way web through time. They consist of unique events occurring one after another; only be deciding that they have some similar qualities does the analyst decide that 'the same' event or relation keeps recurring. He chooses the similar qualities and dismisses any others; as to whether he recognizes the similarities only by perceiving qualities, or also by valuing them, there is often room for argument.

Meanwhile, whether the effect seems continuous or recurrent or once-only, any interested politician may look for its most manipulable (or loved, or hated) relations, to allow programs or imply persuasions.

In a simple and famous example which often attempted both law and persuasion,

was a connection which was alleged so persistently less because its authors saw any vital need to explain imperialism than because they saw a vital need to discredit capitalism. What they often had in mind was

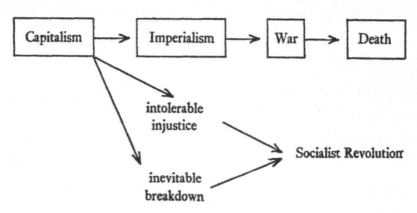

The lower line of consequences were all controversial, both technically and morally. Not everybody thought capitalism unjust or doomed or undesirable. Not everybody thought socialist revolution inevitable, practicable or desirable. Opinions differed about imperialism. But almost everybody did dislike war and death. If capitalism could be convincingly connected to death, then almost everybody might be frightened into getting rid of capitalism. Thus in a narrow view the supposed social consequences of capitalism – injustice, breakdown, revolution – were by-products of the capitalism which was nominated as the explanation of imperialism and war. But in a broader way the whole question-and-answer about imperialism and war may be seen as a by-product of the reformers' campaign to rid the world of those other more controversial effects of capitalism.

While the Left tried thus to establish an unbreakable causal chain from capitalism to war, the Right insisted that any such chain was either longer or shorter. 'Longer' or 'shorter' would serve equally well to destroy the implication that war could be prevented by tampering with capitalism. One sort of conservative saw a chain like this:

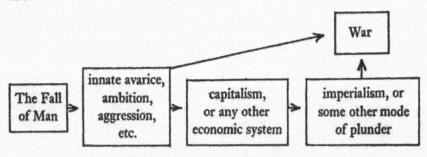

'Man is born to trouble as the sparks fly upward.' Either the chain by-passes capitalism, or capitalism is as unbreakable as any of its other links, or any other economic system in place of capitalism would serve as an equally effective link: do not tribal, feudal or riverine economies organize the same material rapacities as express themselves through capitalism?

Meanwhile other conservatives and many unradical liberals preserved the innocence of capitalism by attaching war to a much shorter chain of causes. If war could be sufficiently explained by some avoidable mistakes of government or diplomacy, then we could satisfy the universal desire to rid society of war while preserving intact the remainder of society's more controversial fabric. These reasons prompted some of the many explanations of World War I which confined themselves to the diplomacy of July 1914 or at least to questions of the national and personal guilt of particular governments. But just as often, other reasons imposed the same limitations: the details of diplomacy can be known more certainly, and footnoted more conclusively, than can those vast causal structures alleged by the Left. Political preference for particular by-products of explanation may have the same effect upon the explanation as scientific preference for particular methods, certainties, or disciplinary conventions. The conservative political motive incidentally allows the scientific certainties; the scientific motive cannot avoid the political implications which result from curtailing the explanation at proximate conditions. Compare the by-products and implications of a typical 'Left' and a typical 'Diplomatic' explanation, for anyone interested in deciding what surgery would be required to rid the world of war:

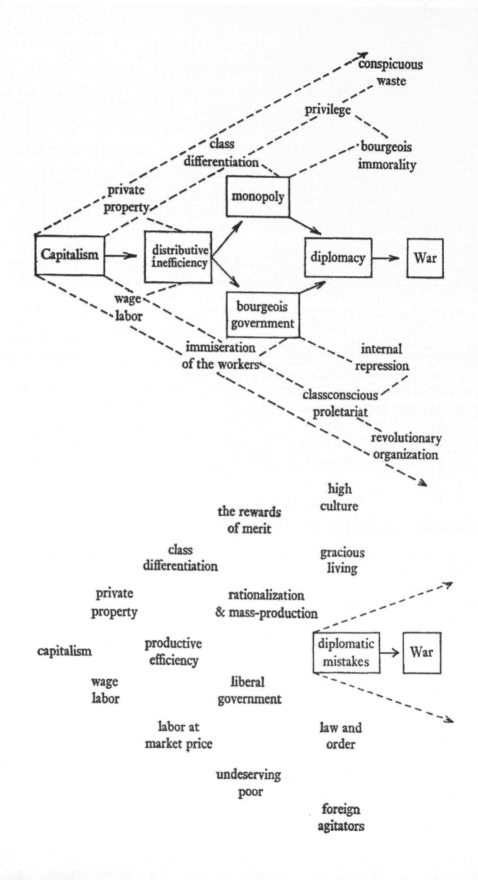

The choice of causal pattern is one method by which investigators' values may order their explanations. Another is the choice of identities. The disagreements between the two patterns above may be expressed more simply if the rival investigators merely distinguish between wholes and parts:

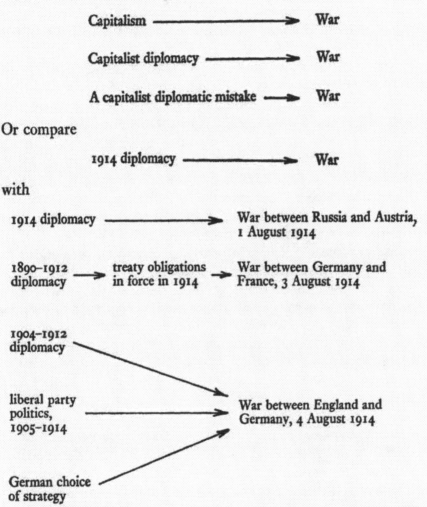

Capitalism ⟶ War

Capitalist diplomacy ⟶ War

A capitalist diplomatic mistake ⟶ War

Or compare

1914 diplomacy ⟶ War

with

1914 diplomacy ⟶ War between Russia and Austria, 1 August 1914

1890–1912 diplomacy ⟶ treaty obligations in force in 1914 ⟶ War between Germany and France, 3 August 1914

1904–1912 diplomacy

liberal party politics, 1905–1914 ⟶ War between England and Germany, 4 August 1914

German choice of strategy

These are facts of different sizes. In obvious ways, political considerations may affect the choice of parts or wholes, 'facts' which are collective nouns for many or few, complex or simple phenomena. Similarly, the 'facts' or 'units' may be identified by particular qualities – as in the use above of 'capitalist'. In much historical and political writing, conceptual identities have causal assumptions.

'Capitalist diplomacy', 'German diplomacy' and 'the Kaiser's diplomacy' do more than date and locate the diplomacy; they imply also something about its causes. Why are British medical practitioners, in 1967, annoyed by their conditions of work? One explainer says 'too much paper work'; another says 'too much socialism'. These explanations do not disagree about the facts or their relations; for manipulative or polemical reasons, they group less or more things into smaller or larger identities.

In most of the above examples, explainers choose a pattern of many causes for a single effect. Similar principles apply when they trace the many ramifying effects of a single cause, or when they explore some 'area of relationships' for patterns of relation which do not center on any particular single cause, or single effect. From a single event, or condition, or other social fact, chains and interactions of effect may reach out in innumerable directions, and which of these a researcher chooses to follow and record will be affected (just as his choice of causes is affected) by his particular values, curiosities and scientific or engineering purposes. There is no special promise in some sociologists' attempts to classify all such effects as either 'manifest' or 'latent' functions. There was none, either, in the efforts that used to be made to distinguish single 'effective' or 'predominant' or even 'immediate' causes. The attempt to distinguish categories of regular relations, for strictly scientific purposes, is discussed in later chapters. By historians still, and by many other social scientists whether or not they admit it, explanations have to be chosen by some principle of value, fashion or chance; no 'scientific' principle can replace them.

Among economists such large and crude analyses are out of fashion nowadays, for good enough reasons, in both the capitalist and the richer communist countries. But however sophisticated, economists and their clients still behave in one respect in much the same way. The very number and complexity of the factors whose interactions they try to measure are sufficient to rule out all plausible possibility of an exhaustive explanation even of such specific phenomena as recessions or particular levels of employment or rates of growth. Explanations of such phenomena are usually therefore frankly manipulative: they single out controllable factors or balances to explain what these have done in the past and may therefore be made to do in the future. There are innumerable alternative ways to enlarge or restrict such things as credit, imports, consumer demand, capital formation. Most of the methods are alike in achieving their primary object, but they are all different in their social incidence, their political practicability and their economic side-effects. They are almost invariably chosen, by the economists who propose them and by the politicians or planners who adopt them, as much for their side-effects as for their primary purposes. Indeed, what is primary purpose for one voter may be by-product for another; on such over-lapping patterns of purpose, political programs as well as economic therapies are built.

To each alternative choice of economic therapy an appropriate diagnosis or explanation may be attached. The therapist who wants to attack the recession by increasing old age pensions will 'explain' the recession by reference to a lag in consumer demand attributable to the attrition of the real value of welfare handouts. The politician whose electors could use some highway and defence contracts will explain how the recession resulted from defence cutbacks and unadventurous expenditure in other public sectors. Private enter-prisers who would like themselves or their customers to be able to borrow more freely will ascribe the recession to the conservatism of the reserve bank. Tax-haters will ascribe it to high taxation. The relevant facts and their inter-connections are agreed, but are so numerous that not even econometricians can feed them all into computers. So the choice of explanations, when they are offered at all, which they more often are by politicians than by the economists themselves, is more candidly manipulative than in most social sciences.

Sometimes their known pasts or futures attract notice to causes whose present importance would scarcely earn it. Effects continue to be respectfully attributed to the British monarchy, the Calvinist spirit, the owner-entrepreneur, long after their heydays have passed and it might be more useful to look for other causes for social cohesion or hard work or industrial innovation. Anticipation is as common as retrospect. Many things which contributed to the slow improvement of central power in eighteenth-century France might have rested unnoticed, but for their later effects upon the revolu-tionary and Napoleonic centralizations. The peasants of the Habs-burg empire probably had as much effect upon its progress and its difficulties, as Russian peasants had upon the Russian empire. But the Russian peasants' 'causal activity' in the nineteenth century often gets more attention, because their causal activity in the twentieth century is going to be regarded as crucial. Much the same might be said of the Habsburg and Romanov monarchies, which in the nineteenth century had as much effect as each other upon the fortunes of as many people. If the first communist regime had later been established in Austrian territory, then the effects of Habsburg dilemmas and inefficiencies in earlier centuries might now be getting the attention which is focused instead, because of their 'causal future', upon the Russian Tsars.

These examples illustrate R. G. Collingwood's suggestion that the historian's principle, in his selection of causes, should be to look for manipulative opportunities. Of course he cannot alter now the past that happened then; but by discovering who made it happen so, and who had opportunities to make it happen otherwise, he may develop a general wisdom about the latitude for social choice. The point is simpler in any science of the present, whose search may be for options which are still open. In applied economics, the sociology of social problems, studies of crime and delinquency, and a dozen other fields, the principles which direct research and choose its explanations are those of social engineering, appropriately governed by social and political values. The virtues of such principles of selection are best discussed after watching them in action in the next chapter's array of examples; notice meanwhile that present values and manipulative interests can organize explanations of remote events and societies almost as readily as they organize the investigation of present, still-open situations. Issues persist, problems recur, analogies are possible, present values and factions are compared with their past equivalents.

Obvious political interests, of course, are far from being the only ones at work. Social and historical explanations are written to interest, to entertain, to sell, to illuminate private experiences and unpolitical problems. Many causes are selected (out of the seamless web of necessary conditions) because of the intrinsic interest or value of the causes themselves. Some people simply love to write or read about heroes, villains, abstractions, sex, eccentricities or inevitabilities. Other causes are selected by apparently technical principles, because they are easy to discover, or to measure with certainty. Historians select conditions for which the sources are good, or hitherto unused. Scientists select whichever conditions can most readily be quantified, known by observation without subjective understanding, or computerized. The chosen pattern of causes still has its political implications, whether political or scientific motives chose it. Some academic and disciplinary considerations will be noticed in the next section, some strictly scientific ones in Part 2. Meanwhile the obvious political interests, illustrated by the examples so far, serve merely as representatives of the much wider variety of social, artistic and entertaining purposes which allow one or another kind of 'extra-scientific' valuation to select the reportable causes of social and historical effects, and to decide which collections of detail, or qualities of detail, shall be lumped together and identified as single 'facts', 'effects' or 'qualities'.

Between rivals within one discipline, values and purposes may thus prompt very different explanations. When the rivals belong to different disciplines, professional politics may complicate general politics and professional ethics may well declare war on intruding ideologies. Their academic as well as their social values may then need to be understood, if we are to account for the differences between the explanations which different investigators offer.

2. *Disciplines, ambitions, audiences*

A discipline of study, especially when practised by a profession, develops social characteristics. Rules define membership, including the 'member' types of knowledge. Even where the methods and subject-matters of neighboring disciplines overlap, they may have very different rules for the use of similar knowledge. A political scientist or a theorist of economic growth may present without penalty 'facts' about eighteenth-century society which would make a historian blush; the historian may present better-certified facts in an ungeneralized disarray that would disgrace a political scientist or economist. When the facts are figures the roles may be reversed, and the scientists measure and count what the historians are still content to guess at. The separators of a distinct discipline of Economic History have often refused to employ scholars who use economic information to explain political events, while welcoming those who use government policies to explain economic events. Scientifically, this defines the discipline by the type of event it explains; politically, it may well ensure its conservatism. Among general historians, American promotion committees welcome readable popular histories which might spell professional death in England, while in specialized monographs the English curiously demand readable prose while the Americans, more logically, do not. Some schools of sociology require genetic or narrative connections to be disguised as behaviorist correlations. Some schools of psychology require that connections inferred from behaviorist correlations be disguised as psychoanalytic explanations. The same ignominious end (in some Teachers College deep in the sticks) awaits the first historian who puts the probability of his inferences into symbolic terms, and the first sociometrist who doesn't.

Such examples need not be labored. However purely scientific their purposes or purely conventional their forms, no two arrangements of social knowledge have quite the same practical uses or political implications. Political or scientific motive may organize an explanation; whichever does, the explanation may still have either or both of political and scientific promise. What are some of the ways in which the rules of the disciplines affect patterns of explanation?

Different disciplines may deal in different facts. When two disciplines explain the same phenomenon, each may concentrate on such necessary conditions as happen to lie within its field of skill.

Different disciplines may deal in different aspects or abstracts of the same facts, which may allow the discovery of different relations between the same facts. Even when different explanations seem merely to give different names and groupings to the same things, there may still be subtle differences of implication. 'Crime', 'delinquency' and 'deviation' do not strike most people as calling for the same remedies. Its undoubted 'function for the integration and persistence of the system' may not commend to all alike what another discipline calls 'secure one-party monopoly of all means of production, indoctrination and violence'.

Different disciplines may have different concepts of 'explanation' itself. Historians and psychiatrists are popularly supposed to explain things by reference to their origins and growth, sociologists by reference to their continuing supports and functions. Some disciplines think things sufficiently explained when identified as cases of laws or members of classes. Others require regular recurrences to be explained by a theory or an understanding of the connecting mechanisms.

Within each discipline there are rewards for original work. In ascending order of rarity and acclaim, 'original work' is the application of usual methods to some untouched tract of their usual subject matter; the correction of earlier work; the successful application of old methods to novel material; the improvement or invention of the methods themselves. The best work often does a bit of all of these. If its methodological invention is remarkable enough it may even found new disciplines or split or reunite old ones.

Two simple examples will illustrate what diverse relations are possible between what may be crudely separated as the political and the professional motives of explanation.

The old-style tammany machines once controlled enough American city governments for 'boss-rule' to be thought of as a general phenomenon requiring a general explanation. Political scientists explained how the bosses gerrymandered city boundaries, exploited slum-dwelling voters (or saved themselves even that effort by inventing the false-bottomed ballot box), suborned public officials by abusing the spoils system of appointments; and financed it all by corrupt contracting and simple theft. Lawyers connected the bosses with syndicated crime, showed how they could exploit gaps and overlaps between federal and state legal systems, and pointed to weaknesses both in enforcement and in the law itself in the matter of city accountability – one Philadelphia machine had a picnic when it discovered that in all the piecemeal improvement of the laws requiring true city accounts, nobody had thought to require that the balance sheet should actually balance. Economists and muckraking journalists showed how the bosses were sustained by corrupt links with private business which allowed franchised public utilities to be provided at a criminally high cost to taxpayers and consumers.

Most of these explanations implied remedies in the form of simple prohibition, excisions of corrupt growths from the body politic. But when social historians and sociologists inspected the phenomenon, they pointed out that all the folksy ward-heelers' opportunities to attract support depended on the absence, inadequacy or cold officiality of public welfare services. They found that the local party, if only as 'fixer' of jobs and school places and hospital beds, could give its clients some sense of membership in an otherwise alien and hostile society. They found in the party machines themselves an alternative to crime as a 'way up' for unprivileged talent. These explanations, and their implications, differed from those which his discipline would encourage a lawyer or public administrator to publish. They could appropriately have been motivated by a desire to reform welfare services and educational opportunities; but in fact they were offered (long after the event) by professionals who may have been more interested in proving the fertility of their disciplines and adding to their own publications. Their disciplines required them to ask of any institution questions like 'What integrative or disintegrative functions is it actually performing for the system of which it is a part?' or 'Which of its social effects are valuable or dangerous enough to be worth reporting?' They were thus led to add a new condition to the list of those seen to be necessary for the persistence of boss-rule. The new condition indicated another possible remedy for the disease, and also a warning to rival therapists: boss-rule could not merely be *removed*; if society was to remain as before, the useful social functions performed by boss-rule would have to be *replaced.**

Similar explanations, with similar implications, had been offered elsewhere by anthropologists: missionaries should not blindly attack unchristian customs and ceremonies without first discovering what real, perhaps irreplaceable, functions those customs performed for primitive societies.

The purposes of able investigators are seldom so simple or so pure. If the last example served to separate professional from political motives, and the disciplines from each other, the next example is to show how profitably all may sometimes operate together. Until 1929 it was widely supposed that, in the eighteenth century, England had a political system appropriate to a stable aristocratic society, but a good deal corrupted by faction and bribery, and fatally corrupted after 1760 when a reactionary king used most improper methods to maintain in power a Tory party whose out-

*This sketch is unjust to the muckrakers, who in fact saw the sociological implications of the system – as many of the bosses themselves did – before any academic social scientists approached it. But the muckrakers made less of it, perhaps because the implied radical social reforms looked less practicable in their day.

dated authoritarian ideas and low political morality lost the Empire its American colonies. This portrait had been painted by historians who were mostly English or American, academic, liberal, uneducated in anything except history and classics, and somewhat puritanical. The subject was then approached by L. B. Namier. He was not English, or liberal, or puritanical, or (until then) a historian. As a business man he had different views of corruption and of the face value of parliamentary speeches, and as a Viennese he was not wholly ignorant of psychology, sociology, political science or work in modern foreign languages. In his chosen historical field he found four interesting features: first a 'disciplinary gap' – no sociology of the parliamentary classes; second, a link missing from a chain – the aristocratic society had not really been connected to its aristocratic policies by any knowledge of the detailed system and process of politics; third, a literature full of indignant Whiggish guesses about these unexamined areas; and fourth, boxes of unexamined documents of exactly the kind his discipline was conventionally expected and professionally skilled to use as evidence. Adding a fifth ingredient – very hard work – he established the sociology in simple but detailed form; he analysed the politics as a going system, not as a deformity of some ideal or unborn system; he found that causes within that system explained how men got power, and explained it sufficiently without mentioning a political party or a political idea. His explanation of the political phenomena of that period was thus organized partly by his general views of life and human nature; partly by the rules of several disciplines; partly by the desire to wring the maximum possible credit from some neglected necessary conditions and some neglected documentary evidence; partly by a temperament which found delight in flaying others' work. His explanation had features of all the types sketched above – it filled gaps, it corrected predecessors, it added a new 'disciplinary' segment to the pattern, it applied old methods to new materials, it invented some method of its own. For those who accepted it as sufficient – who were prepared to forget or persuaded to disconnect all the other conditions which had to be present for those politics to occur as they did – it had implications as various as its organizing purposes. For example: politics is rarely a rational, policy-oriented business. Its motives rarely include the high purposes professed in public speeches. If people ever do plan deliberate social action they miscalculate, often with disastrous and always with unforeseen results. Former historians of this period were lazy and incompetent. Their methods, like their reputations, are beyond repair and these new methods are established. Just as, since Marx, nobody has explained social change without at least a glance at its economic background, so after Namier few will dare to explain political conduct without first understanding the mechanics of the political system within which the conduct occurs.

Altogether it was a rich harvest, both for Namier's view of life and for his choice of technique. Shortly before he got his knighthood he uttered two aphorisms: 'Never work in a field until a fool has been there before you' and 'Never do *anything* without at least five purposes'.

Thus either or both of professional and political motives may prompt the disciplines now to segregate, now to join, in the work of explanation. It is obviously sensible for each to explore the segment of conditions it is skilled in understanding. But in practice the disciplines sometimes become self-assertive. Separatism can then be developed into disciplinary imperialism.

The first step is for a discipline to forget or deny that 'its own' causes or conditions are merely contributors to a sufficient set, whose effect would be very different without the other contributors to the set. The explainer insists instead upon an unbreakable and sufficient chain from his own starting point to the effect-to-be-explained: given (say) his own chain of economic determination, he insists the effect would occur in *any* political or social or psychological circumstances.

But this proposition is vulnerable to others like it, especially if this specialist argues not an unbreakable chain of his own but a breakable one. He may see ways in which war could be avoided by reform or revolution in the economic system, only to be confronted by the psychologist's assertions on behalf of *his* sector: perhaps that war will be inevitable on one pretext or another, economic or not, as long as American fathers drink milk and Russian mothers swaddle their babies. The economist will have shown how to remove his own operative causes of war only to see the war occur anyway, from several other converging causes each alleged to be sufficient in the explanation offered by its appropriate discipline.

This will not do at all. An invulnerable disciplinary empire requires that causes of all other types be seen as mere products of causes of one imperial type, so that the explanations offered by all other disciplines shall become servants – local and specialized parts, perhaps – of 'the' explanation organized by the imperial discipline. Thus for example in a Marxist view, many conflicts may issue from the superstructure of institutions and ideas, and such conflicts may be the occasions for war; but the ideas and the institutions are themselves products of the economic system, mere intermediaries between the primary economic causes and their final effects. With less emphasis on the nature of social processes and more on the nature of the disciplines by which social processes are studied, similar claims have sometimes been made on behalf of sociology, as the discipline which studies society at the highest level of generality and should therefore aim to organize, as its servile or specialized sub-divisions, the particularizing disciplines like politics or economics which deal with limited aspects of social action at subordinate levels of abstraction and generalization. If there were in truth any features of capitalist organization which provoked war, they should be seen as cases within a larger category of disintegrative social mechanisms all of which – not merely the capitalist or merely the economic species – should be subsumed under some general and parsimonious theory of social integration.

While some dream thus of systems which would relate all explanations to each other, the disciplinary necessities of other authors can have an opposite effect. What teacher of history has not read the result of sending a sophomore to an overcrowded library to write, before noon next Monday, an essay which shall explain, say, The Causes of World War One? The first three books on his list are 'out', the fourth has been stolen. In the fifth, an old-fashioned work, he is somewhere between Sarajevo and the Wilhelmstrasse when he sights a girl who needs a cup of coffee. Later he catches a chapter – an 1892 chapter – of Langer's *Diplomacy* and borrows the notes of a friend who once read J. A. Hobson. His own lecture notes include a piece on the Russian general staff but he cut the lectures before and after that one – after all he intends to major in psychology. So the essay contains: British (but no other) capital export, unconnected to British diplomacy; the Franco-Russian (but no other) military alliance, unconnected to the step-by-step mobilization of 1914; the shot at Sarajevo, unconnected to Serbian nationalism or anything else about the Habsburg empire; the irreversibility of Russian mobilization but nothing about Austrian or any other soldiers; a passing compliment to Sir Edward Grey (whose powers are unidentified); and a conclusion, beginning 'Thus we see . . .', about the subconscious springs of aggression which make war possible. He knows his instructor will not regard the last as acceptable History but he puts it in defiantly because he is majoring in psychology and because every Visiting Lecturer has applauded the cross-fertilization of the disciplines.

Reader, do not smile. Consider a certain sort of school textbook – not yours or mine perhaps, but nonetheless numerous. It is conceived not by an author but by a publisher. He has an officer who knows the requirements of all relevant educational authorities, and the state of obsolescence of all their current textbooks. (This obsolescence is governed by various factors: Is the author dead yet? If alive, is he still on the prescribing committee, or is anyone else on it in receipt of a commission on sales of the current book? Does his publisher still maintain a traveller in the area? Do we? How long has the book been on the list? Are the teachers sick of it? Is this one of the systems in which it makes any difference that the teachers are sick of it?) The publisher finally sends the printed curricula of three examining authorities to an experienced hack, with the suggestion that a little ingenuity should produce one book acceptable to all three. Explanations included in this book should preferably offer no less than two and no more than six causes, arranged so that the reader can number them in pencil in the margin. Similarly, effects. They should include the results of the latest research, especially if by local authors, but not at the cost of omitting factors the teachers are accustomed to expect or factors currently selling in the rival texts of other publishers. Cultural and intellectual factors are currently popular but economic factors could be shortened. Factors capable of offending religious or racial minorities, or political majorities, should of course be excluded. The explanations which arise from these commercial necessities may have no more coherence than those that arise from the vicissitudes of campus life. Nor, unhappily, are hacks and college students the only authors who keep one eye on the market and the other on the clock.

It would nevertheless be absurd to expect authors to write without thought of their audiences. Why should a textbook serve one only of the ten religious interests represented among its users? Or the explanation of a social problem explore only the therapies that appeal to one political faction? The point of social science is to communicate with its subjects. Should it 'serve' or persuade them? Should it follow its subjects' interests or its author's, as often as the two disagree? These questions are for argument later. Here it is appropriate to insist that all explanation is eclectic, even if what it chooses to do is to relate facts by class or law; no explanation can achieve neutrality by sufficiently including all the remotely-related facts; the best that any can do, is justice to most of the interests of most of its audience. But insofar as the explainer chooses his audience, and chooses which of its disagreed interests he will serve most helpfully, to that extent at least his own responsibility is inescapable. It applies whether the researcher chooses how and what to look for, or the popularizer chooses what to report. The choices of both should be criticized, not only for their many technical qualities, but also for their 'fairness' or 'justice' to interested parties: for the quality, not merely the inevitable presence, of their values.

It is right to acknowledge at once the limitations of this whole approach to explanations. It says nothing about the connections themselves which are alleged to relate facts to one another. It asks only what prompts an investigator, in real life rather than in a manual of methodology, to choose a particular pattern of causes or conditions or classifications, as if he were free to choose whichever he fancied from some common stock. It is moreover a misleading division of labor to discuss the selection of causal relations in Part 1, and their discovery in Part 2 – these choosing and knowing operations are not as separable as they seem. Nevertheless these present chapters concentrate on such differences and disagreements as can be seen simply as rival choices of explanatory patterns, as if all were drawn from a common stock of established facts and connections.

This is a familiar inquiry. Its discussion is usually illustrated by some simple model, such as a motor accident. A drunken driver skids his car into another which has been unwisely parked on an ill-lit corner on a wet night. Is the 'correct' explanation of this event the drink, the unwise parking, the slippery road, the bad light? Should we go into the social habits that make for drinking, or driving, or the slack regulation of parking? The rain was a necessary condition, but who wants to explain it in a *social* science? Must we go back to the original invention of internal combustion engines, electric lighting, local government, and distilling? Neither the facts nor their connections are in dispute, but 'the *real* explanation' may still be disputed at length by lawyers in court, by those who want to defend or reform drinking or driving or parking or street lighting, and by several rival social sciences.

Models like the motor accident, or the simple sketches offered earlier in this chapter, are the usual material of inquiries into the nature and purposes of explanations. They are useful, but in some respects their simplicity is misleading. Real investigators often have more complex purposes, and express them less directly in inquiries into more complicated events. If this present book is to be justified, it must be by patient survey of the widest possible variety of 'real' researches.

Instead of a motor accident, the next chapter's examples are drawn from the classical controversy about the nature and causes of imperialism. It offers good examples because it was joined by men from so many disciplines with such various purposes and faiths, and such different valuations of the imperial events they sought to explain. Of course they did not share a common conceptual system or a common stock of facts and they certainly disagreed about the connections between events. But efforts to prove the connections of events are left for discussion later. Meanwhile, imperialism is as far as possible treated as a motor accident, with agreed facts, but disagreed explanations and responsibilities and proposals for action or inaction. Of each explanation we may accordingly ask, not whether it was true, but why its author *wanted* it to be true.

4

For example: What caused Imperialism?

1. Joseph Chamberlain

To explain Chamberlain's decision about pensions, the biographer Amery selected the facts of Chamberlain's situation which seemed to map and limit the choices open to him. Chamberlain himself certainly thought that he could distinguish the necessities from the liberties. He professed a lucid, cutting view of history, full of implications for the future, which we may see as his explanation of his country's predicament, and of the need for his own program. Its dramatic and political attractions make it hard to guess how genuinely he believed in it, but he certainly committed his later career to its implications, and it is interesting because it did distinguish the areas of necessity and choice so clearly, and so clearly identified the choosers – Chamberlain among them.

In an industrial capitalist society, for all its promise, Chamberlain saw two related dangers. As a national system it might be destroyed from within by its work force, or from without by its competitors. Technical progress made different defences possible against these distinct dangers. In order to avert revolution from within, the system must maintain between capital and labor a harmony based on balance and conciliation and fair shares. But to avert defeat by external competitors, a national economic system must beat those competitors outright – *between* systems, in the long run, no balance or harmony or mutual advantage could be expected.

Chamberlain had abundant business experience and no formal education in economics. He had not been persuaded by Ricardo that a capitalist economy must inevitably prosper nor by Marx that it must inevitably fail. Neither Marx nor Malthus had equipped him with any iron law of wages. He did not expect proprietors to surrender their unequal relative advantages; but he did not see why increasing productivity should not bring absolute improvements to the workman's standard of living. These improvements could come from natural economic growth, from collective bargaining, from political intervention to regulate industry, from tax and welfare policies. To pay this ransom to the working man was a matter of choice. A stupid, inhuman or shortsighted upper class might refuse the ransom and invite the revolution. Chamberlain thought that any such revolution would be destructive, impoverishing all classes. So he looked to a mixture of economic growth (to provide the ransom) and industrial and political wisdom (to pay it with good grace). But this internal need for continuously increasing wages and welfare was not the only reason why economic expansion was necessary.

Enough has been said of Chamberlain's experience as an industrial competitor. He was a competitor against competition, a take-over man. What held for firms would soon hold for national economies. He saw no possibility of a 'little England' standing still: only the choice to take or be taken. So continuing expansion was a condition of mere survival, and his idea of the expansion of a national economy was predominantly geographical and imperial. The colonial economies must be reunited with the British into a single imperial economy, which would then be strong enough to extend its command to the markets of Asia and Africa, by competition or by war. China, in particular, had such numbers that whoever won it should be big enough to win all the other economic and military battles of the twentieth century.

In both campaigns – for harmony at home and victory abroad – Chamberlain eventually decided that a British tariff was a necessary weapon. It had an effective political simplicity: a single measure would achieve so much. It would protect British industry. It would give Britain a retaliatory weapon against protectionist competitors. It would make possible an Imperial tariff, and free-trading imperial reunion inside it. It would increase and protect the economic advantages to be derived from overseas empire. Its revenues would resolve the financial and political difficulties which still dangerously withheld the 'ransom' at home: the poor could contribute a good deal to the payment of their own ransom, and for many of the rich, the tariff offered compensating benefits which did not attach to property or income taxes.

As an 'explanation of a future', all this is interesting in two ways: first, as an effort to distinguish the historical necessities from the opportunities of effective political choice; second, as a selection (from the innumerable candidates) of certain necessary conditions for a particular imperial development.

Industrial capitalism was not one of the inevitabilities; Chamberlain took seriously the possibility that violent revolution might destroy it. The whole class of proprietors, to a lesser extent their employees, and to a greater extent their political leaders, had to choose and act to preserve the system. But as long as the system was preserved, some important features of it were strictly determined, especially the trend to fewer and bigger firms, fewer and bigger national economies and eventually empires. In the international competition for empire, national fortunes were not determined. At the level of international diplomacy and internal legislative reform, and at the level of industrial management at which technical advances and wage decisions occur, there was real freedom of action and – between nations – free competition.

Chamberlain the historian defined that freedom of action very conveniently for Chamberlain the politician. It was a freedom to win or lose, with no middle course. It offered to voters and cabinets both a carrot and a stick. And it distinguished Chamberlain's policy sharply from the policies of his immediate political competitors. An increasing proportion of the Liberal Party did not want vigorous national action in the imperial competition. Among Chamberlain's conservative colleagues were many who wanted to beat off the domestic reformers and conciliate the imperial rivals. Chamberlain's identification of the historical necessities and opportunities of his time was nicely constructed to support his own policies and to make all rival policies look dangerous or ineffective.

Chamberlain was not consistent through his lifetime, and he did not organize his historical explanations as lists of factors, or sets of necessary conditions. Much depends on what you group together as 'a factor' or 'a condition'; but it would do no violence to his later utterances to list some of his necessary conditions for British imperial success and to arrange them in the pattern sketched below. The shaded part is historically determined; the rest indicates the scope for choice and action. It could of course be matched with another, showing the disastrous alternative sequences that Chamberlain professed to fear.

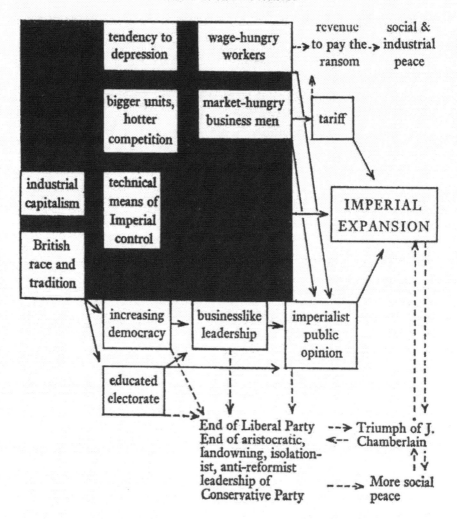

This pattern might have a place in two different exercises. If Chamberlain's policies had succeeded as planned, the pattern might afterwards be offered as an explanation of what had happened; as such it would be open to any tests of its truth. But since its 'future' parts never did happen, it is only useful as representing Chamberlain's thoughts in an explanation of his attempts, as part of an explanation of the actual (though unintended) results of those attempts. In this capacity it only invites tests of the truth that Chamberlain did think or utter such thoughts; though it may still be useful to understand where he erred or failed: erred in prediction or failed in persuasion.

2. *Bernhard von Bülow*

Prince Bernhard von Bülow was German Secretary of State for Foreign Affairs from 1897 and Imperial Chancellor from 1900 to 1909. Through those years he shared responsibility for a new course in German foreign and imperial policy, and when he was dismissed there were critics who thought he had much to answer for. In 1890 Bismarck had left Imperial Germany in treaty relations with the Habsburg and Russian Emperors – *à trois* in a five-power system with the fourth and fifth powers, France and Great Britain, isolated even from each other. Before Bülow took office, that system had already suffered some damage. The Reinsurance Treaty with Russia was allowed to lapse and Russia joined France in a military alliance. But Bülow's share of responsibility included the German naval programs, the revival of Imperial interest in East Asia and elsewhere, the failure of two negotiations with members of the British government, and a Moroccan crisis which did what French diplomatists had never been able to achieve unaided – it appended secret military arrangements to the Anglo-French entente. Bülow gave other inadvertent help to the French efforts to strengthen their English connections, and he did nothing effective to hinder their patient completion of the triangle by the Anglo-Russian understanding of 1907. Thus he left Germany in the situation Bismarck had dreaded: *à deux* in a five-power system, with the hostile three in strengthening combination. Bismarckian critics blamed him for overreaching Bismarck's continental objectives. Imperialist critics blamed him for the imperfect success of his imperialist policies. Socialist and some liberal critics attacked him for being an imperialist at all. In his retirement he wrote his defence: *Imperial Germany*, a short book whose English translation was published in 1914.[1] The book has been surprisingly neglected by critics of the more famous twentieth-century theories of imperialism. In it, this eminent imperial practitioner offered a deep-rooted, coherent and clear explanation (how true, is another question) of his own imperial activities.

Bülow was not explaining the same imperialism as interested Chamberlain. He did administer colonies, but his idea of empire was the imperium exercised by the King of Prussia, now Emperor of Germany, over his subjects in Europe. Bülow did acknowledge technical differences between the foreigners and the domestic subjects with whom the Imperial power had to cope; but in a broad sense, the French and the Bavarians, the British Navy and the German Social-Democratic Party, such Russians and Prussians as might both for different reasons want a 'little Germany', all had equal status as enemies of State. The Empire must confront them all.

The book opens and closes with the sex of this Prussian State. The feminine Germany of the west and south has made German culture; that Germany can think, feel, create, sing, love. It has just been captured by the masculine Germany of Prussia, a 'rude and thoroughly prosaic State of soldiers and officials' who 'prepared the future of Germany as a State in battles and privations under the rule of heroic and politic kings'. The shotgun marriage is not yet a true union. 'The Germany of Bismarck, Blucher and Moltke' and 'the Germany of Schiller, Goethe and Lessing' still repel each other. Nor is that Prussia's only problem. The older European powers resent the newcomer and would be rid of him if they could. So the Prussian Imperial State faces war on two fronts. Will internal strife so weaken and expose it to foreign enemies that it will lose the justification and the power with which it maintains internal unity? Or will the foreign challenge stimulate a unity strong enough to defeat the foreigners and at the same time obliterate the internal disunities? 'The Prussian State may be compared to a man and like any man worth his salt is full of violent contrasts and only capable of great achievements when animated by a strong purpose.' Bülow's explanation of imperialism is an extensive analysis of the 'violent contrasts' to which his government felt compelled to oppose an imperial 'strong purpose'.

Bülow said his countrymen were natural individualists, and separatists. They were loyal not to national but to factional leaders. They would form associations not for national but only for private and local purposes. When they did form national associations, it was for the worse nuisance of bullying the government. The Pan-German League wanted to censor foreign policy, the Navy League wanted to prescribe naval policy, the Association of Farmers wanted to dictate every national policy that touched its interests. What many romantic democrats have celebrated as twin glories which explain each other – the combination of military heroism with civilian individualism – struck Bülow as a fundamental contradiction in German character.

Only too often with us, the union dictated by necessity was followed again by disruption into smaller political associations, states, tribes, classes; or in modern times, into parties that preferred their own narrower tasks and aims to those of the nation at large, and degraded the great deeds of national unity by making them the object of ugly party quarrels. (110)

Regional separatism, which had troubled Bismarck a good deal, no longer frightened Bülow. Instead, the separatist spirit, after 'the unification of Germany, sought a new field of political activity, and found it in the struggle of political parties.'

Party warfare is more bitter and destructive in Germany than in other countries. The parties are irreconcilable because they are immovable: they will never adapt their leaders, their programs or their moods to changing circumstances – 'even the radical factions are thoroughly conservative as regards the planks in their platform and their methods.' Why is this so? Forgetting for a moment his earlier answer in terms of a separatist national character, Bülow offers a more pragmatic explanation: since the German government is not constitutionally responsible to the Parliament, the parties know they will never have to govern. So their programs need not be practicable, their criticism need not be responsible and there is nothing to be gained by their compromising with the government or with each other.

This general damnation of factious politics introduces a review of the particular parties with which Bülow's government had to contend.

Conservatives and Liberals could be a nuisance but never a serious danger to the State. Each deserves German gratitude, the Liberals for dreaming of unifying Germany and the Conservatives for doing it. Each has useful functions still, the Liberals to offer restrained and constructive criticism of old institutions, the Conservatives to criticize new institutions. Both have the function of voting money for the armed forces (one of the few effective powers the Imperial parliament had) and though their records are not stainless, the Liberals have been absolutely sound on Navy bills and the Conservatives on Army bills. Government must always keep the support of one or other, and does best when it has both.

Turning to the Catholic Center Party, Bülow at once defines his objection to it. Its electoral support is determined by religion, and no amount of political folly will reduce it. Bülow thinks it unfair that a party exempt from normal political penalties should nevertheless engage in normal political activity. 'For a party which is in an almost impregnable position, such as the Centre occupies, the temptation to pursue a policy of power pure and simple is very great. It is doubly tempting if the Centre is in a position to form a majority together with the Social Democrats, and with their help can prevent the passing of any and every Bill.' On some issues the Catholics might seem to be natural allies of the Conservatives; but even in that safe-seeming combination Bülow sees the danger that it might provoke protestant reunions between Liberals and Social Democrats. Thus the Center has no dangerous opinions of its own but can be dangerous in certain combinations. Policy, Bülow concludes, must be directed 'not against the Center as such, but against the Centre allied in opposition with the Social Democrats.'

This brings him to the villains themselves.

Different passages of the book present slightly different pictures of the German working man, and different degrees of hope for his redemption. Bülow does not always despair of convincing him 'that the actual provisions for the poor made by the existing society are worth more than the promises of the Social Democrats which can never be fulfilled.' After all,

The monarchy . . . has sufficient insight to mitigate and remove, as far as is possible in this imperfect world, those evils which, together with much good, are due to modern development, evils which are found in all countries, and which are comprehended in the words, "social problems."

. . . Since the beginning of the new century we have continued and in part completed the magnificent structure of our social legislation, not because we have such a strong Social Democratic party, but in spite of that fact. The clearer our conscience towards the working classes, because with a social policy on such a large scale we have done all that is humanly possible to alleviate their economic conditions, the better is our right to take up the battle necessitated by reasons of State against the Social Democrats and their political aims. (197–8)

Elsewhere, 'We remember that the workman is our fellow countryman. In him we also honour God's image.' But he remembers it rarely, and this distinction between the honest worker and his evil advisers is only fitful. More often Bülow lumps the two together as 'the Social Democratic proletariat.' He regards the Social Democratic party as a greater danger to the State than any foreign power, and a better justification for his imperial policies. He sees it as alien and irreconcilable, not a member but an enemy of the Empire, more dangerous than socialist parties elsewhere precisely because it is German: disciplined, obstinate, inflexible in policy, unquestioningly loyal to its brilliant organizers. 'From first to last during my term of office I recognized that the Social Democratic movement constituted a great and serious danger . . . [since their] programme is incompatible with the existing state, the German Social Democrats are irreconcilable.'

What could be done about them?

First of all, could they be destroyed by force?

No – at least it would be risky to try until all other methods had failed. The attempt would provoke retaliation, and the Social Democrats might just possibly win. To proscribe them legally as Bismarck had done was to do them a service – 'the recruiting power of a cause is greatly increased if it has the luck . . . to be able to point to martyrs.' The party would go underground where it could not be watched; and liberals would sympathize, and defend its civil liberties.

Could the leaders be reconciled to the regime by what has since been dubbed 'the aristocratic embrace'?

There were encouraging foreign examples. French socialists had become Ministers, 'and good Ministers too.' Briand became 'a determined guardian of public order' and Millerand an excellent Minister of War. Similar experiments had some success in Italy, Holland and Denmark. But in Germany 'we have a different political system, and, above all, different Social Democrats.' French socialists descend from the revolutionary patriots, Italian socialists from the heroes of the risorgimento, and both (Bülow implies) also have some saving venality. The German socialist movement has neither patriotism nor any capacity for corruption or compromise. 'It is so dangerous to us because it is so typically German.'

If the leaders cannot be seduced by office, can the followers be reconciled by improvements in their economic welfare?

In spite of the hesitant hopes he expressed from time to time, Bülow did not really think they could. It had already been tried, without success. Some social problems were insoluble, and anyway the workers were implacable. 'If, in spite of everything, we have not achieved industrial peace, if the antagonism between different industrial classes continues to be violent, if on the contrary passion runs higher in industry, and the quarrels and hatred between the various industrial classes are bitterer than ever, the cause does not lie in any defect or any lack of adjustment in our economic policy.'

Thus one could neither destroy the movement by force nor seduce either its leaders or its ranks. That left a fourth solution, Bülow's own. He would do to the workers what Bismarck did to the French: isolate them.

He first disposes of a common argument *against* isolating them, the argument that they should be encouraged to put themselves under respectable middle-class leadership and into alliance with middle-of-the-road political parties, from whom they might learn moderation.

Such a belief is contrary to all experience. The educated men in the Social Democratic movement do not form a bridge by which the proletariat may approach the representatives of the existing order, but a bridge by which intellect passes over to the masses. But it is when the educated classes join a revolutionary movement that it becomes a serious danger. (193)

This is the crux of his imperial argument. He repeats it often and supports it from history. It was illustrated in the first French revolution, and in each of its successors:

In 1830 the legitimate Monarchy, scarcely fifteen years after it had been restored, succumbed to a like coalition between intellect and brute force. The March revolution of 1848 was successful because the masses found support and guidance in the educated classes. Wherever the proletariat has fought alone, as in the June battle in Paris and during the Commune, it has always been defeated. (194)

What is true of civil war is true also of elections – 'an isolated proletariat, however numerous, is always a minority in the nation.' Thus he introduces the principal political task of an Imperial Chancellor:

If left to its own resources the proletariat cannot attain a numerical majority in the nation. It can only do so if aided by the middle classes. This is what must primarily be prevented. The Social Democratic party can only be isolated if Liberalism is kept away from it and is drawn towards the Government and the Right. (194)

But the isolation of the proletarian class from the middle classes, and of its Social Democratic party from their political parties, is not an easy task.

Bülow first recommends some minor or negative aids. Politics should be exciting, but not so as to needlessly annoy middle-class individuals into opposition. Especially in small matters, government should avoid 'our ancestral faults of pedantry and caste-feeling', the sort of Prussianism in administration which is bound to irritate the sensitive heirs of Schiller, Goethe and Lessing. In another passage, technical means are suggested by which the steady increase in Social Democratic votes may be prevented from finding full representation in the Reichstag. But the Social Democrats will not be permanently neutralized by such negative methods, and their isolation remains the central task of German government. Unhappily there are no significant domestic issues which will either divide them from the rest of the Reichstag or unite the middle-class parties against them. Bülow emphasizes that each half of this operation is as necessary as the other. It is no good separating the Social Democrats if what ought to be the governing majority continues to divide within itself. But on almost every domestic issue, it squabbles like a babel of bad children. In long passages (for example, pp. 237-9) a bitter and querulous Bülow stamps his foot about the play of interests in politics. He simply can't stand politics, and he can't isolate the Social Democrats either, while this undignified wrangle goes on about questions of trade, industry, agriculture, tariff, taxes and social welfare.

To unite the warring factions, to unite them in support of a monarchical executive, and to be sure that the Social Democrats will exclude themselves from the union, one course remains. The only issues which will divide Reichstag and nation into those unequal camps are what Bülow constantly calls the 'national' issues: foreign relations, colonial policies, armaments. On these issues the Social Democrats define themselves by their acts as traitors, all others as patriots. So these had better be made the permanent subject-matter of politics, to the exclusion of as many as possible of the internal problems of an expanding industrial society. But even 'national' issues can be unsafe in quiet times. Liberals and Catholics will not always increase the arms vote, or concede the Kaiser's constitutional right to determine the size and disposition of his armed forces, unless the nation is in plausible danger. The foreign, colonial, military and naval policies must therefore be not only 'national' but also 'vigorous'. Though Bülow usually stops short of saying it in plain words, his virile metaphors leave no doubt that the Social Democrats can be isolated and the middle classes united in support of the monarchy only if German foreign relations are kept in constant tension – tension, but without serious territorial ambitions and without actual war. An irritating condition of permanent tumescence.

From March, 1905, when he landed a reluctant Emperor from a warship onto the beach at Tangier, until the Moroccan crisis was resolved by the Algeçiras conference late in 1906, Bülow had just that sort of tension. Nevertheless, in 1906 the Catholics voted with the Social Democrats to defeat a military supply bill. 'Principles of State were at stake which could not be sacrificed.' Bülow contrived 'The Block', a rare alliance of all the other parties. Liberals and Conservatives cooperated, Ultra-Liberals joined, the influence of government was used to the limit at a general election, and a battery of anti-democratic devices converted an increased Social Democratic vote into a drastically reduced Reichstag representation. The Center-Social Democratic combination was now a minority and the Center learned its lesson:

The temper of the people, when success was assured, was not such as would be roused by a triumph in party politics, but as would emanate from a feeling of patriotic satisfaction. . . . Even though the Block could only be kept together for a few years, yet the possibility remains that it might be formed again if the Centre should fail to come up to the mark in a national question, or should, by siding with the Social Democrats, defeat a Bill for the furtherance of national aims. . .

That there has been such a development of the national idea, and that such a change has come over the attitude of the parties towards Imperial questions of protection and armament, must fill every patriot with joy and confidence. Fifty years ago, King William found himself alone with his Ministry and a small Conservative minority, in the struggle to reorganize the Prussian Army. . . [but fifty years later] The Armament Bills of 1912 were passed by the whole of the German middle-class parties in the Reichstag. . . . Not one of the middle-class parties, from the extreme Right to the Ultra-Liberals, even thought of making their consent to the Armament Bill [of 1913] dependent on the difficulties and differences of opinion in the question of meeting expenses. The national idea has taken firm root among all the middle-class parties. (155, 164–5)

Thus Bülow illustrated the historical success of his policies – policies, pursued for reasons, which stand as his own explanation of the German imperialism of his generation, and which he summed up in general injunctions at the end of his extensive treatment of the Social Democratic problem:

The idea of the nation as such must again and again be emphasised by dealing with national problems, so that this idea may continue to move, to unite and to separate the parties. . .

The Government must not leave this battle to the parties, it must fight it itself. For the Social Democratic movement does not only threaten the existence of one party or another; it is a danger to the country and the monarchy. This danger must be faced and met with a great and comprehensive national policy, under the strong guidance of clear-sighted and courageous governments which, whether amicably or by fighting, can make the parties bow to the might of the national idea. (199, 204)

Of this whole explanation, three features are especially interesting. First, it is a practitioner's explanation which joins the actor's analysis of his situation to an account of the values, feelings and calculations that led him to act as he did. Second, it is an explanation offered by one sort of conservative. Third, it is an explanation chosen partly for its by-products, of the adoption of a policy which was also chosen deliberately for its domestic by-products.

It is, first, a politician's explanation. With a few vital exceptions, noticed below, its author analyses the surface rather than what others would call the foundations of politics. Social and economic problems, however deeply rooted, present themselves to government as political demands or obstructions issuing from some configuration of political parties. That is the level at which Bülow analyses them – it was the level at which he had to deal with them, and perhaps the only level at which he had any real confidence that he understood them. He is content to accept, as part of nature, most of the structures and problems of economy and society, and to analyse only the changing ways in which, out of these unchanging raw materials, politicians attract support by espousing fancied interests and formulating unnecessary or mischievous issues for political resolution. Some social problems are not problems at all, but part of nature's harmony. Others, being permanent features of man's human predicament, are not soluble, nor fit subjects for politics. Within society it is the politicians, rather than any real conflicts of real social interest, who 'make' politics. The only important conflicts of real interests are between kingdoms or nationalities. The conflicts of German and Pole in eastern Prussia, of German and French on either side of the

Rhine, are real conflicts, to be resolved only by victory or defeat. There is not a sentence in *Imperial Germany* to suggest that the conflicts of worker and employer, of farmer and manufacturer, of rich and poor, have the same 'reality'. Even the conflict of the two Germanies, depicted with such romantic metaphor, is unreal: both Germanies will prosper best if they will overcome misunderstandings and join in union with each other.

Although internal problems are thus unreal, internal politics make them real enough. People are misled into thinking the problems are real, and these illusions lead them to act dangerously. The function of fatherly government is to control and restrain, the function of politics ought to be to educate, such a populace. 'The true means of restraining the majority of the nation from pursuing the revolutionary aims of Social Democrats and from adopting the seductive belief of the Socialists in an infinitely better future, is to pursue a courageous, wide-minded policy which can maintain the nation's satisfaction in the present conditions of life. . .' Thus the politician explains his choice of imperial policies as being necessary to keep the people's minds on issues which were 'real', capable of uniting them and of convincing them of the military necessity for them to be governed from above, while diverting their energies from the fruitless domestic squabbles which they might otherwise have supposed they could resolve better by governing themselves.

There is only a small, though vital, difference between this explanation and the translation of it which almost any radical might offer: 'Bülow chose his imperial policies as the only ones which could excite or terrify a majority of Germans into submitting to military monarchy and brutally conservative social policies; he thus diverted them from the fundamental social and industrial conflicts which cried out for action, but whose resolution would probably include the destruction of the monarchy, of Junker privilege, of the Prussian domination of Germany, and perhaps of some of the fundamental bases of capitalism and private property'.

Bülow's own explanation expresses his particular variety of conservatism by proposing one unbreakable causal chain and denying the existence of one other. He insists that the racial and historical inheritance of German human nature leads inevitably to military monarchy – inevitably, because the alternative is a chaos so hideous that none but a deluded German would choose it. But the unruly individualism which is another part of the same national character makes sure that the German will not submit quietly to a quiet monarchy; in its own interest and in his, the monarchy must incessantly excite, bully, discipline, and aggrandize him. In the chain from national character to imperialism, the links include the party faction fighting which the government must quell by preoccupying the parties with patriotic concerns. The faction fighting does not arise from genuine social problems or conflicts of interest; it arises from the strands of group loyalty, overdone logic and quarrelsome individualism in the German human nature of the party members. It was obviously important that Bülow should deny the existence of any causal chain – whether unbreakable, or breakable by deliberate political choice – which might connect the aggressions of monarchy with the fundamental facts of German capitalism. The by-products of *that* explanation, offered by all the Left since J. A. Hobson, are obvious: imperialism is made to appear both undesirable and avoidable, and could be avoided (according to your distance left of center) by the revolutionary eradication of capitalism, by democratic socialist reform, or by peaceful free-trading arrangements under a responsible government of 'little Germans'. By ascribing both the imperial policies of the government and the political activity of the parties to immutable qualities of national character, Bülow establishes his own by-product instead: the monarchy is historically necessary, and so are the powers and privileges of caste and of Prussia, of which the monarch is the only imaginable protector.

There may be confusion in references to two levels of 'by-product'. Bülow himself insists that he chose imperial policies partly for their domestic by-products: the grouping and isolation of parties, the avoidance of divisive issues, the education of all in the National Idea and in submission to government. But if his policies had these by-products, his explanation of his policies had others. The need to isolate or unite parties, to avoid domestic disputes and to procure unity and submission, were offered as proximate, 'understanding' explanations of his own imperial actions. But for the situation in which he acted – for the form taken by German unification, for the characteristic bitterness of party faction, for the violence of 'unreal' divisions of interest and class – for these he offered, as their single explanatory cause, the German national character. If the reader accepts this explanation, then by-products accompany it which have been explicitly argued little or not at all. The Prussian conquest and rule are inescapable. There is nothing alterable, or indeed undesirable, in Germany's industrial and social arrangements. There is nothing seriously wrong with an imperialism without actual territorial aim, justified by its necessity to a monarchy which in its circular turn is justified by the necessity of the imperialism – both, perhaps, psychological necessities for a national character which needs both, but can only with the greatest difficulty and the strongest leadership be persuaded that it needs either.

3. Theodore Roosevelt

Before Theodore Roosevelt became President, and comparatively discreet, he used to be the best of all exponents of the simplest of all explanations of imperial expansion: it is *fun*.

He began as a skinny, shortsighted, asthmatic child who read a great deal in books, watched birds, interested himself in natural history and was disgusted by bloodsports. Adolescence brought dramatic changes. He started fighting, hunting and talking. He became a disgraceful egotist, in dress and speech something of a dude. After a period in New York politics as a radical republican he went out west as a gentleman rancher. There he developed his health, his horsemanship, and a romantic and chivalrous view of violence. He almost fought a duel with a degenerate French marquis in the Dakota badlands; and after some years he almost made the ranch pay though that, as with all his imperial adventures, was secondary. He also wrote books, quick and superficial but full of cheerful bravado. One of the best-known, a two-volume history of the extension of the frontier beyond the Alleghany Mountains during the war of independence, *The Winning of The West*, traced the colonization of Kentucky back to its beginnings when the Germanic peoples

went forth from their marshy forests conquering and to conquer. For century after century they swarmed out of the dark woodland east of the Rhine and north of the Danube; and as their force spent itself the movement was taken up by their brethren who dwelt along the coasts of the Baltic and the North Atlantic. From the Volga to the Pillars of Hercules, from Sicily to Britain, every land in turn bowed to the warlike prowess of the stalwart sons of Odin. Rome and Novgorod, the imperial city of Italy as well as the squalid capital of Muscovy acknowledged the sway of Kings of Teutonic and Scandinavian blood.

What caused Imperialism?

. . . The day when the keels of the Low-Dutch sea-thieves first grated on the British coast was big with the doom of many nations. There sprang up in conquered Southern Britain . . . that branch of the Germanic stock which was in the end to grasp almost literally world-wide power, and by its overshadowing power to dwarf into comparative insignificance all its kindred folk.

With Kentucky duly settled, the latest expressions of Teutonic energy are the British and German empires. The next is to be the American; the discipline of the frontier is the preparation of the people for the task. Racial superiority equips them for it, and the opportunities for courage in violent endeavor attract them to it. As a practical expression of these general views Roosevelt spent a good many of his spare moments trying to get the United States into war. Almost any war would do. In 1886 there was some trouble with Mexico; he proposed to organize his ranch-hands into a cavalry battalion. In 1892 he wanted war with Chile. In 1894 he wanted to annex Hawaii and Nicaragua. In 1895 he wanted the United States to build the biggest navy in the world. Also to conquer Canada. In 1897, once again in order to annex Hawaii, he wanted a war with Japan. In almost any year he was willing to start something with any or all of the European powers who still had North or South American possessions. As Assistant Secretary of the Navy in McKinley's administration he did all he could to ensure that there should be no compromise with Spain over Cuba.

When critics called him a jingoist he took it as a compliment. When they criticized jingoism he called them 'the futile sentimentalists of the international arbitration type'; they had 'a flabby, timid type of character, which eats away the great fighting qualities of our race.' Anti-imperialists were 'men weak in body or mind, men who could not be soldiers because they lack physical hardihood or courage . . . who would become utterly appalled by slaughter in the field . . . a sentiment of preposterous and unreasoning mawkishness.' In 1897, when he was already in office and the Cuban dispute was already hot, he told the Naval War College: 'Peace is a goddess only when she comes with sword girt on thigh', notwithstanding which, 'no triumph of peace is quite so great as the supreme triumphs of war.'

In 1898 he got his war, went west, and raised and trained his Roosevelt Rough Riders in Texas. It was a bad time for him – on half a dozen occasions the war was nearly won before he got to it, and he praised the Lord for each American reverse. But all was well. He got to the war, and with his dozen spare pairs of spectacles slung around him he had the marvellous opportunity to lead a charge against a well-defended hill near San Juan. He thought it, ever afterwards, the greatest moment of his life. 'I doubled up a Spanish officer like a jack-rabbit . . . I rose over those regular army officers like a balloon.' He was proudest of all that his own losses were many times greater than anyone else's, including the Spaniards'.

It is clear enough what his idea of imperialism was not. He was not interested in the profits of war – he was inclined to think bankers and traders slothful pacifists who corrupted America's primitive vigor. He was not trying to divert attention from domestic problems – he enjoyed domestic problems, and grew if anything more radical as the years passed. He was not after cheap popularity, much as he enjoyed popularity – whatever his personal valor may have done for his political career, it is doubtful whether his imperialist and jingoist views were, on balance, assets. His interest in the national advantages to be won by conquest was more romantic than rational. Even in those days most people thought that war was justified, if at all, by its gains. Roosevelt seemed rather to think that the gains were justified by the opportunities they made for war. In the jargon of this chapter, his ends might be called a by-product of his means. But his imperialism has been explained better and without jargon by three contemporaries:

One observed that 'Theodore Roosevelt's life was the ultimate dream of every typical American boy: he fought in a war, killed lions, became President, and quarrelled with the Pope'.

A lady who knew him as Assistant Secretary of the Navy thought him 'as innocent as Toddy in *Helen's Babies*, who wanted everything to be bluggy'.

A future British Ambassador explained to a journalist who was having some difficulty in getting on with Roosevelt 'You must always remember that the President is about six'.[2]

4. Frederick Jackson Turner

Chamberlain and Roosevelt were prophets and preachers. They explained – and advocated – an imperialism yet to come. Their contemporary Frederick Jackson Turner also explained a forth-coming imperialism, but unlike them he saw no choice about it and he feared it. For present purposes there is no need to rehearse those parts of 'The Significance of the Frontier in American History'[3] which related the moving frontier to unique qualities in the society upon which Turner thought it had such important effects. It was a theory of the consequences rather than the causes of expansion and in any case neither Turner nor many others except perhaps the Red Indian theorists of imperialism have regarded such unresisted expansion as 'imperial'. But the paper's last pages, and fragments of later writings, did hint at a theory of imperialism: of the imperialism that must inevitably follow the closing of the free frontier.

Turner thought that the frontier gave Americans the habit of greed, but while it moved it fed them all they could eat. It made them look ahead always to the next step, but while it moved the next step was towards a retreating horizon that concealed no enemies. It enabled them to turn their backs, for a century, on the European competition for territory. It kept their businesses small because whoever wanted one could go out and start one; so that while it moved no business grew big enough to be dangerous in national politics. It kept government small, because most of what anybody wanted could be won by his own unaided, individual endeavor. At the same time it united and integrated America and made her democratic, and while it moved it kept her so. Now in 1893 'The frontier has gone; and with its going has closed the first period of American history'. But for four hundred years

The people of the United States have taken their tone from the incessant expansion which has not only been open but has even been forced upon them. He would be a rash prophet who should assert that the expansive character of American life has now entirely ceased. Movement has been its dominant fact, and, unless this training has no effect upon a people, the American energy will continually demand a wider field for its exercise.

When the frontier closes, what follows? Business turns from multiplying new enterprises to monopolizing old ones; its size and power and tendency to restrictive combination all increase. Workmen do the same; their leaders turn from radical individualism to the organization of labor unions and the adoption of socialistic ideas. The interests of capital and labor diverge, their conflict grows bitter, and both sides for the first time ask of Government not that it leave them alone, but that it protect them. By both sides therefore democracy is threatened, especially the independent, libertarian elements in Turner's frontier democracy. In spite of these restrictive tendencies the society is still geared to expansion and will still expand – but with a difference. The next expansion cannot be into free land. It may not include migration and settlement. It will probably not attract American labor but it will certainly require much concentrated capital. It will no longer promote peace and democracy, for it will have to be taken by conquest and governed by force. As the open frontier has allowed Americans to ignore both Europe's territorial contests and Europe's imperial methods, so the empire may soon compel Americans to enter that competition and to imitate those methods. The political forms developed on the frontier were generalized to the whole society, with good democratic effect. Perhaps they will now be replaced by the political forms of a militant imperialism.

Why should Turner predict such an empire at all, or offer such an explanation of it? He was first of all a radical democrat who valued personal and national independence and freedom of action: why should such a man prophesy such an historically-determined catastrophe? Second, why should he expect the bad habits bred by the frontier to overpower the good ones? He believed that the habit of expansion, though now admittedly a deep-rooted habit, had arisen from the Americans' perfectly rational, enterprising and fruitful responses to the presence of free land to the west of them. Why then did he see an unthinking, unbreakable 'habit of expansion' rather than a 'habit of rational and wise response' to circumstance, a response which might be expected to adapt intelligently even to such an important change in circumstances as the exhaustion of free land? And why should the habit of expansion also overcome those others which were the great subject of his work – the habits of insularity, democratic independence, mutual forbearance and dislike of authority which the frontier had in one way or another instilled into all Americans?

The first question is the simplest. Turner was a considerable determinist, but there was no necessary conflict in his seeing impersonal historical forces produce a society in which individual action was very free. Indeed the 'uncontrollability' of the historical forces had a lot to do with the freedom of the individuals. The movement west was the aggregate of a million independent responses to a common situation. Each was a free response precisely because there was no central power capable of replacing the million individual choices by a single social decision binding on all.*

Although Turner obviously saw the habit of expansion as being in various technical ways built into economic and other institutions, he must also have seen it as an aggregate of individual appetites, the more potent in effect because of the individuals' democratic powers. We may still wonder why he should expect their regard for expansion to lead them to vote like Gadarene swine for the imperialist destruction of their other values and liberties. Short sight, perhaps; Turner might be romantic about the frontier but he was not sentimental about the frontiersmen. What they followed into the west was their noses, their private and immediate interests. It was luck and free land, rather than anybody's long-sighted vision, that knit the selfishly-impelled movement of each into the broad and beautiful pattern of social results discerned after the event by Turner. The same short sight, now helped by greedy habits, might entice them into an imperialism whose broad and beastly social results not one of them intended. One of the great attractions of Turner's paper was its discernment of the hitherto inscrutable process which connected the motives of the frontiersmen to such ramifying social results. It was no more 'deterministic' to expect an unintended imperialism to issue from the same process. Turner himself suggested that it was his understanding of the effect of the frontier that compelled him, by its logically inescapable implications, to predict that the empire must begin when the frontier closed. He may also have been influenced by

*In discussions of historical freedom and determination there is very often confusion between the notions of contrived unanimity, natural unanimity and either human or natural coercion. If enough people freely choose to do the same thing at once, whether deliberately co-operating or each in ignorance of the other, the historian is apt to describe as 'an impersonal force' or 'an historical trend' what he would see as a freely-chosen act if only one or a few did it. If for each individual his 'choice' is between alternatives of unequal attraction, like working or starving, the unanimous response of all will be declared 'predictable' by cautious historians, 'determined' by others. If a migration is carried forward by flood-waters or a flow of volcanic lava, it is perhaps 'determined' but not 'historically'. If on the other hand the migration is carried by cattle-trucks bound for Buchenwald or Siberia, it may look very 'determined' to the migrants but some historians will see it as a powerful illustration of the historical freedom of choice of governments or powerful individuals.

ten years' contemplation of the robber barons, whose most spectacular decade coincided with the frontier's end.

There is another way in which Turner's predictive explanation of imperialism 'fits' and serves his frontier thesis. One cannot know whether he consciously intended what follows, but wilful or not it appears to be an important part of the unity and elegance of art and argument which distinguish the famous paper. In explaining the frontier's effects upon American society, Turner's argument distinguishes both cause and effect as unique: only America had such an experience of such a frontier, only America enjoys the special blessings that result from that experience. One example is enough: the contemporaneity of the whole frontier experience. Other societies have progressed through migrating, hunting, trading, mining, pastoral, agricultural, industrial and metropolitan phases. But only in America do these many levels of civilization coexist within one society, and continue to coexist through a century of time, so that the effects upon society of Indian wars, of trapping and trading frontiers, of the open range, of land-grabbing and gold rushes, are not the residual, embalmed effects which other societies retain of finished and forgotten causes; in America they are effects which continue because their causes continue. 'American social development has been continually beginning over again on the frontier', assuring the 'perennial rebirth . . . of American life.'

Of an effect which puzzles because eccentric, the most attractive explanation is often one which relates the effect to an equally deviant cause. This allows any determinist to keep his regular laws intact, while at the same time the isolation of both erratic phenomena, the one occurring only with the other, may be persuasive evidence of their relation to each other. For Turner, democratic individualism distinguishes American from comparable European society, and so does the 'contemporaneity' of the frontier experience. It is a plausible inference, and for an American democratic individualist a satisfying one, that the one phenomenon is explained by the presence of the other. But what if Americans are *always* democratic individualists – before, during and after the frontier period? For its perfect isolation Turner's pattern must be distinguished not only from contemporary European societies, but also from its own past and future – from America before the frontier opened, and from America after the frontier closes. In Turner's meaning of American society there *was* none before the frontier opened – the first immigrant opened it. His pattern has to get the best beginning it can from Independence, the date from which both the frontier, and the differentiating characteristics of American society, could develop in full freedom. For isolating his variables from the American past this can only be half-satisfactory; even if under restraint, each tendency did begin in the colonial past and besides, doubters might suspect that Independence itself gave impetus to each independently of the other. Their connection can be certain only if it can be shown that in a mature and independent America, the one still cannot survive without the other; and in 1893 that could only be shown by prediction. The whole force and originality of Turner's thesis is in its insistence that the American social character is not a 'once caused' effect that can survive its causes, but is an effect which endures from day to day only because of the daily rebirth of its causes at the frontier. If a closed frontier could leave durable effects, then many European societies would possess them too. Turner had two reasons to insist that the character would not survive the disappearance of its cause: the paired isolation and control of his variables, and the special 'daily' nature of the connection he asserted between them.

So to enclose his thesis suitably between a beginning and an end, to distinguish its central pattern from the American past and future as well as from foreign contemporaries, to 'prove' the link between the great cause and its great effects – for all these purposes, now that the frontier had closed, Turner had to predict what America would be like without it. It was precisely useful for his thesis that he should hint at a European style of imperialism, probably to be accompanied by illiberal European values and institutions. He had set out to prove that the Europeans who peopled America were made different there only by the frontier that they found there. His concluding prediction, of their sad reversion to type when their circumstances should revert to type, was too necessary to pass as mere afterthought, or artless pessimism. This explanation of imperialism looks as if it was written to repair, as its by-product, some shortcomings in the theory of the frontier.

5. J. A. Hobson

Hobson and Turner had so much in common that they might have been expected to write very similar explanations of imperialism. Both saw the thing-to-be-explained as a geographical, economic and military expansion being attempted by every mature society big and strong enough to try it – a product not (like Bülow's) of peculiar national circumstances, but of a particular stage in any rich nation's development. They both hated and feared it, believing it would bring no good even to most of its protagonists. Both knew what they wanted instead, and their visions of good were alike. Each believed in a 'small' democracy: a democracy of small businesses and small holdings and small government, with a minimum of regimentation and the maximum number of nuttily independent households. Perhaps Turner, with the small-town and country household in mind, saw grandmother secure in a corner of the family hearth while Hobson with the industrial midlands in mind saw her secure on an old age pension; perhaps Turner would have accorded a bigger role to natural abundance in assuring good wages, Hobson to a strong trade union movement; perhaps Turner's independent citizens enjoyed a more fluid and adventurous, Hobson's a more settled and cosy, existence; but these were no more than the differences between prairie and seabord, country and city, in one and the same free-speaking, free-voting, free-trading, peaceable, liberal paradise.

When these brothers in faith, who identified and hated the same imperialism as an enemy of the same utopian possibilities, nevertheless ascribed it to wholly different causes, that was partly because of yet another similarity: neither of them was primarily interested in explaining imperialism. Turner in a few paragraphs gave it the explanation whose implications offered logical support to his frontier thesis. Hobson in *Imperialism, A Study* (1902)[4] gave it the explanation whose implications would attract popular support to his underconsumptionist economic theory. Turner's purpose being to convince intellectuals of a point about the past, his pessimism about the future (though doubtless sincere) cost him nothing. Hobson's purpose was to reform the future, radically. It was utterly convenient to these respective purposes that Turner should foresee an inevitable imperialism springing from the habits and appetites of everyman, while Hobson ascribed an avoidable imperialism to two easily alterable causes: the distribution of incomes, and the machinations of a few conspirators.

Hobson's *Imperialism* is famous enough to need no summary here, the more so since the gist of its economic argument, its relation to his general economic theory, and some objections to its truth have been well summarized in a recent article. D. K. Fieldhouse points out, what it is a main purpose of this section to emphasize, that *Imperialism* is an argument not so much about empires as about domestic English society:

In a sense, this book was primarily a vehicle for publicizing the theory of 'underconsumption', which he regarded as his main intellectual achievement, and which he expressed more fully in *The Evolution of Modern Capitalism*, and other works. In brief, the theory, which was an alternative to the Marxist concept of surplus value as an explanation of poverty, saw excessive investment by the capitalist, with its concomitant of underconsumption by the wage-earner, as the root cause of recurrent slumps, of low interest rates, and of permanent underemployment. Hobson thought there were only two answers to this problem. The correct one – which would also be the answer to the 'condition of England question' – was to increase the buying power of the workers by giving them a higher share of the profits of industry. The wrong one, which was no answer to the social question, was to invest the surplus capital overseas, where it could earn a high interest rate, and thus sustain domestic rates of interest, without benefiting the British worker. And this, he held, was what Britain had been doing since at least the middle of the nineteenth century.[5]

The by-products or implications of this explanation of imperialism were not (as for Turner) additional proofs of the underconsumption theory. *Imperialism* explored some particular consequences of underconsumption, but added little or nothing to Hobson's already-confident view of the causes of economic malfunction, except perhaps in emphasizing the role of foreign investment as an evil alternative to better methods of balancing investment and consumption within the home economy. Whatever Hobson's intention, the great achievement of the book was to improve not the structure but the popularity of his economic theory. Perhaps the domestic ills of inequality and underemployment were too controversial (or too uninteresting) by themselves. Perhaps Hobson's argument about them could never be popular as long as it appeared in technical form as economic theory – but *anybody* could understand, and be moved by, *Imperialism*. Like 'The Significance of the Frontier', it was constructed and written with rare elegance, deceptive clarity and genuine and infectious emotion. It was well-timed in the last year of the

Anglo-Boer war, at the climax of decades of accumulating liberal concern about imperial policies. Besides these general charms, its argument also offered a marvellous variety of attractions for particular people and points of view. If an explanation may have one sort of by-product in its logical implications, it may have another sort in its points of popular appeal, its collection into a coherent scheme of so many matters of popular misgiving.

What made *Imperialism* such good propaganda? Basically, it took the old complaints against inequality and poverty, which only a minority (the poor and their few sympathizers) could be expected to worry about, and by connecting unequal incomes with the flight of capital, with periodic depression, with various kinds of capitalist racketeering and colonial plunder, with arms manufacture and imperialism and war, it sought to enlist in one army in a single crusade what had hitherto been scattered minorities who each objected to only one or two of those evil phenomena. There were business men who worried about depressions, but not about the empire or the poor. Some Fabians who worried about the poor were still imperialists. Cobdenite opponents of public expenditure on the colonies often saw no need for public expenditure on social services either. Some socialists were socialists only because they did not think capitalism could ever be purified. Hobson's argument offered to all these the doctrinal basis of an alliance.

Its effect should not of course be exaggerated. Some of the suggested alignments were altogether too unlikely. It was probably not until the first world war and the Russian revolution had made their impressions on public opinion that *Imperialism* achieved its widest popularity, and even then the disillusion with imperialism was by no means all Hobson's work. Most of the connections alleged in *Imperialism* had been alleged by others before ever it was written – there had always been free traders who connected protection, imperialism, public extravagance and 'big' government, and there were Marxist and other socialists who alleged more connections between more abuses than Hobson did. But first, Hobson did it very attractively; and second, he did it more safely. Classical economic thought still offered no comfort to the poor and no plausible explanation of depression, while socialist thought tended to allow no cure for anything except by the dangerous alteration of almost everything. The overwhelming attraction of Hobson's argument was its implication that so much ill could be eradicated by such gentle and viable measures of reform, measures with such respectable intellectual parentage, to be undertaken in the name of such familiar and re-assuring values.

Much of Hobson's originality lies in his unique combination of so many ideas each, in itself, familiar. His method of reform is Fabian, though its single comprehensive theory is not. There are Ricardian assumptions about the possibility of a self-adjusting economy together with many of John Stuart Mill's admissions of the need for marginal corrective action by the state. There is all of Cobden's belief in free trade without any of his cruel insistence on *laissez-faire*. The contempt for aristocratic interests and orthodoxies, the sanguine confidence in the state's capacity to accomplish what-ever novel scheme it thinks expedient, might be Bentham's own, but there is no insensitive trace of Bentham in Hobson's compassionate understanding of human nature and spirit. Hobson's theory, if valid and acted on, would rid the classical liberal ideal of its cruelties and technical shortcomings while preserving all of its freedom, its values and its hopes; and preserving, above all, its magical identification of selfishness and virtue, of private interest and public good.

He asked the English to stop plundering colonies not as an act of self-sacrifice, but only in order to get richer quicker by surer methods. All that was required was the taxation of a margin – a very small margin – of savings that could not be invested profitably at home; the redistribution of this margin to consumers; and some trade union pressure to keep wages pressing hard on productivity. The taxation would remove half the problem of overinvestment. The consumers' expenditure, by increasing the demand and opportunity for profit-able investment at home, would remove the other half of the problem of overinvestment. By the elimination of depression and under-employment, and by the redistribution of purchasing power, stability and social justice would be secured. The rich would have lost only a small part of what they could not spend, and might well be compen-sated by the greater prosperity of all their other investments. Reasonable inequalities, quite sufficient to sustain all existing social differences and social certainties, would continue; so would the old institutions of the state, and everybody's rights and liberties in and under them. Only a useless and dangerous empire would have been traded for peace abroad, and growth, wealth, social justice and satisfied consciences at home.

Here, apparently, was something for almost everybody with penalties for almost none. A final attraction of Hobson's explanation of imperialism was its deft choice of scapegoats. There is a familiar propagandist advantage in nominating, as the authors of all evil, as few conspirators as possible; thus you make the division between your supporters and your enemies as victoriously unequal as you can. The ideal scapegoats should be few, foreign-connected, readily recognizable and already disliked. (Like the Nazis, Hobson included international Jews as the most sinister of all.) Marx, by contrast, was compelled to indict far too many for comfort. His middle classes might be personally innocent instruments of the capitalist system, but that would not save them from real loss in the socialist revolution. His enemies of progress might even add up at times to a majority of voters; they would certainly command all the civil and military arms of the State which was scheduled for destruction. Altogether, a very painful revolution was indicated against an uncomfortably numerous enemy. Hobson's villains by contrast, though not negligible, were not a whole class, and many of them were not *necessary* enemies. His fourth chapter identified them: those who made and sold armaments, built, coaled or owned ships, clothed and fed armies; the great manufacturing exporters who pushed textiles and hardware into colonial markets; contractors for colonial public works; colonial civil servants, army and navy officers, missionaries; and above all, one group of financiers – not the genuine investors, but 'the great financial houses, who use stocks and shares not so much as investments to yield them interest, but as material for speculation in the money market . . . These great businesses – banking, broking, bill discounting, loan floating, company promoting – form the central ganglion of international capitalism.' They are a mere fraction of the population, a small proportion even of its middle and upper classes, and even of this short list a fair proportion could adapt themselves to be as gainfully employed without imperialism as with it. In manner of life, not one need suffer in Hobson's gentle revolution. As long as they earned it in less harmful trades, he had no objection to their getting all the money they could spend – his only design was against a small part of the surplus that they could *not* spend.

What caused Imperialism?

There are of course all sorts of objections to Hobson's economic theory, to the viability of his proposed reforms, to his 'facts' of overseas investment, and to his connection of investment with imperial policies. They were well summarized by Fieldhouse. Here it is enough to reiterate the point that this account of imperialism was chiefly an analysis of the domestic political economy of capitalist society. Directly stated, that analysis attracted very limited support. Built into this explanation of imperialism it acquired an untechnical simplicity, it was extended to account for a larger range of evils, it brought hitherto scattered reformers into an alliance of purposes, it concentrated their fire upon scapegoats, and it showed how the moderate action needed to bring domestic prosperity and social justice would also bring justice and peace between nations. These implications are built into the explanation with such economy and art that it would be absurd to suppose that the author's only motive was a single-minded curiosity about the causes of imperialism.

Hobson was an impressively 'unlimited' economist. He did argue that certain economic interests and processes might control or exploit the many other conditions and activities that made for imperialism. But he allowed to those other conditions and activities their own life and reasons – economic interests might direct them towards imperialism but economic interests were not the causes of their existence – and he wrote about them with catholic perception. If he thought he saw economic interests exploiting people's religious or patriotic or class feelings, or their voluntary or political institutions, he did not conclude that economists should become the organizers of the other social sciences. He was not a disciplinary imperialist. The disciplinary imperialists who later sought to replace his explanation by proposing a single economic, or a political, or a racial or a sociological condition as the sufficient single cause of all effects were neither as sensitive as Hobson to the mutual dependence of those aspects of life, nor, sometimes, as original as they claimed to be. Most of their ideas were already in Hobson's book, neglected by critics who concentrated on his economic analysis and his dubious connection of economic interests to political acts. But even his economic argument is rarely about abstract economic men, and he wrote with humane intelligence of the motives of economy, religion, charity, sociability, adventure and patriotism. The 'sociology of imperialism' appears in many passages about the relations between education, social ambition and jingoism, between public opinion and methods of taxation, between hostility to other classes and to other races, between primogeniture and the disposal of younger sons. The popular view of imperialism as an atavism is foreshadowed in Hobson's discussion of 'lusts of quantitative acquisitiveness and of forceful domination surviving in a nation from early centuries of animal struggle for existence'. Imperialism as a political racket, a product of party political warfare, appears in his account of its use as a device for avoiding reform. Its connection with particular constitutional forms is the subject of a long chapter about militarism, democratic liberties and the authority of the state. It would only be necessary to sever some of Hobson's organizing connections, to lift from his book as much as was ever very sensible in the subsequent contributions to this topic of Lenin, Schumpeter, and a host of others.

6. V. I. Lenin

'Theory is thought about action.' Propaganda, he might have added, is thought *in* action. It does not seem likely that it was to occupy spare time (as most of his biographers suggest, except D. S. Mirsky and Christopher Hill), or from idle curiosity or any merely didactic itch to correct Hobson's or Kautsky's errors, that Lenin gave some months of 1916 to writing *Imperialism, The Highest Stage of Capitalism*.[6] As an explanation it was constructed as if to meet an urgent and practical need to split the socialist movement, to give unity and determination to the half that Lenin wanted to lead out of the split, and to discredit all rival candidates for the leadership.

But if the following pages are all about the book's pragmatic purposes, this is not to suggest that Lenin wrote it cynically. His circumstances made theory, for the moment, exceptionally important; but they made it at least as important that the theory be historically true and reliable, as that it be attractive or plausible or orthodox.

International socialism had fallen part, as had most of its national components. Of whatever unity the Second International had appeared to achieve before the war, little had survived August 1914 and through 1915 and 1916 too little (for Lenin's purposes) had been rebuilt by the Zimmerwald conferences and other such means.

Within Russia, Bolshevik and Menshevik organizations were each troubled by internal divisions. At almost every level from international organization to party cell and trade union shop, these divisions arose from and were expressed as disagreements and uncertainties about the true nature of the war and the correct socialist response to it. Besides posing its own questions, the war also gave new urgency to older theoretical problems, problems of revolutionary or reformist strategy which could previously wait, but could wait no longer, on continuing reflection and debate. Bills for war finance and conscription confronted socialist MPs. Antipatriotic organizations and publications became illegal. Call-up papers or demands for overtime work in factories and transport services confronted the rank and file. Socialists had to stand up and be counted. The pressure to stand up in the lawful rather than the revolutionary ranks was formidable; but those patriotic, lawful and generally popular ranks were also the ranks of militarized capitalism at its worst. Despite polemics like Lenin's it was seldom a simple choice between courage and cowardice, fidelity and desertion. Was it so obviously a more revolutionary act for the Russian worker to fight against rather than for his government – for the victory of German rather than of Russian monopolists? If the war was indeed a breakdown of capitalism, did that necessarily alter pre-war judgments that socialist revolution would be premature in a country not yet sufficiently industrialized? If the Tsar was a feudal remnant, should socialists help capitalists to remove him, or avoid that entangling alliance and fight the capitalists immediately? If history had still to work out a remainder of its capitalist phase, would socialists hurry it on more effectively by supporting or by scragging the bourgeois parties, or should they retire to prepare the next revolution from hiding, or use their agitating power and industrial organization to build some of the work of the next revolution into the texture of the present one?

At the same time as he agonized about such historical strategy, the party leader had at every step to remember also his revolutionary program and his party tactics. Whatever the personal motives and ambitions might be, it was chiefly by doctrine and program that the illegal parties were split or united, strengthened or weakened. Even in the most naked contests for party power, the leader's principal weapon was the formulation of conference motions which would unite or divide opinions (and followings, and units of organization, and often funds) in ways advantageous to himself. At the base of the movement, however widespread and efficient his party machinery for recruitment and communication with the masses, the machinery was only there to propagate theory and to organize the action indicated by theory, and it would gain or lose its mass support according to how convincing the theory sounded and how satisfying the action felt. Party support was seldom secure or usable without continuous exercise, and this in itself could pose problems for leaders. Some mixture of successful reformism and agitational industrial action was really the only way to keep a mass party following in being; but what if such methods were at times *historically* wrong? In all such dilemmas, theory had to be the socialist leader's Intelligence and Operations Branch as well as his Propaganda Department. It had to be plausible, or there would be no ranks to lead. It had to fence off rivals, or the ranks might be led by others. But at the same time it had to prove right, not wrong, or it would lead all together to destruction. For various reasons, in 1916, Lenin needed some new theory urgently.

A very large majority of European working men, together with most leaders and members of most socialist parties, were supporting or at least not opposing their own countries' war efforts. Even more distressing to Lenin was the disarray of the left-wing minorities who did oppose, for these were what ought to have been his own team. All socialists of course opposed the war in the sense that they 'opposed war'. The majorities were mostly demanding peace by negotiation, peace without victory, peace without annexations. But many of the left minorities who did make active efforts to avoid war service or war work, and who did try to keep illegal party organizations alive, were likewise demanding only 'peace'. Worse, the genuine socialist aversion from war and national aggrandizement was being made the basis of all sorts of efforts to rebuild a broad socialist unity. Worst, everybody wanted the shooting to stop at the earliest moment, at all costs, as a matter prior even to the socialist revolution itself.

Lenin saw the war as an incident in the breakdown of capitalism, an incident which had *armed* twenty million workers and peasants. Far from laying down their guns, they should turn them on their officers and their national ruling classes and effect the international socialist revolution just as soon as a sufficient organization existed to direct them. Such an organization could only be built *by* experienced incorruptibles like himself; but even the most personally incorruptible of them, the stalwarts of the Zimmerwald peace movement for example, were straying into every variety of pacifist or procrastinating heresy. Such an organization could only be built *upon* a willing, correctly educated section of the proletariat; but it was becoming less and less possible to educate the proletariat in the circumstances of war propaganda and censorship and the imprisonment or defection of their leaders. The task for the left was therefore: to split European Socialism decisively, fencing off the reliable revolutionary left and identifying all the rest as members of the capitalist camp; to rebuild illegal organizations throughout industry and the armed forces; and through those organizations to educate a revolutionary proletarian phalanx which should refuse the temptation, when it came, to lay down its arms in peace, but be ready to turn them on its masters in revolutionary civil war.

The sum and substance of Social Democracy's practical programme in this war is to support, develop, extend and sharpen mass revolutionary action, and to set up illegal organizations, for without them there is no way of telling the truth to the masses of people even in the "free" countries. The rest is either lies or mere verbiage, whatever its trappings of opportunist or pacifist theory.[7]

As his effective correspondents dwindled, his channels of communication narrowed, the leaders of his Russian network were imprisoned, the journals in which he could publish diminished in number and circulation, Lenin still hammered away at these themes through 1915 and 1916. He won what he could at the Zimmerwald peace conferences, not much in September 1915 and only a little more in April 1916. In letters, articles and pamphlets he denounced the majority socialists of every European country in turn, in every case enjoining the hard left to split, to fence off, to avoid any part in the war but also any campaign that was merely for peace. Most of these messages were short, and they were declaratory rather than analytical. Pacifism *was* a form of chauvinism. Socialist unity *was* nothing but a device to get socialists to fight for capitalist causes. Pacifists, defeatists, defencists, gradualists, reformists, democrats –

all *were* one and the same (social-chauvinist opportunists) working together whether they knew it or not for the same end (the continuation of capitalism and war).

It was all very well to say so. But why should anybody believe the nearly incredible – that Kautsky and the Fabians, the martial Millerand and the gentle Martov, were in the same camp? Looking to the objective effects of their actions, Lenin even put them in the same camp with the Rothschilds, the Krupps, the Kaiser and the Tsar. Only a particular Marxist view could make such bedfellows, and half the bedfellows were themselves the most eminent of Marxist theorists, offering Marxist reasons for their positions, and describing Lenin if they spared him a pamphlet at all as wrong, mad or megalomaniac. And still almost every conflict of policy, every split or alliance of groups, every choice between legal and illegal organization, every effort to end the war or to turn it into revolution, seemed to spring from honestly held convictions or differences of theory, or was at least defended publicly by reference to theory. The most immediate tactics appeared to be connected directly to the most profound historical views. Exactly what stage had Europe reached, in what historical process, to be understood by which of the analyses which claimed descent from Marx? Plekhanov's Marxist analysis saw in the war an opportunity for socialists to join in the destruction of German (the worst) imperialism; for a German victory would merely give back a truncated, deindustrialized Russia into the firmer grip of its landowners. Martov's Marxist analysis saw peace as the organizing aspiration which might reunite Russian socialism for the still long and arduous task of preparing the proletariat for revolution; both in Russia and in the European democracies, the same peace program might divide the bourgeois ranks and attract democrats and radicals into socialist alliances. Kautsky's Marxist analysis saw imperialism as a choice rather than a necessity of capitalism, a choice which might imaginably introduce a phase of ultra-imperialist peace in which socialists need only capture one world trust instead of a dozen national centers of state power. Whatever Lenin might say, their Marxist credentials, their proletarian loyalties and their ultimate revolutionary intentions were at least as plausible as his own. It was their different extensions of Marx and their different views of history that were dividing for piecemeal defeat what ought to have been the united forces of progress.

Recognition that a war is being fought for national liberation implies one set of tactics; its recognition as an imperialist war, another.[8]

Even when Lenin conceded that they had set off on the right track, it was to point out how detailed theoretical error could still lead many into wrong turnings –

There is evidence that even today the indisputable fact that capitalism is progressive, when compared with the semi-philistine "paradise" of free competition, and that imperialism and its final victory over "peaceful" capitalism in the leading countries of the world are inevitable – that this fact is still capable of producing an equally great and varied number of political and apolitical mistakes and misadventures.[9]

Through the winter of 1915–16 the misadventures multiplied, nourished by the copious springs of historical and theoretical error, and diverse understandings of Marx.

Without pretending to penetrate Lenin's mind, we can at least borrow one of its devices to identify an 'objective' need for a general restatement and up-dating of Marxism. He had been denouncing error and asserting orthodoxy, but in no real theoretical sense had he done much to demonstrate or explain the errors, or establish the foundations and prove the reasoning of his own position. We can also see, again without pretending to know that he did, the conditions which such a re-statement needed to satisfy:

First it must stick to Marx and be as invulnerable as possible to charges of deviation.

Second, it must nevertheless repair some wear and tear in the Marxist system. There were embarrassments: accelerating productivity in the mature economies which 'ought' to be reaching the stage of ungovernable internal conflict and decay; the apparently peaceful transcendence of frontiers by the international monopolies which 'ought' to be finding national states an intolerable strait-jacket in restraint of the internationalization of production; the long years of comparative peace from 1870 to 1913; the extent of labor organization and of piecemeal industrial gains and social reforms in the richer countries, and the persistence there of merely reformist working-class parties. There were various rival denials or explanations of these phenomena, each method pregnant with deviant thought and action; they must give way to a single authoritative canon.

Third, something must be done about the two most fertile begetters of error, two trends that seemed to contradict Marx flatly. The advanced countries' workers were not being 'immiserated'; and their middle ranks of skill and income were thickening where Marx had predicted sharper division and a widening gap between capital and labor, rich and poor.

Fourth, the enemies of history and of the working class must be identified, simplified and lumped together. The most dangerous – those who represented themselves as friends in order to lead the workers to destruction – must be shown to be, not bad or mistaken or uncertain socialists, but no socialists at all – as bourgeois and anti-historical as any capitalist.

Fifth, the universal war-weariness was such and peace movements of every kind so enticing, that people must be given really compulsory reasons to go on fighting, to turn straight from one tired, bloody war to another. Immediate peace must appear as not merely a wrong but an unattainable aim, one whose pursuit by the wrong methods, with the wrong allies, could lead only to more and worse wars.

Sixth, more was needed than a positive new analysis. Its negative implications must not be left to chance. If it was to show the error of their ways to the followers of Hobson, Bernstein, Kautsky, Legien, Plekhanov, Axelrod, Martov, and all the rest, then its destruction of their theories must be explicit and unmistakable.

Finally, the analysis must offer a positive role for socialism and the working class – a role with no possible alternatives, a role easy to understand, simple (however hard or brave) to pursue, and bound (because historically determined) to succeed, just as soon as leaders and workers discerned it clearly enough to play their parts.

The 'unbreakable chain' was a metaphor doubly appropriate to Marx's historical and economic analysis of capitalism. One chain led through time from primitive society to mature capitalism. Within capitalism, another connected its present foundations in physical nature and human technique to its accumulating contradictions. Nobody had any choice about its development; nobody could alter its essential internal relations to cure or purify it; nobody could prevent its contradictions from destroying it. The first six chapters of Lenin's *Imperialism* explained imperialism by extending both chains – what had happened to capitalism since Marx, and what made its new contradictions as incurably self-destructive as the old contradictions which also, of course, it still incorporated.

Since Marx, Lenin pointed out, production had been further monopolized and its control had passed, through a group of monopolist banks, to an oligarchy of financiers. To the old contradictions between capital and labor, between increasing capitalization and falling profit, between competition and monopoly, between productive capacity and its underemployment, there were now added the special contradictions of finance-capitalist imperialism. Production was in one sense socialized but the relations of production were not. Production was internationalized but the state system – the proprietors' enforcement arm – was not. Each international cartel and each imperial alliance registered a momentary balance of the actual wealth and powers of the participants, but their wealth and potential fluctuated so that the balances frozen in trust or treaty had constantly to be revised by force. Insofar as monopoly inflated profits these could only be re-invested, soon to intensify the old effect which monopoly was designed to ward off – the effect by which over-capitalization depressed profits, put pressure on wages and intensified the war of capital and labor. The escape by capital export allowed a breathing space, but not for ever. It merely exported the old process into new areas, in which the class war would soon have to be policed by ever-increasing military expenditures, while at the same time the monopolist groups sent their national armies into successive world wars with each other in their competitive struggles for territory. At a higher and more destructive level the old contradiction continued between competition itself and its inevitable product of bigger monopolies; and as ever, the function of monopoly was to inflate profit by restricting production, so that the greater productive potential of the new international units was flatly contradicted by the restrictive functions which were (under capitalism) their only reason for existence. This central contradiction comprehended all the rest; in it lay the dialectical necessity for the international socialist revolution which alone could unleash the new productive capacities of mankind.

So far, the positive explanation of imperialism. Unbreakable and impeccably Marxist chains were extended into the present and future. It had been impossible to prevent imperialism (so much for Hobson). Imperialism could neither be undone, nor unify the world, nor find for itself any stability by peaceful self-regulation (so much for Kautsky). Its wars were its own and none of its uses of changing combinations of national armed forces could possibly be mistaken for old-fashioned 'national' wars for the advantage of the nationals (so much for all social chauvinists). Its wars must follow each other incessantly until its capitalist foundations were destroyed by socialist force in the bloodiest war of all (so much for Martov and all pacifists, gradualists and procrastinators).

But it was not enough to show all rival explanations of imperialism to be wrong; not enough, even, to show that mistaken interpretations bred strategies and tactics which put their exponents 'objectively' (but still surely by honest mistake?) on the side of the enemy. They would be more murderously discredited if their existence could be explained in an orthodox manner – if they could be shown to be, not workers misled by mistake into the enemy ranks, but bourgeois making no mistake at all: genuine, economically-determined bourgeois-to-the-backbones, doing naturally what bourgeois are historically determined to do. (That should take care of any more talk of 'bringing them back to the fold', of 'socialist unity' with them.) It happened that the theoretical device which would thus identify them would at the same time complete the necessary repairs to Marx, by incorporating into his analysis the only facts of history which still appeared to contradict it, the rising living standards of western European workers and the increasing moderation and patriotism of their political parties. The concept of parasitism, employed by Marx and enriched by Hobson, got Lenin's eighth chapter to itself, and his ninth and tenth spelled out its felicitous implications.

The export of capital and the division of the world by the monopolists of a few advanced territories not only accounted for the years of peace before 1914 (then for the war, as soon as the spoils were all seized and had to be re-divided); it accounted also for areas and periods of enormous monopoly profit.

The receipt of high monopoly profits by the capitalists in one of the numerous branches of industry, in one of the numerous countries, etc., makes it economically possible for them to bribe certain sections of the workers, and for a time a considerable minority of them, and win them to the side of the bourgeoisie of a given industry or given nation against all the others. The intensification of antagonisms between imperialist nations for the division of the world increases this urge. And so there is created that bond between imperialism and opportunism . . . (301)

The monopolists' provision for a pensioned petty-bourgeoisie is the economic and historical cause of the persistence of that class of supporters of capitalism. But the monopolists are too shrewd to suppose that they themselves, or any other honest reactionaries, can organize these new clients. They get organized instead by reformist parties who profess to fight against *particular features* of capitalist society, thus implicitly accepting and effectively defending its bases. In a paper written for another purpose while *Imperialism* was in progress, Lenin put it tersely:

What the capitalists and their diplomats now need is "socialist" servants of the bourgeoisie to deafen, dupe and drug the people with talk about a "democratic peace" so as to cover up the real policy of the bourgeoisie, making it difficult for the masses to realize the real nature of this policy and diverting them from the revolutionary struggle.[10]

Imperialism elaborates this message less quotably at greater length, just as it does the historical growth of parasitism which Lenin also summed up more briskly in another contemporary paper:

The relatively "peaceful" character of the period between 1871 and 1914 served to foster opportunism first as a *mood*, then as a *trend*, until finally it formed a *group or stratum* among the labour bureaucracy and petty-bourgeois fellow-travellers. These elements were able to gain control of the labour movement only by paying lip-service to revolutionary aims and revolutionary tactics. They were able to win the confidence of the masses only by their protestations that all this "peaceful" work served to *prepare* the proletarian revolution.[11]

Now in wartime, as in any other revolutionary situation, the parasites betray the working classes by keeping them loyal to their slave-masters, thus fulfilling the role for which the opportunist parties were founded and which their leaders' parasitic class-status makes appropriate for them. To have anything to do with such leaders or with their 'limited' objectives is to assist their purposes. Their purposes are more vile than their masters' purposes. Their masters act their own bourgeois role which, though it is now nearly played out, is yet their appropriate role in history. But the labor leaders, reformists and opportunists, Marxists who deviate by a hairsbreadth from Lenin in any legal, cautious or pacifist direction, these prolong the slaughter by corrupting the working class so that it shall *not* enact its historical role – the next, the most vital, the most liberating role in human history.

The wrangles with Kautsky have often been passed over lightly by critics of *Imperialism*, stripped off like 1916 barnacles so that the 'pure' argument of the book may be held up for admiration or contradiction. I think they do too little justice to the craftsmanship of Lenin, who generally wasted no words, muddled no purposes and encrusted his weapons with no barnacles. The wrangles with contemporaries appear to me to be the sharp point of the book, its preliminary theory the force required to drive the point home. Every step of the general theory has its tactical implications for 1916, and none of the implications is left implicit. It is merely trite to reiterate that for Lenin the only purpose of theory was action. He might still have used those few months of his life during which action was impossible, to write a general appreciation of modern capitalism and a strategic guide to action in the decades to come. That was probably among his purposes, especially because he was insisting at that time that the revolutionary situation, though it might break next day, might equally not arise for a decade. But the connection of theory to the immediate divisions among his socialist contemporaries, the insistent connection of its every step to the immediate need of a particular split and regrouping of parties, make it hard to believe that this was either a by-product of the author's main intention, or the fussy intrusion of day-to-day controversies to interrupt the 'pure' flow of general theory. Two passages from the last chapters may illustrate the reasons for supposing that the general theory was constructed at that time as a weapon for the party warfare of those years. The first exemplifies the instant and constant connections which Lenin made between each step of theory and its tactical imperatives:

Kautsky's theoretical analysis of imperialism, as well as his economic and political critique of imperialism, are permeated *through and through* with a spirit, absolutely irreconcilable with Marxism, of obscuring and glossing over the fundamental contradictions of imperialism and with a striving to preserve at all costs the crumbling unity with opportunism in the European working-class movement. (298)

The second is especially telling because it is part of the book's final peroration and because it was directed at Martov. Of all political rivals, Martov must have been one whom Lenin in his heart could least suspect of parasitism. Martov had been his close friend, had fought with him against what they had once agreed on as 'opportunism', was brave, honest and gentle, and was to retain some of Lenin's personal affection and respect until his death. Perhaps it was just such qualities of some of the old revolutionaries that made them dangerous to Lenin. At any rate it was upon them, the very nearest Marxists to his own personal position, those whose fighting opposition to imperialism was unquestionable, that the whole argument of *Imperialism* was made to converge in its closing pages. In the matter of 'the extraordinary rapidity and the particularly revolting character of the development of opportunism',

The most dangerous of all in this respect are those who do not wish to understand that the fight against imperialism is a sham and humbug unless it is inseparably bound up with the fight against opportunism. (302)

That fight against opportunism – against all the efforts of European socialism for unity and peace – is surely what this explanation of imperialism was 'inseparably bound up with'. The explanation was so constructed that, if believed, its implications would serve to found the Third International, kill the Second, recapture for Lenin both branches of the Russian Social Democratic Party, and put all to work in illegal organizations to transform the war into an international revolution.*

7. J. A. Schumpeter

An English translation of Joseph Schumpeter's 'Zur Sociologie der Imperialismen' (1918–19) did not appear until 1951,[12] leaving time for its argument to be misunderstood for different reasons by both Marxist and liberal English-speakers. E. M. Winslow, in *The Journal of Political Economy* (Vol. 39, No. 6, December 1931) and in *The Pattern of Imperialism* (1949), expounded it fairly in direct

*This guesswork is based on Lenin's character, his situation, and the text of *Imperialism* and contemporary papers. My colleague Israel Getzler suggests that the guesswork may be supported by the history of Lenin's rivalry with Kautsky since 1914, and by Lenin's correspondence about the publication of *Imperialism*. Editors, thinking to publish it legally in Russia in 1916, insisted on deleting some passages which attacked Martov and, especially, Kautsky. Lenin wrote insistent, angry and despairing defences of his footnotes against Kautsky – 'they are extraordinarily important to me'. See Lenin, *Polnoe sobranie sochinenii*, Vol. 49, letters to M. N. Pokrovsky of 2 July, 14 July, August, and 21 December 1916.

exposition but in other passages made opportunities for the unwary to misunderstand it. Though he did not literally misrepresent it either, it is easy to see how the misunderstanding was encouraged – and widely propagated – by juxtaposing two sentences of Hans Morgenthau's *Politics among Nations, The Struggle for Power and Peace* (1949, p. 32):

We have seen that imperialism is not determined by economics, capitalist or otherwise . . . historic evidence points to the primacy of politics over economics, and "the rule of the financier . . . over international politics" is indeed, in the words of Professor Schumpeter, "a newspaper fairytale, almost ludicrously at variance with facts".

Schumpeter would not have forgiven the careless reader who inferred from this that he equated 'capitalist' with 'economic'. Marx himself was not more insistent that capitalism was a passing phase in man's economic development. Schumpeter's explanation of imperialism, its language drawn from the education he shared with Bauer and Hilferding, Marxist in the categories of its analysis of almost every historical phenomenon except capitalism, at one with Hilferding in its connection of tariff and monopoly capitalism with imperialism and war, had as its central theme the economic provenance of imperialism by modes of action and organization which were generated quite rationally by one economic system, but survived to operate in and upon later systems to which they were no longer 'rationally' appropriate. Schumpeter himself may have feared his misinterpreters, for he reinforced his text with two methodological footnotes:

Imperialism thus . . is an element that stems from the living conditions, not of the present, but of the past – or, put in terms of the economic interpretation of history, from past rather than present relations of production*

* Imperialism is one of many examples of the important fact, already alluded to in the beginning, that the application of the economic interpretation of history holds out no hope of reducing the cultural data of a given period to the relations of production of that same period . . . For example, the constitutional and political order of the Normans in southern Italy cannot be explained by the relations of production prevailing in that country. The very economy of the Normans in southern Italy becomes comprehensible only by reference to their capacity and wishes. But this does not actually refute the economic interpretation, for the mentality of the Normans was not something that existed outside the economic sphere. Its sources are found in the economic background from which the Normans came to southern Italy. (84–5)

And on another page, the footnote,

methodologically, it is interesting to note here that, though nationalism and militarism are not "reflexes" of the capitalist alignment of interests, neither did they emerge as what they are today during the periods in which they had their roots. Yet they do not necessarily escape the focus of the economic interpretation of history. They are the forms assumed in the environment of the modern world by habits of emotion and action that originally arose under primitive conditions. (127)

It might indeed be Marx himself identifying some crust of class, idea and institution surviving from earlier relations of production, now restraining and distorting the full potential of the new relations of production, but soon to be burst and sloughed off by the irresistible development of those new relations. That, precisely, was Schumpeter's view of the relation of imperialism to capitalism.

'The Sociology of Imperialisms' was nevertheless what its title indicated, more a sociological than an economic analysis. Why did such a famous, and very technical, economic theorist digress into sociology? In his preface to the 1951 translation, Paul Sweezy offered a reason:

Any theory of capitalism which leaves [the phenomena of imperialism and war] out of account is unquestionably incomplete. More, it is *prima facie* inadequate and even wrong. Now Schumpeter's theory of economic development not only does not explain imperialism and war; it leads to the expectation that the advance of capitalism will push them further and further into the background and eventually relegate them to the scrapheap of history. It is perfectly clear, then, that unless this contradiction between theory and reality is resolved, Schumpeter's whole system would be, to say the least, suspect. The essential point of the essay on imperialism is precisely to resolve this contradiction, and in this sense it forms a crucial part of his entire structure. (xiii)

This suggests for Schumpeter's explanation of imperialism the purpose attributed above to Turner's – the logical repair or completion of a theory about something else. For Schumpeter's second excursion into sociology, 'Social Classes in an Ethnically Homogeneous Environment' (1927), Sweezy suggested a similar function –

A complete theory of capitalism . . . would have to consist of three parts: the theory of origins, the theory of functioning and growth, and the theory of decline . . . Origins are important not only for their own sake but also because they explain much that does not belong to the pure logic of the system . . . At the risk of being somewhat overschematic, I would say that the essay on social classes is Schumpeter's central work on the theory of origins, while *Capitalism, Socialism and Democracy* [1942] occupies the same position with respect to the theory of decline. (xiii–xiv)

This line of speculation should perhaps be taken further than Sweezy took it. Schumpeter's system of thought about capitalism relied heavily, at every point, upon differentiating real life from a pure, free-trading capitalist model, an 'imagined alternative' (of which more later) to reality. Schumpeter, of course, wanted to insist upon the essential reality (and not at all on the 'imagination') of his model. Both the innocence of capitalism, and the value of the Schumpeterian system of studying it, depended on the plausibility of thus separating 'it' from the surrounding circumstances which were accused of never having given 'it' a fair go. Schumpeter's *Social Classes, Imperialism* and *Capitalism, Socialism and Democracy* are exactly alike in performing this essential service. *Social Classes* shows how entrenched aristocracies became capable of surviving to bedevil and distort the early growth of capitalism, while at the same time the effect of capitalism on the class structure must eventually transform it into a structure both efficient and just. *Imperialism* shows how the violence and aggression to be found in mature capitalist society were carried into it partly by the survival of pre-capitalist classes, and partly by the corruption of the capitalist classes themselves by their original subordination within feudal structures; and shows at the same time how capitalism itself, far from generating any of the violence and aggression, works for their gradual attrition. *Capitalism, Socialism and Democracy* shows how capitalism must decline, not from any technical or intrinsic fault of its own, but because its very energy and rationality will breed a generation bored and annoyed by it, a generation cured of any reverence for past or present and so well imbued with the habits and values of innovation that they will restlessly, perhaps irrationally, innovate some replacement for capitalism itself. Throughout this whole historic process, a sceptic may perhaps be forgiven for seeing Schumpeter's capitalist reality, that 'essence' of capitalism which is such a logical necessity of so much of his argument, as a sort of ghost at the party – never a thing observed, always a possibility imagined but unrealized, aborted by its uncomprehending parents, plaintively prayed for by Schumpeter (and of course by a distinguished company of other mourners, from Ricardo through Hobson to Hayek).

These complaints about Sweezy's modesty and Winslow's emphases should not be exaggerated; each, undoubtedly, had his point. In the first place both noticed a simpler aspect of Schumpeter's *Imperialism*, its expression of a scholarly Austrian visitor's dislike of the German regime of 1914–18. When Schumpeter describes how monopolist trusts and tariffs are forced upon an unwilling capitalism by the surviving power, ethos and class structure of eighteenth-century absolute monarchy, a historian may tremble with one emotion or another as he considers this explanation of the Hawley-Smoot tariff or the nineteenth-century origins of Canadian or Australian protection. But of William II's Germany, of the Empire whose tariff had been introduced by the old aristocrat Bismarck to reconcile Junker and industrialist, whose seven- and twenty-year armament markets for steel were written and rammed through the Reichstag by the courtiers of absolute monarchy, in which Ludendorf was commanding the economy while Schumpeter was writing the essay, it was perhaps less stupid. Bülow's own account of his and the Junkers' reasons for their imperial policies could not be more succinctly summed up than in Schumpeter's explanation of the imperialism of the late Roman republic –

The alternative to war was agrarian reform. The landed aristocracy could counter the perpetual threat of revolution only with the glory of victorious leadership . . . it was an aristocracy of landlords, large-scale agricultural entrepreneurs, born of struggle against their own people. It rested solely on control of the state machine. Its only safeguard lay in national glory. Its only possible course was preoccupation with the foreign-policy contingencies of the state . . .

. . . Such things never rise into full consciousness. An unstable social structure of this kind merely creates a general disposition to watch for pretexts for war – often held to be adequate with entire good faith – and to turn to questions of foreign policy whenever the discussion of social problems grew too troublesome for comfort. The ruling class was always inclined to declare that the country was in danger, when it was really only class interests that were threatened . . .

History offers no better example of imperialism rooted in the domestic political situation and derived from class structure. (68–9)

As Schumpeter watched the final disaster of Bülow's Germany it was not absurd of him to see those 'class interests' as the interests of a pre-capitalist class, 'rationally' formed in the Prussian conquests of eastern land, now made into a redundant and dangerous nuisance by the growth of capitalist society, but offering corrupting temptations to the new class of capitalists – an artificial market for weapons and textiles, a tariff, an effective labor discipline, the physical devastation of foreign competitors. Schumpeter did not mention this regime under which he was writing – perhaps he mentioned the Romans much as Lenin, expecting censorship, wrote 'Japanese' when he really meant Russians. But his situation up to 1918 may have done more for Schumpeter's thought than merely to give his *Imperialism* two separate purposes, a tract for the times as well as a contribution to his theory of capitalism. His whole, life-long effort to disentangle an innocent essence of capitalism from its guilty associations with monopoly, restriction, war and class may have owed a good deal to the fact that the capitalism which he actually observed, throughout what he always regarded as his one formative and creative decade, was a capitalism struggling for growth and freedom under an unhelpful Habsburg or a corrupting Hohenzollern absolutism, each complete with the military aristocracy which had won each its empire in pre-capitalist times.

In any case Winslow was right in one point – Schumpeter certainly meant to exonerate capitalism. To do so, he abstracted a narrow 'essence' of capitalism – a model with free trade, perfect competition and no frictions – and opposed to it a narrow definition of imperialism, excluding all aggression for 'rational' gain unless the gain was merely a pretext for the aggression: 'imperialism is the objectless disposition on the part of a state to unlimited forcible expansion'. By definition, an objectless imperialist could not have pursued any of the objects that Hobson or Lenin – or pure capitalism – had in mind. But Schumpeter required more of his explanation than that it merely disconnect capitalism from imperialism. He needed not a disconnection but a complex reconnection. For his purposes a satisfactory explanation had to include among its qualifications (besides truth) the power to show, first, that capitalism did not cause imperialism; second, that imperialism was rationally explicable by reference to other, non-capitalist causes; and third, as Sweezy suggested, that imperialism itself caused as many as possible of the undesirable phenomena which seemed to discredit capitalism.

It was in pursuit of this third aim that Schumpeter conceded so much to the neo-Marxist Hilferding. He repeated, as vividly as Lenin had just repeated it, Hilferding's picture of a protected growth of monopolist cartels and trusts making fortunes by price-maintenance at home and dumping abroad, directed by a new oligarchy of finance-capitalists.

Here capitalism has found a central organ that supplants its automatism by conscious decisions . . . the customs area of a trustified country generally pours a huge wave of capital into new countries. There it meets other, similar waves of capital, and a bitter, costly struggle begins but never ends.

[This did not have to arise from any inner necessities of capitalism itself.] Nevertheless, the situation . . . is really untenable both politically and economically. Economically, it unleashes storms of indignation among the exploited consumers at home and the threatened producers abroad. Thus the idea of military force readily suggests itself. Force may serve to break down foreign customs barriers and thus afford relief from the vicious circle of economic aggression. If that is not feasible, military conquest may at least secure control over markets in which heretofore one had to compete with the enemy. (107-9)

There follow two pages of description of the nightmare that follows – in Schumpeter's view, *had* already followed – this development. The imperial opportunities are exploited as fully and profitably by Schumpeter's finance-capitalists as by Hobson's, Hilferding's or Lenin's, and at least in a direct sense they do not represent any irrational instinct from the racial past: 'The conflicts that have been described [are] born of an export-dependent monopoly capitalism'. That sort of imperialism is made possible by tariffs. 'And it is true that this circumstance thoroughly alters the alignment of interests. It was neo-Marxist doctrine that first tellingly described this causal connection (Bauer) and fully recognized the significance of the "functional change in protection" (Hilferding).'

But there could have been no 'export-dependent monopoly capitalism', no imperialization of capitalism or capitalization of imperialism, without protective tariffs. Protective tariffs are no part of a pure, free-trading capitalism and were not generated by it. For Schumpeter this was an historical observation, to his critics it seems a childish trick of definition, but whatever it is, it is the device by which he reconciled his neo-Marxist view of what was happening in the world with his more famous, anti-Marxist but nevertheless economic, explanation of *why* it happened so.

Since we cannot derive even export monopolism from any tendencies of the competitive system toward big enterprise, we must find some other explanation. A glance at the original purpose of tariffs provides what we need. Tariffs sprang from the financial interests of the monarchy. (118)

For its own purposes the monarchy enlisted and corrupted the bourgeoisie and produced a hybrid economic system: monopoly-capitalism as described by Hilferding, and rightly blamed for imperialism.

Nationalism and militarism, while not creatures of capitalism, become "capitalized" and in the end draw their best energies from capitalism . . . And they, in turn, affect capitalism, cause it to deviate from the course it might have followed alone . . . (128)

'*The course it might have followed* . . .' Capitalism is exonerated for two reasons: first, because Schumpeter can imagine a different course 'it' might have taken (which we can rephrase, if we step outside his essentialist thought: Schumpeter can imagine history having taken a different course to produce a different kind of capitalism); and second, because he still expects its inner, dynamic logic to win in the end. Man cannot be rid of imperialism by deliberate political choice, but capitalism will rid him of it by its inner automatism. 'It' only acquired its corrupt imperial purposes, after all, when 'it' 'found a central organ that supplants its automatism by conscious decisions'. To restore its health, remove its brain.

The objections to this theory are partly matters of fact and concept, and partly belong to the problem of historical norms or 'alternatives' to history. Neither is the concern of this chapter; a good, brisk, representative attack by Murray Greene can be found in *Social Research*, XIX, (December, 1952), reprinted in H. M. Wright (ed.) *The "New Imperialism"* (1961). Enough has been said here of the apparent purposes and obvious by-products of this explanation. We can conclude by briefly comparing its form and practical message with Hobson's.

That most critics have depicted these two as opposites, the one a wholly economic and the other a non-economic explanation, can perhaps be attributed to the critics' indifferent stamina as readers – the two authors approached their subject-matter from opposite ends. Hobson wrote his first hundred and twelve pages about economics, then two hundred and fifty-six about the politics and sociology of imperialism, including extensive theories of parasitism and of both psychological and institutional atavism. Schumpeter opened with (in the English edition) eighty-two pages of politics and sociology, then closed with forty-six of economics including an extensive theory of monopoly-capitalist imperialism. Apart from obvious differences in length and elaboration, choice of examples, and merely detailed variations in theory, their disagreements are only two. One is a conceptual difference about what shall be called 'capitalism'. The other is a real difference of opinion about the capitalist process, a difference which led Hobson to require some political adjustment of the system, Schumpeter to expect it to adjust itself unaided. The systems they wanted to see in operation in the end were, in all but one essential, identical.

Where Schumpeter insisted upon opposing 'pure' capitalism to its imperialist accretions of tariff, etc., as different things under different names, Hobson was content to bundle them all together as one corrupt form of capitalism; but what Schumpeter excluded by definition from his concept of capitalism was roughly the range of phenomena which Hobson wanted to exclude from capitalism by deliberate legislation. They both saw the same 'capitalized imperialism' or 'imperialized capitalism' at work, the same profit motives of the same powerful groups making for expansion and war, and they agreed that the whole business was less profitable than peaceful free trade would have been.

Their real difference concerned saving and investment. Hobson saw a tendency to over-saving which needed to be corrected by political intervention. He also accepted as motives arising naturally enough from any profit system the special interests which put the state to work – against the majority interest – for their private imperialist purposes. They too should be dealt with politically, though only by omission – a well-educated democracy would refuse tariffs, refuse armament expenditure, refuse to annex colonies. Schumpeter on the other hand saw in a free-trading capitalism no possibility of over-saving, and various automatic checks which would limit the optimum size of firms well short of monopoly. Indeed he was particularly anxious not to interfere with savings. Short-run redistribution for social purposes would restrict the capital available to the innovating entrepreneurs on whose function two things depended: long-run economic growth, and the principal originality of Schumpeter's professional contribution to economic science. He therefore agreed with all the political abstentions recommended by Hobson, but would add one more: abstention from Hobson's political redistribution of income.

That one difference of policy was connected by rigorous logic to the one important difference between their explanations of imperialism. Within the complex of capitalist-monopolist-imperialist behavior, both saw profit motives as the present-and-active engines of modern imperialism. Except for the conceptual difference of which so much has been made they thus agreed that a corrupt *historical* capitalism had indeed caused imperialism. They disagreed as to whether an (unhistorical) 'pure' capitalism would have caused it, and consequently they disagreed as to whether it should be pure capitalism, or a capitalism adjusted by deliberate tax and welfare policies, which should now be allowed to go ahead and dissolve imperialism. They differed, that is to say, about the conditions necessary for over-saving and under-consumption, about the conditions and importance of the innovators' contribution to growth, and about the long-run prudence of short-run social justice; but not, as far as I can see, about anything else of importance. Each wrote the explanation of imperialism whose implications, if acted upon, would establish the particular variant of classical free capitalism which each respectively thought workable.

8. *Jacob Viner and E. M. Winslow*

How can capitalism recover its respectability? Even its best friends, Hobson and Schumpeter, want to strip it of its characteristic forms of organization.

Perhaps there are not in fact any connections between capitalism and imperialism; or if there are, perhaps other conditions for imperialism can be manipulated instead. Even if they included the latter purpose, the effective attacks on Hobson and Lenin have generally begun with some historical hard labor. Cairncross corrected Hobson's statistics, Feis showed that Germany could scarcely spare any capital for export, Langer inspected the detail of diplomacy for signs of financial control, Viner examined international lending to find abundant signs of political control, Hancock compared British operations in areas as different as Ireland, West Africa and Palestine, Gallagher and Robinson and MacDonagh investigated the paradox of annexations by free-traders – all searched for the facts which ought to be there if the theorists' causal connections were there.[13] But for these arduous exercises another school had meanwhile found two more comfortable alternatives. It was easy to make a different selection from the conditions necessary for imperialism; and it was easy to reclassify knowledge – often the same old knowledge used by the economic interpreters.

Almost any student of modern imperialism would, if pressed, acknowledge an indefinite list of necessary conditions which had to be present if imperialism was to occur at all; but most of which for one reason or another, he saw no need to mention in composing his own explanation. The facts of geography; the technical resources of transportation, communications, weapons; the technical capacity to govern conquered territories; the facts that human beings have legs and arms, can walk and fight. Even Schumpeter, with a consuming interest in technical innovation, forgot to mention steam or steel or telegraphs or rifling or explosive projectiles when he explained and dated modern imperialism – but he would scarcely have denied their necessity to the effects he was explaining.

Many necessary conditions are thus left 'asleep' in all explanations. They sometimes offer rewards to the investigator who notices them and wakes them up. A really obsessive investigator will sometimes wake up a sleeping condition, or find some forgotten link in a causal chain, and declare it to be not merely necessary but *by itself* a *sufficient* cause, thinking to distinguish himself by his originality and at the same time kill off his competitors by his implications.

If we would explain why nations expand and make war, then a sleepy but necessary condition is that they should exist in the first place. Our very concept of 'war' requires them. For fighting organized in other ways we have other words like riot or revolution. By definition there can't be war without nations; by observation there have seldom been nations without, at some time or other, war; it is a short, glorious step to the conclusion that the existence of nations is the only and sufficient cause of war. As the present method of inquiry would lead any cynic to expect, 'the existence of nations is the only cause of war' usually means that it is the only cause with which that investigator personally wants to interfere.

This particular sleepy condition was woken up and brushed up by Jacob Viner in 'Peace as an Economic Problem' (1944).[14] But that short paper is no subject for cynicism. Its immediate purpose was indeed, like Schumpeter's, to defend free-trading capitalism as a force for peace; but far from narrowing the conditions for war to one, it insisted on their infinite variety. In its imposition of some order upon that variety, it is the most intelligent short general essay on the causes of war that I have read, showing an unbeatable sophistication both about the substance of history and about the fruitful methods of studying it. Viner thought that war might arise, and had at times arisen, from combinations of almost any of the human propensities: from the pursuit of land, money, women, unity at home, excitement abroad, racial purity, religious uniformity, strategic or cultural empire, sentiment of every kind. Nor was there one war for each cause, or one cause for each war, or the same causes throughout the same war. 'Major wars are never voluntarily entered upon for a single reason, or for petty reasons, and never have single and simple objectives. Whatever the predominant factors may have been in bringing a nation into a particular war, its members during its course will acquire a diverse set of moral, political, sentimental, religious, or economic reasons for wanting, or not wanting, to go on with it to a victorious conclusion; and these may well be different from those which led originally to its entrance into the war.' From this miscellany Viner did single out politics, not as a privileged cause, but for a special causal function: whatever other factors might make for war, they could only do it by procuring political action.

In my view, therefore, war is essentially a political phenomenon, a way of dealing with disputes between groups. Every kind of human interest which looks to the state for its satisfaction and which involves real or supposed conflict with the interests of other peoples or states is thus a possible source of contribution to war. Every kind of interest which can conceivably be served by successful war will be in the minds of statesmen or will be brought to their attention. Given the existence of nation-states, the factors which can contribute to war can be as varied as the activities, the hopes and fears, the passions and generosities and jealousies, of mankind, in so far as they are susceptible of being shared by groups and of being given mass expression. (248)

In that passage can be discerned, I hope without impertinence, the three main purposes of Viner's paper: the first and third overt and familiar, the second original but smuggled.

First, it insists on the multiplicity of factors which may make for war. If so many, then any economic factors need have no unique importance, and much of the paper argues that some of the capitalist influences actually make for peace.

Second, the implications of the phrase 'which looks to the state for its satisfaction' add a point to the case not merely for international free trade but also for internal *laisser-faire*. It was a point which Gladstone made in the Don Pacifico debate, but he made it about citizens abroad; Viner generalizes it to the citizens at home as well. The bigger government becomes, the more of its citizens' wants it accepts responsibility for satisfying, then the wider is the range of the citizens' wants which the government will feel compelled to represent, the more numerous the resentments and complaints and jealousies which it must therefore make its own. The cupidity or fear or bellicosity that were harmless in the heart of the impotent individual may become deadly in the brief of the government which represents him, and carries a gun.

Third, Viner wishes to argue that political manipulation may prove, not a sure cure, but still perhaps the most fruitful practical approach to the prevention or reduction of war. It is for this manipulative purpose that he points to politics, not as the sufficient or only source of war, but as a necessary last link in the chain by which *any* factor leads to war. Viner, a wry, perceptive and not-entirely-resigned conservative, thus employs both the very long and the very short causal chains which are typical of conservative explanations. On the one hand he regards war as 'natural' – 'in the same sense in which crime is natural'. There are chains from human nature, through almost any of its forms of social organization, to war. But not all their links have the same strength, and they all converge upon the same last link, the proximate political one, which may prove to be the most malleable –

I should explain that I do not believe that the form of political organization which leads to war is permanently bound up with the nature of human nature or that transformation of this form to some form or forms at least much less conducive to war is beyond the capacity of man to achieve if he can be brought to will it strongly enough. (247)

This argument, precise in the hands of its author, could become a most explosive blunderbuss for others who supposed it could be used to shoot down all other explanations of imperialism and war.

It is unjust to single out a few follies from the long article and the book,[15] *The Pattern of Imperialism*, which E. M. Winslow contributed to this controversy. Most of their pages were given to a much more extensive and scholarly review of the controversy than has been offered here. But here, it is Winslow's own explanation of imperialism that is interesting. He agreed with Hobson that capitalism could be made to work for peace; he agreed with Viner that the liberation of capitalism and the prevention of war were political tasks; he agreed with Schumpeter that imperialism is an atavism and also (apparently) that definitions can be extraordinarily serviceable. But whatever Viner's propagandist purposes and Schumpeter's definitions, both did keep an eye on the real life they wrote about and neither forgot the customary rules of discourse. What happens when an enthusiast mixes Hobson's program for the reform of capitalism, Viner's view of politics and Schumpeter's definitions with a fourth ingredient: the conviction that from page to page he can jump in and out of the Aristotelian categories of knowledge, at will?

Winslow dreamed (but not absurdly: not with much hope) of ridding the world of war by Gandhi's methods of organized non-violence. The last pages of *The Pattern of Imperialism* accordingly explain war as caused by the propensity to resort to force. But another explanation of imperialism occupies more of the book:

. . . imperialism and war are to be explained as general phenomena in terms of themselves, as kindred self-generating institutions and indeed as atavisms. (226)

Here is the marriage of Viner's 'essentially political phenomenon' with Schumpeter's atavism, to make the explanation which singles one link out of its chain, one condition out of its set, and declares that one alone to be sufficient:

That the organization of peoples into regionally segregated political groups is the most potent cause of modern war is the one proposition which today claims the support of those who are unable to accept the Marxian theory that war is a product of capitalism. (237)

This implies a proposition about society, even if it has the form of a statement about scholars. Scholars cannot accept the Marxian explanation. Why not? Many passages of Winslow's book explain why not, and include some exposition of Schumpeter's and Viner's reasons why not. These latter were evidently imperfect, perhaps because the mere existence of economic systems (which neither denied) might always tempt somebody or other to blame wars on them. But whatever shortcomings he may have sensed in others' demolitions of Marx and Hobson, Winslow moved to repair them by the simple method of definition.

He first distinguished from imperialism any expansion which was unresisted, or economic in aim, or democratic in management, or naval in method.

On the whole and in the detail-obliterating perspective of history, we have come to regard all this colonial activity and conflict as colonialism rather than as imperialism. (4)

Thus the Athenian, English and American empires were acquitted of imperialism without the arduous business of inspecting them. But might not the Portuguese and Spanish empires claim the same indulgence? No, because they were militarist. 'We shall use the terms "imperialism" and "militarism" repeatedly, and it may as well be said first as last that they are coeval terms, representing the same general pattern of thought and behavior in the ordering of human relationships. . . It is not a synonym for colonialism . . .' (3) 'First as last' proves right enough – all definitions in Chapter One reappear as conclusions in Chapter Nine. But most of them have meanwhile been contradicted first by a neo-Hobsonian argument about capitalism, and then by Winslow's own Ethical Explanation of imperialism.

Winslow agreed with Schumpeter that monopoly and tariff were imperialist phenomena which had been foisted upon capitalism by pre-capitalist influences. But he agreed with Hobson that to purify capitalism would require art as well as nature: not the non-interference that Schumpeter wanted, nor the interference with incomes that Hobson wanted, but in Winslow's view, anti-trust laws and the strict control of credit and investment were required. This was not merely (as Hobson's was) a proposal for reform. It also served, like Schumpeter's 'essential' model, to prove that capitalism had never caused imperialism at any time. Any malpractices of capitalism were extrinsic, atavistic inflictions upon it from outside itself – from the 'dim past' which in Winslow's version transmitted forces more brutish and primordial, more from the depths than from the past of human nature, than Schumpeter's once-useful habits which merely outlived their utility.

The implications of this argument, however odd, are inescapable. When in Winslow's words imperialism 'captures and uses capitalism . . . to further ends which are not themselves economic', it does so by means both negative and positive. Besides introducing tariffs and controlling trade for political ends, politicians also refuse to control credit and refuse to bust trusts. The 'capture' of capitalism turns out thus to be accomplished partly by omission. 'The failure of organized society, through the agency of government, to provide and enforce rules of the game for free enterprise in business . . . and the failure of society to devise a positive system of control consistent with free enterprise, places a major share of the blame for the breakdown of capitalism on what, for lack of a better name, we call politics.' Failure to interfere is thus an atavistic weapon of interference with a system which without such interference (i.e., failure to interfere) could be imagined in pursuit of peaceful ends; therefore the existing system, victim of a brutish noninterference, cannot have been the cause of its own warlike acts. Among other things, this seems to require that tariffs were forced on capitalists who did not want them, but who did want credit control, which was forcibly withheld from them. Not even Winslow had this impression of historical capitalist behavior. His argument could really be rescued only by some further definition: insofar as he wants free trade and controlled banking a capitalist is a capitalist, but insofar as he wants controlled trade and free banking he is not a capitalist at all but an imperialist. His ideas of free trade and controlled banking spring from the internal logic of the capitalist system within which he works, but his ideas of controlled trade and free banking spring atavistically from the warriors from whom he is descended.

This last, I confess, was not Winslow's resort. He resorted instead to another kind of definition: not of the words that describe the world, but of the words that classify our descriptions of it. It would be unfair to set out the Ethical Explanation in any but his own words:

Reduced to its simplest terms, the economic interpretation of conflict visualizes a person, or a nation, desiring some object, such as territory, goods or raw materials. It thus assumes to have set up at one stroke the economic motive and the economic end. . . . Yet if economics is to be regarded as a science . . . the economic motive can never be associated with concrete ends . . . It is basic to any science that the data with which it deals shall remain fixed, or constant. Without such data, analysis and prediction are impossible. The desire for concrete things . . . does not fulfil the scientific requirement, because of the instability of such data . . . Whether anything is desired and the degree of desire are matters of choice between alternatives, which depends upon the exercise of value judgments. Such rejecting and choosing belong to the field of ethics, not economics . . . The economic motive, therefore, emerges with the fact of scarcity and the need to economize, not with the ethical problem of choosing between alternatives . . . An economic motive, therefore, is not directed towards some specific end, and there are no ultimate ends which can be called economic. (217–9)

This argument is summed up in an example:

The desire of a nation to obtain such concrete things as oil fields or iron mines cannot be regarded as an economic motive, and war to obtain such specific objects cannot be regarded as based on economic causes . . . the desire of another nation to possess these resources and the act of going to war to obtain them constitute neither an economic motive nor an act of economic warfare; the desire has the nature of an ethical valuation, and the act the nature of plain theft. No economic content is observable in the whole affair. (221).

There are interesting conclusions to be drawn from this. First it would appear to be open to other disciplines to play the same game as Economics. If Criminology achieves scientific status, we will be able to say 'The criminal method, therefore, emerges with the fact of scarcity and the need to steal, not with the ethical problem of choosing which bank to burgle . . . the action of a burglar in obtaining such specific objects as gold bars cannot be regarded as a criminal act for criminal motives; the desire has the nature of an ethical valuation and the act the nature of plain transportation . . .' But whatever shall we do when Ethics sets up as a science? A second interesting conclusion is that imperialist wars are fought for things like oil-fields, although the book's initial definitions were agreed that 'in the detail-obliterating perspective of history' such rational adventures were not to be called imperialism.

Neither of these conclusions was Winslow's; he seems to have intended this passage about science and words to be applied, with a slight adjustment, to life. The pursuit of particular objects was not 'economic'; thus wars could not have economic causes; thus the pursuit of property (which is economic on all the other pages of the book) could not be a significant cause of war. Those who wished to reduce or avoid war should not, therefore, waste time tampering with the economic system. Poor Aristotle.

9. D. K. Fieldhouse and William L. Langer – objective science at last

Three separate contributions to this controversy are summarized in D. K. Fieldhouse's ' 'Imperialism': An Historiographical Revision'.[16] First the connections between finance-capitalism and a new imperialism, alleged by Hobson and Lenin, have been attacked by the direct historical investigation of the connections themselves. Second, Hobson is said to have misunderstood the pre-history of his period. He thought that the old mercantilist imperialism had ceased early in the nineteenth century and therefore asked 'what are the new reasons for this new imperialism late in the century?' Fieldhouse reviews the work of Gallagher and Robinson which points to a continuing British commercial imperialism throughout the century, and this part of his article may be seen as explaining the reasons which led Hobson to ask wrong questions. But third, he cannot accept that Hobson was entirely wrong, that there was no new thing at all to explain. 'In sum, the most obvious facts of the new phase of imperialism cannot be explained as the logical continuation of the recent past, nor in Hobson's terms of a new economic factor. What, then, was the explanation?' Fieldhouse is imprudent enough to continue 'An answer is not, of course, hard to find' and thus to introduce, with acknowledgments to 'the vast literature now available', his own explanation.

If his substantial explanation of imperialism is disentangled from his many returns to the explanation of Hobson's mistakes, Fieldhouse appears to nominate the following as the present and active causes of imperial activity at the turn of the century. The first two are paraphrased, the third and fourth quoted from his text:

What caused Imperialism?

1. A continuing old-style economic imperialism, chiefly commercial, getting changing kinds of political support as demanded by changing circumstances.

2. Contiguous and defensive annexations, undertaken to secure existing possessions.

These two have a continuous history through several centuries. Though both still at work, they explain only that part of imperial activity which is also continuous. The novelties – the entry of new imperial powers and the leaps of old ones into new, non-commercial, non-contiguous territories – result from two new conditions:

3. The significant fact about the years after 1870 was that Europe became once more an armed camp . . . [its] imperialism may best be seen as the extension into the periphery of the political struggle in Europe.

Such economic motives as the politicians had were merely the instrumental motives of a new mercantilism, directed to increasing national wealth and self-sufficiency for purposes of power and war. 'Yet, if the first, and territorially decisive, factor in the imperialism of the post 1870 period was this unemotional, almost cynical, policy of the statesmen, it cannot be said that it was the only new feature, nor in the long run, the most important one.' That most important one was

4. . . . millions of people for whom an empire had become a matter of faith . . . the politicians, pressed on now by a public demand they could not control, even if they had wanted to, continued, with increasing bellicosity, to scrape the bottom of the barrel for yet more colonial burdens for the white man to carry . . . In the new quasi-democratic Europe, the popularity of the imperial idea marked a rejection of the sane morality of the account-book, and the adoption of a creed based on such irrational concepts as racial superiority and the prestige of the nation.

Putting the last two together, therefore,

In its mature form [imperialism] can best be described as a sociological phenomenon with roots in political facts: and it can properly be understood only in terms of the same social hysteria that has since given birth to other and more disastrous forms of aggressive nationalism.

How would this explanation be plotted on one of those converging-chain patterns sketched in the previous chapter? If Fieldhouse's thing-to-be-explained is accepted, and his 'old' causes of the continuing element of 'old' imperialism omitted, then for what is new in the new imperialism his explanation offers one short causal chain, and an unconnected link of one other.

The short chain has at least the virtue that it connects its cause all the way to its effect – this is the chain from the armed camp to its effect of territorial competition overseas. The further lengths of the chain – whatever the causes were that turned Europe into an armed camp – are not mentioned. Lenin's, Hobson's, or any other capitalist causes? Developments of population or technology or ideas? Social hysteria? Monarchic atavism? Never mind.

The second condition is one link in a chain whose origins are social: 'the politicians pressed on now by a public demand they could not control. . .' This popular imperialist hysteria is given almost no causes, and almost no connection with its alleged imperial effects. At least two explanations of the popular enthusiasm were offered in books referred to by Fieldhouse: its manufacture by imperial profiteers who influenced newspapers and financed patriotic associations (Townshend, Hobson) and its development to ameliorate the social strains engendered by industrial and slum life (Strachey, Hobson). Fieldhouse does not argue to disconnect these suggested causes, he just leaves them out. He also leaves out any real link between the popular enthusiasm and the imperial effect. 'Pressed on' in the passage quoted above has no footnote and is related to no evidence-based connection of popular enthusiasm to diplomatic or political acts – there is instead a leaping inference of a kind that Fieldhouse is quick to condemn in others' explanations.*

* It might be argued that the popular jingoism of those times is so well known and its political effect so obvious as to need no tedious 'evidence-based connection'. The unfought victory of this notion never ceases to surprise me. Whenever the connection is alleged it tends to have the same few, scattered and English foundations, borrowed and exaggerated from the chapter on English policy in William L. Langer's *The Diplomacy of Imperialism*. It often uses Mafeking nights – enthusiasm for winning wars once engaged in them – as evidence for a passionate desire to start them. Certainly there were times in the 'eighties and 'nineties when politicians felt 'pressed' to annex, or not to relinquish, colonies. There was bellicose feeling on both sides during the Fashoda crisis, though when they lost, the French diplomatists did not find that public opinion hindered their

patient work for an English agreement. From the date on which the English finally entered that negotiation, Joseph Chamberlain forgot the natural supremacy of the Teutonic races and discovered instead the natural and peaceful affinities of the liberal democracies – no frenzied public even noticed the change. Meanwhile the 'sane morality of the account book', having inspired the Belgian king to rape the Congo, was preparing in England to dismiss the imperialists, their imperial tariff schemes, and their imperial 'methods of barbarism', in a landslide election. On balance there is more politicians' testimony about the *difficulty* of getting support for imperial policies, as Chamberlain, Bülow, Roosevelt, Witte and the French imperialists constantly complained. Quite apart from its ill-proven connection with policy, the evidence is even sketchier for the existence of any general or *predominant* popular imperialism. You could sell news of war, as Northcliffe is invariably quoted as testifying, and you could sell jingoist entertainments in the music halls. Less of the latter in other countries than England. But modern pacifist newsreaders are just as interested in news of war, just as Victorian readers were interested in its serious competitors for headlines: bestiality, cruelty to children, treason, arson, murder, and other things which people always desire to read about but seldom desire should happen. Everywhere, at all times, in newspapers addressed to every social class, war has displaced other headlines and sold more copies; this cannot be evidence of the bellicosity of particular populations at particular times. There was in any case more English newspaper opposition to the Boer war than to any other British war of the last century and a half. Of course, strong currents of imperial feeling did exist. Most evidence suggests that they were strongest in the richest and oldest-established classes. There is little real evidence about the feelings of the masses in England, and less elsewhere. If the masses nevertheless had such frenzied feelings, it is strange that they could bring them to bear so effectively upon national leaders without *their own* political leaders and organizations hearing of it. If Fieldhouse's case is ever to be established it must really cope with some of the contrary evidence, including for example: (1) the anti-imperial policies and electoral support of the German Social Democratic Party from its foundation to 1913; (2) the policies and membership and electoral support of all other significant working-class parties in all European states before 1913; (3) the non-jingoist policies, numerical strength and social composition of all significant European trade unions before 1913; (4) the more usual, rather than the occasional, behavior of such middle-class or non-class parties as the German Centre and Ultra-Liberals, the British Liberals and Labour Party, and the various Dreyfusard forces; (5) the history of French majorities from the Dreyfusard triumph to 1913; (6) the defeat of the imperialist party in the British elections of 1892, 1905, 1910–11; (7) Italian politics from Crispi's fall to 1910; (8) the Habsburg rather than popular origins of most Habsburg aggressions during this period; (9) the unpopularity, and the deliberate anti-popular intent, of most Russian imperialist adventures during the period. Perhaps Fieldhouse used the phrase 'quasi-democracy' to suggest that the irrational social hysteria was found only in the upper, voting classes of the countries that still had limited franchises – but the franchise was universal enough in England, France and Germany, so I am driven back to the conclusion that his hysterical majorities must have included all those Liberal and Labour voters against tariffs and 'the methods of barbarism', those German Social-Democrats and Centrists, those followers of Gompers and William Jennings Bryan, those French anti-militarists and anti-clericals, those notorious imperialists the Russian proletariat and peasantry, those Dutch and Belgian burghers red in tooth and claw . . .

So we have one short chain and an isolated link of one other – and that is all, of all the conditions which had obviously to be present for Fieldhouse's 'effect' to occur at all. But it might be argued that he did not set out to nominate *all* the necessary conditions. His purpose was to explain a change, a change carefully delimited as being less than Hobson had supposed it to be. For that purpose he needed to nominate only the new intervening variables which so altered the balance of the whole set of conditions as to produce this particular, limited change in their combined effect; the remainder of the set, the vast number of continuing, unchanging, 'sleeping' conditions, could justifiably be left asleep. Quite so; but there still remain a lot more candidates for nomination than Fieldhouse chose to include – the very large number of novelties which *were* new in that century of European history, and which might plausibly be thought to be conditions necessary for the occurrence of the new imperial events. Fieldhouse offered good historical reasons for disconnecting one such candidate: capital export. But he offered no reasons of any kind for disconnecting others – for example, the growth and movement of populations; scientific advances and a related history of ideas about society and religious belief; the appearance of new aims and techniques in the government of existing colonies, especially in India; the extension of the capacities and functions of government in Europe itself; the whole imperial technology of steam and steel, railroad and telegraph, including its dramatic effect upon the military economy of rich against poor soldiers; changes in the domestic economies, social structures, educational arrangements, literacy and other skills, and political systems of the metropolitan societies. Fieldhouse did not move to disconnect these. He could not claim to have merely 'let them sleep' since they were not present at all with the 'old' imperialism. He just left them out.

I do not mean to suggest that he should have put them all in. Nobody – least of all, in six journal pages – could possibly put them all in. I mean only to reiterate that old and ill-remembered cliché, that almost every human event is conditioned by almost all of human history, so that any explanation has to be selective, and according to its particular purpose, *ought* to have its selection rationally organized by that purpose. Fieldhouse's first purpose was corrective, and he summed up admirably an effective attack upon some of the 'connections' alleged by others.

But to suggest that Hobson and Lenin were mistaken in thinking that the need to export capital from Europe after 1870 was so intense that it made the colonization of most of Africa and the Pacific necessary as fields of investment is merely to throw the question open again. The essential problem remains: on what other grounds is it possible to explain this sudden expansion of European possessions, whose motive force is called imperialism?

Disconnecting capital export has left a gap. What is needed is consequently a gap-filling explanation, with perhaps some irrational but understandable psychological expectation that the new piece shall be roughly of a size and shape to plug the particular gap left by the extraction of the old. This would make sense if the whole of Hobson's or Lenin's surrounding pattern of explanation remained acceptable, and it was only a particular mistake about capital export that needed replacing. But that cannot have been Fieldhouse's view: indeed, his paper implies that it was not merely the technical causal function of capital export which had to be replaced, but also as far as possible the whole manipulative implication of Hobson's and Lenin's contributions. Fieldhouse's own explanation leaves the economic system innocent, and directs the manipulator to the state system, the arms race, and an ideology vaguely ascribed (if to anything) to 'nationalism' and to the new 'quasi-democracy'. I doubt if that was his conscious intention either, for if it were, a great many other connections and disconnections needed to be established. It is much more likely that he was a disinterested scholar engaged in a disinterested search for truth – one whose values, prejudices or manipulative interests as a private person were as far as possible excluded, as a matter of professional integrity, from intruding any bias into his professional work. That undoubted detachment and integrity are indeed the only reasons for including Fieldhouse's explanation among these examples. Chamberlain and Bülow, Hobson and Lenin, Schumpeter and Viner had shameless purposes, to justify or alter policies. These purposes certainly led some of them into error. They asserted facts carelessly or dishonestly. They asserted wishfully, instead of carefully investigating, the interrelations of facts. Or they ignored 'their own' facts' connections with others, and thus undermined the usefulness of their work to their own purposes, seeing possibilities of managed or natural improvements which in reality were limited by those other facts and connections which the blinkered investigators neglected. It was nevertheless those same purposes which gave their explanations their only organization and principles of selection; which showed each investigator what to study and where to stop; which gave each explanation whatever it had of order, coherence and usefulness.

When a disinterested scholar substitutes his professional integrity, his detached objectivity, for the political values of Hobson, what then organizes *his* explanation?

Answer: Hobson still does, through the responses of correction and gap-filling; or some *unconsidered* patchwork of contemporary purpose and convention does; or nothing does. Fieldhouse's explanation relies on a little of each. As organizers of a substantial explanation of his own all three are worthless.

But this is unfair – not to Fieldhouse perhaps, but surely to the ambition of scientific neutrality? The effects of that aspiration should be studied in the work of a more formidable exponent.

William Langer may not want a value-free science but he is the most reliable avoider of wishful thought, or any other substitute for the hard work of discovery. Of thirty years of European diplomacy, as far as one man could, he read everything in all languages, knew everything in all archives. So when he selected, it was deliberate. If he simplified, it was not from ignorance of the facts' complexity. In the third chapter of *The Diplomacy of Imperialism 1890–1902*[17] he wrote a short general explanation of the springs of the British imperialism of those years.

As Hobson and Schumpeter had, Langer gave about half his pages each to the economics and to the sociology of imperialism; but was readier to hesitate, to doubt one-way causes, to write of reciprocations. 'Perhaps the most remarkable feature of late Victorian imperialism was its popularity with the lower classes'. For many, the 'feature' has become a cause; for Langer, this requires argument:

It is always difficult to determine what is cause and what is effect in a case like this, but it does appear . . . that the public was more excited than the government. There is surely some room for argument that popular pressure was more important in the growth of imperialism than was the action of the ruling classes. (80)

That 'room for argument' perhaps expresses the caution of a diplomatic historian accustomed to more detailed certainties; perhaps

Langer emphasized popularity as a somewhat neglected, somewhat original argument. He emphasized it again in the book's concluding reflections, but left it out of the preface:

With two groups of powers fairly matched [after 1894] the old European issues were reduced to a deadlock. This fact, together with the growing economic pressure and the increasing competition for markets, stimulated and facilitated that outburst of overseas expansion which we call *imperialism*. (vii)

Here and elsewhere commerce, or mistaken thought about commerce, gets more emphasis than popular pressure. They get equal emphasis in Langer's own admirably balanced summary of his third chapter:

There we may leave the discussion of British imperialism in the late-Victorian period. It is hard to theorize about it and of the many explanations that have been offered no single one is entirely satisfactory. At bottom the movement was probably as much economic as anything else. It resulted from the tremendously enhanced productive powers of European industry and the breakdown of the monopolistic position of England through the appearance of competitors. The feeling that new markets must be secured was very widespread and the need for new fields of investment, though not much discussed at the time, was probably even more important. These needs, however, had been met in the past without any corresponding expansion of territory. It was the embarkation of France, Germany, and other countries on the course of empire that brought the British to the conviction that only political control could adequately safeguard markets.

But this economic side, whatever its importance, must not be allowed to obscure the other factors. Psychologically speaking, I imagine, the prevalence of evolutionary teaching was perhaps crucial. It not only justified competition and struggle but introduced an element of ruthlessness and immorality that was most characteristic of the whole movement. The rise of a popular electorate, quite without culture and only semiliterate, underlined the crudity of the expansionist movement. It called forth a cheap newspaper press and a raw literature of action. In the larger sense, I suppose, it is perfectly true that the industrial system, which was tending more and more toward the mechanization of humanity, made inevitable the yearning for escape and action. Just as, at this very time, people were beginning to seek an outlet for physical urges, even if only vicariously by attendance at huge sporting events, so they tried to find some expression for the combative instincts of the race through the encouragement of aggressive action and adventure abroad. At the same time the religious strain was too strong in the English to be left out of account entirely. The profound conviction of their superiority as a governing race, of their divine mission to improve the world, was not only a rationalization of other motives, it was in itself a primary moving force. (95–6)

This is Hobson's array of information, without all Hobson's inter-relation of it. Langer sees converging upon the imperial effect the same causes as Hobson saw, Langer sometimes softening, sometimes denying, the directive hierarchy into which these causes were ar-ranged by Hobson, who in any case was not quite the single-causer he has been made out to be. Like Marx, Hobson allowed plenty of independent life to ideas and to 'soft' social forces; more than Marx, he allowed independent origins as well as independent life to many of them. But he did see inequality, his 'taproot of imperialism', and the conspirators who throve on it, as stimulating and coordinating the other imperialist tendencies of high and lowly thought, of industrial and urban tedium, of evangelists and younger sons. Langer sees these as separate, independent causes of imperial effects; and although he does not pry very far into their origins, he allows that many of them may well have arisen from causes in the recent in-dustrial experience of English society. Generally, he takes Hobson's pattern of facts, but shakes it hard to loosen many of its connections and certainties. He does not deploy much criticism of Hobson's connections, of the detailed kind published later and summed up by Fieldhouse. But on the other hand he never forgets the connections, which Hobson observed and Fieldhouse forgot, between imperialism and the traditional, technological, military, religious, intellectual and social patterns of English life.

The loosening of Hobson's connections is justified by considera-tions of truth. It becomes less helpful as this argument proceeds, to discuss the selection of causes without reference to their truth; but Langer's selection is still much the same as Hobson's. It is fair to set the loosening to the credit of Langer's more detached mind, free of Hobson's intent political purposes, free of his wishful imagination of villainous influences and viable alternatives; but fair also to add, that detachment gave Langer no apparent advantage as a *selector*, and no reason for serious dissent from Hobson's selections. His chains of cause and consequence, though more fragile, run about as far and deep in the same directions as Hobson's, stopping short only of the inequality of incomes.

The best features of Langer's explanations are perhaps his incomparably good fact-finding, and his unfailing awareness of the complexity of social action. He does not assert that causal chains 'end' wherever it suits him to drop them. He sees reciprocal relations, free choices and genuine uncertainties. He doubts most causal dictatorships and hierarchies. Like Viner he sees, but remains unterrified by, the need to select. Except insofar as Hobson's errors were self-fulfilling, Hobson would have done better by his own good causes if he had possessed more of Langer's caution and patience, more sense of the simultaneous and equal necessity of many of the conditions for imperialism, a greater awareness that he *chose* his explanation from the seamless networks of relationships (some repetitive, some unique) objectively present in history, a greater sense of deliberation between open alternatives in his choice of a cure. After all, the revulsion of feeling against imperialism came sooner and from other causes than Hobson proposed: greater pecuniary equality may have had a little to do with it but there are many more immediate and plausible candidates, including the effect of Hobson's book (and others) on the distribution of thoughts and valuations and votes, rather than of incomes. Much purposeful, radical explanation would do its work better if illuminated by Viner's principles and Langer's industry.

But Viner's principle, it should be remembered, was to see a choice of explanations as a choice of strategy, to explain war politically because there seemed a best chance of preventing it politically – a judgment which needs to be supported by exploring the operation of other causes of war and the chances of preventing war by other means, in case other means should be more practicable (as Viner denied) or more desirable (as Hobson believed). This is to ask the radical to make a better-informed, a more deliberate choice from the widest range of valuable alternatives that he can make himself aware of. He should follow the ramifying effects of action in all possible directions, with all possible completeness, if he would apply any morality of consequences or 'morality of systems'. This is not a matter of moralizing, passing 'clergymen's judgments'; more a matter of putting value-systems themselves to tests of consistency and practicality and implications-in-action. In the end he must still know less than everything. He must still choose, and nothing can direct his choice any better than his radical purposes and values can do. 'Complete' explanation would in principle be coextensive with much of human history in much of its detail; so voluminous, as merely to pose the problems of selection all over again. Meanwhile in all common sense there are enough very obvious patterns in reality, and enough values shared by investigators of the most diverse politics, to make sure that a lot of the knowledge gathered in different interests will prove useful to everybody. But this follows from the sharing, not shedding, of values. What the radical, like anybody else, needs is to know more, skilfully; not to know all, neutrally.

The relation should certainly be reciprocal, his radicalism as well as his explanations suffering and responding. In practice to 'be radical' is to govern, vote, teach, preach, or by research to discover and organize knowledge usefully for those who do: in any of the divisions of labor, to commit action to moral purposes. It is a trite reminder, that the quality of valuation must arise equally from the values and from the technical understanding of the action valued. Any such purpose is likely to be served well, in proportion as the investigator grasps more of the complex, ramifying consequences of action. Not by forgetting his organizing purposes, but in order both to serve them and to refine them, he may need to search widely and not always in obvious directions, to attend respectfully to his rivals' choices, to see through party labels and good intentions to the actual, factual consequences of action. Radical purposes will not be well served by blind or wishful substitutes for research; but not by purposeless research either.

Perhaps after all Hobson's rules were best. They recognized no disciplinary boundaries. They related choice not stupidly but intelligently, not narrowly but with full awareness of social complexity, to the investigator's moral and political purposes. They allowed Hobson to uncover a network of relations for imperialism some of which have since been disconnected or corrected – *but which have scarcely, in seventy years, been added to.*

Such rules cannot be acceptable to any value-free inquirer. For Part 2 the question is, what rules can he use instead? Before turning to that formidable question, the next chapter sums up some general implications of Hobson's rules for social science.

5

A Model of a Moralizing Science

Even if Turner and Chamberlain, Hobson and Lenin and the rest had all agreed to explain the same events and had made no mistakes of fact, then their explanations might have differed materially from those just reviewed, but it should still be clear that they would have continued to differ from each other. It should also be clear that their divers purposes – to reform or conserve societies, to condemn or justify past policies, to reinforce theoretical structures – might well have been better served by a stricter regard for truth, but could scarcely have been *replaced* by it. Even Langer's detachment could provide only detailed criticism of an explanation shaped still by Hobson's politics. However desirable as qualities of observation, 'objectivity' and its last-ditch rearguard 'intersubjectivity' still seem to be unable to organize an explanation or to bring men of different faith to agree about the parts or the shape, the length or breadth or depth or pattern, that an explanation should have.

If social science were fairly represented by these examples, its political and moral valuations would be integral parts of its work; analytically separable perhaps, but not removable. It would be silly to criticize the values for being present; instead, it would be good to criticize their quality and the manner in which they performed their indispensable work. 'Value-free' aspirations would be absurd. The ideals of objectivity and cumulation would require drastic revision. Science could be no more unanimous than politics.

A great deal of social science, though much improved in many details, has still the structure of those old explanations of imperialism. All general theories of political or social stability, of social cohesion or conflict, select controversial indicators of those effects, and select incomplete or insufficient causes for them. So do all explanations of social mobility, the recruitment of elites, deviance and delinquency and divorce, personal alienation or anomie, party and class and group behavior, urban location and communications, traffic accidents, social change, and economic growth. Some of the implications of this may now be summed up in (1) some broad categories of values expressed as political purposes – categories even cruder than those used in earlier chapters; (2) some equally rough categories of scientific purposes and methods; and (3) a model of relations between the two.

1. Purposes

It suits the shamelessly political purposes of *this* argument to classify political attitudes and values as Conservative, Radical or Liberal – three categories which will presently be reduced to two.

Since it is the politics of social scientists that are being classified, and there are scarcely any social scientists in static societies, 'conservative' cannot include do-nothing or stand-pat attitudes. Rather it defines, and distinguishes from liberals, those for whom 'conserving' is an activity – those who see dangers in deliberate revolutionary or experimental change, but who also see dangers in the natural trend society seems to take if left to itself. To preserve more valuable social achievements they are prepared to interfere with less valuable trends which may threaten those achievements. They may interfere by governing, legislating, litigating, fighting, preaching or educating – or by social research. This category may often coincide with the commoner definition of a conservative as one who values such things as security, refinement of culture, organic unity and social peace and thinks that various traditional controls are needed to preserve those qualities. But the coincidence is not invariable and if anybody thinks that those organic and orderly qualities grow naturally, he is here classified as a liberal, i.e. one who wants to leave society alone.

What sort of investigations should we expect of such interventionist conservatives? They will want to see the social structure 'whole', and to emphasize the multiple interconnections of its parts. They will search it for weaknesses, and search social processes to see how far they accommodate, and how far they create or intensify, strain. Where they find weakness or strain, they will look for points at which safe intervention or control are possible. They will generally want such intervention to be as specific, as economical, as possible; they are (of all political types) the most sensitive to the unintended side-effects of social intervention, which makes them excellent critics of radical proposals even when, as sometimes happens, they agree that the primary purposes of the radical proposals are good ones. Being sensitive to the variety of the human weaknesses and needs which society must take care of, they will not want all social institutions to be geared to maximize a single function (such as material production) and they will not be willing to analyse society by differentiation from a pure, such as a power-seeking or a wealth-producing model; but insofar as such a model may be made real either in life or in radical plans, they will be quick to connect it to its by-products in the neglect, frustration or destruction of other human capacities and needs. For all these reasons they may be expected to try to develop analytical methods which can expose the maximum interconnections between social parts, but at the same time to expose those parts as 'deposits of history' and as contributing (or not) to the future persistence of the social system. Their explanations may run as deep as any radical's, but ramify more widely. To explain the presence of features they wish to preserve, they will connect those features to the very foundations of society. They will do the same, as far as they can, to features they wish to excise or control, so as to enjoin extreme care in the choice of surgery or regulation.

Radicals are more simply defined. They want to interfere with society in order to improve it, perhaps inventively, perhaps in imitation of more just or more advanced societies. At one extreme are real revolutionaries; at the other, where left approaches center, J. A. Hobson can be the limiting case. He is a little hard to classify because he expected such mild interference with 'natural' society to have such radical effects. By itself his reform program would classify him as merely liberal, as also would his vision of an *almost* self-regulating progress. But because his modest marginal transfers of income were to have the effect of ridding the capitalist world of unemployment, empires, wars and revolutions, he had better be classed as radical. But not as typical of the class – typical radical surgery is more equally related to the magnitude of intended change.

The magnitude of the change intended, and of the measures

required to produce it, will obviously affect the radical investigator's choice of scientific methods and of patterns of explanation. Ideally, his investigations should be politically the most creative and scientifically the most inventive, even if in both departments they also tend to be the most risky. He must certainly adopt methods which will enable him to search social structures and processes for the moments of choice they manufacture, for points from which they can be controlled or altered. He will have to investigate at least as much of the social structure as he wants to remove or replace, together with any surrounding conditions which either protect it from, or expose it to, manipulation; and probably also the historical development which got it into its present deplorable condition. Explanation-by-origins is a popular radical pastime. In developing societies a great many institutions outlive the causes (or else the respectability of the causes) which originated them. If the death or discredit of those causes can be made public, to that extent the surviving institutions can be made to look undesirable or unnecessary. Of course while the radical explainer is busy thus, the conservative for political reasons and the sociologist for professional reasons may be equally busy, explaining the new functions which the old institution has acquired since the days of its origin, in order to show why it does persist, or why it ought to be allowed to persist, or why if it is abolished then not only its manifest and official functions but also its many unofficial and unnoticed functions had better be replaced, if unintended social damage is to be avoided.

It will be evident by now that these arguments are converging upon the eminently democratic and unbiased conclusion that social research needs the services of both radical and conservative investigators. The work of each should complement and correct the work of the other. The work of both should include profound and complex social analysis, with attention also to the historical origins and processes of change. Both have strong incentives to improve methods of dynamic analysis. Neither can achieve his extrinsic political purposes by working within the limitations of a single discipline (unless perhaps history, but each will see the need to improve *that*). Each can be expected, if there is conflict, to let his political purposes override his profession's rules – especially its boundary rules. There are sometimes, moreover, affinities in their guiding values. Both radicals and conservatives have imagined collective or organic societies. They often share enemies – the business-man, money-based class structures, the impersonal exploitive relationships of the cash-and-contractual society. They have had occasional, though seldom durable, alliances in practical politics. But however far their aspirations diverge from one another, they ought ideally to produce such similar or complementary social science that for our present purposes they might as well be joined in a single activist or 'Interventionist' category.

While not everybody would want to classify them together in that way, few would quarrel with the conclusion that social research needs both its radical and its conservative wings. A more quarrelsome question is whether it has any real need of its liberal middle.

It may have, of course, in the usual meaning of 'liberal'. If the liberal is defined by his valuation of individual liberties, and his hope that men will use them well, then his 'attitude to society' will depend on the society. In a liberal but endangered society he will be a conservative. In an illiberal society he will be a radical. Only in a society whose liberal characteristics seem both natural and stable will he be a liberal of the kind defined here: one who wants to leave society alone.

Perhaps liberals within this narrow definition, since they do not want to interfere with society and should consequently have no urgent need to understand its workings, do not become social scientists at all. But most prosperous Americans are liberals and most social scientists are prosperous Americans – there must be *something* wrong with the argument. Why assume that the social scientist's work need have any connection whatever with his politics?

Social science is a job, it pays, it satisfies plenty of unpolitical curiosities. Without deprecating these attractions, there may still be relations between a liberal's social science and his liberalism. He may wish to justify his liberal views, or more practically to defend his society against the efforts of right and left to arrest or advance it. Might this not lead him into social analysis so profound and general as to demonstrate all the harmonies, all the maximum unimprovable economies, of his social system? At first sight, yes; on second thoughts, no. For it is every part and function of his society that he has to defend; but all analysis and explanation have to be selective.

Will he therefore select the features of his system that exhibit the most satisfying harmonies? Indeed he will – until recently there were several dozen celebrations (though rather fewer analyses) of American affluence, for every radical explanation of poverty in America; several dozen celebrations of British tolerance, for every explanation of the racial attitudes of British emigrants to Rhodesia, or residents in Notting Hill. The impulse to celebrate does not *compel* analysis in the way that the impulse to attack or defend compels it. More commonly the liberal resorts to analysis only when parts of his system are attacked, and carries his analysis only as far as necessary to repulse the attack. This may be a long way: some of the liberals who defended capitalism from the accusation of imperialism looked as deeply as any of their attackers into the foundations and the history of both phenomena. So might the defender of any attacked institution, or any attacked theory. But what should the liberal do if nobody attacks him? Perhaps liberal social science owes all its depth and originality to the initiatives of its enemies. As Winslow and Fieldhouse both remarked, most explanations of imperialism have continued to be organized by Hobson.

None of this holds for liberals in the wider sense of the word. In *that* sense, Weber and Hobson and Keynes were liberals; but Weber was a liberal in an illiberal society, Hobson in an imperial society and Keynes in an unemployed society. In these environments, all were interventionists. It is a very narrow definition which makes 'liberal' mean no more than 'complacent'. To save that other and honorable liberalism from slander, it will be better from now on to call the merely complacent social scientist a 'Non-interventionist'. Of his work, the accusation of unoriginality, of shallow or facile analysis and facile or proximate explanation, is half-justified. Insofar as it is not justified, the complacent social scientist must derive his organizing purposes from one of two sources: from the initiatives of his enemies, or from within his scientific discipline. He would probably welcome the last suggestion as more charitable than the others, and agreeable to his professional ideals of scientific objectivity. But it leaves him dependent on his discipline for a supply of organizing purposes. What supplies does it offer?

Suppose his discipline is controlled by a majority as complacent as himself. Either they have no interventionist colleagues to other-direct them, or else effective sanctions compel any conservatives and radicals to exclude political prejudice from their professional work. If the complacent majority are to run a proper profession, to prescribe curricula and evaluate work and select and promote people, they will have to set up non-interventionist, non-political criteria for judging professional work. They may borrow criteria from pure science, and judge new knowledge by its heuristic and parsimonious qualities. Does it unlock new areas for inquiry, does it lock up old knowledge into fewer, more universal generalizations? From the same source they may learn that even the practical fruits of 'pure' research are not improved by bringing the research under the control of practical motives. But in physical science, research is usually under the control of one practical motive: that speculation should be organized for testing. 'Testing' for the social scientist too often means social engineering, and to organize knowledge for *that* would be a breach of non-interventionist rules. So in physical science experiment follows promptly, and usually with consensus of purpose, upon the heels of pure inquiry; but in social science this seems to be true only of the least pure, of the policy-oriented and empirical branches. Application follows theory smartly enough in market research or psychiatry; but experimental tests of high sociological theory seem forever to await the syntheses of its ever-receding maturity. In the meantime the waiting generations must continue to evaluate knowledge by criteria unanchored to application or, as a rule, experiment. The higher and purer the theory, the more of social structure and function it systematizes, the less its non-interventionist author *wants* it to be 'applied'. Its only practical function is as an argument against wilful manipulation of society, and such abstinence cannot serve it as experiment. Perhaps its predictions of 'natural' developments will test it, but that also may take some generations. Perhaps it can justify existing social structures; but usually, it is busily claiming to be value-free. Meanwhile life goes on and neither political nor experimental tests can be the non-interventionist's criteria for the judgment of knowledge or the promotion of its authors.

Two criteria remain, one high and one low. The high one is originality. Unfortunately anybody can be original by being merely silly, unimportant or obscure; it is precisely the tests which could distinguish useful from useless originalities, that have had to be abandoned as improperly political or 'impure' tests. So the ambitious scholar can pick up any old causal chain and trace it back a few links further; wake up any old sleeping condition and build a career on the voluminous description of it; light upon any new level of abstraction, invent a conceptual scheme appropriate to it, and devote a lifetime to the re-classification of all the old social facts under the new arrangement of collective nouns. If there are no satisfactory criteria for ranking these various originalities, there always remains the low test, which has the great advantage of precision and objectivity: the much-criticized judgment of work and its authors by the quantity and frequency of its publication. Of this judging procedure the profession retains considerable control, in its editing of professional journals and university presses; but some is confided to the officers of the commercial and 'vanity' presses who may also, of course, apply professional among other criteria.

The profession is now ripe for social analysis by an anthropologist or a Namier, for it is possible to explain the whole process of knowledge-production as merely a function of the career-system of the profession. Any society has to have mechanisms for distributing its members into hierarchies without intolerable strain. If we were to construct a 'pure' model of a non-interventionist social science, its production and publication of social knowledge should rationally exist to perform ritual, promotive and judicial functions within the professional society, but no others.

Such a model would have little relation to reality. If there is anywhere a 'pure' non-interventionist social scientist, he is unlikely to behave as in that model. He is more likely, if he does not want to manipulate society himself, to sell his discoveries to those who do. Not to those who would (contrary to his non-interventionist faith) engineer any fundamental changes in society; rather to those who would manipulate themselves some profit out of society's existing arrangements. Social research can help to sell soap or automobiles, to adjust neurotics, to improve the public relations of politicians, to reorganize the factory floor on more harmonious principles, to streamline management, to rationalize decision-making, to provide material for college courses and examinations – in a hundred ways, most of them saleable, to lubricate and harmonize, advertise and congratulate and entertain, the society whose general structure the complacent social scientist does not want his discoveries to upset or undermine.

Thus the non-interventionist can generally get his methods and explanations organized in one of three ways: by the initiatives of his enemies, by ritual requirements established by his colleagues, or by the various commercial requirements of the public to whom he sells his products. An interventionist would describe these products as being, socially speaking, consumption goods rather than capital goods.

2. *Methods*

Methods could be classified in a number of ways – by the disciplines that use them, for example, or by some classification of the human activities they describe, or by their logical types or levels of abstraction or generality. The last-mentioned will do as well as any.

There is direct observation and description of conduct, differing only in methodical accuracy, if at all, from laymen's descriptions. Most disciplines do plenty of it, not only to get material to generalize about, but also as the best way of knowing many causal or functional connections. In the course of it, the plainest language already does a good deal of organizing and relating, with nouns like state, institution, result, personality, group, game, idea; verbs like cause, organize, represent, conform, rebel, recover, relate. Only the disciplines of Law and Philosophy take much real care about the raw observations they pack into these portmanteaux.

Then there are more deliberate grouping concepts, which class things by some common quality or some system of internal connections discerned in them all: concepts like democracy, revolution, scapegoat, authoritarian, inner-directed. Into these any bit of raw experience will be classified by a few only of its characteristics or its supposed causes or effects or functions. The choice of such features will determine the company the experience finds in its new box. One aspect of cannibal raiding classifies it as sin; I recognize it as being like my own sins. Another aspect of cannibal raiding identifies it as war and perhaps sub-classifies it as defensive or aggressive war; I know which civilized wars it thus resembles. Another aspect classifies it as food-gathering; I see myself picking lemons from my tree or buying a can of beans in the local supermarket. Another aspect – based on some less obvious causal propositions – identifies it as a release of social tensions; I see myself kicking the cat, driving aggressively, or penning that sentence 'most social scientists are prosperous Americans'. Another aspect classifies it as a mechanism for establishing individuals' qualifications for manhood or social promotion; I see myself learning to shave, cramming for my B.A. examinations, trying to make the serious bits of this book more original and the original bits more serious. It took an abstract and subtle social science to make these last identifications, and they all have different manipulative implications. One makes the abolition of cannibalism look easy, another hard, another nearly impossible. Some imply that it could be simply abolished, others that its functions would need to be replaced. One suggests abolition by moral abjuration or religious conversion, another by police prohibition, another by economic development, another by social reconstruction.

Then there are 'higher' levels of abstraction, classification and relation – levels at which the functions common to social systems can be identified but their ways of performing those functions can be differentiated; levels at which the performances also look alike; levels at which millennial civilizations can be compared and differentiated, levels at which their histories appear identical. Knowledge ordered thus may offer more opportunities for contemplation than for social intervention or control.

There are many other ways in which methods and their different arrangements of social knowledge might be classified, in order to notice the manipulative possibilities of each type. Two more will be enough: differences between narrative and analysis, and differences between disciplines.

Historical, sequential, causal knowledge is the natural stock-in-trade of the reformer. But too often it takes the thing-to-be-reformed out of its context. Because its past explains it, its present relations get neglected, and with them the less obvious effects, the by-products and side-effects, which may result from interfering with it. These latter connections are revealed better by 'simultaneous' analysis, whether of social structure and function, of political or economic systems, or of systems of ideas and expectations. Yet such analytical knowledge, even if organized to expose the parts of society at work rather than at rest, can seldom tell the manipulator much of what he needs to know about the processes by which systems themselves are changed, whether by natural growth or by deliberate intervention. This is something like the difference between a revolutionary theory (what's wrong with the society you've got, and what sort of society you want) and a theory of revolution (how to turn the one into the other). The manipulator obviously needs both sorts of knowledge, and usually knows that he needs both. The 'pure' non-interventionist scientist may be satisfied that he understands both natural and deliberate processes of change by means of purely sequential explanations; or he may be content to understand the internal relations of society by means of purely analytical and functional explanations. He may be satisfied because, either way, he apparently has an internally coherent body of knowledge and he does not mind its being useless. Only the interventionist has a conscious and over-riding need for both sorts of knowledge. It was the historians of the left and the frightened right – Engels and Beard, Tocqueville and Namier – who most often stopped their narratives to analyse the internal relations of society. It is the uncomplacent sort of sociologist who most insistently relates social analysis to historical processes, to economic changes and political interventions – Tocqueville again; Ostrogorski, Veblen and Michels; Mannheim and Titmuss and Riesman and Wright-Mills.

No discipline is self-sufficient – none is the expert on *all* the determinants even of specific types of social conduct.

Perhaps the lawyer comes nearest. A lot of the conduct he studies is deliberately controlled, and his knowledge of it is well-organized for daily and practical use. He can predict how a change in law will affect the behavior of judges, and therefore perhaps the conduct of policemen, public accountants and other predictable folk who have to keep their eyes on the probable behavior of judges. He is less certain about taxation lawyers, who may be too clever, or burglars or juries who may be stupid or lucky or humane. He claims no special knowledge at all of the broad social foundations and effects of laws, or of the best methods of persuading legislators to change them.

For similarly limited purposes, including much regulation and adjustment of going systems, Economics has the same character. But it generally refuses to organize most of the knowledge necessary to make large changes in systems, or to make systems grow or to understand why they grow. Growth economists refer increasingly to the non-economic conditions for growth which are the business of sociologists, psychologists, political scientists and historians. So with political scientists. They study the chief instrument of social intervention, and should surely organize all the knowledge needed by manipulators or anti-manipulators – yet they readily hand over to others whole areas of the conditioning of politics, chains of cause and effect which run off into the territories of psychologists, sociologists, economists and historians.

Sociology is perhaps the extreme case – like the United States a century ago, advocating free-trading interdependence in theory and erecting some formidable trade barriers in practice; perhaps for the similar reason, that it is industrializing late but fast. Some sociologists organize knowledge very usefully for a range of minor or adjustive purposes of business or government; others expose sources of strain and stability at both controllable and uncontrollable levels of social structure. But at the levels likely to interest conservative or radical interventionists, sociology has seldom much to say about the practical choices open to would-be manipulators. It is also at these levels – in the sociology 'of the middle range' – that the discipline suffers most from what its law-seekers used to call interloping variables. A sociological hypothesis at this level has to make a double abstraction: from 'whole life' it has to abstract societal aspects, and from whole systems it has to abstract parts – perhaps groups of one type, or functions of one type. The recurrent association of features within these limits cannot be expected unless the forces that bear upon them from 'outside' are 'fixed'. Too often, to 'fix' all the foreign variables will reduce the hypothesis to a description of a unique, or very locally recurrent, association. If it refuses to retreat thus to historical description, the inquiry may be driven to quite uninteresting heights of abstraction before it can find many significant regularities in social structures and functions, simply because these aspects of social activity are too variously affected by others, for example by changing modes of production and uses of power. To abstract one sort of conditioning from others is appropriate to an attempt to measure them all, and to relate their converging 'influences' to the conduct which they all condition; but it is hopeless if other conditions are to be ignored while conduct is expected to show regular relation with one sort of condition only. Even if relations be there, and be regular, they will be discovered only by systematically distinguishing the effects of the 'ignored' conditions – in this case, by becoming an economist, political scientist, psychologist and lawyer, as well as sociologist.

Perhaps these difficulties are acute in sociology because its subject-matter includes so much thoughtless behavior. Men seldom set about building social structures as deliberately as they plan legal or political or even economic institutions. Social structures arise some-what inadvertently from men's efforts to get or build other things; the sociologist must abstract for study the societal aspect of conduct which was rationally directed to other ends. Unless he crosses disciplinary boundaries to study those rational directions and those other ends, he must find it hard to establish reliable behavior or sufficient explanations of societal phenomena, or explanations which include what a would-be manipulator of the social structure would need to know.

Sociology may be unusually vulnerable to the mysterious disturbance of its subject-matter by interloping variables, but all well-disciplined disciplines suffer in some degree. To prove even their most domestic causal or functional propositions, they must either insist on the primacy of one type of cause without reference to the rest of the 'undisciplined' (or other-disciplined) conditions in the 'set'; or they must work on model assumptions about the rest of the set, assumptions which real life or other disciplines may any day uncertify; or they must forget their disciplinary boundaries, and go trespassing. The further they stray the more inexpert they are likely to become, and before them stands the awful warning of the general historian, demonstrating his inexpertise upon each in turn of the economic, the sociological, the psephological and the psychological factors which he insists on including in his wide-ranging, synthesiz-ing explanations.

To the investigator whose motives are predominantly scientific, it may seem better to present whatever disciplined conclusions he has, with a note of their unexplored dependence. It may seem safer to find some better-contained area of study. To the pure scientist any original work, if as 'big' and novel, is as good as any other. In the familiar dilemma between the value of knowledge and the certainty with which it may be known, the pure scientist, especially if in a branch of science in which 'no interference with society' means both 'no urgency for knowledge' and 'no experimentation', may well find that the balance of temptation leads in the direction indicated by Kurt Lewin when he advised –

Only ask the questions in your research that you can answer with the techniques you can use. If you can't learn to ignore the questions you are not prepared to answer definitely, you will never answer any.[1]

Social science may thus avoid the really perplexing, uncertain and valuably important problems of social life. It may also set out on what has been called the drunkard's search –

A passer-by finds a drunk on his hands and knees under a street lamp, and asks 'What are you looking for?' 'A dime I lost.' 'Where did you lose it?' 'Up that alley there.' 'Well why look for it down here?' 'Because there's some light down here, stoopid.'[2]

For the scientist who really wants to find the dime, whose overriding motives are extrinsic to his professional career and his discipline's rules, the balance of temptation should usually lead him, groping but rational, up the dark alley. It has often done so in fact. Radical and interventionist-conservative sociologists stray into history, as noted above. Many of the extensions of historians' interests into economic, social and psychological fields have been begun, or provoked, by interventionists. The economists who disliked and wanted to alter their economies, or who saw a need to defend them actively, have been the chief trespassers into politics and sociology: Smith, Marx, Hobson, Schumpeter, Hayek, Keynes, Balogh, Hansen, Boulding, Galbraith. In political science it has been the left who, since Marx, have related politics most insistently to history and economics; the right, since Plato and Hobbes, to psychology.

R. H. Tawney said 'the poachers often get the fattest rabbits'. Such trespassers are many and distinguished; none was complacent about his own society; together they make a majority of the great founders, discoverers and innovators in their disciplines. This is scarcely surprising. It arose partly, of course, because the classical innovators lived when, if you did not care a damn about society, you had no reason to study it – outside the church there were few well-paid publish-or-perish careers for disinterested academics. But it is by no means clear that the requirements for innovation have changed with the changing career-requirements of social scientists. To organize knowledge for interventionist purposes will often require the sort of poaching which stimulates scientific as well as social imagination. It will often require work in several disciplines. But not guesswork. In proportion as deliberate social action becomes possible or urgent – as revolutionary situations menace or entice, as free resources become available for new disposals, as public opinion swings in new directions, as unemployment or racial tension or other strains increase – as the opportunity for action approaches, so will the interventionist be motivated to make sure that his knowledge is not only suitably organized, but also reliable. For unlike the pure scientist, he is prepared to stake more than his academic fortune, and probably many more fortunes than his own, upon the truth and sufficiency of that knowledge. Its truth and sufficiency, moreover, may be tested by judges more severe than the publishers, prescribers and promoters within the pure scientist's profession.

3. Model

Real scientists are not like this chapter's simple types. Such types are sketched as guesses at the parts played, in the complex and untidy conduct of real scientists, by their 'pure professional' and their 'pure political' motives respectively. With this purpose in mind, all these unreally pure types can now be put together into a model as pure and unreal as themselves.

The model has only three moving parts.

First, it is the model of a complex advanced society. This part of the model is real – the society has many millions of citizens, who form some millions of families, scores of thousands of groups and organizations, hundreds of major institutions, several political parties; 'social events' occur in millions every hour, 'social facts' are practically innumerable. Desires to understand and to preserve or change this society are distributed much as we know them to be in our own real societies. The only ideal feature of the model is the assumption that all these social facts, and all their connections or relations with each other, are in principle discoverable; but only by hard work and scarce methodological ingenuity, so that a familiar and realistic need exists to economize scarce research resources.

The second element in the model has already been described. It is the whole array of social scientists, some interventionist and some pure, together with all their technical resources of alternative languages, concepts, methods, and systems for organizing their researches and their results.

The third element is the Ideal Director of an Ideal Social Science Research Foundation. He commands (in the form of money which he can spend as he pleases on hiring and equipping social scientists) a fraction of the society's scarce research resources. It is his business to economize these resources. He, like those who established his Foundation and appointed him, is an absolutely pure scientist. He is utterly satisfied with the society in which he lives. Besides his own career, he cares for nothing except the quantity, importance and truth of the social knowledge produced by his Foundation. He is even prepared to make its heuristic propensity to subsume old and generate new knowledge the only test of the 'importance' of new knowledge. The only test, that is, except truth. In a competition which is about to be conducted between his own and all rival Foundations – a competition which will promote the winning Director to be National Director of All Foundations – the umpires will admit only knowledge verified by test or at least organized so that it could in principle be tested.

When he hires his staff, how will the scientifically pure Director discriminate between the pure and the impure, the professional and the political, the detached and the passionate, the objective and the biased candidates for research appointments?

He will pick the impure every time. They have stronger motives, and originating rather than merely defensive or responsive motives, for pressing their explanations of social events further backward into history, further outward into social context. They are more strongly motivated to ignore disciplinary boundaries, but at the same time to get the most reliable truth by the most appropriately disciplined methods. They are thus appropriately motivated, as the purist or the careerist is not, to make an economizing judgment between the marginal need for the trespasser's poached goods, and their marginal quality. When poaching fails, they have stronger motives for cooperating with colleagues from other disciplines. They have stronger motives for organizing knowledge into testable form, and stronger motives for hoping it will survive the tests, and soon. They often need knowledge more quickly. They are often saved from certain difficulties of personal and scientific indecision, by having extrinsic tests of the relative importance and urgency of social-scientific problems. Finally they can be assumed to have all the pure scientist's motivations – they earn their livings in the same way and are presumably no less ambitious – but to his careerism and his pure curiosity they add their third and distinguishing motive, and three is more than two.

The pure Director, for his pure purpose, must therefore hire the most passionately impure researchers he can find.

There remain two flaws in this model. First, the researchers may all turn out to be passionately impure in different political directions, reducing the Foundation to confusion as each fights to organize its work in a different way. One way around this difficulty is to hope that the works of conservatives and radicals will complement each other, as in theory they should. A better way is to relate the model, not to a Research Foundation which in real life would differ sharply from it, but to any single social scientist's mind. It is a real enough model of the best minds, whether they be judged admirable by the goodness, the usefulness, or the scientific originality and fertility of their work.

The second flaw in the model is not removed by thus getting rid of the first. However dearly the biased researcher may desire true and useful discoveries, that merely describes his motives; it does not follow that it will describe his work. The world is full of wishful thinking, the libraries are full of wishful social science. Won't the interventionist's impatient purposes divert him always from scientific to engineering problems, and even with those, won't his hopes and fears, his values and his ideological blinkers, distort everything he does from formulation of theory through choice of method to detailed observation and understanding? I concede that they can, and that they often do; and further, that the way to guard against these ill effects is to practise about one half of the conventional wisdom on the subject of scientific objectivity. But it is difficult and very important, as Mr. Wanamaker said of the wasted half of his advertising budget, to know which half.

In research there are apparently distinguishable problems: what to select or search for, and how to know it is there when you find it.

The nature and discovery and proof of the causal relations between social facts have been systematically neglected in this argument up to now, which must often have given it an air of frivolity. A researcher's values have obvious scope in choosing the connections he would *like* to discover; but the tougher business of knowing and proving them is surely an exclusive field for objectivity? It is time to turn from the choice of explanations for use, to their choice for truth. Can neutral scientific rules replace valuations as selectors? And quite apart from its selection, is the hard knowledge of causes always as value-free as it seems?

Part 2 - Truth

If social scientists won't value what they study, what principles of selection can they use instead?

The following chapters argue that they cannot avoid valuing. Those who try to avoid it discover less, and also worse because they substitute bad judgment for good.

Much of what follows is argued as a debate between pure and applied, between scientific and engineering principles of inquiry. 'Scientific' can mean an organizing preference for more general over more local knowledge; 'engineering' represents every sort of political, social or entertaining purpose, and the organization of research to serve such purposes directly. The distinction no longer interests the best philosophers and methodologists, who rid themselves ten years ago of dreams that a 'high and pure' social theory should try to imitate the triumphs of physics. Such thought should trickle down in time into the daily practice of the professions. But tens of thousands of young sociologists, political scientists and even a few modernizing historians are still told by their books and teachers to be as abstract, general, objective, quantitative and unfeeling as they can. In their usual meanings these instructions more often hinder than help the discovery and understanding of social facts.

If the following chapters resume some methodological arguments of the nineteen-fifties, their unoriginality does not make them less important. Even where the arguments seemed conclusive, the winners' triumphs are no use if the masses still follow the losers. Those tens of thousands are not yet convinced that it pays to value knowledge for its truth and use, not its form. In social science it may not always be fruitful to value general above particular knowledge, to value scientific yield above social consequence, to value scientific un-animity above disagreement, to value facts above valuations, to value certainties above uncertainties, or to suppose that avoiding valuation will necessarily improve the yield of fact or fertile theory. In any scientific work there are relations between its social and scientific purposes, its selections, its methods, its yield, its immediate social applications, and the general social consequences of nourishing the activity. Of these the social effects, and therefore the others as among their causes, are proper subjects for anybody's valuations. Are the above relations likely to be the same in social as in physical sciences?

In physical science selection for uniformity, generality, certainty and scientific agreement is richly justified by results, and value-freedom generally comes without trying. Physics goes far, geology as far as it can, but both in the same direction. It is still worth asking whether the same old map will lead the social sciences to the same bonanza.

6

Scientific Selection of Causes

1. Scientific selection

Natural scientists abstract and select (especially, they select abstractions) comparatively untroubled by problems of objectivity. Matter includes as many individual items as human society does, and to a layman the items look as various. In their behavior, scientists nevertheless discover numerous identities in regular relations with one another. Because most of these regularities are reliably unaffected by being discovered, discovery allows the controlled rearrangement and use of matter – by humans, not so far by inanimate matter itself as a result of its better education. Humans value each other above other materials; they permit each other to experiment with the non-human world and, when its regularities are discovered, to exploit it without misgiving. Few would deny that *eventual* social use is what chiefly justifies the activity of science, and we sometimes exaggerate the extent to which the detail of research is divorced from thoughts about its social use. Nevertheless their unanimous valuation of their regular subject-matter allows scientists to agree upon many rules of search.

A most important rule is to look for regularities: for methods by which, levels of abstraction at which, identities and correlations and recurrences will appear, and for theories to generalize and explain them, base prediction on them, and indicate how more of them might next be discovered. For social as well as scientific purposes these rules work better in natural science than others would do. 'What will feed this family, heat this house, cure this disease, win this war, rearrange natural energy to perform this task or that?' – these socially-directed questions are engineering questions. They will usually be answered at all only if they wait upon, often to use without augmenting, the discoveries of a science whose own rules exclude such questions just as they generally exclude valuations in any moral or political sense. Though it rests on some underlying valuations, and values the order of importance of problems for study, nevertheless physical science serves the values of society best by being, in its day-to-day research activity, comparatively 'value-free'.

There are various ways of approaching the question why social science has not followed this model, and the question whether it should try in future to follow it more closely. We can try, in turn, a formal approach, an understanding approach, a practical approach, and a rebellious approach.

A formal approach: social science might simply borrow the theories, or the rules, of natural science.

There have been some very detailed imitations. Darwinian theory was thought by some to apply with negligible adjustment to the development of national societies. Others inferred from Cannon's *The Wisdom of the Body* that societies were like enough to bodies to allow sociologists to apply, intact, the methods of physiology. Another popular loan was a rule that causes may only be inferred from behaviorist correlations.

It is more usual to borrow more general rules: 'Search for regularities; make explanation deductive whenever you can; terminate explanation when you identify a case of a law; dismiss from selection whatever cannot be so explained, or search for new ways by which it can be so explained.' Or if even these prove unhelpful, still more general rules are available: 'Seek rules which (like the search for regularity) are derived by scientists from their scientific experience, not from their other social experience. Design rules to select knowledge for its values of quantity or elegance or fertility (for use or admiration by other scientists) not for any other values (for use or admiration by other people).'

This last is the rule which most clearly relates the imitation of science to the avoidance of social valuation. Indeed, the intrusion of values and engineering interests is often blamed as a chief cause of the present low yield of social science. We are easily blinded by our immediate interests, beliefs and values. We do not find what we do not want to find; we will not recognize unpleasant facts; we would hate to see our minds sufficiently simulated by machines, or to find that our children were likely to be criminal in proportion as their parents were virtuous; and so on. But the argument is not conclusive. Bad eyesight may make a man a poor prospector, but does not by itself prove that the gold is there. Many social scientists are well aware of these blinding capacities of their human feelings. They would delight in any iconoclasm. They desire authentic discoveries, and desire to be the discoverers, more passionately than they desire almost anything else. They know that there are richer rewards for discovering than for being good.

Moreover, it is a two-edged argument. The social scientist's desire to find enough uniformities of behavior to support the physicist's type of general theory may blind his observations and misguide his selections just as effectively as any social values could do. The desire for the form and social authority of science is for some people more imperative than is any desire for its real yields. On the other hand many social discoveries, though they may have offended conventional values, have been more helped than hindered by the investigators' own.

But if personal feelings do not obscure the right answers, perhaps they prompt the wrong questions. Social problems prompt engineering questions which could never elicit 'high and pure' scientific answers. But of this, too, able men are well aware; much modern social theory expresses a hopeful and imitative quest for 'high and pure' questions. (This may be dubious imitation, for example of physics whose earlier 'pure' questions arose directly enough out of engineering problems.) Perhaps the low yield of high and pure questions arises from the nature of society rather than from the shortcomings of its scientists. Instead of asking how scientists should imitate each other, we can try to understand how society fails to imitate nature.

Values limit experiment. While this obstructs inquiry, it may also allow us to go on wishfully misunderstanding what the yield of experiment would be. To imitate the laboratory we might have to divide the human population into unequal classes: the valuable discoverers and exploiters, the valueless discovered and exploited. To some extent this is the historical condition of mankind from which it desires to be *rescued* by social science. But the division would present technical as well as moral difficulties. The discovered may discover the discovery; they may have to be taught it to fit them for engineering; but they may use their new learning to resist the engineering, or by changing their ways to falsify the science. The last is merely one case of the most general misgiving of those who distrust social imitations of natural science. Whether from 'free will' or from incomprehensible complexity, human social behavior may include an intrinsically unpredictable element. That some people desire it to include that element, is no evidence that it does not. There are plenty of unstable and unique phenomena in nature; the question is whether they are more extensive in society, and its regularities fewer, less useful or less reliable. As I wonder how to spend this day, how to construct this book, how to vote, what to learn, when to fight, what values to put on this and that, I am not behaving quite like anything a physical scientist studies: so why should his rules be expected to improve any study of *me*? My choices seem neither perfectly predictable nor perfectly inscrutable. They are among the causes of action; they are unlike most causes in nature; they are often more directly understandable than causes in nature. Behavior is full of predictable similarities and repetitions. They are reliable enough to support some science and a lot of experience; but not, apparently, to replace much of the experience by a science of, *merely*, regularities.

To determined imitators this is merely a challenge to intensify the search for scientific principles of selection which will at last isolate the identities whose relations *are* regular. If there are no such underlying regular systems, then it seems to such men that there can be no real science; so the scientific endeavor must be – can only be – a gamble on them, organized by a search for them. To search, instead, for good or bad or useful or unique things, to let modestly empirical or moral or political purposes join in organizing the search, will simply divert it from its only promising direction. To think of scientific advance as the improvement of investigatory skill, rather than the accumulation of true laws, is to 'descend' to merely clinical or engineering 'levels'. To see imagination and persuasion as the social equivalents of the physical scientist's 'discovery' is to go off the rails entirely.

Most do nevertheless admit that some scientific rules need adjustment to social facts. Strict behaviorism has few champions left.

Perhaps the quest for uniformities is the next to need adjustment. Rules which define the variations as random are merely obscurantist, since many of the variations are understandable and some (for example, by understanding intentions) are predictable. But the variations are so various that, where regularity cannot work as selector, selection may usefully be guided by political as well as scientific valuation.

Two conclusions might be drawn from these circumstances, one primarily moral and the other primarily technical.

First, if the investigator may not be tyrant and engineer over his subjects, if the subjects' values are valued equally with the investigator's, and if the subjects' values are not unanimous but are many and factional, then perhaps investigators should represent factions – their work will overlap in practice, because the faction-fighting value-systems in practice overlap in wide areas of consensus, and share needs for large quantities of neutral information. In this scheme for social science, different values will select different explanatory patterns, as in the example from imperialism.

Second, technical reasons may support the same scheme, if it is true that human choice and social complexity are such as to render unnecessarily limited any science of 'regularities only'. Even if underlying systems are discerned, they may be 'weaker' than natural systems. What may be required of investigators may be skill with irregularities, in a science of probabilities and possibilities; a mixed technical and political judgment, a rational approach to problems not merely of practical and moral, but also of logical uncertainty. International theory is not alone in developing, already, sophisticated approaches to uncertainty. But the choice and use of statistical methods, the understanding and predictive use of human intentions, the choice of programs worth exploring, the gaming approach to others' calculations, the 'feed-back' from science to the game-players, all require valuations of one or another 'non-scientific' kind. Such a science will not be purified but dismembered by rating its valuations lower than its other thoughts, or by trying to limit them to 'given goals', or by trying to exclude them altogether. I can see what values led Hobson to select the parts and shape of his explanation. I can test many of its factual and connective statements technically. But when these are corrected I cannot then subtract the valuations to leave a neutral residue of 'scientific' explanation. I may leave a neutral heap of information; but I can only employ other values to reorganize it into other explanations, or to extend research in other directions.

For a more practical approach to value-free selections, recall the example of boss-rule in city government.

In considering this phenomenon, suppose that I hesitate between the broad alternatives of a value-charged 'engineering' attack, and a value-free 'scientific' attack. Valuation does at least supply ready rules to guide my selection of the reportable conditions for the persistence of boss-rule. I disapprove of boss-rule and of many (though not all) of its effects, so from its conditions I want to select those which could be manipulated; but they must at the same time be conditions whose own value, and whose other effects or by-products, could either be done without or (if valuable) replaced. By such rules, most of the innumerable conditions necessary for boss-rule can immediately be dismissed. The existence of cities is a condition necessary for their government by bosses, but I do not want to do without cities or the many good things they supply. The existence of a monetary system is another condition undoubtedly necessary for boss-rule, but I do not want to do without money either. The same applies to a list of conditions which range from traits of human nature through features of the citizens' culture and values and technology and economic organization, to many detailed and local facts of city government. It must be emphasized that it is the number and variety of these necessary conditions, in practice uncountable, which make *selection* necessary both in directing research and in reporting its findings. My engineering rules have the virtue that they work – they organize and terminate my inquiry, and their product may well enable something to be done about boss-rule. They express scarcely anything except my scale of political and social values (or my client's, or somebody's); but they work with a particular economy. The same rules which govern engineering application, govern also the scientific search. They may limit inquiry but they avoid waste.

What might be the alternative, the scientific approach? Without much doubt its first step ought to be to avoid asking questions about phenomena like boss-rule – or delinquency, or education, or marriage, or religious behavior, or democracy, or political parties, or group dynamics or social stratification or conflict or consensus. But in practice many social scientists do ask about such things, and do seek value-free rules to elicit value-free answers. So for understanding the causes of boss-rule, can I imagine any rules which would be independent of my moral or social values, but which would select more fruitfully than my political rules will select – would lead me, perhaps, to discover laws?

I try some obvious candidates. Simple regularity does not seem to help. I can find no general attributes of modern cities which are invariably associated with boss-rule, nor any single attributes of the boss-ruled cities which are invariably absent from other cities.

But the search for single attributes may be a primitive mistake. Bosses may associate not with singles but with particular combinations. Try: poor social services + insulation of local from central government + majority left school by age 16 + contradictory real and expected mobility chances + franchised public utilities + plurality of religions. All were present with Boss Hague in Jersey City. But so they were in Hartford, Conn., without a boss. (Indeed, because they were present in Liverpool, England, Lincoln Steffens once 'deduced' that a boss must be somehow concealed there with them.) This is the trouble with all such combinations I can think of: if they fit the cities where bosses are, they also predict bosses where bosses are not.

Perhaps I should use regularity as a means of isolating irregularities. I appear to need a selector of those causes which (a) connect with boss-rule but (b) distinguish Jersey City from Hartford and Liverpool. A model of the configuration of forces common to all cities without bosses, if juxtaposed with the facts of Jersey City, should indicate which of Jersey City's facts are eccentricities. The boss will be one eccentricity and the scientifically interesting members of the set of conditions which 'cause' him will presumably be among the other eccentricities. This may narrow my search, though not far. To begin with, how shall I exhaust (without selecting?) all features common to unbossed cities? But suppose that I somehow arrive at a model of unbossed cities. Where my political selector would dismiss from explanation the conditions for boss-rule which nobody wants to manipulate, this value-free, law-seeking selector will dismiss, instead, whatever Jersey City conditions appear also in unbossed cities. But the remaining irregulars in Jersey City may be quite insufficient to account (without their regular companions) for the boss.

It is hard to understand what scientific yield can be expected, at this level, of any 'regularity-related' rule at all; and of engineering yield, there will of course be even less. The necessary conditions for Boss Hague's rule which *distinguish* his city from other cities are no more likely than are any other conditions, to be those which engineers will wish to manipulate. Other conditions such as the state of the law or the welfare services, conditions common to all cities, necessary to boss-rule in some but without the converging conditions which would make a sufficient set for boss-rule in the others, may well be more easily manipulated, or manipulated with more reliable and predictable effect, or manipulated with more valued by-products. However general such conditions may be, any explanation of boss-rule ought to include them. If explanations of boss-rule did not include the poverty of welfare services before the New Deal, we would be quite unable (for either a scientific or an engineering curiosity) to explain the fall of the Philadelphian and many other machines in 1933 and after; but welfare services were much the same in Hartford and Liverpool and Melbourne. Yet it would seem that only a manipulative interest – real or hypothetical, direct or disguised in conventions of analysis – can select welfare services into the explanation of boss-rule but leave the monetary system out.

Regularity and irregularity are not the only value-free selectors available. Try proximity – it would be non-evaluative to select causes by their immediacy to their effects. But this has only a deceptive possibility in historical studies, and none for functional or analytic studies. The contributions of human apathy or social alienation, of the existence of cities and money, of systems of production, distribution, exchange, law and crime, of Boss Hague's individual mixture of blarney, avarice and religiosity, all seem to be equally immediate, equally proximate to the persistence of his rule. So also for 'efficient' causes and 'predominant' causes. 'Efficient' causes usually disguise a political judgment of responsibility, or a political choice of the link at which to drop a causal chain, or mere ignorance of the other necessary conditions. 'Predominant' causes do not in practice choose themselves by their power or size. 'Power' and 'size' usually have to be valued as well as measured. The conditions in which the cause will 'predominate' are seldom either constant in fact, or exhaustively named in explanation. There *are* commonsense technical things that can be said about the 'force' or 'weight' of particular causes, but they usually express engineering considerations and require prior valuations.

In 'Some Issues in the Logic of Historical Analysis'[1] Ernest Nagel suggested five objective tests by which particular necessary conditions could be distinguished as 'more necessary' or 'more important' than others. None of the tests seemed universally reliable, practicable or even applicable, but Nagel was only concerned to show that such tests were, in logical principle, possible. Even if workable, it is still not clear what might be their advantages – how, for example, they would help to discover 'laws'. As alternative principles for the selection of any one explanation, each would of course organize an explanation with different implications, including knowledge useful to different interests, though economically organized (except by chance) for none. Each is also exposed to the valuing involved in collecting its primary material – grouping and naming the 'conditions' or 'factors' in the first place, and in some cases establishing their causal relations to each other.

Other value-free selectors will be discussed below, especially some functional candidates – rules which would select, as the causes of Boss Hague's persistence, only the conditions which also caused other nominated facts about Jersey City (or the U.S.A.) to persist – and some candidates which would replace the investigator's values by those of the people investigated. But none of these will make it any less foolish to demand scientific rules for engineering problems, problems to which such rules would be no more appropriate in physical than in social science. If ever a pure science explains boss-rule, it seems unlikely to be a science of bosses or cities as such, any more than the pure science which contributes to the improvement of bridge-building is a science of bridges. If such a pure science ever emerges from – say – neuro-physiology, its engineering application will still require a *social* science, and 'social' will be what distinguishes this science from 'pure' – as well talk of a pure social science as of a pure applied science. On society's few comparatively reliable constants of love and avarice, demography and economics are – somewhat unsteadily – built already and each demonstrates its maturity as much by its frank engineering interest as by the fertility of its general models. Few of the models last long. They obsolesce with social change.

Finally: even if valuation *could* be exorcised, why *should* it be? Good and evil, wish and ought, were declared to be dirty words in the first place only because they were expected to encourage quarrels and inhibit inquiry. But perhaps social science is – not surprisingly – like other social activities. Social scientists are supposed to discover and teach a better understanding of society to the citizens and politicians. What sense does it make to imagine a unanimous social science in a freely disagreeing society? Perhaps we should not ask for less valuations in social science, but for better ones – for questions that will yield not more unanimous answers, but more valuable answers.

Perhaps, for example, the scientist should search past and present for social opportunities: for the alternatives men saw, and the better alternatives they might have seen if better informed; also for the stricter limitations they might have seen if better informed, and the mistakes they might then have avoided. As noticed above, R. G. Collingwood recommended this principle of selection to historians. It is not necessarily inconsistent with scientific principles; it merely depends how indirect you hope to be, and how much law you hope to find. But in its more direct, engineering form, it is often disliked as a variety of historical relativity: causes must be selected for their double relevance, both to the effect they joined in causing, and to the social interest of the historian. This scarcely differentiates the method from the physical scientist's, except insofar as his manipulative interests are more stable and unanimous. William Dray notes (without approval) another objection: 'a historian cannot sensibly ask himself how *he* could have produced or prevented the defeat of Napoleon or the outbreak of the Civil War.' He can still sensibly ask *who* might have prevented it, and when, and how, in the interest of a general wisdom of prevention; and if the historian suffers from the options being already closed by history, the scientist of present society does not.

A related suggestion, which Dray develops in his own work[2] and notices in that of Hart and Honoré on *Causation in the Law*, is that historians look for 'responsibilities'. They do not first find who caused events, in order to praise or blame them; they first decide who could be held responsible for events, in order to give to responsible action a special causal significance. It does seem appropriate that the human study of human society should accord strong and independent causal force to deliberate action, whether by individuals or multitudes. Dray finds this view promising, but raises some philosophical difficulties. It also has its practical and political difficulties. It is only a preliminary, or a general quality for rules of selection. Its rules in detail will have to be like Hobson's or Bülow's, expressions of somebody's detailed judgments of 'responsibility'. It may seem to oppose constants to 'opportunities', as alternatives to search for. But the opposition is unreal. Constraints and opportunities define each other, neither knowable without the other. Do you search the haystack or seek the needle? In either case you find mostly hay that you don't want, but must still inspect for needles.

There is likely to be more serious tension between the choice of valuable and regular causes, since they seem inconveniently unwilling to coincide, and are unlikely to do so if 'valuable' is defined as 'freely chosen'. People's free choices may of course show regular patterns; but many valuers of freedom give special attention to exceptions to the pattern, so that even a search for 'valuable regulars' may seem to them to be a contradiction.

Among modern philosophers of history, only Dray and Morton White have given much attention to these problems of selection. In *Foundations of Historical Knowledge* (Harper and Row, 1965) White describes very well how historians must make valuations in choosing things to be explained, and in choosing their causes and effects. White calls these valuations 'extrahistorical'. He means that they cannot de derived from the historical facts; he does not mean that valuations are outside the investigator's business as historian. Among other things White sees the historian's values determining his notion of 'normal', and his selection, therefore, of causes because they are 'abnormal'. This is indeed one, but is only one of the jumble of selective principles at work (and often at war) in most historians' minds. In many passages of rapid social change, so much is new that abnormality would be a capacious net that caught too much. Often, too, abnormalities have importance in some conditions that they would not have in others. As suggested by the example of boss-rule, either a preference for irregular causes or a preference for regular ones may yield useless or unsatisfying explanations. An invention or a new law, or a general's single brilliant departure from Clausewitz's principles, or some spontaneous unexpected riot, may have important effects just because, and only if, everyone else's behavior is predictably regular.

Irregularity may appeal to those who like their selectors to appear value-free. But in social life, as White argues, such a principle can seldom be based exclusively on observed regularities, and usually has to rest also upon an element of valued 'normality'. White does not extend his argument to other social sciences, but it applies truly enough to the 'engineering' majority of them. As a method of letting valuation assist selection, a search for abnormalities does not appear to have any special social or scientific advantages over other methods – for example, over the selection of 'intrinsically valuable' causes and effects, or causes fertile in by-products or futures, or opportunities to manipulate social processes.

The same search for opportunities can organize the explanation of quite determined effects. We have rough expectations, either general or particular to the time and system, of where and when and for whom such opportunities are most likely to arise. The 'manipulative' explanation of what is judged after inquiry to have been an unmanipulable process, is one which closes one by one the 'opportunities for opportunity', the chances for choice thought likeliest or most desirable. Such an explanation must be organized by a mixture of scientific expectation and political intent. Men of different faith or interest will disagree, as noticed earlier, as to which were the desirable locations for opportunities. They will disagree in judging which *were* opportunities and which (for reasonable ordinary men) were not. They will disagree about where to go and when to stop: about which causal chains to search, how far and in which directions, for links which were choices.

Thus Collingwood's principle does not replace the rules employed by the explainers of imperialism, it merely introduces and applauds them. A vast amount of social action is, by few or many people, deliberate, even if less often what most of us would call 'free' or what Collingwood would call 'rational'. To narrow the search to a search for choices is not to narrow it far, until one adds 'for important choices', which adds another to the tasks of valuation. The various attempts to avoid this last by specifying 'important for what' never remove the problem far. To choose causes for their fertility is to value their other effects as well as the one you began with; it is not to avoid valuation.

A determined scientist may well respond by insisting that his own search is for patterns of uniformity in the 'free' choices themselves; and then, for their correlation with patterns of the circumstances in which the choices are made. The sciences may well sort themselves out according to the extent to which strict enough uniformities are indeed present in the behavior which they respectively study. But wherever observation reinforces the probability that they are not, then a determined limitation of selection to 'uniformities only' may be simply stupid. It will certainly not build a 'regular' science upon irregular subject-matter. What it may do instead, in the worst cases, is to replace the intelligent engineering principles of selection which seem right for the study of irregular systems, by principles whose application to those systems is irrational.

For example: avoid socially-valued identities, lest you be accused of valuing them yourself. For the same reason, do not report qualities or quantities whose recognition or estimation does require an element of your own valuation. Choose classes and identities for their regular relations, but suspend this rule whenever it would require valuation to classify and identify cases; whenever that danger threatens, choose other classes and identities (regardless of regular relations) for the operational certainty with which they can be employed. Avoid reporting things which are unique to one or few systems, lest you be accused of writing history, or of untheoretical empiricism. *Some* common qualities always occur in otherwise-dissimilar systems. Report those alone, even though *for each particular system* this produces a random selection of facts and relations which constitute *neither* sufficient law-based explanations *nor* intelligently chosen, socially useful ones.

The alternative to this folly is seldom a blind retreat to art and superstition. But any historian or general sociologist or political scientist who values the form and generality of scientific statements more than their useful correspondence to valuable facts may do best to turn to some branch of some discipline in which the two are less at war: to econometrics or demography, perhaps, or physiology or experimental psychology.

These very general observations might be referred to any number of illustrations and cases. The following sections offer two examples only. First, cannot functional analysis substitute purely scientific for partly political principles of selection? Then in a very different case, is detachment easier in explaining the ideas of remote or uncontroversial societies?

2. *Explaining functions*

The various usages of 'function' all seem to include the notion of an activity or effect which continues because its causes continue. Durkheim made clear the functional analyst's duties:

When, then, the explanation of a social phenomenon is undertaken, we must seek separately the efficient cause which produces it and the function it fulfils.[3]

This suggests that functional analysis should deal in two-step explanations which answer two questions: 'what caused the things which in their turn caused a system to exist or to persist?' R. K. Merton usually neglects the first question, but insists that the second is a question about 'objective consequences' whether or not 'intended' by the actors or 'called for' by the system:

Functions are those observed consequences which make for the adaptation or adjustment of a given system; and *dysfunctions*, those observed consequences which lessen the adaptation or adjustment of the system. There is also the empirical possibility of non-functional consequences, which are simply irrelevant to the system under consideration.[4]

These seem clear instructions if I approach a social fact and ask 'which of its *effects* must I report?' I must report whichever effects are part of the adaptation or adjustment of the system. But if instead I ask the other question – 'of this fact or effect, which *causes* should I report?' – then functional analysts are unhelpful. Neither Durkheim nor Merton offers rules for the selection of causal explanations, rules which might replace the personal valuations which helped to select the explanations of imperialism. They recommend societal facts rather than the facts peddled by other disciplines, and Merton is alert for reciprocal causal relations. That seems to be all.

A school educates children. The school may be seen as a system for functional analysis, or it may be seen as part of the structure of a larger social system, performing functions for that system. In either case the structure of the school is one among the conditions necessary for the performance of its functions, but is certainly not the only or sufficient condition. It may sometimes be convenient to distinguish 'origin and development' from 'continuing conditions and present effects', but the distinction is crude and often misleads. An investigator can relate the school's functions to the structure of the school, to the institutional complex of which it is part, to the demand for education, to the structured roles and expectations of parents and teachers, to conflicts about those roles and expectations, to the interests and actions of ruling individuals or classes, to necessary conditions in culture and human nature, and to innumerable other connections which link educational processes as causes or effects to other features of the whole social system, and to its history.

If a functional analyst seeks the causes of the school's performance, he can search any sector of its necessary conditions. He can follow chains of cause and interdependence outward into the social system or backward in time, just as historians do. Just as historians must, he must decide how far to follow chains of either kind. Except for some prejudice against temporal sequences, his rules say no more than historians' rules do, about how far he should go, or in which directions. He may be guided by his values, or by other people's values expressed as consumers' demands or disciplinary conventions; or by what for any one system may prove to be an irrational preference for whichever links and chains recur in most similar systems. As in historical explanation, no choice (including the last) will have quite the same political implications or uses or persuasions as any other.

There have been many attempts to rescue the investigator from these awful moral responsibilities. Personally, I do not want him rescued. In any case it is specially difficult to exorcise valuation from functional social analysis; besides this neglected need for rules to select causes, there is the much-debated difficulty of specifying the system or equilibrium which shall serve as the functional effect.

In any institution or social system, many things occur, big and little, intended and unintended, which are differently advantageous to different people. Which effects – and whose satisfactions – represent 'the system'? Functional analyses are all too likely to differ with the different analysts' valuations of the interests which respectively suffer and prosper, endure or change. So functional analysts feel the familiar need for some more objective organizer, to replace their own values in selecting reportable functions. Some have hoped that a few comparatively abstract qualities might be disciplined for this purpose. For example, 'integration' and 'persistence' are present in all groups and systems, and it might be possible to index them. Functions within a system could then be sorted out according to their causal contributions to these measurable effects.

I hope later to show that the investigator's values would still have to play a technical part in the connection of cause to effect, or structure to function, in the first place. But besides such neglected difficulties, there are already more familiar ones. How can 'persistence' be measured? Adaptation may be necessary for persistence – some systems persist only if structural change is flexible and continuous. When is 'adaptation of old system' really 'failure and replacement by new system'? In more archaic language, when does a quantitative become a qualitative change? In practice we choose some social features that we fear or value or find convenient to measure, if they persist we declare that the system persists, and we require the rest of 'the system' so to adapt as to enable the survival of the qualities thus valued as important. An American social system has persisted since 1607 or 1776 or 1866 because its constant qualities impress us; or we are so pleased or upset by the advent of polyglot immigration or motor cars or anomie or other-direction that we identify some break, some change of system along the way, dated according to taste – according, that is, to our taste in persistent qualities. Any index of persistence must value some social goods and discount others.

So also with 'integration'. There can be no value-free rule to guide the choice of the frequency of (which?) social contacts, the effectiveness of communications (between whom, about what?), the uniformity of (whose?) norms (about what?), the comparative importance of voluntary and coerced participation, the comparative importance of the social as against the legal rejection of deviates, the anger expressed in riot as against the anger effectively repressed by fear. Any index of integration is an index of somebody's values. It need not necessarily indicate his social values. He may index what he thinks measurable, 'value-free', neglected by his competitors or impressive to his reviewers, but these values have neither scientific nor social advantages over the social values – justice or lovingkindness or equality, for example – which might be built by other investigators into other indexes.

Thus qualities like persistence and integration require systems of values – or sheer caprice – for their abstraction from systems of society. But if not neutral, might they not at least be consistent? Does an eccentric measure matter, as long as it is used consistently in all cases, to permit reliable repetition and comparison, albeit of wilfully chosen features of societies? But for scientific purposes persistence and integration have limited interest since they index or control little else in society; and from any valuer's point of view they are like plumbing and police forces – they are consistent with all varieties of social condition from good to horrible. Within any social system they are of utterly different interest and profit to rich and poor, master and servant, bureaucrat and bohemian, winner and loser. They may usefully preserve societies or uselessly arrest or calcify them. If these are to be the qualities which replace the investigator's personal values as organizers of functional knowledge, if they are to be the terminal consequences which sort out significant from insignificant functions, if they are to determine the only permissible destination of reportable causal chains (though still saying nothing about the length or directions from which the chains converge), then functional analysts will be valuing with a capricious and erratic vengeance. It will usually be, as has often been remarked, a conservative vengeance.

The most-quoted defence of functional analysis, as value-free in the sense of being a neutral method available to any ideology, is R. K. Merton's in *Social Theory and Social Structure* (rev. ed. 1957, The Free Press, Glencoe), pp. 37–54. The method, Merton argues, is apt for studying both functions and dysfunctions. Conservatives can concentrate on functions, to illustrate the good harmony of society and the necessity of its established institutions. Radicals can concentrate on dysfunctions, on the strains and tensions which show society to be both imperfect (thus justifying change) and inefficient (thus making change objectively likely).

The shortcomings of this defence seem to me, as to many others,[5] to be principally three.

First, the good and bad things in society have an almost random relation to their functional characteristics. There can be integrated, perfectly functional systems of tyranny or inequality or exploitation. The radical does not necessarily want to change something because it is dysfunctional, because it engenders strain or weakens some system's persistence. He just as often wants to replace one perfectly functional social mechanism by another, because he thinks the other would be more just or pleasing or originative of further change. The conservative does not always want to preserve things because they function well; he often wants to preserve things, for the values they serve, in spite of the fact that they function very badly. Neither values the processes of society chiefly or always for their functional contribution to society's persistence.

Second, radicals and conservatives have strong, if different, interests in change; and the understanding of social change can sometimes be translated into functional language, but really only after the event – after the changes have first been understood and explained by conventional historical methods. The understanding may gain little and lose much in the translation. As will be argued later, the springs of change are certainly not all understandable as dysfunctions. Technical and economic innovations, for example, arise in perfectly functional 'going' systems, as gratuitous improvements, as often as they arise as problem-solving efforts to cope with scarcity or conflict. A large proportion of social change in the modern world arises from the intercourse (in war, goods, skills, technologies and ideas) *between* systems. If some of the causes of change are external, and if its internal causes include functional, dysfunctional and non-functional features, and if the understanding of change requires the study of processes through time, studies of which periodic instantaneous analyses are only one and often a weak variant, then it seems absurdly unpromising to try to cram all dynamic analysis into a structural-functional model, however refined or reformed.

As a third defence, Merton has insisted that 'the system', meaning a whole social system, need not be the only terminal consequence by which functional analysts distinguish reportable causal chains or reciprocations. Within systems, there are sub-systems and groups and individuals; things can be functional or dysfunctional for them, too. This last defence is the purest common sense, but self-devastating. Once the analysis of society becomes an analysis of all or any patterns of interest and self-service of all or any groups and classes and individuals, then the last distinguishing characteristic, the last selective principle, of structural-functional analysis disappears and only its language remains. It becomes, as Merton rightly argues, available to all ideologies; only its vocabulary distinguishes it from history and economics, and the functional purpose of its vocabulary has disappeared. The effect of a social process upon a group may be to give the group less or more of money, power, joy, dignity, long life, righteousness, or any of innumerable selfish or selfless satisfactions. To distribute these as 'functional', 'dysfunctional' and 'non-functional' either for the whole system or for the recipient group, is a procedure whose scientific promise is obscure. Many groups and individuals, considered as systems, may have no desire to persist, and may not direct their actions to the end of persisting, if to persist means to stay as they are. Functional effects, as Merton insists, need not be the satisfactions of felt desires: but what is to be the dialogue between the individual's and the analyst's valuation of the effects of structure that converge upon the individual's experience? By this departure from 'whole system' analysis, Merton is driven to begin again where Bentham began, defying a century's criticism of Bentham's calculus:

This more exacting form of functional analysis includes, not only a study of the *functions* of existing social structures, but also a study of their *dysfunctions* for diversely situated individuals, subgroups or social strata, and the more inclusive society. It provisionally assumes, as we shall see, that when *the net balance of the aggregate of consequences* of an existing social structure is clearly dysfunctional, there develops a strong and insistent pressure for change.*[6]

This language will not avoid, but may unhelpfully obscure, the investigator's problems of valuation. As will be argued later, the connection of structure to function must still be done by historical methods; it will be done better if all those methods are available, rather than a ritually restricted few; it may need an enlarged, but not a ritually restricted language for its expression. Except to expose or conceal it, the choice of language will not affect the work done by the investigator's values.

* What if the solitary beneficiary of everyone else's dysfunctions happens to have the only gun? As in Haiti? Or a monopoly of education, or wealth, or religious authority?

The organizing effect of one variety of functional method was demonstrated in a recent argument about the 'functional necessity' of social inequality. One exchange between Wilbert E. Moore and Melvin Tumin may serve to illustrate the nature of this extensive controversy.

Each investigator declares his values. Moore does not favor equal social rewards for unequal work. He thinks rewards should be unequal as social contributions are unequal. Tumin would reward conscientious and bad work unequally, but not contributions of work which are made unequal by unwilled heredity, or social scarcity, or custom.

Each investigator, in order to assert that his own values are practicable, chooses a different set of causes for existing American inequalities. Not unnaturally Moore chooses the unmanipulable causes, to forge the conservative's unbreakable chain; they are also causes whose by-products nobody would wish to do without, so they discourage surgery. Tumin chooses manipulable causes, though he finds them deep in most existing societies – he asserts causal chains of typically radical length.

To display these different causes, each adopts a different method of analysis, and a good deal of the argument is about the methods of analysis. In this the parties differ. For Moore, there is perfect concordance between his valuation of the structural-functional method and his valuation of inequality. Tumin, working under a local hegemony of structural-functional disciplinary rules, argues against them, but argues as far as possible on their own assumptions and in their own language – only thus can converts usually be attracted from within closed or self-sufficient systems of thought.

Beginning with some corrections of his earlier views, Moore argued:

It was admittedly wrong to say that all rich rewards were for helping to maintain social systems, or that the rich would always form distinct social classes. Innovators usually get extra pay, even though they help to change social systems. Unequally paid people do sometimes fail to form separate social classes; but they are not for that reason any less unequal. I am not arguing that societies necessarily require class systems, only that they necessarily require unequal pay.

The causes of unequal rewards are two things which no society could do without: (1) the division of labor and (2) the need for incentives.

It is because of his quality, efficiency and achievements that a man gets a good job; after that, it is because of the social importance of his good job that he gets good pay. You could not reward *only* the different conscientiousness with which people do their jobs, because conscientiousness cannot be reliably judged. You could not pay unequal rewards in esteem only, because most people could not be trained to be that unselfish, and because managerial people can usually fiddle other advantages for themselves anyway . . . ('But Some Are More Equal than Others', *American Sociological Review*, 28, 1, February 1963, pp. 13–18, tr. H. Stretton).

There follows more argument about the injustice of equal pay even if it were practicable. Melvin Tumin replied –

There are not two but at least five causes of inequality:
(1) Except for the different roles of husbands, wives and children, most job-differences merely specialize labor, without making one job harder than another or giving one any authority over others. This distribution of duties can be achieved without unequal rewards; but in some societies unequal rewards are nevertheless given.
(2) People, and also jobs, differ in their intrinsic characteristics. The people with particular skills go into the jobs which require those skills. This could be done without ranking either the people or the jobs. Most societies however do rank both the people and the jobs and reward them unequally. This cannot be generally necessary, because each society ranks them somewhat inconsistently, and different societies sometimes rank them quite differently.
(3) Some people behave themselves and others don't. Good people have to get more rewards than bad people get, if society is to survive. This causes personal inequalities but in advanced societies it does not sort people into social classes.
(4) People and jobs get ranked and rewarded according to somebody's valuation of their contribution to society. (4a) Society needs shared values and ideals, so it rewards people who specially strengthen or exemplify its ideals. Some such rewards are necessary for social cohesion, but the particular ideals to be rewarded, and the type and scale and social effect of the rewards, can vary widely from one society to another. (4b) Some divisions of labor do cause unavoidable inequalities of authority, and probably of pay. Some men have to organize and co-ordinate the work of others. If some skills happen to be scarce, incentives may be necessary to get the scarce people to do the skilled jobs. But in their ways of indoctrinating people to expect that managers and unusually skilled persons should get rich rewards, societies are already internally inconsistent, they already differ from each other, and they could imaginably vary much more.

(5) When people get money or authority, whether or not they get it for some socially useful reason, they then use it to get much more money, authority and other rewards, for themselves or for their friends and relations – rewards which serve no socially useful purposes at all. (*ibid.*, pp. 19–26. Same translator.)

If these are the causes of inequality, they support a number of conclusions.

In one sense, most of these few causes are manipulable, and so therefore are many of the types and degrees of inequality itself; but only in the utopian sense, that a society can be imagined, as productive of both economic and social goods, but without generating great inequalities. Tumin's explanation of inequality was *not* organized (as for example Marx's or Hobson's was) to reveal also the moments at which, the methods by which, or the agents by whom, reform might be attempted.

Second, Moore's structural-functional method does seem to select (from the countless candidates) only those causes of inequality *which also cause the social system to persist or to disintegrate*. In a generous view, his explanation of inequality is organized either by his valuation of inequality, or as a by-product of his explanation of the persistence of the social system. Less charitably, one might suppose it to be a by-product of efforts to establish certain disciplinary rules either for their own sake or for their supposed heuristic promise. But there is no need to guess so impertinently at the author's motives, for any one of the four will discover knowledge of interest chiefly to conservatives, and organize it for use (if at all) by conservatives only. I do not mean to suggest that Tumin is right in thinking equality possible; only that if it *were* possible, the possibility could never be discovered by Moore's methods. On this point Tumin needs no translation –

It must be clear by now that the criterion of social survival is useful only as a beginning touchstone for social analysis. Little is learned about human society by asking what is required for minimum social survival . . .

Following another line of analysis, we must ask, "Under what conditions do we get more and less of various forms of inequality, and why, and with what consequences for whom?" If we put our questions that way, we shall not be beguiled into seeking rational accounts for the existence and continuity of various cultural forms, most of which seem to be accidental products of human social history which arise very much by chance, and persist often simply by virtue of impersonal social drift, or inertia, or by the contrivances of various elites who find the social situation to their liking and wish to preserve it.

Some 'human social historians' might see their subject as less accidental but few would quarrel with Tumin's conclusion, except to point out that his conclusions must remain as utopian and unusable as Moore's, as long as his method remains as unhistorical as Moore's.

This sketch has become unjust to both contenders. Recent years have seen a widespread repentance of functionalists. Tumin's party is on the way to majority. But much of the repentance is vague, no more than a pious change of aspiration. Static systems may be out, but the statics tool-kit is yet to be replaced. What use are refined methods of studying covariance if the new subject of change gives little promise of obeying 'laws of change'? If not regular functional relations, or regular recurrences, or regular tendencies of change, what else is a regular scientist to look for? There is some rueful acknowledgment of the poverty of much fashionable sociological purpose and method in Moore's presidential address to the American Sociological Association, published in the *American Sociological Review*, 31, 6, of December, 1966:

It is this addiction to discontent and to the search for a better future that I want to explore here, particularly as this activity of the laity relates to the enterprise of sociology as the generalizing science of man's social behavior. Have we, in short, any obligation as social scientists to start taking account not only of the changeful quality of social life but also of the fact that some portion of that change is deliberate?

1966 seems a late year in which to 'start' considering that question of obligation. Moore's argument seems to imply that sociologists are now at last driven to it not by their moral senses, but by the technical inadequacy of the methods available to any scientist who seeks (in generality and value-freedom) to evade that moral question.

3. *Understanding strangers and ideas*

Must an investigator's values do the same work when he investigates ideas to be explained by relation to one another, or societies remote from the concerns of his own time and place?

There is some reason for putting these two questions together. If the native investigator of his own society can use many formal, quantitative methods, and talk confidently of causes, this is often because the meanings of action in his society are so familiar to him that he sees no need to begin by 'understanding' them. The initial tasks of understanding language and social rules and the meanings of actions become more obviously necessary the less familiar the society to be studied. Thus the study of deviance at home may look very statistical, while the study of deviance in primitive societies may consist largely in learning to understand those societies' expectations of conformity. In the end, the same choices may have to be made between the important and the unimportant conditions for, or causes of, action; but along the way, the investigator of unfamiliar societies may sometimes develop more diffidence or sensitivity in his efforts first to understand them. Anticipating some arguments which have to be repeated for other purposes later, it may be asked whether political detachment and a greater need to 'understand' are likely to affect the way in which an investigator's initial purposes and values direct his choice of explanations. Suitable examples can be found in modern histories of medieval Europe, which include much functional, as well as sequential, explanation.

There are obvious ways in which present ideology can still affect the explanation of events or functions in remote societies. First, directly: some of the same problems may appear to exist in both societies. Second, the problems of past and present may be related to each other by analogy or descent. In medieval society the Marxist historian does not find the crisis of capitalism, but he does find its origins, and also an analysable economic system, hierarchical relations of production, class conflicts, and useful examples of the economic determination of social change. Conservative historians may take similar advantage of similar material. In explanations of serfdom, the 'bond' has different attractions and implications according to whether it appears as a chain from serf to soil, a chain from serf to master, or with utter respectability as one of 'the bonds of society'. One historian explains it by its function for the owner of the means of production; another explains that the serf accepted it in the first place because it gave him valuable rights to land, food, shelter and protection at a time when freedom was more a state of exposure than a set of rights; another explains its persistence as a sociologist might, by reference to its function for the persistence of the social system as a whole. Each explanation, intentionally or not, is likely to imply a different valuation of the modern as well as the medieval balances of order and liberty, stability and change, share of work and share of product.

Present concerns may influence the explanation of remote events in a third way, if the remote events are studied by methods which were really designed to cope with present problems. The historian of 'the origins and growth of the present' carries his analysis of causes as far as the points or levels at which he believes that present changes or continuities have been or ought to be determined. Not all historians of the origin and growth of the present, of course, agree about these points and levels. One terminates his explanations at the study of the personal skills and ambitions of political leaders; another follows chains of cause and consequence into electoral behavior or the standing rules of the political system; another relates action to what he may see as an autonomous history of ideas; others connect political and social events to social structure, or to developments within the economic system. But between them the historians of the origins of the present are nowadays so numerous that their conventions of explanation, born of their interests in present systems, may tend to become the general conventions of the historical trade. Nobody really expects that a Marxist's first questions about medieval society will be: what conceptual scheme does *this* society seem to require for its analysis? What were the determinants peculiar to *it*, what were *its* springs of change, to what points therefore should I press my explanations? On the contrary, everybody expects before the Marxist starts that his explanations of events in *any* society are likely to extend all the way to some terminus in that society's productive system. Similarly the free-willingest of liberals may become reluctant to limit his explanations of medieval wars, as he used to limit them, to diplomacy and family interest, since it became conventionally unsatisfactory to explain modern wars that way. After Britain got a civil service, Tout started to investigate medieval administration. After Tocqueville analysed the bonds of society in modern France, tenures and knighthoods and serfdom were discovered to have been bonds of medieval societies. After Marx had published an elaborate analysis of the growth of its own gravediggers within capitalism, some historians began to test his earlier guess that an analogous pregnancy had expanded the feudal economy. Not only moral judgments but also explanations of the conduct of King John and King Richard III have changed with changing valuations of military success, personal morality and administrative skill in modern government.

Not that most applications of present methods to past societies are stupidly mechanical. In a historian's mind and in his choice of methods, past and present prompt and question each other as in any comparative study; such promptings get the historian started more often than they tell him where to stop. This is certainly true of some influences of a more general kind. Marx and Tocqueville are often taken as exemplifying distinct scholarly traditions, searching societies respectively for the sources of conflict and for the sources of consensus. The same pair might also epitomize the narrative search, for moments of revolutionary or qualitative change in one tradition, and in the other for continuities. All four of these general attitudes of expectation and quest could be found at work in the study of medieval history, each after its development in more modern studies.

In any of these ways – in the search for origins and analogies and old solutions to recurring problems, in the use of methods devised for one society to investigate others unlike it – the sort of extrinsic, present purposes and values which guided the explanation of imperialism may also, strongly or faintly, affect the explanation of apparently remote and unprovocative events. Insofar as he lets this happen mechanically or obtusely, an investigator may be accused of one form or another of a sin denounced in *The Whig Interpretation of History* by Herbert Butterfield, who thought such present interests must distort perception of the past, unless restrained by a humble attitude to the past. Butterfield's distinctions have to be subtle. It would be nonsense to expect men of the twentieth century to put other than 'twentieth-century questions' to the past. But questions may be in different degrees limiting and directive to their answers, or they may be hesitant, inquisitive, open. 'What did Norman knights think about the class structure?' should shed, at the very least, either its first or its three last words.

Whatever the force of Butterfield's argument there are certainly historians who work as if they believe in it – whose attitudes to past societies seem to be as uninterfering, as merely observant as they can be made by a sophisticated consciousness of Whiggish sin and its insidious disguises. Many of them are also reluctant to write about causes. The relation between these two self-denials seems as often temperamental as logical. It may partly be that causal analysis was not an eleventh-century preoccupation. The humble scholar wants to find what were the preoccupations of the people of that century, and when he finds them, wants to enter into and understand them on their own terms, rather than 'explain their occurrence' in terms that would satisfy the philistine curiosity of another age. The curiosity of another age is acceptable – why else would it have historians? But the philistinism may consist in refusing answers unless they come in modern categories – state and society, national and international, rational and irrational, religious and political and economic – categories which may hinder understanding of a life in which they were scarcely recognized. There is also something cocksure about announcing causes, especially causes which people of that age were unaware of. While the social scientist tries to understand people better than they do themselves, the diffident historian is more ambitious – to understand them as well as they understand themselves. Examples of the deliberate attempt can be found in R. G. Collingwood's *Roman Britain*, in C. V. Wedgwood's books about England in the seventeenth century, or in medieval histories like those of Helen Waddell or – for different reasons – Richard Southern. More historians than these, of course, make the attempt. Perhaps all historians do; these four, like Butterfield, announced their intentions formally.

Can the historian enlist the values and preoccupations of the society he studies, to organize his study of that society? If he can, should he?

At least three reasons why he should have been suggested. First, pleasure. He may simply be absorbed by medieval scholars or juvenile delinquents or Polynesian islanders. One anthropologist says 'When I say I love the Polynesians, it's an active verb'. But these, motives of much research in many fields, need not distinguish one from another.

Second, there is an argument at once like and unlike the familiar argument for a general social science. Native historians and sociologists of their own societies, like Freud, are said to be ill-placed to distinguish constants from accidents, universals from peculiars, in their too-familiar subject-matter: their studies are apt to have the limitations as well as the advantages of introspection. Not only may the insider tend to generalize his results wrongly to the world outside his sample, but he may misunderstand the internal arrangements of the sample itself because he may not discern which of its parts are specific to that system, which of them would arise from the structural necessities of a numerous class of systems, and which belong to some unchanging residue of human nature. If Freud had analysed motherless orphans or some wartime generation which grew up without fathers, and found the same characteristics as he found in his well-mothered and fathered Viennese patients, he might not have attributed the characteristics of either to their mothering and fathering.

Satisfactory 'controls' are rare in social science. Experienced imagination is often more helpful than particular comparison, and the language of imagination more precise than the language that 'isolates and controls variables.' A direct comparison of the profit motive in modern society with its absence from some monastic economy would rest on absurd assumptions about the identity of all the other aspects of the two societies; it would certainly break all Butterfield's rules. But an understanding – a proper understanding – of life in some of the more productive and inventive monastic economies is still useful knowledge for whoever wants to know how inherent the profit motive is, or how North-European or how class-related, or how necessary to innovation; or what, in what conditions, might imaginably be produced without it. Even this is too mechanical a comparison. It is better to put the argument in entirely general terms: whoever has studied man in the greatest variety of cultures and social systems ought to have the best general judgment of man's social capacities and – at least until tomorrow – his incapacities. This should make him the ablest student of any one society. He will have more questions to ask; he should know how universal or how unusual the answers are; he should be better able to imagine what might be achieved by what kinds of organization, and what on the other hand can only be achieved (if at all) by inventing what has not been done before, or not in like circumstances, or not without intolerable costs.

Is this just the familiar case for a general social theory whose categories can comprehend all the significant varieties of social system and experience? That, surely, is how to prepare for controlled factorial comparison and for scientific generalization just this sort of general knowledge of the range of social variation? For reasons that must wait, I doubt it; the subject is too complex, the regularities too unreliable, and the study too dependent upon whose values organize it. But certainly few gains, whether discoveries of regularities or enrichments of imagination by experience, will come from merely Whiggish, crudely present-centered studies of past or strange societies. When Macaulay searched the seventeenth century for the origins of whatever interested him in the nineteenth, he missed much that the seventeenth century might have taught him about whatever social and intellectual capacities of man chanced to be unexercised in early Victorian India and London. Butterfield and Miss Wedgwood recommend an opposite approach. The scholar should not search strange societies for their differences from his own society, nor for their similarities to it. He should not ask only how they perform those functions which are performed in his own or in all societies, nor only how they approach the problems unsolved in his own society. Instead, he should approach the strangers with an open curiosity, almost as a supplicant for membership, and give their preoccupations equality with his own in organizing his study of them.

This is still, in a roundabout way, a 'present-centered' interest in the past. Insofar as the historian is stimulating the imagination he brings to the problems of his own day, even his humility could fairly be described as instrumental. But that is scarcely true of a third reason for deference to the values of remote societies: the idea that for their own sakes they are as well worth understanding as one's own.

The advertisements of modern social science are not likely to attract many recruits to the profession as a contemplative one. But there remain a few contemplative historians. Apart from pleasure (which curiously is seldom argued for) what are the rewards of the contemplative life? *That* is a Whiggish, present-directed question. Contemplation is not a way to rewards, but a use for lives – for your own, and for the others' lives you contemplate. You may study men, especially unfamiliar or remarkable men, in order to know more about Man; more about yourself perhaps; perhaps more about the squalor or divinity of your nature, or about the nature of divinity.

Anselm, like you, was a man. *How* like you? If you can understand him, will you perceive a richer nature in yourself, or a poorer nature but enlightened by a more deeply-felt humility? Whoever knows Anselm is in some way a richer man than before, but only if he feels and understands as Anselm did; not insofar as he performs modern operations upon Anselm, classifies him into modern analyses, 'explains' him as a member of a class or an effect of a cause. If Anselm can be disposed of in those ways there was, for purposes of contemplation or self-knowledge, no need to study him at all. There is as good material here and now, the material on which the classifications and analyses were based. Disposed of in that way, Anselm may serve to generalize or limit our modern observations, but he won't enrich them.

Nor are other souls the only objects worth contemplating. Other values, other ideas, other societies, may offer similar rewards, if they are studied with the same receptivity, to the scholar who does not hope to fool about with his own world, but only to reflect upon his relation to it, his identity in it, what conduct in it is to be regarded as virtuous; or to guess how his image of god is refracted by the local circumstances of his material life. Such a scholar may well use modern techniques to find out how Anselm lived, what he thought and wrote, at what dates, under what discomforts – but when the scholar has uncovered the thing he came to contemplate, he has to empty his mind of as many as possible of the assumptions and habits peculiar to his own generation, while he contemplates it. After all, one purpose of his contemplation is that it may free him further from his bondage to these local habits and assumptions. The rules of science may have to go out with the rest. Rather than work of equal use to all, the exercise is likely to produce work uniquely personal. If such a scholar exists in 'pure' form, I think he is the limiting case: the one who may discover most with the least direct organization of his work by the rules of his profession or the preoccupations of his present society. He is also the least likely to be accepted as a social scientist by other social scientists. Paradoxically, he may approach nearest to their ideal of scientific detachment; but it is not moral neutrality that gets him there.

All three of these interests – delight in medieval men, an interest in the range of man's social capacities, and the contemplation of Man

himself through others' examples and understandings of him –
seem to be present in Richard Southern's *The Making of the Middle
Ages*. So also, of course, are plenty of conventional modern interests
– the mechanics of medieval societies have to be made clear to
modern readers, by explanations that do not differ in principle from
Marx's. But inasmuch as these three 'unmodern' interests are
present, what sort of explanations do they prompt?

They include the fitting of ideas to each other and into systems of
thought, sometimes by other logic than ours; the description, therefore, of those other logics. They include the recognition of affinities –
of a nascent humanism, for example, discernible independently in
politics and painting and theology. This understanding and relation
of ideas is more than a descriptive exercise in 'the history of ideas'.
It is a method of identifying a society and its principles of unity, a
method apparently different from any mechanistic study of society's
causal origins or division-of-labor integration, though still not without parallels among the more 'understanding' methods of functional
sociology. In one sense not necessarily tied to any idealist philosophy
a society is defined, and its unity exists, insofar as it is comprehended
and articulated in the minds of its members. A peasant may live in a
society as old as he can remember and as broad as he can walk, a
society whose principle of unity is the division of labor between
summer and winter, man and wife, cultivator and blacksmith.
Within walking distance, feeding and clothing himself in the same
way off the same land under the same laws, a scholar may live in a
society as old as writing and as extensive as Christendom, a society
whose principles of unity may be the authority of the Church and
the order of the Empire and may include the harmonies which
Aristotle laid down for works of art and God laid down as Laws of
Nature. A society gets that name only insofar as the various experiences it offers to an individual member impress him as *related*; it is
within his mind that the relations are perceived or made, so it is only
by exploring his mind that an outsider may perceive the more
important internal relations of a strange society, or indeed discover
whether 'a society' is there at all. A traveller after all, scarcely speaking the language of the territory he travels, can enjoy all the mundane
benefits of law and order and the production and exchange of
necessaries, and still feel entirely a stranger, not knowing in what
sense if any the strange land is inhabited by 'a society'. In some

sense, certainly, as its material culture tells him; but for all he knows he may be travelling down the Rhine, each port the outpost of a separate state; or each town may be a sufficient society, conducting foreign trade and foreign relations with neighbors whom it finds as strange as the traveller does; or all may be part of some universal empire, in social as well as political fact. Language, faith, a sense of community, and the writ of government may not be coextensive; each may run less far or farther than the next. I suspect that the most complete description, analysis and 'explanation' of a strange land by the more mechanistic methods of political and economic science would leave Southern feeling a stranger still, in a land as unknown as before.

The political and economic scientists in their turn, if they were ever to read Southern's precise account of the significance which the notion of freedom had for some serfs, or of Anselm's particular mutation of the image of the ladder to heaven, might dismiss it as quaintly antiquarian or indulge it as literary relaxation – might fail to notice in it a nearer approach than their own, to their own ideal of scientific objectivity. There is, as has been suggested, a paradox, which may be expressed in various ways. This near-perfect understanding, which leaves its object comparatively undistorted by the observer, is achieved by just those humanists who most insist that their work is a moral exercise; it is achieved not by detachment from the 'object' studied, but by moral and humane respect for the people studied. Scientists who on the other hand insist on abstracting, classifying, indexing and comparing – precisely the activities which make valuation inescapable – are determined as far as possible to choose *without* choosing, to 'evaluate' without valuing. Or again: objectivity is not an unreasonable aim for anyone who is content that his work should be useless in any mundane sense, yet moral neutrality is rarely among the ideals of such people; while scientists who insist that their work be useful – that it has no other purpose whatever than to be useful – also insist that all thought of its uses should be excluded from the process of inquiry.

Values can be objects of research (which all scientists approve) or its organizers (which many disapprove). The distinction is clear in work on unfamiliar societies, but easily obscured in work on familiar societies whose values may be much the same as the investigator's. If societies 'possessed values' unanimously there might seem to be no problem in the latter case – it could not matter whether the organizers of research were the investigator's or the society's values if the two were identical. But the investigator who wants to study values as objects does not mean that he wants to surrender the organization of his research to them. He appears to mean something which is clearer when the object-values are unfamiliar. One can distinguish a few of Anselm's values from Southern's and more of both from the values prevalent in Southern's twentieth-century society. The purist presumably wants *none* of the three to interfere with Southern's study of the first of them. If some impregnation is unavoidable, he wants full disclosure, so that readers may discount whatever values are present. He will not admit that the problem is really to choose which values will guide which parts of the investigation most fruitfully – and 'fruitfully' calls for a mixture of moral and technical valuation, unlikely to be unanimous.

Southern at least knows what he is doing. His own ideal of objectivity might be summarily expressed in advice both moral and technical: 'Stop shoving people into pigeon-holes and *watch* them; shut up for once, and *listen* to them.' The aim is still more than a photograph, and far from 'value-free'. Selection is at work from the beginning. Abstraction and interpretation are only deferred, to wait upon better understanding. If a similar spirit of humanism is discernible, though unremarked by them, in both theologians and painters, it takes abstraction, valuation and choice to recognize it. The selection is not Anselm's. Nor is it dictated to Southern by British Television and the London *Times*. It is his own, a response to understanding both societies, and his book is only as subtle *and original* as the values that organized it. Does this mean that it can be useful only to those who already shared Southern's values before they read it? Not quite: the book is among other things, as most social science ought to be, an effort at persuasion as well as discovery. To scoff at this, is probably not to notice which parts of anthropology and sociology are imperfect, ritually restricted rediscoveries of this traditional manner of thought. There can be few more remarkable explorations of the strains imposed by his complex role-set on a multiple member of several intersecting status- and reference-groups, than Anselm's reflections upon his identity, his situation and his duties.

Some of Southern's interests and values, and the style of explanation which they prompt, are indicated in a few sentences from the opening pages of the final chapter of *The Making of The Middle Ages*:

These changes are hard to define and their connexion can more readily be felt than explained. Indeed, in a strict sense, these changes defy definition, and the connexion between them cannot be explained – it can only be exemplified in the lives of individuals. At the deepest levels of experience, in intimations of the nature of God and the economy of the universe, in new insights into the powers and powerlessness of man, the changing scene of history has its focus and its justification.

Those are not hard to locate among preoccupations and values present though perhaps unfashionable in the modern world. They are plain on many other pages of the book, not hindering the technical work of discovery, but directing it to whatever, in the eleventh century, Southern's complex moral sense judged it valuable for twentieth-century readers to know.

Even if there were no great difficulties in the way of discovery, what scientific selector would do better than that moral perception and judgment? A privileged effect – social integration, economic distribution, an indexed rate of change – to be the terminal consequence for all investigations of all systems? A twentieth-century classification of social facts and causal mechanisms, which should terminate inquiries into all systems when their classifiable parts were identified and correctly boxed? A rule that for any effect, causes should be chosen for proximity, weight or certain knowability, regardless of their intrinsic interest, moral message, or manipulative potentiality? The last scheme is always stupid. The first two may serve some specialized purposes of inquiry, usually to test the universality of facts and relations observed here and now; but they will usually prohibit more valuable discoveries, of unsuspected options and potentialities, and prohibit also the less expected, more surprising illuminations of comparative study.

Southern's values are exposed, in many ways, by the way they work for him. It seems right that they should thus organize what are, in part, explorations of their own practical – or impractical – implications. Among other things, they lead him to study some interesting or valuable networks of social relations as these were understood – and existed because understood – in the people's ideas of their identities and roles. Sociologists attempt similar understandings of similar structures in modern societies; but many also attempt unanimity, by substituting what are often technically crude and unperceptive selectors, like 'contributors to the system's integration and persistence'. These were meant to be justified by a yield of law: by the discovery of identical functional performance in whole classes of systems. Failing in that, they became instead rules of method, directing selection in each study of each partly-unique system. In this capacity they do facilitate some comparisons, though they probably prevent more valuable contrasts than they expose reliable similarities. Inescapably, they import their built-in valuations. Where Southern chose perceptively what he judged valuable, these rules apply, often less reliably, values in which few sociologists believe. The yield of such cross-purposes is seldom valuable to anybody.

Neither the natural scientists' regular subject-matter, nor their consensus of values, can be reproduced by the upside-down method of fabricating a consensus about methods of selection which neither discover uniformities or new options of behavior, nor choose deliberately its valuable causes and qualities.

7

Scientific Knowledge of Causes

The last chapter attacked some imitative methods of choosing causes. This one attacks some imitative methods of knowing them. The next attacks an opposite opinion, that for understanding human society the methods of science are no use at all. Mixed methods seem best, and the mixtures have political characteristics. Chapter 9 is then about functions of imagination and valuation in estimating effects, however their causes are known.

1. Plain facts and fancy philosophies

How are causes known?

The question is for philosophers. Most of their problems are beyond the scope of this book. For example, social scientists seldom try to do without an idea of causality. If processes seem to occupy continuous time but to be observable only at discrete intervals, few social scientists understand whatever philosophical and mathematical problems arise from this. If 'action at a distance' were approachable by some imaginable microanalysis of the times and spaces between, a science which tried the microanalysis would scarcely be recognized as social. Similarly, of those who want laws to 'cover' statements of cause, some allow that the laws might be on another scale, many and microscopic. 'This insult caused this quarrel' may not need cover at all. But if it does, it may not be by a law about insults and quarrels, but by a host of laws for the many connections summarized by the statement of conclusion. Social scientists usually neglect such intricacies. Talk of intentions and purposes may be 'as if' thought, shorthand for something else; but again, it is the shorthand social scientists still use.

Those problems can be avoided. The subject of this study is not 'what sort of knowledge is it?' but only 'who chooses and organizes it for what purposes?' But many of the social scientists, though no more philosophers than I am, do argue for one sort of knowledge rather than another, or for one rather than another logical description of the knowledge they have got, and they often do so for the practical purposes, and with effects on their principles of selection, which *are* the subject of this study. To understand their choices you have to know their theories about the knowledge of causes.

Does knowledge of causes require, or imply the existence of, laws on the same common-sense, macro-social scale as the statements they are supposed to cover? If it does, how should social scientists divide their time between observing the cases and formulating the laws? If choices and intentions count as causes of action, should scientists understand them in people's minds, or infer them from people's actions? Or should they infer causal relations from patterns of actions without any assumptions about mental acts or any other 'causal mechanisms'? Philosophers regard these as stale problems (though they dropped rather than solved some of them). But many social scientists propagate strong views about them. These opinions affect methods, inspiring prohibitions and imitations and scientific aspirations, so they are the subject of this chapter.

In these old-fashioned terms, are causes in human society like causes in non-human nature? How like or unlike are the human methods of knowing each? Both like and unlike, obviously. This chapter supports the social scientists who emphasize the unlikeness, who design methods to take advantage of their subjects' unique capacities to talk, intend, invent and introspect. These days there is plenty of support for this policy. But even its supporters desperately resist, still, one of its implications. For knowing causes, most social scientists, whether they like it or not, rightly use the logic and methods which historians use. Both scientists and historians need to improve these methods, not replace them.

Many relations between people or events remain visible and understandable to common sense through all arguments about the logical structure of common sense. To common sense, many connections between facts are 'facts' themselves. I see an insult provoke a fight which ends with a victory and a corpse. I see each of the four with the same certainty, even though each may be a concept of different type – the insult is only intelligible in a learned language and culture, the fight is a unity I impose on a succession of events, I may infer the victory from one fighter's thoughts and the other's posture, the corpse means the same to beast as to man. The causal links are not obscure, though some are in mental acts and communications, some in physical motions, some in both. The whole thing may be bundled into one word – a brawl – or it may be analysed into many parts and the parts re-connected by causes or other relations, but whatever such talk is about, it seldom raises doubts about what happened, or how, or even why. An enormous number of the relations studied in social science have this simplicity. If there is doubt about them, what is required is that they be more carefully observed, or counted, or reported, or understood in the reliable sense that a language is understood, or reasoned by universally accepted rules of inference.

There can also be great certainty in re-relating the parts of wholes which common sense might never have dismembered in the first place. Some of such 'causes and effects' could be described indifferently as invariably regular dependent associations, or as artificial products of an analytical method. In them, as in the logical relation of ideas to each other, causes come nearest to mathematical proof.

This is to make two points. For practical purposes a great many causal relations can be simply and certainly known; but this 'visibility' is not unique to one type of relation, nor known by one privileged logic. Both points are obvious, and are reflected throughout the practice of social science; but not always in its aspirations.

2. *Stories, cases and laws*

There is one methodological program which its friends describe as scientific and its enemies as superstitious or aesthetic: whatever its purpose or subject-matter, all respectable scientific knowledge should look alike, use the same logic, order abstractions in the same hierarchy, judge the same relations to hold between usefulness and universality – and know causes (or do without them) by the same reasoning.

Readers who already avoid this belief can skip this section to the less familiar contents of the next. But among the young, and in the minds and manuals of many who teach them, scientific faith and ritual are catchy and tenacious; they beat scientific method, any day. In reputable universities in three continents, year by year, professors of sociology and political science can be heard to preface their selections of historical knowledge with declarations that 'history is the mere description of one unique event after another', 'the comparative method is for social science what controlled experiment is for physical science', 'unfortunately we are still relying here on prescientific impressionism', 'of course these intuitions are mere guesswork until we have some verified general laws', and 'empirical generalizations from observed covariances are the building blocks from which real theories will eventually be constructed'. So this section is to repeat an orthodoxy which is yet neglected in many journals' jargon and many teachers' practice: the quality of physics which social scientists should imitate is the excellent relation of its methods to its purposes, problems and subject-matter. That relation was not achieved by applying to the problems of physics methods appropriate to different problems, nor by indulging aspirations in theory which contradicted the most fruitful methods in practice.

The strongest desires have been for a deductive science; for the inference of causes from regular recurrences only; and for scientists' causes to be different from historians' causes.

We have only one way to demonstrate that a given phenomenon is the cause of another, viz., to compare the cases in which they are simultaneously present or absent, to see if the variations they present in these different combinations of circumstances indicate that one depends on the other . . . We have seen that sociological explanation consists exclusively in establishing relations of causality . . . Since, moreover, social phenomena evidently escape the control of the experimenter, the comparative method is the only one suited to sociology.[1]

Long after Emile Durkheim thus exemplified the social-scientific revolution, Maurice Duverger looked back to applaud its outbreak:

In the eighteenth century . . . the idea appeared that social phenomena have a regular character, and are therefore subject to natural laws more or less analogous to those which govern the physical universe: the conception of social laws marks a decisive step forward as the purpose of science is to look for laws which can be tested by experiment.[2]

Lest the idea be thought specially old-fashioned, Marxist, or French, the up-to-date English-speaking believers can be represented by two young American sociologists who, after editing scores of contemporary papers in the field, still declare that

it is only through a comparative approach that useful causal explanations can be achieved, since it is impossible to assess the validity and reliability of any causal interpretation that is based on a single sequence.[3]

To judge the promise of these recommendations, and of any social science which excludes whatever knowledge the recommended methods will not yield, we may begin with an example of the varieties of knowledge which one unregenerate discipline still admits to its journals. The text is from Murray Groves, 'Dancing in Poreporena', a student's essay published in the *Journal of the Royal Anthropological Institute* (84, 1954, 80–82). Though long, the quotation is economical – it includes in terse style a fine variety of the observations, understandings and inferences to be found in the 'primary observations' of most social sciences.

Poreporena was a Papuan village inhabited by extended family groups called *iduhu*, each a 'patrilineal and patrilocal group residing in a single line of houses'. Groves prepares to explain one function of their dances:

Poreporena had no government, but it did have leaders. In each *iduhu*, leadership was usually hereditary . . . the incumbent was called the *iduhu kwarana* . . . and in Motu the word *kwara* was used, as in English, to denote both the head as a part of the body and the senior man in a group . . .

The Motu also have a word, *lohia*, to denote a chief, leader, or man of power. Usually the *iduhu kwarana* was also known as the *iduhu lohia* . . . but sometimes two different men might be called *iduhu lohia* and *iduhu kwarana*, respectively. The language allowed a clear distinction to be drawn between formal status and *de facto* power. When two different men within one *iduhu* each enjoyed one of these two different kinds of leadership, it was probably only a temporary arrangement; either the *iduhu lohia* would break away to form a new *iduhu* of which he could also be *iduhu kwarana*, or on his death his challenge to the hereditary line would die with him, or else in time his victory over the hereditary line would be recognized in a new popular view of the succession . . .

The *iduhu kwarana* lived in the front house of the *iduhu*, and his verandah was the ceremonial focus of the *iduhu*. On it . . . decisions were taken and agreements reached . . .

Apart from the advantages inherited by an *iduhu kwarana*, other attributes that distinguish powerful personalities anywhere – wealth, military prowess, intelligence, and cunning – gained one man within an *iduhu*, rather than another, ascendancy in the public eye . . . Those men of Poreporena who sought ascendancy and renown might use various means to their end; trading expeditions, offensive raids on other villages, attacks on canoes at sea, gardening, marriage and sorcery all provided opportunities for enlarging a man's standing in the community. There was only one way, however, in which a man might visibly display and commemorate his ascendancy over others; namely, by sponsoring a dance. The people of Poreporena say, even today, that only a strong man can hold a dance. And when asked why a man is holding a dance, they often give the surprising answer that it is because he has quarrelled with someone else.

. . . This account of the dance makes little sense today because the modern village context no longer contains the key to its meaning. Now there are many formal devices for fixing and proclaiming the relative standing of rival public figures . . . In the past, none of these devices was available; there was only the dance.

. . . The ingredients of worldly success – a man's wealth, the number of kinsmen and allies owing him allegiance, and the power of his *iduhu* – were all brought to a focus in the dance . . . A *turia* [a minor dance] was more or less successful according to the number of people who attended, the amount of food distributed, the duration of the dancing, the skill of the drummers, the variety of dances offered, the beauty and amiability of either sex in the eyes of the other, the splendour of the head-dresses displayed, the weather, etc. A *hekara* [a cycle of dances] was fought out until one man had no further food to distribute. Success thus depended on the wealth, talent, range of acquaintance, ancestral power, and magical resources (or luck) of the sponsor and his *iduhu*. Like the Kwakiutl *potlatch*, the Motu dance was a device for adjusting personal standing; it was part of a battle that never ended.

How did Groves know that Poreporena had no government? He lived there, read accounts by others who had lived there, and found no orders issuing from any regular source. An expectation generalized from other societies led him to look for such a regular source. For the hypothesis that it wasn't there, independent opinions were better than the Poreporenans'. Though they doubtless agreed, they might have no word for government and might misunderstand questions about it. But Groves' next sentence might need different foundations, depending on whether it was to report or predict. To know that leadership would continue to be hereditary, independent evidence about the past might be less useful than the Poreporenans' own opinions, which might well determine the next inheritance.

Groves next distinguishes two sorts of leadership. That two exist is made likely by the existence of language for distinguishing them. About the functions of one, much is learned by watching and understanding what does and (with more expectations generalized from other societies) what does not go on, on his verandah. About the other sort of leader, a mixture of evidence is indicated in the next paragraph. By observation and interrogation – by watching acts, asking questions and understanding ideas – Groves has discovered people's present understandings of each other's status. Partly from their present beliefs, but also from his and others' historical observations, he adds narrative accounts of how such leadership could be won. A man might rise by piracy but be respected now for his big gardens and his fictitious heredity. To understand this, you have to know both true history, and present opinions however false.

In one paragraph (and in unquoted parts of the paper) Groves notices that other devices have recently replaced dancing as registers of social standing. This helps to support two inferences: that dancing did once perform that function, and that *something* usually performs it. An historical comparison thus provides an imperfect but helpful shuffle of variables. But Groves' belief that dancing did perform the function still rests more securely upon his original direct observation and understanding, than upon this ill-controlled association of variables. When social phenomena vary together, such 'control' can rarely be an observer's strongest reason for concluding that one causes the other. Social life is complex and some unnoticed variable may be causing both. Effects may recur, but from different causes each time. Knowledge is strongest when it has both foundations: regularity, and an understanding of the mechanism.

If an indignant missionary protests that the dances do nothing for anybody's status, Groves can no more argue from regular association than can a scientist whose law is accused of resulting from observations through a faulty microscope. Both have to respond by proving, not that something happened regularly, but that it ever happened once. That the dance performed its function on any one occasion can be known more surely by Groves' mixed methods (or by improved methods of the same kind) than by regular association alone, or any other single method alone. Groves understands what the Poreporenans experience and think. He adds some 'genetic' knowledge. (The metaphor indicates another mixture: for primitives, laws based on regular association connect a child to its father, but to see it born once is to know one of its relations to its mother. Its connection with its father is known better, not worse, as physiologists improve their understanding of the mechanism.) It is in Poreporenan minds, *once*, that Groves first understands the connection between the dance and the status of the host. The valued, selected, understood and historically explained causation of effects, which is called the function, does not appear to depend in practice on any law about recurrence of that function. Moreover if some more general law treats this whole functional process as one phenomenon, and relates it to another as for example to a particular type of social structure, it is equally likely that this larger law will rest less surely on the regular association of the two phenomena, and more surely on a direct understanding of the mechanisms which relate the two. Repeated observations may still be appropriate. But their purpose will be to get a better look next time, or to see if different observers discern the same things, more often than merely to see whether the same actions recur regularly in the same circumstances.

The functional substitution of modern devices for dancing, in Poreporena, is a reminder of the limitations of functional analysis for explaining change. No dysfunction led to the replacement of dancing. No measurement of strains, no 'net balance of dysfunctions' nor 'excess of demands over support', could predict or account for change in Poreporena over the last eighty years. Foreigners have caused Poreporena to change, partly by direct intervention but chiefly by altering its environment, informing it of social alternatives, offering it new technology, and implanting a new capacity to invent. As observed earlier, imports of power and ideas and techniques are difficult to explain functionally, so is gratuitous innovation, and so are their effects. Poreporena is only an extreme case.

But these are once-occurring causes of change. Functional analysis is meant to explain the continuing causes of continuous effects in stable societies. Are these functional relations different in kind from other causes, or discoverable by different methods?

Functional analysis was discussed earlier as a system for selecting causes by their relation to certain terminal effects – a system which may limit the effects to be reported or explained, but which offers no rules to tell the analyst how far or in what directions he should look for the causes of those terminal effects. For selecting causes the functional analyst's rules leave him as free – and as unhelped – as any historian. It may now be noticed that the two have the same task and use the same methods in finding and proving the causal connections themselves.

R. K. Merton insists that functions are 'objective consequences'. Consistently, that is what all the functions and dysfunctions mentioned in his writings are. They are causal (including reciprocal, interacting) relations established exactly, if not always as carefully, as historians would establish them. Thoughts, intentions and responses are understood; irrational actions are referred to dispositions; motives are sometimes declared by the actors, sometimes disbelieved, sometimes inferred from actions. Aggregative or unintended effects are traced, understood or measured by variously appropriate methods. One of the few features which these various methods have in common, is that they rarely depend much upon regular association. But the literature of sociology, both theoretical and empiricist, is full of hints that most of these messy methods should soon be replaced by fewer and better ones. What will these better methods be?

For Hans Zetterberg the better methods will be those of physics:

As is well known, we explain something by demonstrating that it follows the laws of other phenomena . . . In physics, atomic theory is an inclusive theory in terms of which most laws of physics can be explained. Since it can explain most laws it also can explain most phenomena. The final goal of the scientific enterprise is to know such a theory . . . Sociology like many other sciences in a Liberal Arts college has not yet reached this level.[4]

For Ernest Greenwood, the better methods will be directed to the theoretical illumination of regular associations:

An empirical generalization may be defined as a proposition about a class of units which describes the uniform recurrence of two or more factors among them . . .

In constructing theory, the scientist uses empirical generalizations as building blocks . . . Law is the summarization of the theory in causal terms . . . Predictability is the scientist's criterion of validity . . . therefore, a research hypothesis in science is a deduction from a theory, and its verification is a validation of the theory from which it sprang.[5]

For R. K. Merton the better methods will have the logical structure of all the physical sciences, but detailed similarity to physiology:

The *logical structure* of experiment, for example, does not differ in physics, or chemistry or psychology, although the substantive hypotheses, the technical tools, the basic concepts and the practical difficulties may differ enormously. Nor do the near-substitutes for experiment – controlled observation, comparative study and the method of 'discerning' – differ in their *logical structure* in anthropology, sociology or biology.[6]

I doubt if the method of discerning belongs in that logical company, but it depends on one's reading of the ambiguity of the last sentence. Merton's own proposals for verification always require some observation of regularities, but not necessarily of regular associations between otherwise discrete phenomena. What else the regularities will be which within the logic of experimental science will verify or replace the impressionist 'discernment' of unique causes, is not always clear:

So well established is the logic of functional analysis in the biological sciences that [the] requirements for an adequate analysis come to be met almost as a matter of course. Not so with sociology. Here, we find extraordinarily varied conceptions of the appropriate design of studies in functional analysis.[7]

For the right conception, Merton appears to recommend his own outline of an 'adequate analysis' in physiology. In this the causal relations are different, and differently discovered, from Zetterberg's. Causes are not inferred from associations at all, but are discerned by inspecting and understanding sequences and causal mechanisms.

Theory based on this sort of causal understanding is likely to generalize descriptions of processes, processes uniquely understood. If the processes recur regularly in particular circumstances, they will probably be connected to those circumstances by the same sort of understanding of the connecting links or mechanisms, rather than by unaided inference from the recurrent association of the process and the circumstance. To be consistent, any surveying or quantifying of the recurrence will not be directed chiefly at establishing the causal links; it will be directed at measuring how widespread is the occurrence of the process. If it proves to be a reliably recurrent or persistent process, it may sometimes become safe to infer its presence from simple indicators; but this is different from inferring the causal relations themselves from the regular associations of the 'linked' parts.

Merton does not offer this advice, though it seems to be implied by much of the advice that he does offer. For knowing causes, he seems to reject both the physicist's method and (whenever it is so named) the plain man's or historian's method, but without committing himself to any clear alternative, unless it be merely the historian's mixture of methods under another name. He emphasizes the persistence and recurrence of processes as the ground for inferring causal knowledge, yet rejects the inference of causal links from 'some regular association of parts'. This can make sense. An understood process of cause and effect may recur or persist; one may infer from its persistence, something about the regularity of people's habits, including their 'free' choices. It is by such methods that historians conclude that Russians are inexperienced democrats, that sermons won't change white attitudes to Negroes, that different states pursue different notions of national interest, that industrial innovation spreads faster than agrarian innovation in some conditions, slower in others. Why recommend that the elements of selection and 'unique' understanding in these methods should give way to new (but always nameless) methods, or that causes inferred from the repetition of a process are necessarily known more surely than causes well-understood by understanding the process once? Merton's functional theory includes a simple *non-sequitur*: abolish historians' methods of *knowing causes*, but replace them by functionalist rules for *selecting effects*.

By contrast, there was never any doubt what knowledge the eminent anthropologist A. R. Radcliffe-Brown aspired to, or how he theorized that causes might be known. It was perhaps the absence of any relation at all between his sensitive methods-in-practice and his methodological utterances that allowed the latter their simplicity:

. . . there are certain general "physiological laws", or laws of function, that are true for all human societies, for all cultures. The functional method aims at discovering these general laws and thereby at explaining any particular element of any culture by reference to the discovered laws.[8]

With no laws at all, he discovered and explained a great deal about his Andaman Islanders. But faith resisted experience to testify again in his famous final lecture:

For social anthropology the task is to formulate and validate statements about the conditions of existence of social systems (laws of social statics) and the regularities that are observable in social change (laws of social dynamics).[9]

Many people who no longer write such absurdities continue nevertheless to imply a good many of them whenever they patronize as 'insightful', or damn as 'impressionist' or 'prescientific', any statements about lawless causes observed (and understood, and selected) in single cases. Such hunches inspire hypotheses, they admit; but only successful prediction in other cases, or controlled repetitious observation, can verify them.

The opposite of this is, in the *practice* of social science, a more usual relation between correlation and 'understanding'. Correlations often provoke hypotheses which are confirmed by the internal inspection and understanding of particular cases. Such hypotheses usually describe or assume something about processes of thought and feeling. These are not sufficiently understood by any regular association of parts. One reason for the continuing scarcity of verified sociological laws is probably a lack of objective regularities for such laws to describe; but there is also this other reason, that most candidate-hypotheses are not verifiable by their rigorous authors' own rules.

If causes are inferred from association, then statements of cause are justified by associational laws, which are verified by repeated observation. But most sociological hypotheses assert (if often in disguise) more than the mere association of otherwise discrete phenomena. They assert the nature of the relation rather than merely the regular association. They need more than regular association for their proof; but at the same time their authors, perhaps mistaken about physical as well as social science, regard anything beyond regular association as 'impressionist'. For example it would require the logical connection of ideas with each other and with action, and valuation to establish some of the identities, as well as regular recurrence, to verify these candidates:

Suicide is a function of the degree of group integration which provides the psychic support to group members for handling acute stress.

The greater the division of labor is in a society, the less the rejection of deviates in the same society.

Insofar as subordinate or prospective group members are motivated to affiliate themselves with a group, they will tend to assimilate the sentiments and conform with the values of the authoritative and prestigeful stratum in that group.[10]

The first is so vague it can mean almost anything you like. The others, in that there are important exceptions to both of them, are simply false. But even if the proposals were more plausible, 'be motivated', 'assimilate sentiments' and 'conform with values' are unlike any concepts by which matter is understood. We can understand more about their causal relations with each other than could ever be inferred from their 'association' with each other. Statements about their relations are accordingly different from most natural-scientific statements, and must be differently verified.

Those are formal objections to a social physics. There are also practical objections. Unhappily the practical obstructions are *too* famous. As long as quantification and experimental or comparative control of social data are obviously imperfect, their lack of yield can be blamed on the imperfections. Practical difficulties let true believers continue in the faith – and also, meanwhile, in some of the pre-revelation methods.

Suppose I guess that there may be relations between deviance and social mobility. I index deviation, index real upward mobility chances, and index people's expectations of mobility. After the notion 'upward' has been given content by learning and understanding people's valuations, some quite objective facts from the population's biographies can be collated to indicate real chances of upward mobility – i.e. the past real chances of people present now. Their present expectations must be discovered by understanding what they think. Identical expectations may arise from different thoughts. Some people extrapolate their inaccurate impressions of past chances – they 'invent the past and remember the future' – but others predict their chances by other methods – well or ill, they invent a future. Those differences I can only know by understanding, but such different reasons for identical predictions may have some causal interest for science now, and some practical importance later if my results are to enlighten any social engineering.

It now takes a further mixture of methods to show that a *difference* between the indexes of real past chances and expected future chances indicates a *cause* of whatever is indicated by the statistical occurrence of deviations. Did unknown common causes make the population both misjudge its chances and commit its deviations? Or did people's deviations (causes still unknown) reduce their upward chances below an otherwise well-judged expectation? Or did reality confront false expectations to produce frustrations which caused the deviations? Or did the last two, started by undisclosed historical causes, then combine to perpetuate each other?

Do I now initiate the studies of covariance, whose complexity would multiply with every invading variable they had to incorporate, but which appear necessary to answer these questions? Of course not. I get to know some orthodox and some deviant members of the population and try to understand how different factors meet and mix and operate in their mental experience to affect their conduct. That is to say, I try to understand the causal mechanisms themselves. This does not necessarily mean that I abandon sociology for psychology; it means that I have decided to study the nature and operation of societal forces at the point where their causal inter-relations are most visible, accessible and understandable to me. This happens to be precisely where, and how, the medieval historian Southern would study them. If I can discern and understand the meeting and interaction of societal forces in this manner, I may well know more about them, and know it more reliably, than I could ever discover by more 'objective' or behaviorist methods, or even by 'regularly associating' well-understood but still discrete parts of thought and behavior. Measurements, surveys and statistical counts may still be important; but their purpose will be to show how many of the population behave in the way I have now understood, for the reasons and causes I have now understood; their purpose will not be to show what those causes are, nor to verify my understanding of what they are.

At the end of an illuminating review of some explanatory theories of juvenile delinquency, Cohen and Short observe:

There does exist, to be sure, a considerable literature that seeks to relate various aspects of the social and cultural order to delinquent behavior by comparing the backgrounds and experiences of official delinquents and of those not officially defined as delinquent . . .

They deal largely with correlations, that is, the observed tendency for delinquency (as defined) to be associated with certain other events and circumstances. They do not, as a rule, deal with these correlations within the context of a general theory of delinquency which would be necessary to *explain the correlations.* The theories we have presented at some length, on the other hand, suggest ways in which the findings of these studies can be explained. Either Cohen's or Miller's theory, for example, helps to make sense, although each in a different way, of the correlations that have been found between membership in the lower class, school experience and delinquency.[11]

Cohen's theory says that many working-class homes produce children who find it hard to conform to rules laid down by middle-class authorities – rules for the good behavior and advancement of all, including working–class, children. But children who deviate from these rules lose the approval and praise which children desire; so they organize a society of their own with rules of their own, a society which *will* approve and praise the conduct which they *do* find possible. Because of the particular circumstance which makes this gang sub-culture necessary, its rules are often drawn in direct reaction against the middle-class rules. One reference system has been replaced by another, the second made stronger by being also a membership group.

In contrast to Cohen's theory which has the children reacting against the values of the middle class, Miller's theory says that the children get into trouble by conforming to the values of the working class. A general lower-class culture values such things as ' "trouble", "toughness", "smartness", "excitement", "fate" or "luck", and "autonomy". There are different ways of realising these values – none of them is intrinsically and necessarily delinquent – but their pursuit is highly conducive to delinquent behavior'.

These rivals have the form of many everyday and most historical explanations. Each, as Cohen makes clear, makes a narrow selection from the conditions necessary for delinquency. How might each be tested for truth? Only marginally, or negatively, by any factorial analysis of the association of variables. For areas where gangs exist, the gang theory would not be much damaged by evidence that similar delinquency occurred where gangs did not. We are used to people doing similar things for different reasons. The tests required are tests of understanding: how well do we know how the boys themselves relate their various experiences, see options, feel about the options, predict rewards and penalties? How faithfully do we follow and understand the systems of ideas we call 'the sub-cultures'? These are not problems merely of primary observation or operational procedure; they are also problems in the heart of the causal theories, and of their appropriate verification. We may find similarities from boy to boy, from city to city. We may learn to rely on indicators, to know when probably one understood experience is being enacted, and when another. But this is to measure or map the incidence of a causal pattern which has first been understood quite otherwise than by inference from the regular covariance of its parts.

But the imitation of physics dies hard. If physicists were reciprocal imitators, they would ask the molecules to talk to them, and distrust knowledge got by any other method. The social scientist's 'primary observation' and understanding of causal relations may lack the perfection of deduction or the working certainty of the well-tested simple association. Historical and 'genetic' explanation, the recognition of causal influences in uncontrolled life, the understanding and interrelation of reasons and motives in action, are all imperfectly reliable; but good is better than bad. Bad is unlikely to be made better by anyone who regards his mixed bag of methods as a temporary, prescientific substitute for revolutionary methods to come. He won't bother to improve the shameful old tools he's going to throw away. Faced with the irregular but specially accessible phenomena for which the old tools were developed, the idiot will still trade them for methods which can only discover causes at all where there is regularity, and can even then discover less about them.

This is not to say that social life has no regularities, and social science no capacity to generalize. There are some very regular aspects of social behavior, and some of them persist long enough to support some 'cumulative' science; though even the 'universals' of economics are local, and which of them stay true becomes increasingly a question for social choice. But suspend, for a moment, the faith that underlying regularities invite a social physiology. If we turn from such aspirations to the actual stock of anthropology, sociology and political science, we find their general wisdom in much the same condition as the general wisdom of historians. Except for those patterned by the spurious selectors discussed below in Chapter 13, most of their explanations resemble historians' explanations (which are as often functional as sequential). How are those explanations related to more generalized knowledge?

The nature and use of generalized knowledge in particular social explanation has been well explored by philosophers of history; better, perhaps, than by most of the few philosophers of social science. (Social scientists are more prone to supply their own do-it-yourself philosophy; professional philosophers have sometimes neglected social scientific practice to analyse its methodological programs instead). Much of the recent philosophy of history[12] fits the practice of most anthropology and sociology and political science, and the fit suggests that these differ from history in their efforts to formulate their general knowledge, but not really in the *kind* of general knowledge of causes they can expect to accumulate.

The historian's skill relies on a stock of experience, which itself supplies some reasons why he should not try too hard to formulate it. He does formulate a great deal of it, in limited generalizations about causal patterns within national social systems at particular times. Halévy's generalizations about social stability in Victorian England or E. H. Carr's about change in modern Russia[13] assert more uniformities of behavior, of more people in more complex circumstances, than do many social-scientific hypotheses. Beyond that, and especially between systems, the historian usually hesitates. There are too many exceptions to every law he can think of. Processes recur, but not identically. They are processes of ideas-in-action, of action-in-the-light-of-ideas, and only primitive societies or illiterate peasantries live for long on a fixed stock of ideas. So the constants are complex and local, or the more abstract, general ones are such that their operation cannot be reliably abstracted from the local 'mixtures' in which they operate. For any likely or interesting general laws, the identification of cases would be difficult; and it would require choices and valuations unlikely to be unanimous.

The historian nevertheless has in his head plenty of tentative generalizations and expectations. The relation of these to particular explanations does seem to be in many ways unlike the relation between strict laws and cases of those laws. The historian's 'laws' prompt and hint and warn – they suggest where to look for a process, or what sort of process to look for; what to trust and what to suspect. They rarely establish, unaided, important relations.

One school still argues that laws are logically necessary to historians' causal statements, which are that much weaker whenever the laws are unknown, unproven or unmentioned. This was Carl Hempel's view, in 'The Function of General Laws in History' (*Journal of Philosophy*, XXXIX, 1942); it was endorsed by Karl Popper, modified and elaborated by Gardiner, and provoked much philosophical controversy ten years ago. In *Explanation in Social Science* (London: Routledge and Kegan Paul, 1963), Robert Brown returns to Hempel's simplicities:

When we look . . . at the answer given to the question 'Why have the peasants ceased to look to their chiefs for help?' it is plain that a number of generalizations are presupposed. These are such psychological or sociological statements as: the disappearance of services rendered by a superordinate group (the chiefs) lessens the demands made for further aid by a subordinate group (the peasants); the demand for aid lessens with the decrease in face-to-face relationships; and the demand decreases as the superordinate group increases its economic exactions. Each of these is crudely stated, each requires testing. But without something like them we are left with gaps in our account. Unless, for example, we know that the imposition of economic hardships upon a group of people somehow modifies their requests for help directed to the oppressing group, we have no reason for concluding that the peasants ceased to request aid because their potential helpers were identical with their actual oppressors . . . The importance of implicit generalization of this crude type for explanations given in terms of historical origins and development is well known. (50–1)

Well known or not, it has been often and expertly doubted.[14] Even if laws do perform the function claimed for them by Hempel and Brown, they will surely perform it well or ill according to their truth, not their universality. Brown seems to equate truth with universality. He sketches missing laws true of any 'group of people', not merely of the Ganda people whose conduct is explained in his example. Why should such laws be true of Ganda people only if also true of other people? Even if laws of regular recurrence be required, why should they not be Ganda laws based only on repeated observation of repeated Ganda behavior? Knowledge of one man's disposition will often predict – or 'complete an explanation' of – his conduct more reliably than would knowledge only of what is common to all men's dispositions, especially if in response to situations of the type in question there proves to be practically nothing that is common to all men's dispositions. Social laws may similarly prove as reliable as they are limited. Once this is admitted, reliability may sometimes increase as the limitations of the law contract until the law applies to one society, one period, one short-lived group, or even one person or one case, at which point its legal status is curious. In practice many particular causal relations seem to be known before, and more certainly than, whatever laws they may eventually help to build.

Nevertheless, however unformulated and merely statistical, generalized expectations do direct most research, even if for historians their formulation is not its chief product. This limited service of law to explanation is as common in sociology, political science and anthropology as it is in history; just as all four rely heavily upon their more direct methods of discerning causes. Both features signify the special difficulties and opportunities in their subject-matter, rather than any scientific 'immaturity'. (Whatever sense it makes to call them 'high' or 'general', it makes no sense at all to call sciences 'mature' simply because their subject-matter is regular, independent and simple). But if history and the social sciences must use logically similar methods, it can still be for different purposes. A sociologist may well do his best to formulate all the law he can. It is likely to be more statistical, local, and unreliable than most of the theory of physics, or even physiology. And he will not get it right if he imitates their methods. Instead, he must learn languages and understand ideas and the local rules by which ideas are related in specific systems of ideas. He must explain processes by historical method; compare similar processes after they have been similarly understood; exercise a typically historical and valuing judgment in identifying and abstracting any regular and interesting similarities between processes; exercise more of the same judgment in distinguishing the surrounding conditions which have to be stated from those which can for his particular purpose be left asleep; count and measure whatever is measurable (to the vast improvement of a great deal of historical research); and provide repetitious verification when appropriate, remembering that this may often require the original painstaking explanation of case after case rather than any brisk check of some visible indicators or associations. The 'laws' that result, besides being vulnerable to social change, can only be as reliable as the original understanding of cases was reliable.

What generalized knowledge may political science and sociology hope to accumulate? There may be a few determinate laws. There may be many statements of probabilities. There will be model processes, with exceptions and variations sketched but not exhausted. Many may be skills, rules about investigation rather than about its subject-matter. Most will be severely limited, to particular times and places, nations and cultures, classes and groups. The bewildering volume and marginal uncertainty of such knowledge offers compensating advantages to anyone who can do without a Calvinist election of generalizations as either saved or damned, perfect or worthless, universally true or unimprovably pre-scientific. With a stock of 'guarded generalizations' subject to continuing refinement rather than formal verification, not so much 'cumulating' as obsolescing and adapting to social change and innovation, with applications and exceptions requiring an experienced clinical skill – with these it will be easier to abstract from untidy life, to make the best of too many variables, to use imperfect knowledge carefully, and to trace particular strands of cause and effect through complex networks with less anxiety about 'invading variables'. The result will be unlike most physical sciences, unlike the natural history they sprang from, and unlike any intermediate state they ever passed through. It may be more like a mixture of history and clinical medical research made contentious by party politics. By the tests that knowledge should be as true as possible and ordered most rationally for its intended use, it will still be science. For much of it, Michael Scriven once suggested the name 'normic statements' and the following description –

Normic statements are useful, where the system of exceptions, although perfectly comprehensible in the sense that one can learn how to judge their relevance, is exceedingly complex.

. . . Essentially, a causal explanation of an individual occurrence must use normic role-justifying grounds because (a) there aren't any true universal hypotheses to speak of and (b) statistical statements are too weak – they abandon the hold on the individual case. The normic statement tells one what had to happen in *this* case unless certain exceptional circumstances obtained . . . An event can rattle around inside a network of statistical laws, but is located and explained by being so located in the normic network. Not with mathematical exactitude indeed, nor beyond all possibility of error, but often as exactly and certainly as our observations are exact and certain.[15]

An imperfect arrangement for such 'normic knowledge', but at least a better model for it than any from physical science, is suggested in the next section.

3. Lawyers and laws

Lawyers predict. They have to, in order to regulate social conduct. They organize for ready use a complicated volume of rules about conduct. Of all the disciplines of social science, theirs is the oldest, the most used and the most exact. There are daily tests of their efficiency, and a watchful public will not tolerate much error in their predictions. They are reliable judges of each other's skills, and of the limits, locality and effect of their laws. They specialize, but without serious conflicts of method or conflicts of laws, or panic about invading variables. It is a little surprising that other social scientists, whose time is so often spent in envious contemplation of physics or biology, should dismiss Law as if it were a primitive 'natural history' of ungeneralized detail, or as if prescription were unrelated to description, understanding and prediction. In fact prescription is thickly textured with prediction. In common prudence, the level of generalization of such a skilled profession should attract respectful attention, and some inquiry into its reasons.

As the draftsman of a statute writes each clause, he must predict (in order to proscribe) inventive evasions of it. He must also predict (in order to avoid disturbing) the range of innocent activities to which, if written carelessly, the clause might be applied – the rights and duties it might inadvertently create, the new forms of conduct it might inadvertently provoke. The lawyer has been professionally alert to the 'latent dysfunctions' of law for many centuries. To be precise, the draftsman must predict how the citizens will respond to his and their own predictions of how courts will respond to what he writes. The court or opinion lawyer often has similar tasks. Besides knowing what the law says, he must predict to what class of acts a court will assimilate the particular facts in question. This is a problem of simple abstraction. Which qualities of which acts will a court bring under which rule of law, assimilate to which 'legal act'? The law deals only in abstractions. Even murder, whose law is child's play compared with most laws, is an abstract composition of death, type and proximity of causation, state of mind, and the absence of various excusing circumstances such as war, lunacy, minority, various public employments, or the apprehension of a need for self defence. No executioner has yet been tried for murder, for maliciously throwing the switch a few seconds in advance of the governor's order; until it happens, we will not know which aspect of his conduct will be brought by a court under which rule of law. When it happens, the court's problem will be akin to the problem confronting any sociologist who must decide, on the same facts, whether the executioner has helped society to reject a deviate, or become a deviate himself.

The accuracy with which the conduct of courts can be predicted depends partly on the precision with which the rules of law themselves define the abstracts of conduct to which the court is instructed to apply them. In practice, few codes or statutes have much success in this; the necessary definitions have to be refined by accumulating precedent. These refinements are commonly very local. Though American courts are sometimes bolder than British, the law-making judge in a court of record usually keeps his *ratio decidendi* as narrow as he can; though this limits his extension or refinement of the law, it also reduces doubt as to the sort of facts to which the refinement must in future be applied. For to be sure which law, or none, a court will apply to any set of facts is to predict how a court will distinguish one abstraction from all other possible abstractions from the same facts. That courts work to strict rules, and assist in coercing many citizens, makes them different only in degree from ordinary society, which also has its rules and coercions. When a court distinguishes one from all rival abstractions from the same facts, its procedure has much formal and practical likeness to the procedure by which a scientist must decide of which law (in a scientific sense) a particular set of facts contains a 'case'. It is therefore interesting to notice the lawyer's and the generalizing sociologist's opposite attitudes to simplicity of law.

Nobody's *words* are more sparse and clear than a good lawyer's. But this economy does not spring from any hope that fewer, shorter, simpler, more general, more abstract or more axiomatic laws will make prediction surer. On the contrary the lawyer is driven to save what words he can by the weary certainty that for surer prediction of the effect of laws on conduct, and of conduct on courts, the law must usually be made longer and more complicated. In double contrast with some theoretical sociologists, lawyers are parsimonious with words but not with laws themselves. Even consolidation and codification seldom shorten law, though they may get it into better order. Nor is the Law a million unrelated, detailed rules; most of the rules attempt to explicate, for application to conduct, comparatively general principles. But the principles will not serve by themselves. Case-law must continue to define, with ever-increasing, never-perfect reliability, the rules for identifying regular legal acts in tracts of irregular human conduct. Even if the growing and changing complexity of industrial society and its social purposes did not do so, the mere quest for certainty would still drive the lawyer thus to complicate his laws. Nor does this complexity mean that the law is 'merely descriptive', a natural history of unique details. The notion of 'contract' abstracts a simple identity from millions of exceedingly diverse transactions; but to make the identifications predictively reliable, it requires a large and complex volume of law. Though different in some logical respects, is the problem much different in form or practice for a social scientist whose rules are meant to indicate which regular, abstract features or qualities (subject, though in a different sense, to law) are present in each unique variation of behavior?

In proportion as a sociologist writes simpler and more general laws, hoping that fewer may subsume more local laws and cover more cases, to that degree will he usually weaken his identification of cases. Uncertain identification of cases does not merely limit the clinical use of laws, a prospect which might not worry a pure scientist; by uncertifying their primary observations it uncertifies the laws themselves. The sociologist's safest resort may prove to be like the lawyer's: to complicate his laws; to abstract them less and limit them more precisely; to classify more detail in finer categories instead of dismissing more detail from fewer principles. The complex laws that result from such efforts are never final. They must accommodate new variations of behavior, including the evasive and inventive variations to which people may be prompted by knowledge of the laws. They must grow with the societies to which they relate. They must have their refining case law. Some men, some societies, will still break them. It may be well to arrange them as the lawyer does, with broad statements of the normic sort about the expected general tendencies of conduct, serving to classify the volume of minor rules and instances which distinguish cases from exceptions more precisely, and which must constantly adjust their distinctions to changes in the modes of conduct to which they relate.

Lawyers' law and prediction may be less or more certain, and its certainty estimated, without recourse to the notions 'scientific' or 'impressionist', 'idiographic' or 'nomothetic', 'axiomatic' or 'inductive'. Despite some conservative rituals, the courts have developed rules of evidence and inference pragmatically, not imitatively or dogmatically; they mind what the law should do, not what it should look like. They thus accommodate events and processes, sequences and analyses, rules and constructs, states of mind and states of things, things to be counted and concepts and ideas to be understood and intentions to be inferred and emotions to be empathized, all by diversely appropriate methods. The concentration of law schools and courts of record upon the marginal uncertainties of law and conduct should not lead us to forget how faultlessly lawyers draft the many statutes that quietly work well, and predict in the innumerable standard cases which never get to court. Its tradition, its interest and its customers all press the profession to predict as well as it can – to adjust its methods instrumentally to requirements of truth, certainty and justice. This, also, offers a neglected good example to other disciplines.

There are thus similarities of form and practice between the Law and other disciplines, and there is a practical integration of prediction and prescription within the discipline of the Law. Whether there is also a logical integration of prediction and prescription, may be more doubtful. The draftsman of a statute or the adviser of a client may be seen as, purely, predicting the citizens' and courts' responses to the facts, including the law. But in another view he may be seen as solving conceptual problems – 'does this law include or exclude acts of this sort?' – problems from which the tasks of prediction can perhaps be analytically separated. The question is one for philosophers, but its solution will not affect the practical lessons which other social scientists might draw from the lawyers' long experience in developing rules for selecting predictively-reliable identities from the messy-looking diversity of social behavior.

Much of the generalized wisdom of a mature social science might thus be like the laws of the land, and its schools and libraries be like the great law schools and libraries. Sociologists might then predict and contrive behavior as many economists and demographers and lawyers do already – roughly but well within local limits, and inventively when required. Meanwhile the Law has principles, but no grand theory. Its principles are moral, political, admonitory. They are also commentaries on, guides to, organizers of, its detail. But the general principles by themselves are rarely reliable for deduction, and they clearly never could be. Lawyers do not dream that a few parsimonious, overarching laws may one day subsume all others. They know the difference between Locke's subject-matter and Newton's. They neither suppose their science to be young, nor sit industriously under apple trees.

8

Understanding

1. The very idea of a social science

It has been argued that knowledge about society must include a great deal of understanding and valuing. Some people think that it should not include anything else. Benedetto Croce thought that

if we really do make live again in imagination individuals and events, and if we think what is within them . . . history is already achieved: what more is wanted? There is nothing more to seek . . . The fact historically thought has no cause and no end outside itself, but only in itself, coincident with its real qualities and with its qualitative reality.[1]

R. G. Collingwood made it clearer:

. . . the historiar need not and cannot (without ceasing to be an historian) emulate the scientist in searching for the causes or laws of events. For science, the event is discovered by perceiving it, and the further search for its cause is conducted by assigning it to its class and determining the relation between that class and others. For history, the object to be discovered is not the mere event, but the thought expressed in it. To discover that thought is already to understand it. After the historian has ascertained the facts, there is no further process of inquiring into their causes. When he knows what happened, he already knows why it happened.[2]

Isaiah Berlin summarized a great deal of careful argument, depending less on idealist philosophy and more on the practical difficulties of a science of history, in a sentence:

The historian's primary need is the knowledge that is like knowledge of someone's character or face, not like knowledge of facts.[3]

These are modern representatives of a tradition of thought whose earlier leaders included Vico, Hegel, Dilthey and in many ways Weber and Freud. Collingwood and Freud emphasized the effect of human consciousness upon the explanation of individual acts. The others gave more time to its implications for the understanding of systems: systems understood as patterns of rules and roles and expectations, techniques and skills and styles and understandings; each to be understood only by learning its very own language and pattern and 'inner logic'.

Because the argument is often dismissed by misrepresentation, it is worth summarizing one lucid version of it in Peter Winch's *The Idea of a Social Science and its relation to Philosophy*.[4] From a particular social theory of language, Winch goes on to propose 'that the notion of a human society involves a scheme of concepts which is logically incompatible with the kinds of explanation offered in the natural sciences.' Social conduct may only be understood as that of men acting according to rules, in a special sense of 'rules'. No useful knowledge of it can arise from observing acts without understanding rules. Their meaning and context are what make acts social. To abstract the observable act from its understandable rules will not make the study of society more scientific; it will avoid the study of society altogether. Just as the modes and rules of action are what constitute society, so, in a narrower professional context, are they what constitute sociology. But the relation between the sociologist's rules and the social rules which he studies is not such as to allow the former to require that the latter be lined up and counted, as required for 'science'. As one example,

statements of uniformities presuppose judgments of identity. But . . . criteria of identity are necessarily relevant to some rule: with the corollary that two events which count as qualitatively similar from the point of view of one rule would count as different from the point of view of another . . . Those rules, like all others, rest on a social context of common activity. (83–4)

The natural scientist's professional social context affords the rules which allow him to identify similarities in nature. The sociologist's difficulty is that his 'nature' is a society whose own rules supply criteria of identity; but are themselves the objects of study; must contribute criteria to the rules of study; and will suffer understanding but not measurement. It follows that 'his understanding of social phenomena is more like the engineer's understanding of his colleagues' activities than it is like the engineer's understanding of the mechanical systems which he studies'. Some of the social investigator's activities, like some of his subject-matter, may be made similar to the natural scientist's, but even when this happens it will still be true that

although the reflective student of society, or of a particular mode of social life, may find it necessary to use concepts which are not taken from the forms of activity which he is investigating, but which are taken rather from the context of his own investigation, still these technical concepts of his will imply a previous understanding of those other concepts which belong to the activities under investigation. (89)

If the investigator ignores the society's own rules about identity and difference and applies, from without, criteria that do not relate to those rules, then it ceases to be society that he studies. Whatever aspects he may see of human activity, he will not see its social aspect, for its modes and rules of conduct, including its conceptions of similar and different conduct, *are* that aspect. Of what he has already understood of that aspect, he may make his own arrangements, perhaps; but for that initial understanding he cannot substitute any statistical association of externals.

The difference is precisely analogous to that between being able to formulate statistical laws about the likely occurrences of words in a language and being able to understand what was being said by someone who spoke the language. The latter can never be reduced to the former . . . (115)

The required understanding need be no more intuitive or unreliable than is the learning of a language; but it 'is a notion far removed from the world of statistics and causal laws; it is closer to the realm of discourse and to the internal relations that link the parts of a realm of discourse'. Lawyers always, economists sometimes, understand society in this manner. Sociologists' work can be as reliable as theirs. If at first unnerving, 'it will seem less strange that social relations should be like logical relations between propositions once it is seen that logical relations between propositions themselves depend on social relations between men'.

This is not to argue that society exists only in idea, or understanding only through language. The analogies with language remain analogies, to indicate a view of society as including the acts, ideas and rules which the investigator must study, and also the ideas and language of study which he must use. In another analogy,

The relation between sociological theories and historical narrative is less like the relation between scientific laws and the reports of experiments or observations than it is like that between theories of logic and arguments in particular languages . . . One does not have to know the theory in order to appreciate the connection between the steps of the argument; on the contrary, it is only in so far as one can already grasp logical connections between particular statements in particular languages that one is even in a position to understand what the logical theory is all about . . . Whereas in natural science it is your theoretical knowledge which enables you to explain occurrences you have not previously met, a knowledge of logical theory on the other hand will not enable you to understand a piece of reasoning in an unknown language; you will have to learn that language, and that in itself will suffice to enable you to grasp the connections between the various parts of arguments in that language. (134-5)

This 'understanding' is differently understood by its advocates. For Collingwood, a hard labor of imagination must be based on some pre-existing affinity between investigator and actor. For Winch, and perhaps for different reasons for Weber, it is more like the scholarly labor of learning a language. For Berlin it is at once more scientific and more intuitive – whole life has many regular abstracts accessible to science, but the reconstitution of the whole requires an understanding more imaginative and elusive than is required in learning languages.

2. Knowledge

The idealist argument shocks many of the new scientists out of their value-freedom. They snort and sneer. Some understanders snort back. Each mutters of abolishing the other. Stereotypes abound. Scientists say: the understanders are afraid of cold fact, and are also too lazy to get out of their armchairs to look for it. They are afraid of being shown to resemble animals or machines. They don't want their cherished values and irrationalities brought into the light for inspection. They fear their own technical and personal obsolescence, when all their ritual humanistic mumbo-jumbo is replaced by an efficient social science. They nestle into the past and fear truth. Understanders say: the scientists are intellectually lazy and morally evasive and technically mis-directed. They want machines and research assistants to save them from the challenging difficulties of understanding, and also to save them from moral responsibility for their acts. They hate human freedom and morality and creativity so they dismiss these distinguishing glories of man, as 'irregularities', from their so-called science of man. 'A man who lacks common intelligence can be a physicist of genius, but not even a mediocre historian,' says one. Says t'other, 'In frequent contrast to this public character of codified quantitative analysis, the sociological analysis of qualitative data is assumed to reside in a private world inhabited exclusively by penetrating but unfathomable insights and by ineffable understandings . . . In some quarters, the very suggestion that these intensely private experiences must be reshaped into publicly certifiable procedures if they are to be scientifically relevant is itself taken as a sign of blind impiety.' 'Like the perpetual motion machine,' the first insists, 'the attempt to construct a discipline which should stand to concrete history as pure to applied, is not a vain hope for something beyond human powers, but a chimera, born of a profound incapacity to grasp the nature of natural science, or of history, or of both.'

These passages are unacknowledged because unfairly ripped from context. In more tolerant moods, both parties have at times suggested divisions of labor to their own advantage. For Berlin, the sciences analyse and history synthesizes. 'We can make use of scientific techniques to establish dates, order events in time and space, exclude untenable hypotheses and suggest new explanatory factors, but the function of all these techniques, indispensable as they are today, can be no more than ancillary . . .'[3] The sciences order information about some of the more rational, regular, specialized activities of men. When in whole life these mix with each other and also with the more inventive and irregular propensities of men, historians attend to what issues from the mixture.

Sociologists disagree. Some think that the historian's guesswork is being replaced bit by bit by reliable techniques, and that his diminishing remainder of unregenerate methods have no claim to use the newcomers as ancillaries, and no reason to expect that the same mortality and replacement will not overcome themselves. But other sociologists simply reverse Berlin's roles: historians will gather facts, sociologists order them. 'Understanding' observes, science synthesizes and predicts.

Perhaps there are horses for courses. Perhaps regular behavior should support law and scientific explanation, while irregular behavior need not be dismissed as it might be from natural science – if it is socially important we can try understanding it instead. Or perhaps those tables should be turned and science allotted the residual function: only when our best efforts still fail to understand conduct, should we resort to inscrutable (but perhaps predictive) correlations. Unhappily neither of these plausible arrangements happens as smoothly as perhaps it should. Persistent understanders take the most reliable laws as merely challenging their understanding: why *do* children learn, divorce and delinquency associate, the rich invest, societies possess religions and inequalities and incest-bars? Meanwhile persistent quantifiers and law-gatherers correlate items whose relations seemed plainer without it: if hunger drives me to riot they index me into a social tension curve, or field, or calculus; if I work and walk alone but carouse and sleep in company they average me for outgoingness and cross-classify my affectivities and rationalities.

What *are* the right relations between these methods of thought?

The heart of the idealists' argument is right. To retreat from understanding to inference from behaviorist observation, is wilful obscurantism, a stupid abstention from useful knowledge. More strictly, as all understanders argue, it is senseless – the actor's consciousness is part of any concept of action, especially social action. But the idealists' objection to science, though true enough of a lot of bad science, is still wrong in principle.

Actions, properly and thoroughly understood, do often show similarities and repetitions. Why should sociologists and historians be any less interested than economists are, in whatever regularities *do* appear? Actions, properly and thoroughly understood, do have consequences, especially the aggregative, systematic consequences which arise unintended from conjunctions of the independent acts of many actors. What conflict is there between understanding these acts and tracing their consequences? Actions, properly and thoroughly understood, are performed in situations, situations whose provenance cannot always be discovered by the most 'critical' rethinking of the actors' thoughts about them. Why should the understanding of an actor's thought prevent an investigator from offering, also, causal explanations for the occurrence of his situation? Or of the actor's upbringing and experience which may have disposed him to act as he did? To the objection that the situation and all its causes are themselves composed only of other people's conscious actions, to be understood by similar re-thinking, there are two answers. First, it is often false; not all causes, situations or consequences are understandable through actors' consciousness alone. Second, even if they were, there might still be room for causal analysis as a shorthand substitute for detailed understanding, in economizing time and sketching the out-of-focus context of action. Some of the trouble springs from confusing the use of regularities to support general theory and prediction, with the use of regular associations as the foundations of causal knowledge. There is nothing wrong with understanding a causal process directly, then generalizing and predicting its recurrence. But exclusive understanders may refuse to call it 'causal' in the first place, because oddly enough they seem to accept the scientists' exclusive concept of causality.

Recall Croce, satirizing Taine:

Facts are brute, dense, real indeed, but not illumined with the light of science, not intellectualized. This intelligible character must be conferred upon them by means of the search for causes. But it is very well known what happens when one fact is linked to another as its cause, forming a chain of causes and effects: we thus inaugurate an infinite regression, and we never succeed in finding the cause or causes to which we can finally attach the chain that we have been so industriously putting together.

Some, maybe many, of the theorists of history get out of the difficulty in a truly simple manner: they break or let fall at a certain point their chain, which is already broken at another point at the other end (the effect which they have undertaken to consider). They operate with their fragment of chain as though it were something perfect and closed in itself . . .[5]

Croce's argument against tracing causes has no logical connection at all with his argument in favor of understanding actions. He offers no reasons why the inner understanding of action should make the discovery of causes impossible, nor why it should make the discovery of causes uninteresting. His only argument against tracing causes, is that nobody will know when to stop. Thus he himself indulges the fallacy of a value-free science: unless the science is unanimous and of equal use to all, it must be no use to anybody. The first part of this book was meant to show that it is only the non-citizen, the non-social

social scientist, who can't know when to stop. As soon as the social scientist *values* either his own or his studied society, he should be able (if intelligent) to judge which chains to carry and where to peg them.

Croce and Collingwood wrote only of history, and were imperialists for it. Other understanders have more sense. So do some scientists. In *The Conduct of Inquiry* Abraham Kaplan suggests that there are two kinds of explanation, both scientific. Whenever deductive explanation won't work, what he calls 'the pattern model of explanation' will. The investigator is satisfied when he discerns, in whatever he studies, a satisfying pattern. Patterns are patterns of relations; 'relations may be of causal, purposive, mathematical, and perhaps other basic types, as well as various combinations and derivatives of these.'[6] That mixture of relations, it seems to me, will have to be put together by a corresponding mixture of methods, in which understanding will not exhaust its duty in primary observation, the duty Kaplan seems to assign to *Verstehen* on other pages. It will be apt to enter into every stage of the investigator's work from his first questions through his observations to his formulations of theory. Really, the idea of 'pattern explanation' says that investigators may do what they like, barring only mistake or falsification, and mix what methods they like. What is interesting is that a pragmatist who praises so many of the harsher scientific novelties should call this, also, 'science'. Perhaps it was a suave attempt at defensive incorporation.

Few scientists still claim the whole social territory – not at any rate for strict behaviorism or universal laws. Approaching the armistice tent from the other camp, Berlin concedes the scientific possibilities. 'Comte was not altogether mistaken: mathematics, physics, biology, psychology, sociology are indeed rungs in a descending order of comprehensiveness and precision and in an ascending order of concreteness and detail.' But the order is in the subjects, not the youth or maturity of the sciences. The strict methods won't prize any secrets from the more luxuriant and irregular subjects. '. . . Versatility, richness of content, capacity to deal with many categories of problems, adaptability to the complexities of widely varying situations – all this may be purchasable only at the expense of logical simplicity, coherence, economy, width of scope, and, above all, capacity to move from the known to the unknown.'[3] Max Weber found he could generalize intelligently from direct, discerning understanding of unique systems. Most social problems demand complex mixtures of observation and understanding, direct penetration and indirect inference.

But for some problems (and some factions) 'science' and 'understanding' are still alternative methods. As such, have they any interesting politics?

3. Politics

Is science for uninterfering scientists, but understanding the method for moralists and politicians of all persuasions? Or is understanding the method for radicals, and generalizing science the method for conservatives, or vice versa?

'Social science can only be objective in proportion as it is abstract and rigorous. Work done by private understanding must always express the investigator's bias.' Thus the conventional wisdom to which both parties often agree, though the advocates of understanding would say 'judgment and responsibility' for 'bias'. Its opposite, though not quite true either, comes nearer: Understanding can be very direct, complete, reliable (like learning a language). Abstraction and classification require a judgment often imaginative, often political (like deciding which killings are murders, which values are basic, which solitaries are alienated, which policies are bourgeois-deviationist, which sciences are nomothetic). The humanities are observant, photographic, matter-of-fact: they describe life as it is. Science is moral and fanciful: it patterns and dismembers and rearranges life. Understanding avoids the drunkard's search, the blinkered selection of whatever will yield to convenient mechanical methods.

Little about a young executive's experience in a golf club is difficult to *understand*. There need not even be much difference between radical and conservative, Christian and Buddhist understandings of it, beyond slight variations of distaste. But choice, imagination, judgments of intrinsic importance and prejudices about wealth and conformity may all go to work in the effort to abstract the young executive's affiliative from his rational behavior, his affective from his instrumental behavior, his membership from his reference orientation, his goals from his means. There is wide and realistic agreement in understanding the actors and actions that constituted the crises of Munich 1938, Suez 1956, Cuba 1961 and Cuba 1962. But choice, judgment and the war of creeds enter with the effort to identify and classify: was Cuba 1961 'a Suez situation', was Cuba 1962 a better-handled Munich? Doubtless most Soviet leaders have agreed in *understanding* the behavior of Russian peasants or Marshal Tito or Mao Tse-Tung; but they have taken wavering uncertain courses in assigning these perfectly intelligible phenomena to their correct boxes in the classifications of an abstract political science.

At least this frivolous view is no sillier than its conventional opposite. Both arise from stupid distinctions between science and understanding.

How arbitrary those distinctions often are, can be illustrated from one of the famous Hawthorne experiments.[7] Investigators set out to find some behaviorist correlations by controlled experiment: the output of six workers would be related to exhaustive combinations of such variables as wages, hours, rest periods, lighting, etc. For most combinations of these variables, production continued to increase, taking no apparent notice of the variables. The investigators at last attributed this to the heart-warming experimental interest being taken in the workers, and to their unusual happiness as a group. One can call this the experimental incorporation of two additional variables, and preserve the behaviorist appearance of the experiment. One can call it 'the illumination of covariances by new theory'. Or one can call it understanding: the new theory consisted in understanding, in the workers' minds, how they felt and why they responded as they did. In the discipline of psychology one can say that a fact was discovered: a trait or capacity in the workers' natures. In the discipline of sociology one can say that the novelty was not discovered but invented: a new way of behaving, and getting others to behave as nobody had before. On the one hand, stricter seekers of the laws that govern what *is* might have designed uninterfering experiments which would merely have confirmed the old knowledge of incentives. On the other hand a sufficient general theory of group action might have predicted the behavior of the Hawthorne workers and told the managers how to produce such behavior. But that general theory might have been developed by understanding – that is how Robert Owen developed it a century before at New Lanark – and consist of nothing but generalized 'understanding'.

But it may be useful to use these dubious distinctions for a few more pages, if only to further weaken by further exploring them.

Is understanding the method for radicals, but generalizing science the method for conservatives?

Both the conservative and the radical possibilities of a generalizing social science are implicit in a few words of Paul Lazarsfeld's:

. . . it is unlikely that any surprising "discoveries" will be made for quite some time to come. But it is this very fact that forces the modern social scientist toward his main tasks: parsimonious organization of knowledge through systematic theory, and development of empirical methods to gauge how much regularity there is in the social world . . .[8]

Radical expectations of this enterprise are like those of natural science. The more we know, the more we can control, change, invent. If social science carries risks, for example of new techniques of tyranny and exploitation, they are as well worth taking as were those of natural science.

But what if, in human social behavior, the fundamental regularities are not there? Or are few, uninteresting and unusable? Or respond to discovery by wilful self-change? Many radicals and 'active' conservatives agree in fearing that a single-minded search for regularities, in an effort to imitate science rather than understand society, may immobilize scarce money and talent to discover only few and trivial constants; and that it may dismiss, as too irregular for science, precisely the means and opportunities and morality of innovation which *ought* to be the subjects of a *social* social science. The really useful knowledge of any one society may not be universal in either of two senses: it may not be knowledge of durable regularities which would survive reformist 'rearrangement', and it may not be true of other societies. It may never be discovered – or 'invented' – at all, or perceived as possibility, by scientists disciplined to search only for regularities, and to value them in order of their long life and generality. Those fertile peculiarities, the self-fulfilling and self-averting prophecies, must irritate any law-seeking science, though they need not trouble anyone who sets out, as Weber or Malinowski or Halévy or Carr or Riesman or any working politician does, to learn and understand the internal relations, the directions of growth, the 'logical possibilities' of unique systems. What is social science for, if not to enlarge the number and potentiality of self-fulfilling and self-averting programs?

For example: to demonstrate mathematically what advertising contributes to an otherwise-endangered economic equilibrium, is accepted as an act of value-free science. It reports what happens, and why. To show that advertising diverts appetites from education to electrical goods is already a suspicious act, but the science can still accommodate it: the implied reforms would leave its universals intact. To select those causes and effects of advertising which suggest that it might be better for people to behave more variously, with many no longer wishing to maximize the measurable kinds of income or consumption, is not an economist's act at all, even if committed by an economist. It is a wholly political or immoral suggestion: by persuading people to irregularize their behavior, it might reduce the generalizing capacity of economic theory.

Those are technical objections to scientific purity. Even if they were belied—if for example some social 'particle physics' or 'physiology' were to issue from experimental psychology – there would remain plenty of moral and political objections to any spread of purity to the engineering branches of social science.

Even the most abstract organization of social knowledge is likely (as is much of economic theory) to offer unequal opportunities to different parties. And even its neutral parts promise (like most of economic theory) to be complex. Its engineering application will require educated skill, just as natural-scientific knowledge does. How will the skills have been educated? If in a law-seeking, value-free school of social science, they will have acquired no special moral or political experience; yet almost by definition, political and moral skills are integral parts of the skills required in the application of social knowledge. The more important decisions taken by structural engineers are cost-versus-risk decisions, only a few of which can in practice be referred to clients. In much social engineering the responsibility of the engineer is likely to be greater. It already is, in many branches of education, town planning, social work, psychiatry, economics and management.

Some responsible ethics are built into the education of psychiatrists, lawyers and school teachers. Some schools of economics make room for courses in other moral sciences as well as for some moral discourse within economics; others have abolished both these opportunities for moral exercise. Perhaps the latter have had too little time to produce, so far, any great innovators. They already turn out plenty of specialized skills for the market. If this means professionally irresponsible skill for sale to the highest bidders, it is scarcely a neutral skill of equal use to all. Happily, many young economists still import moralities from childhood, church, parents, peers, or their own reflections; but from the first four they cannot learn much skill in applying their moralities to complicated technical problems.

Debate about the justice and morality of social purposes and techniques and distributions, an awareness of the moral dimensions of social choice and action, should surely be built into any education in social science – as a matter of skill, not indoctrination. Since higher education is some mixture of starting research oneself and learning the research procedures and results of others, this moral awareness had better be built into the process of research itself; which need be no more obscurantist than are laboratory rules about safety or painless vivisection. Its moral dimension is of course already there; but (so radicals and the more alarmed conservatives may agree) the formal, generalizing, indexing and quantifying methods conceal or neglect its presence while the understanding methods expose and emphasize, and are more apt for educating people in, the moral aspects of social action.

For example, the two approaches to the study of delinquency may be recalled. One sought, basically, to infer the causes of delinquency from its associations, by methods of survey and refined factorial analysis. The other sought to understand the causal mechanisms first, then perhaps to map their distribution by survey. The latter method seemed to offer more technical promise. It certainly has more moral and political promise. In animal ecology, even if the understanding method were available, the other might be preferred as disturbing the subject-matter less. In social science, despite some efforts to create it, there is no consensus for that valuation. Some prefer conversational, understanding methods precisely because they disturb the subjects more – from psychoanalysis to social survey, there are many efforts to make the inquiry itself the cure.

The methods have other moral differences. If factorial analysis shows a causal relation between misjudged mobility chances and delinquency, it will still tell little of the subject's experience of that relation. More understanding routes to the same conclusion may, along the way, tell the investigator whether frustrated youth turns to crime as a rational high-risk enterprise, or in short-sighted but cheerful defiance, or in guilt-stricken desperation. Since in practice there will prove to be relations with more factors than misjudged chances – with employment, housing, parentage, education, efficiency of deterrence, etc., – knowledge of the meanings and experience which these present to youth must be vital for whoever chooses therapy: there are *no* morally neutral, single-purpose social therapies without by-products; and no factorial analyses which yield more than rudimentary knowledge of the existential accompaniments of their 'factors' and causes of action.

The same immediate understanding of experience may be as useful to the 'high' theorist as to the 'low' social engineer. In the subjects' most 'subjective' experience of society, much of the society's articulation is visible. Understanding may expose not only values to the valuer, but also causal connections to the most general theorist.

Another paradox: the more exotic and abstract the social science becomes, the less possible becomes that division of labor which would have the detached scientist discover the technicalities, and the citizens then value the items of experience and choose policies accordingly. To choose policies is to choose their by-products as well. Whoever composes a program must usually value many options, hour by hour, as he works. He cannot have the public at his elbow. Even if he could, the public would understand less of the problem, foretell less of the by-products, discern less of the options, than his skill should enable the scientist to do. But the public cannot be at his elbow, nor even give its whole attention to the limited options he chooses to present to it. At best, the public votes occasionally for one or other of a few portmanteaux of options. Often, it does not even vote for choices, it votes (where it is allowed to vote at all) for representatives to choose on its behalf. These officials may be able to spend a little more time than the public could, at the social scientist's elbow; but not enough to relieve him of his responsibilities to devise and choose the patterns of viable options he will present, and the patterns of inquiry and explanation which underlie the options. The people's representatives may see nothing at all of the 'pure' scientist, though his output organizes all sorts of explanations, implies all sorts of policies and is an increasing part of the curriculum in the education of elites.

However democratic, the social scientist cannot hand over each step-by-step valuation to public or politician. If he wants to be democratic, he must learn to represent the citizens himself, like any politician; and like any politician, he must choose which interests of which citizens to represent, and decide for himself when the representative's duty is to follow his constituents, and when to lead them, persuade them, divide or reconcile them, propose inventive options to them.

But he cannot represent people whose experience he does not understand, nor value items and options of experience which he does not understand.

On balance, understanding – especially of the patterns of unique social systems, and of the citizens' experience of them – does seem to promise more scientific yield and social improvement, than does a search for strict universals and deductive explanation. To that extent it should be the method of radicals, right or left. But if a preference for deduction looks reactionary, it need not hang guilt-by-association on other scientific procedures. Counting and measuring and surveying and associating and dissociating can do wonders for any understander's understanding.

The best understandings and the worst misunderstandings of the social experience of capital punishment have probably had less effect on its reform than have causal inferences from statistical associations of crimes, detections, convictions and executions. Or more precisely, and more typically of the relations between association and understanding, reform has followed the *dissociation* of executions from the other three.

Most understanders of the havoc on the highways have shut one eye and ridden one hobby-horse or other – like some of the selectors of causes for imperialism, they have perhaps been less interested in saving life than in inhibiting booze or youth or auto-makers' profits. They certainly accumulated less usable knowledge in several decades, than has now been provided in as many years by neutral statisticians – not neutral between life and death, or perhaps between therapeutic and theoretical promise, but professionally neutral between men and women, age and youth, drink and sobriety, speed and inattention, drivers and pedestrians and manufacturers and repairers and roadmakers. Neutral, that is to say, between valuable identities, chosen for the engineering potentiality of every one of them.

The understanding type of factory sociology is better than 'industrial economics' at exposing and emphasizing the moral and humane qualities of industrial life. But the most impersonal economic theory may discover more than the sympathetic understanding of individuals ever could, about the causes which raise or lower or displace employment, bear on wages, and enable the humane control of many of the things the understander values.

But the distinction itself wears thin. Just as formal theory often conceals a good deal of understanding, and requires more for its practical use, so may the understanding of unique social systems include the accumulation of limited laws which hold at limited times within those systems, laws as hard-faced as any formal universals. Many of them, though, might be hard to distribute. If you know someone well, do you 'understand' him, or 'know laws' about him?

The distinction is like any other model: it selects some qualities of statements about society and ignores others. As a program, much of this book is about the harm it does. But as a descriptive model it fits often enough. This chapter can conclude with one example each of a fit, and a program.

Politics sometimes dictate methods quite crudely, according to whether the investigator wants his society to invent or to imitate or to stay as it is. Until 1957, higher expenditure on American education may have been urged in some poorer states as imitation, but in the richer states and in the country as a whole it was generally urged as invention, as a possiblity peculiar to American society, a possibility discerned by the internal inspection and understanding of its unique wealth, values and institutions. But as the first Russian Sputnik circled the sky, internal understanding gave way abruptly to general law. Success in rocketry (and in war and in productivity and in ideology and in uncommitted Asia) became law-bound consequential functions of educational expenditure. On this topic, exaggeration should be forgiven any author who is Australian. Most arguments for the improvement of Australian education are law-based and comparatively phrased, perhaps because so much of Australian education is comparatively backward. If any unique features of Australian society do make unique educational innovations possible there, they are unlikely to be explored. Understanding and invention appear unnecessary and unpersuasive while even limited laws are available.

The laws are mostly of quantities. It is tempting to ascribe the 'quantitative corruption' of Australian education to the methods by which it is studied and argued about; but more probably the same politics account both for the law-based argument, and for the merely quantitative and imitative improvement which law-based argument suggests.

Just now, in the procession of social change, a curious paradox may sometimes incline both leaders and followers against invention. Followers imitate, for obvious reasons. Leaders outrun law of any simple kind; theirs is the first experience of their predicaments, and capacities. The inventiveness which put them in the lead, should be a habit by then. But, looking only at itself, the most inventive course for social science seems to many at the present moment to be, to reach for laws. In the most advanced societies this may tempt the sciences to transform *themselves*, at the expense of their ever contributing much more invention to the transformation of their societies. Law and imitation still go together – the first law the social scientists attempt, is to generalize the past of natural science to the future of their own.

I conclude that there is sense in opposing some value-free, law-seeking, behaviorist tendencies of science, as non-interventionist, to understanding and the historical type of explanation as socially active or inventive. There is also a special case for emphasizing the understanding components of research because they tend, more often than its other components, to exercise and sophisticate the researcher's moral and political faculties, with technical advantage to as much of his scientific selection as is best done with an ingredient of social valuation. No very subtle or democratic judgment of the morality of action can be built on crude observations or indexes of people's responses to it – on whether they squeal or cheer, fight or submit, buy or save, vote yes or no, stay put or emigrate or commit suicide.

Both conclusions are hesitant, just as both methods usually work best in company with each other. 'Science' should not rank methods for their own sakes; that holy word should dignify the best hold you can get, direct or roundabout, considering the nature of your purpose, problem, and subject-matter.

Nor, the next chapter will suggest, should hard knowledge of either kind always be valued above the fictions of imagination.

9

The Imagination of Effects

1. Two functions of imagined alternatives

For most practical purposes, knowledge of the social effects of social causes depends technically on valuations.

Statements of cause can be turned into negative hypotheticals – 'if A had not happened, B would not have followed'.* Most philosophers of history say this, but few seem to have explored its practical implications.

It is difficult to imagine social vacuums or stationary citizens. If I imagine history or society without one feature, this usually entails imagining some other, some substituted feature in its place. I have to imagine a narrative or a society made different by more than a simple subtraction. I have to ask: without this cause (perhaps a war or a law, perhaps a part of social structure or a trait of human nature) what would people be doing? They would be doing something

---

* Common sense may not always agree that if the cause had not happened, the effect would not have happened. If I am a member of a firing squad when I shoot a man dead, others' bullets will kill him if mine misses. In that case the substitution of one sufficient cause for another may be unimportant, except perhaps to my conscience. In social explanation it may be more important, because of the different values of the different causes either in themselves or in their different by-products – 'if voluntary association did not make this society cohere, then coercion *would*'. In these examples common sense declares that the cause does indeed cause the effect, even though in its absence a similar effect would still arise from different causes. To a few such cases, some of the argument of this chapter may not apply. But if mine and my neighbor's bullet will cause for all practical purposes the same effect, common sense will scarcely allow the abstract 'same effect' in the other example. The cohesion of society caused by voluntary cooperation would be a different cohesion of a different sort of society if coercion caused it. So common sense, as this chapter argues, will take a further step: besides causing this society to cohere, voluntary association also causes coercion to stay away.

different, or differently. It is my imagination of the difference that allows me to measure the effect of the subtracted cause. Merely to establish that a causal relation is present, I need only prove 'if not . . ., then not . . .' But to measure just what it causes, I must ask 'if not . . ., then *what*?' Economists may like to compare their concept of opportunity cost.

At the same time an imagined alternative to reality may do another service. It may indicate how much of reality needs to be explained. I imagine some norm, and need only explain as much of reality as differs from that norm. If my norm is perfectly realistic, there is nothing to explain. But 'norm' is too narrow a word; such imagined historical or social alternatives are sometimes 'normative', sometimes 'normal', sometimes utopian, sometimes nightmarish, sometimes precise models, sometimes vague expectations; 'imagined alternatives' is a better collective for them.

These two services – the indication of things-to-be-explained and the judgment of effects – may be performed in a single explanation by different imagined alternatives, or by the same one. Two examples will illustrate these respective possibilities.

Recall Bülow's explanation of imperialism. What had to be explained was the divergence of Bülow's own imperial policies from Bismarck's policies of German 'saturation' and self-limitation. An imaginary continuation of Bismarck's Germany after 1890 was the fictitious alternative which told Bülow what had to be explained, what effects had to be given causes. Causes had to be found for the divergence of reality from that particular Bismarckian fiction.

But although that imagined alternative defined what had to be explained, Bülow could not allow that same fiction to measure the *effects* of his own divergent policies. He professed not to believe that continuing Bismarckian policies would have continued to have Bismarckian effects, so he would not allow that the effect of his own policies had been to change what would otherwise have continued to be a Bismarckian Germany. Instead, he measured his policies' effects by their divergence from a different alternative, a nightmare of domestic disunity, the fall of the monarchy and the dissolution of the empire. Bülow's policies thus caused real history, including the survival of monarchy and empire, to diverge from the imagined alternative of breakdown. On the one hand the 'breakdown' alternative had some predictive bases. On the other hand it required imaginary assumptions about the policies that might have replaced Bülow's, if Bülow's policies had been 'subtracted'. It is easy to see what mixture of 'science', manipulative purpose and valuation entered into his imagination of alternatives, and thus into his technical judgments of cause and effect in the history that had actually happened.

J. A. Hobson, on the other hand, imagined a single alternative and made it do both duties. He imagined a model capitalism. The imperial, historical difference from the model was what had to be explained, and the only causes that interested him were those whose effects were sufficiently measured by that same difference between imagined model and observed reality. (I leave aside, for the purpose of this argument, the question whether his 'reality' was imagined too, by faulty observation.)

Imagined alternatives perform these services differently, according to whether they are imagined as inevitable, 'choosable', probable, improbable, utopian, or downright incredible. Some seem viable as alternative histories which might well have happened. Others (like Melvin Tumin's vision of social equality) don't claim to be viable in that sense, but they do claim to represent social systems which would work, consistently with all known imperatives of human nature and social necessity, if ways were ever found of getting them set up to begin with.

The number of non-viable alternatives which may be imagined is obviously infinite. Some of them may well be used in the measurement of real effects, sometimes to demonstrate how inevitable these effects were, sometimes for other useful purposes. The alternatives which can be imagined as in some sense viable may also be, on occasion, quite numerous. Some of them can in practice, but some others could not even in theory, be fully tested for 'viability' by reference to present knowledge of present and past societies. Thus the number of imaginably viable alternatives can seldom be limited by technical thought alone. But most of them are open to a great deal of technical criticism, so that their number and viability are not a matter of caprice either – they are not just 'projected values', fantasies without any order of utility, likelihood or explanatory promise. In the imagination and limitation of alternatives, technique and valuation and explanatory purpose mix, necessarily and inseparably, though unequally in different cases. But the imagination of alternatives, explicit or not, is technically necessary to most judgments of the effect of a cause, or the weight of any one in a sufficient set of conditions. It would seem to follow that, in discriminating among imaginable alternatives to whatever actually happened, valuation not only helps to choose which causes are worth reporting; it also enters, in practice if not in theory, into the technical measurement of the effect of each cause.*

Except perhaps the last, these are not revolutionary suggestions. They describe methods of thought already familiar by other descriptions. It was suggested earlier that explanations have by-products. The causes of any things-to-be-explained have usually been busy causing other effects as well. Valuation of those other effects often guides the selection of reportable causes of the original things-to-be-explained. To remove the selected causes would alter their other effects as well as altering the effect-to-be-explained. Many of the explainers of imperialism certainly had such whole alternative histories in mind.

'The imagination of alternatives' may also be a funny way of talking about something more conventionally described as 'the control of variables'. But the special characteristics of the human population, its consciousness, inventiveness, and capacity to be wilfully irregular, commend 'the imagination of alternatives' as language likely to lull or deceive the investigator less often than the language of 'comparative method' and 'the control of variables' may do. For many of the operations which it describes in social science, 'the control of variables' seems a far-fetched metaphor. 'The imagination of alternatives' describes a little more directly what appears to go on in the social scientists' heads; in any case, I ask the reader to be patient with this language, at least as long as may be necessary to decide if it has any advantages in use in practical criticism.

Is it really necessary for an author to make explicit his question-putting, differentiating or effect-measuring alternatives to actual history or actual social systems? Are some such alternatives more fertile than others? Do different values and purposes require the imagination of different alternatives? Is the discovery and discussion

---

* An Appendix, p. 432, is designed to make this suggestion slightly less horrifying to philosophers.

of any social scientist's imagined alternatives a fruitful way to understand and perhaps improve his work? More exercises in criticism are needed – in Part 3 such questions will be put to a variety of complex explanations.

That may be easier if types of alternatives are classified. Some are derived from the comparative study of other situations or societies. Both of these acquire spurious realism because they imagine, as alternatives for one narrative or society, things that were indeed true of some other narrative or society. Third, there are the honestly imaginary alternatives. These are not distinguished by being fictitious, because the first two are that; these are merely more candid about it. This does not always make them less 'realistic' or less 'viable'. They include all sorts of utopias, nightmares, programs, predictions, rational models, ideal types. These categories – imagined alternatives based on pasts, on neighbors, on artificial models, and on programs and utopias – are discussed in turn in the following sections.

2. Pasts as imagined alternatives

If two causes together change a system, its past may serve to measure their combined effects on the present, but won't sort out the effects of one from the effects of the other. The past may not even be reliable for single causes, if those are thought of only as 'external' stimulants. Undisturbed people do not *always* behave repetitively. They sometimes get bored or inventive, change their minds and habits. Nevertheless, variation from an earlier condition is the commonest and often the best basis for measuring the effect of one sort of cause – the once-occurring sort cited in sequential explanations. This is doubly true if it is also linked to its effects by some of the more 'visible' links, such as physical compulsion or rational intention, and if it comes by itself in quiet times to have its effect upon an otherwise undisturbed routine.

If some isolated, traditional and hitherto unchanging island society is visited by a drought, or by a schooner full of trade goods, or by a black-birding raid, or by just one charming but syphilitic castaway, then to trace and measure the effects of any one of these visitations may require no imagination at all, no artificial 'control of variables'. The past supplies a picture of what would undoubtedly have continued to happen if the visitor had not intervened. All variables except one are effectively controlled in the stable nature of the society itself, and need no artful fixing by the social scientist. But if all four of these visitors arrive at once, then the only effect that can possibly be measured against the stable past is the combined effect of all four. In order to attach its separate effect to each, the social scientist will have to imagine alternatives which never existed in the real past. It will not even do to imagine separately the effect each cause might have alone, then to add up a total by simple arithmetic, because the four and their effects will interact with one another. In practice it may often be easy to trace the effect of each by common sense, direct inspection or 'internal logic' if it is the sort of cause that has such a quality – the effects of drought and of axes, if they were the only novelties, might indeed mix as the islanders used the axes to cut cacti or coconuts, and common sense could easily abstract the effects of one from the effects of the other. But plain, unimaginative common sense can do no such thing to the tangle of variables at work in, say, a complex industrializing society.

But this very helplessness which prevents common sense from making theoretical predictions of complex systems, drives it to extrapolate instead: to make the past the chief or only guide to the future, whenever there is no reliably better guide. While John Maynard Keynes was insisting on the importance for economic analysis of business men's long-term expectations, he thought it would usually be safe to ignore the distinction between their short-term expectations and their immediately-past experience –

For, although output and employment are determined by the producer's short-term expectations and not by past results, the most recent results usually play a predominant part in determining what these expectations are. It would be too complicated to work out the expectations *de novo* whenever a productive process was being started; and it would, moreover, be a waste of time since a large part of the circumstances usually continue substantially unchanged from one day to the next. Accordingly it is sensible for producers to base their expectations on the assumption that the most recently realized results will continue, except insofar as there are definite reasons for expecting a change.[1]

As in prediction, so in explanation: the past is a model which the investigator *may* use, but there is no law that he *must* use it. When

Bülow wished to measure the consequences of isolating the German working class, he used a comparative model: the French history of working and middle class alliances. But for the effects of isolating the German Social Democratic political party, he insisted that comparisons would mislead. If the German socialist politicians were allowed to make alliances, they would not be like contemporary socialists who were not Germans; they would be more like earlier German politicians who were not socialists. If you like, Bülow alleged that national character was a stronger factor than socialist thought. But as a reason for doing so, and as a method of doing so, he insisted that the German past was better than the French present, both for explaining why German socialists acted as they did, and for measuring the effects of their acts and the effects of his own acts in isolating them.

If Bülow's behavior appears too artful by half as he imagines alternatives from different passages of the German past or from French or English pasts and presents, all according to their convenience for his dubious purposes, nevertheless his operations illustrate one point very clearly: there is not necessarily much logical or scientific difference between pasts and neighbors, between historical and comparative studies, as measures of causes and effects. Their political differences are often more important than their scientific differences. But certainly pasts (and futures, which can be used in the same way) do sterling scientific service. For explaining change, they are often the safest 'fixers' of all the social features that are prone to be forgotten as investigators – especially historians – concentrate on what does change, and magnify it. Models and comparisons usually hold or fix features noticed as common to all or to a class of societies. Pasts and futures fix these, but they fix others as well – forgotten features common to all societies, and the features that are unique to one society, though general and regular within it: geographic determinants, culture, national character, a multitude of continuing institutions. But they may always, of course, 'fix' too much: it all depends on the facts and on the investigator's purposes. Descendants from any past may fail, in important respects, to resemble either their grandparents or their neighbors; other models may be better than either, and the investigator may have to invent them.

3. Neighbors

Comparative study, richly fruitful in many social sciences, is too often discredited by the false claims made for it, especially by the claim that its only purpose is to simulate the experimental control of variables in order to infer their causal relations from their regular associations.

In a factorial analysis of the interacting effects of drought, axes, blackbirding and disease, their possible combinations would have to be observed in fifteen otherwise identical island societies, and then in perhaps seventy-five more, if half a dozen observations of each combination were thought sufficient to establish that its effects were reliably regular. To control the Hawthorne effect of observation on the observed, seventy-five more should be watched unawares if the original seventy-five know of the observations; and if the original seventy-five don't, the results may not be reliable for other societies which do. In complex societies and their unique histories, there are scarcely any single factors varying in otherwise undisturbed surroundings; and for factorial analysis the innumerable variables do not select themselves, so their 'real' number must be multiplied by the number of ways of analysing and identifying them, an activity requiring art and valuation as well as 'operational definition' and measurement.

Such analyses, like the observations of regular association which they include, are not useless, but their uses are mostly negative. Dissociation is more conclusive than association. Association cannot prove that irreligion causes delinquency, but dissociation, and other implications of comparative factorial studies, may indicate that it probably doesn't. Those who feel sure that immorality caused Athenian culture to decline, or that Christianity or materialism caused the Roman empire to decline, or that Calvinism caused capitalism to rise, or that tyranny arrests science, or that democracy corrupts manners, or that value-freedom accelerates discovery, would do well to test their theses by whatever comparisons are available; but though these may sometimes support negative conclusions, they can seldom do more than hint at positive ones.

Rather than imitating experimental control, a more promising use of comparative study is to extend the investigator's experience, to make him aware of more possibilities and social capacities, and thus to help his imagination of question-prompting, cause-seeking and effect-measuring alternatives, rational models, ideal types, utopias and other useful fictions. The function of comparison is less to simulate experiment than to stimulate imagination.

In a comparison of two, the investigator usually applies to his pair an analysis designed among other things to separate their similar from their dissimilar features. These may first have to be understood and explained, thoroughly and separately, in each society – in much social analysis this will be necessary to establish their similarity to each other or to any wider range of known cases, to identify and fit them for service in law or model. So valuations may well be needed, both to identify and to select similarities.

Not all the dissimilarities need then be dismissed as irregularities unfit for study. Their commonest use is to put questions to each other, to start a search for the causes of dissimilar effects, and to measure the effects of dissimilar causes. In *Work and Authority in Industry*[2] Reinhard Bendix compares the justifications of managerial authority in Russian-East German and in Anglo-American industry. Both industries are bureaucratized, and they are the world's leading examples of industrial bureaucracy. Do their similarities chart the regular, the compulsory degree and kind of bureaucracy required for the optimum productive use of a common technology? Not really. The conclusion that some of their common features are 'necessary', or must be universal to all systems which include the same optimum requirement and the same technology, is not based principally on induction from these two cases. It rests more confidently on 'internal logic', on argument from imaginary rational models, on the dismissal of other models as non-viable – 'How *could* you organize production, without . . .'

But their similarities are nevertheless set aside while their differences question each other. Why only one hierarchy in Anglo-American industry, twin hierarchies in Russian? Why the assertion of common purpose between Russian managers and workers, but of cooperation for different purposes by American managers and workers? Many of the answers lie outside the industrial systems abstracted for study, in the surrounding government and social structure, and in the different histories of the two societies. Different causes operating thence – for example from the Tsarist past and from Communist government – have their effect measured by the different-from-American features of Russian factory society. As causes, those features of Tsarist past and Communist government are of course merely members in causal sets which must include innumerable other necessary conditions as well. These others are left asleep, but their slumber is not determined in every case by their being common to both of the compared systems. Selected differences supply Bendix's imaginary models, each for the other. As question-putting, cause-choosing models, it would be equally sensible to choose them for their political as for their technical interest. As effect-measuring models they are clearly imaginary (for each other) and often unreliable; Bendix rightly supplements their services by direct inspection of causal mechanisms and by uncomparative historical explanation.

Comparison is strongest as a choosing and provoking, not a proving, device: a system for questioning, not for answering. For Bendix the provocation was fruitful, and the book is excellent. It is still worth noticing some minor points which illustrate the vigilance the method calls for. Comparison tempts the comparer to exaggerate both similarities and dissimilarities, to distinguish like from unlike decisively. The temptation is probably stronger in proportion as the user's purpose includes the development of theory or of general models. Thus Bendix contrasts the universal Tsarist authority over landowner and serf, with the comparatively independent, mediating position which English landowners occupied between their government and their servants. Russians of both classes expected the central government to control relations between them; English of neither class expected this. To exaggerate this theoretically welcome contrast Bendix neglects evidence of the extent to which the English poor *did* ascribe similar 'Tsarist' authority and power to the central government, and did expect the same function of it. A study of the tens of thousands of petitions to king and parliament in the first half of the nineteenth century would compel him to acknowledge more similarities and to soften some differences between the compared systems of ideas and expectations. Similarly, in distinguishing the American single from the Russian twin hierarchies in modern management, Bendix perhaps underemphasizes the presence and importance in Western industry of 'twin' or 'watching' agencies. They do not amount to the monolithic twin supplied in Russia by the Communist

Party; but ordinary police, company detectives, government 'company squads' and trust-watching agencies, the scrutineering branches of public and private accountancy, the presence of independent management and personnel advisers, and so on, do put a vigilante at the elbow of a great many officers of capitalist bureaux for whom ideology is not enough.

This is not to attack Bendix's able work, but to suggest that in many comparative studies the direction of theoretical promise as well as practical improvement may be towards finer analysis, with finer and more complex separation of similarities from dissimilarities. The temptations lead the other way, especially when the compared systems are unequally valued, the historical and theoretical yield are unequally valued, and the aesthetic delights to be had from matching twins and cutting distinctions are unconscious, or are mistaken for *scientific* satisfactions. Comparisons have intellectual beauty and lend themselves to beautiful chapter-constructions, to balanced chiasmic styles of prose: I recommend to any willing critic, a comparison of Bendix's *Work and Authority in Industry* with William Faulkner's *The Wild Palms*, in which a similar simplicity of structure is made to accommodate more subtle identities-in-difference and distinctions between universals and particulars. Care and patience are one method of vigilance; another is for the investigator to keep active in his mind a shuffling variety of models and expectations, besides the two which his compared pair supply for each other.

One use of a variety of models within a comparison was Thorstein Veblen's in *Imperial Germany and the Industrial Revolution*,[3] which included a paired comparison of industrial England and Germany in the nineteenth century. Three of its principal causal propositions were justified respectively by a theoretical model, a compared neighbor, and a remote passage of the German past.

Veblen had few and merely formal misgivings about making his imagined alternatives explicit:

What might have come of the new industrial era in the absence of the Imperial frontier and its customs is a speculative question, of course, and can not be answered with any degree of confidence, but . . . may after all be interesting as going to show the nature of the outcome from which the State's policy has preserved the German industrial situation. . . . In the conceivable case that the new era in trade and industry could have been left unregulated by State authority for State ends, it is fairly to be presumed that the outlines of the resulting situation would not even approximately have coincided with what has actually come to pass. (179–181)

Six pages follow of 'alternative history': a free-trading, therefore richer, more equal and more peaceful history. This alternative is drawn from a generalized theoretical model. The model includes many of what are now thought to be theoretical errors. It is very good that Veblen should thus make clear his imagined justification for saying that the real Imperial policies did more harm than good. Other writers make the same or rival claims, but make them harder to test by leaving implicit the logically necessary judgment of alternative effects.

Germany nevertheless prospered. This was embarrassing to any believer in free trade. Some strong and independent cause had better be found to explain such a betrayal of the free-trade model. As such a cause, Veblen selected the double advantage enjoyed by a late industrializer. The late-comer picked up a ready-made technology without the delays and costs of development, and without the encumbrance of a 'capital museum' of plant surviving from every stage of development. To this, Veblen added, more originally, a more important advantage for Germany: the technology was acquired without some social structures which had inevitably accompanied its development in England. In Germany, state and entrepreneur could exploit the new methods rationally, because free of the stultifying vested interests which had been generated in England by the development process itself. To establish this relation between cause and effect, Veblen used England and Germany as both question-putting and effect-measuring models for each other.

Why did the Germans seize their opportunity so late, so expertly, and so dangerously?

If an inquiry into the case of Germany is to profit the ends of theoretical generalization bearing on the study of human institutions, their nature and causes, it is necessary to discriminate between those factors in the case that are of a stable and enduring character and those that are variable, and at the same time it is necessary to take thought of what factors are peculiar to the case of the German people and what others are common to them and to their neighbors with whom their case will necessarily be compared. (5)

Their earliest history shows them to be racial hybrids, expert at cultural theft and adaptation. They put together a 'civilization of workmanship and fecundity' which Veblen regards (because it was their first, and a spontaneous, culture) as indicating their natural and permanent propensities; whenever allowed, it is to these propensities that their behavior will 'naturally' revert.

This past defines a culture alleged to be a constant, to have survived the later overlay of dynastic culture; a 'natural' culture to which Veblen can give full causal credit for the industrial achievements of the nineteenth and twentieth centuries. In one way only – by unifying the area required by the English technology – has the later coercive Prussian culture contributed to industrial prosperity. Was that a once-only contribution, or does it continue as a necessary condition? Veblen used the German past to show that without dynastic interference the natural culture would still cause Germany to prosper; Bülow used much the same past to show that without continuing dynastic interference, the necessary condition of unity would dissolve again. Veblen does not seriously discuss that possibility; but if he did, his argument with Bülow would have to be between alternative causes of unity, judged present and sufficient because of the imagined effects of their absences.

Thus two models – one from the past and one from general economic theory – serve to discredit all that Veblen hates in German government. Meanwhile the neighbor-models supplied for each other by modern England and Germany contribute similar services. Technological borrowing (defined by differentiation from the English model of domestic technological development) joins with the free-trade model and the past-modelled 'natural' German culture, to supply sufficient causes for the otherwise-awkward fact that Germans do prosper in spite of German government.

Whatever he may pretend, Veblen has of course not attempted (nor could anybody) a complete catalogue of the conditions for prosperity. We may see him ask 'What causes German prosperity?' and render a value-structured answer. Or we may, if philosophers prefer it so, see him as dismembering the question into value-structured questions to which comparatively value-free answers become possible: 'Would the good features of prosperity be sufficiently produced by causes intrinsically good in themselves, without any causal contribution from the bad features of this government?' We could substitute factual requirements for each 'good' or 'bad' in these questions. To rid the answerer's task of all valuation, we would have to go further, and nominate all permissible imagined alternatives by which he might choose the causal links and measure the effects in question, or instruct him to choose them strictly for predictive likelihood without regard to social value. These tasks can rarely be consigned to some questioner-client; nor do I understand how science would benefit if they were; but their consignment appears to be among the minimum conditions for a value-free science. It is certainly among the minimum conditions for a value-free choice of comparisons, whenever these fail to promise isolable variations with *all* unstated variables 'held'.

However ill-held the other variables may be, Veblen now makes the Germans' uninhibited exploitation of the new technology serve as a model by which some English facts can be discredited. Those features of English society which the German borrowers abstained from borrowing, and which therefore differentiate England from the German model, become the causes of English industrial decline: snobbery, sloth as a form of conspicuous display, sport, and a too-obtuse uneducated pragmatism. Thus English culture and German government are identified as enemies of economic growth, while English government and German culture are strong among its causes. A mixture of values and technical considerations has led Veblen to shuffle his alternatives from pasts, neighbors and general theoretical models; but there is no imaginable way in which the work could be 'cleaned up' either by expelling its valuations and all their effects, or by insisting that all alternatives be derived from and all questions be put by a single model. Criticism must be directed at the valuable as well as the technical features of the models, and at the values themselves.

Veblen's and Bendix's work seems hopelessly old-fashioned – 'interpretive', 'subjective', 'pre-scientific' – to some modern comparers, whose own comparative studies (now called covariance analyses) are indeed more refined, complex and exact. Computers allow large new ranges of material to be searched for covariance. But when the covariances are established, their discoverers are usually the first to acknowledge that these are merely empirical associations – they still require illumination by theory before knowledge of them is likely to be very interesting or useful. When the theory is mathematical, it seldom does more than express the discovered covariances more deftly or strictly. More often, the required theory is causal. It purports to describe the mechanisms of thought or feeling which produce the repetitive behavior whose parts covary. Like Cohen's and Miller's theories of delinquency (above, p. 209) or Dahrendorf's theory of class conflict (below, p. 339), it selects causal conditions and mechanisms, and has a logical structure, like Veblen's, Bendix's or any other 'understanding' or historical explanation. The theory explains the covariances, but could not be inferred from them. It gains strength from surviving the evidence of covariance without contradiction, but almost all social theory – including the most new-fangled – relies more heavily (though sometimes not confessing it) upon some 'shock of recognition', some direct and convincing understanding of how the subject people think and feel in behaving as the covariance records. Except for many differences of care and generality (not always to the advantage of the newer studies) the new 'covariance' and 'theory' stand for the same things, in the same relation to each other, as did the old 'evidence' and 'interpretation' or 'explanation'.

As a device for proving causal relations, comparison may thus be limited by the unmanageable number and uncertainty of the variables, by the intrinsically irregular nature of some of them, or by our distrust of 'inferred' causes whenever their mechanisms can be more directly understood. The accumulation of comparisons, as of pasts, will continue to do its chief service by provoking questions and sometimes censoring answers, rather than by finding and proving causal relations.

4. Models

In one way or another, most artificial models are selections or selectors, or both. Some are selected out of the material studied – the Ricardian model of the economy neglected much of it to select parts which, by themselves, seemed to constitute a self-sufficient system. Others – organic, mechanical or mathematical metaphors for manifestly different things like societies or personalities – are useful for what they select from life, for what they imagine about it, or more rarely for what they discover about it.

Models like Weber's 'ideal types' may isolate systems or influences, to measure or imagine what their effects would be if 'pure'.

Where the systems in life are reasonably independent, or reliable in steady environments, then mathematical models may represent the aggregate effects of many individual behaviors. Love and hunger are steady enough, and babies and money-values so countable, that demographers and economists can build mathematical models with considerable predictive power. They may also have powers of 'causal discovery'. Constant causal mechanisms in the minds of investors or procreators may have variable social effects, depending on facts about their numbers which are known to no one of them, but which may be measured and modelled by mathematical economists. It is not enough to know what each party in the system will try to maximize, nor merely to gross up their efforts by arithmetic, to see how big the crop will be. Within the aggregates, all sorts of interrelations will feed back to the individuals all sorts of situations. The input of behaviors is turned into an output of offers and situations, by processes of which many are not psychological at all and may be modelled by the logic (not merely grossed by the arithmetic) of mathematics. And yet, such models do usually depend for their power upon the reliability of the psychology which gives comparative strength and independence to the systems they model.

It is an objective social fact that people use money as a medium of exchange for the interchangeable values of a great variety of goods. Sophisticated societies have all learned to be very reliable in the ascription of these money values, and in learning the behavior that goes with them. Increasingly, behavior with money is prescribed by law, which makes it more reliable still. So economists have the double advantage, that they study reliable behavior, and have one important part of their valuing – the part sometimes distinguished as evaluing – done for them by their subjects.

By this, other disciplines are sometimes encouraged to *ascribe* such an exchange-medium to other systems of behavior. This is what many of the more strained efforts at mathematical model-building amount to. A vote is treated as a dollar, each worth as much as the next in a political 'market'. The interaction, activity and friendliness among members of a human group are given quantities such that their relations with each other can be expressed mathematically. The various experiences sought by trustees, members and customers of a public-service organization are equated as comparable – perhaps quantifiable – 'satisfactions'. It may be a fact that

253

people use money to represent the interchangeable values of a wide range of goods – but the actual range, and its limits, may be significant. If people felt some steady exchangeability between their values of love, power, beauty, nonboredom, etc., they might long ago have included these 'commodities' more fully into the money economy. The fact that they don't, or the extent to which they don't, may express their own judgment of the extent to which they do not expect these things to have steady values in different situations, or steadily comparable and interchangeable values for different people. The failure to invent any medium or quantifier for such behavior may usefully warn investigators, that the behavior is unlikely to be steady enough to support useful models either.

By no means all the attempts are unconvincing. There are sensible efforts to quantify aggregate effects, to express unpsychological interactions by mechanical or mathematical methods, and to 'imagine out' simple elements from complex systems. Mathematical economists set brilliant examples. Games theory illuminates strategy, though (like mathematical economics) not in a wholly uninterfering way, if the strategists adopt it as a skill. Communication theory discovers fascinating patterns, though their social and 'causal' significance is sometimes exaggerated in efforts to infer causes from the patterns, or to make them indicate qualities of loneliness, friendliness, urbanity, integration or conformity. Not much good will come of communication theory which steadily ignores the contents of the communications – but that is usually a condition of mathematical treatment. Group theory is more bedevilled than helped by its strain towards quantities and mechanics.

But for too many people, formal models change from discovering devices to become utopias – like Sir Thomas More's original, imagined because desired, however impractically. Enthusiasts long for a social life representable mathematically or mechanically – a desire begotten by another, often more passionate than More's, that social should resemble physical science. There is nothing intrinsically wrong with utopian models. They may do moral and persuasive service. They may also do technical service, for example if causes are sought for reality's difference from them. But they should not masquerade as representative models. If Ricardian or Darwinian models of society had been seen as programs and judged to be nasty ones, there might have been a few less imperialists, a few less worshippers of the robber barons, a few less unfortunates starved or kicked to death. These primitive examples are derided now – often by the authors of sophisticated mathematical models of minds, groups or economies. Yet these too, designed for description or discovery, soon start giving social advice. The modern model has its own method of turning into a program – having failed in its task of modelling predictable regularities, it turns into a selector instead.

For many mathematical or mechanical models, a selective eye can discern *some* similitudes in real life. What non-predicting models select from life for scientific report is now declared to be life's important, or objective, or significant structure. ('Significant', except in specific statistical contexts, is the non-valuer's favorite disguise-word for 'valuable'.) What begins thus as scientific hope for a particular type of model, becomes a preference for a particular type of social fact, without its owner noticing the irrationality of this change of purpose. In the absence of any convincing gain (not merely, promise) in prediction or control, it is just as 'ideological' to select only the quantities out of social life, or only the attitudes out of patterns of thought, or only the selfish or regular interests out of patterns of motive, as it is to select what seems valuable by any other test.

Herbert Simon finds that he can give mathematical expression to L. Festinger's selections from the facts of some groups' behavior.[4] He could not do the same for *all* the relations which David Riesman might select out of the same groups' behavior. None of these eminent three would claim (I hope) that this proved Festinger's selections to be 'more scientific' or 'more significant' or 'more valuable' than Riesman's. But less eminent enthusiasts still teach their pupils to rank selective principles according to their haul of certainties, uniformities, quantities or – best of all – the capacity of the relations selected to be mathematically modelled. By these judges Riesman's principle – of selecting what it would be socially valuable to know – is usually thought to define itself, by its overt resort to valuation, as nonscience.

Sophomores identify and differentiate themselves from inner-directed, other-directed and autonomous models. These are not merely references for the readier recognition and description of real facts. They supply causal explanations for what resembles them.

They select qualities of character, select causes to explain those qualities, and invite the characters to do some selecting on their own account, instead of leaving it all to parents or peers. As Riesman doubtless intended, their ideological potentiality is obvious. But so is Hobbes' or any modern model-builder's counter-selection, of whatever qualities of character can be found reliably in all characters, or represented in mechanical or magnetic models of attraction and repulsion, or of operationally-identifiable attitude and quantifiable affectivity.

A model chosen partly for political purposes may do good descriptive, selective or discovering service, and a model chosen solely to discover is not by that reason emptied of political characteristics. Each is as likely as the other to seduce its Pygmalion, who may forsake life for his model, believe life resembles his model, or try to force life into resembling it better. However imaginary, artificial models are not essentially different from those selected from pasts or neighbors; their use and promise should be judged by the same tests, both technical and political.

5. Utopias and programs

When Tumin and Moore debated Tumin's vision of an equal society,[5] they argued whether such a society could work, and whether American society could be made more like it. But these utopian and programmatic questions arose out of a prior one: what are the actual, factual causes of present inequalities? Does the division of labor cause them? Does the organization of labor cause them? Do they survive from extinct historical causes? Do powerful minorities merely take advantage of the division and organization of labor, to seize an unequal share of its product, an unnecessary and perhaps reducible share? To these questions the answers are not simply visible in a complex society. To identify real and present causes and effects, each debater therefore proposes an imaginary society. The only equal society which Moore can imagine is either patently unworkable, or so primitive that not even the poorest American would desire it. Labor could not be specialized and organized without unequal rewards; so the conditions for producing wealth necessarily include its unequal distribution. Even if other causes do join in to reinforce this one, there would be little point in manipulating those other causes, because this sufficient one would continue to generate substantial inequality.

It will be remembered that Tumin mounts two attacks on this argument, each based on utopian thought, on the imagination of an alternative condition of society. First, he disagrees that the division-of-labor, as cause, is merely replaceable by the others. He does not believe that division of labor and inheritance and opportunist plunder are substitutes, like bullets from a firing squad, such that the same inequality would arise from the first even if none arose from the second or third. He believes, on the contrary, that these causes are cumulative: that each adds its own increment of inequality. Since existing societies do not offer the seven combinations of these three causes for comparative study, he has to assert their separate effects by a mixture of direct inspection, and the imagination of societies without them. Second, he turns from society to its members to reinforce the same argument in another way. He makes an analytic distinction between two or three parts of any man's reward. One part is necessary, a man would not work without it. A second part he would work without, but he will nevertheless seize it if he can. A third part, if he is lucky, he inherits – he would work without that too, perhaps harder. Some of these hypotheticals can be supported by comparisons – within and between existing societies, men can be found doing the same work for different rewards, and some arduous jobs regularly earn less than other easy or enjoyable ones. But many of these 'senseless' inequalities are nonetheless made necessary by people's expectations. American film stars and executives as a matter of fact will not perform for moderate wages, they would sooner starve or marry or sell vacuum cleaners. Tumin has to argue that their expectations are not in the nature of human nature but are implanted by the American culture, a culture much influenced by the profiteers themselves – a culture to which productive alternatives can easily be imagined. So Tumin is again busy imagining, for how little reward a man would still work in the present culture, and for how much less he might work if differently educated and socialized. But Moore is, in this respect, no better. Moore may well be right in what he says, but what he says is no less imaginary than what Tumin says. When Tumin says his alternatives could work, and Moore says they could not, the two are being equally fanciful; yet their different relation of causes and effects in real America do, and must, depend partly on these fancies, and on the values that propose which fancies should be imagined and debated. As in most debates between interventionists and liberals, Tumin's values have the initiative, if not necessarily the victory.

What distinguishes utopias from programs is their relation to life here and now – utopias are to compare, programs are supposed to connect. Utopias may often be the more fertile of the two, selecting the many and deep causes that compel real life to differ from some very valuable, very different alternative. But to that selective principle programs add another: programs are meant to distinguish constants from whatever causes (and effects, therefore) are open to manipulation. They select the *mutable* causes which make real life differ from some alternative judged valuable *and attainable*.

Economists are well aware of the role of valuation, both by the predictor and by the predicted, in economic explanation and prediction. Gunnar Myrdal developed the argument forty years ago. With generous acknowledgment to him, there is a most elegant short demonstration in Paul Streeten's paper 'Programs and Prognoses'.[6] Between program and prognosis, dialogue never ends. Prognosis affects program by indicating the workable options, the different means to similar (seldom identical) ends. As a program is put to the test, earlier prognoses are belied, modified, improved; changing views of what is possible compel changes of valuation and desire.

At the same time, programs determine prognoses, and not merely by error and 'wishing it so'. Prognosis must use, as data, other people's programs and often the prognosticator's own. 'Not value systems in the abstract, not given sets of ends, but programs, in so far as they are backed by power, are an essential element in analysis and prognosis.' Predictions are not necessarily chosen for their statistical likelihood. There are gambling and loss-minimizing considerations – 'an evaluation of gains and losses is an essential prerequisite for prediction, where alternative probability hypotheses are available.' Choices of concepts, theories and models for analytical and predictive duty likewise entail valuation often moral as well as technical. 'A particularly apt example is the means-end model itself. By arranging and presenting the facts in a certain way, policy questions are already implied, which would not have arisen if a different model had been chosen.'

It appears therefore that programs are modified in the light of prognoses, but prognoses also depend upon, and are altered with, changing programs. Valuations depend on what changes are believed to be feasible. But the "constants" which determine what is feasible may in turn be altered by people's valuations. Faith can move mountains.

What has this to do with explanation or with the explanatory functions of imagination? Reasoned predictions (if fulfilled) will serve after the event as explanations; prognosis and explanation have similar structure and the same debt to their valuations. Programs have the scientific advantage of being conscious and honest about their values. To distinguish 'neutral' models (and the means-ends model which they often assume) from program-models as pure from applied, or as science from persuasion, is rubbish. Both types of model select identities and their relations, expose some options and not others, help some programs more than others. Marx, professing objectivity, explained and predicted. Some people worked for the events he predicted, some waited for them, some worked to avert them. The three had different success at different times. Nothing illustrates Streeten's thesis better than the self-fulfilling and self-averting effects of Marx's predictive explanations, and the unnerving behavior of some of the relevant data, which include (among items which Marx failed to predict) the self-helping prognoses of Stalin, Keynes and Elton Mayo.

When historians ask what made people's actions differ from imaginable alternatives, these questions might as well be organized by models of valuable or dangerous, stodgy or inventive options. Even the investigation of the past can be, in this sense, programmatic. It is scarcely necessary to illustrate the uses of programs in searching the present for knowledge to be used in the future. For many including quite technical purposes, programs can be the best of all imagined alternatives. Typically, they are designed to select and discover what causes reality to diverge from viable and valuable alternatives, rather than from unattainable utopias or from the less valuable alternatives suggested by the past, neighbors, or scientific models of no social interest. They encourage rational and explicit relations between facts and values. As discoverers' models, programs prompt mutually improving and reproving dialogue between wishes and possibilities, hard facts and soft options. Such rational intercourse between facts, choices and values is likely to be better, for scientific as well as social purposes, than any unwanted or unnoticed 'impregnation': between models and morals, marriage is better than adultery. Models must have appropriate technical qualities, but whenever it proves possible, they might as well have social attractions as well. There is an economy, a collapse of two stages of thought into one, whenever models *of* man can also serve as models *for* man. If there is sometimes conflict between the scientific and the social promise of alternative models, this is no objection to, but is rather a characteristic incident in, the proper dialogue between possibility and fact, program and prognosis.

An example is offered in the next chapter, in a comparison of the functional analyses of Elie Halévy and Talcott Parsons. At the risk of repetition it is worth anticipating here, as a good example of the technical advantages which a programmatic scheme of inquiry may sometimes have over selections organized by a 'neutral' model. Parsons attempts a systematic ordering of the disintegrative possibilities present in all systems, possibilities which point to, and are warded off by, a matching set of integrative causes. To these two alternative sets, the theory invites the empirical investigator to limit his search. Halévy starts from the other end: within a particular society he sets out to discern the most dangerous potentialities, and then the causes which ward off each danger. Each danger is judged jointly for predictive possibility and social value. This vision of dangers is just as systematic as Parsons', but by a very different system. Halévy plods patiently through a conventional classification of political, economic, intellectual, religious and other institutions; dangers of trifling value are ignored; dangers valued as important are included whether or not they are dangers of disintegration. Parsons' system distinguishes good from bad integrators solely by their integrative effect. Halévy can distinguish them by that test, but by other tests as well. He can for example imagine the bad (though equally effective) integrators which might imaginably replace the actual good integrators; he can imagine the good integrators which might alternatively replace the actual (equally effective) bad integrators. He can thus ask and answer the question 'What causes this society to have socially valuable rather than socially bad integrators?', or *vice versa*; or more generally, 'What causes one stable society to be different in valuable respects from another equally stable society?' Halévy's questions can include all of Parsons', but can dismiss many of them as (for *this* society) uninteresting. Halévy's method can cope better with system-change, with the conditions necessary for valued qualities of the process of change, and with non-disintegrative (or 'non-functional') causes and effects in change. The method is applicable to any society. Essentially, it finds causes for the differentiation of reality from a valued danger-model, which is, perhaps, the liberal's or conservative's rational program model – more appropriate than Parsons' model, since liberals and conservatives have more to fear than merely strain or disintegration. It is a more fertile model technically, since it can cope with mixtures of consensus and coercion, and with mixtures of inertia, dynamic equilibrium, and system-change whether institutionalized or not. But it cannot work at all unless the investigator is prepared to be a systematic valuer, not merely before he starts but at every step of his work. The dangers are not deduced from theory, but from values; they have to be discerned and imagined for each unique society. The value and coherence of such work will depend partly on the value of the investigator's values, on their coherence with each other and with his detailed valuations, and on their coherence with the technical parts of the work.

Pasts, neighbors and abstract models might suffice to discover regularities and internal relations in stable or slow-changing societies. But the constants to be found in social behavior in the twentieth century are too likely to change with a rapid fecundity alternately promising and terrifying. Is it intelligent in these circumstances to aspire to an independent, unwishful knowledge of what *is*, and of the causes which support what is against what was, or against the unvalued alternatives imagined by 'neutral' models? Is the yield of this abstinent search then to be handed over to electors and preachers and politicians to pick and choose what use they make of it, unhelped by science in the tasks of valuing, choosing, persuading, and inventing? This does not seem to me to be, either scientifically or democratically, the most hopeful procedure. As the economic and customary foundations of society change, as the physical bases of personality seem about to be opened to manipulation, we need a science of choices and possibilities. Such a science needs moral as well as technical originality. It must invent as well as discover. Inescapably, it must include political as well as technical debate. It cannot be a science only of durable laws and extrapolated trends. *It must be persuaded to stop indoctrinating its recruits with the peculiarly stupid ideals of generality, objectivity and cumulation.*

This is not to suggest that investigators can merely invent future facts, or that there are no constants to be found, or that past or comparative or morally neutral models may not continue to be useful and prevalent – important elements of them all are built into most program-models. Pasts and comparisons must usually anchor program *and* prognosis. It is in present facts that most potentialities have to be discerned. What I do mean to suggest is that, far from possessing any intrinsic or necessary disqualifications, programs often have technical advantages as scientific models. They have obvious advantages for social purposes. Both advantages increase as social choices multiply and social changes accelerate.

The use of danger-models and program-models in social science is likely to add further to the social choices, likely to make the social changes more deliberate, and likely to reduce the number of constants remaining to be discovered in social behavior by any more neutral, uninterfering science. To these changes, and to the changing purposes and methods of inquiry which ought to accompany them, program-models can adapt as other models can not. Some find it unnerving that the increase of knowledge, by widening choice, may lead to the falsification or obsolescence of much of the knowledge itself. But there is an important sense in which that ought to be the goal of our science, as well as its difference from natural science: for us, the purpose of knowledge is often to erode constants, escape from regularities, reduce the certainty of prediction; or if the regularities seem valuable, then to replace their causes, so that men may now choose what once they suffered from necessity. This is not necessarily a radical message, of interest only to those who want to change the world. Already the quality of life in rich cities, the directions of change in poor countries, the trends of population and hunger and ideology and weaponry all point to a similar conclusion, that it would require a radically inventive social science to enable our generation to preserve much of the world as it is. Programs already have scientific fertility as discoverers; as discovery proceeds, they are adjustable to the work of invention and persuasion, thus keeping in step with the maturing function and purpose of a humane social science.

There is a fable about that maturity. It runs: 'A social science which tries to preach, to solve social problems and reform societies – a normative science, explaining particulars historically and eclectically – is young. When it learns value-freedom it is adolescent. Only when it has an exclusively cognitive, abstract and sufficient general theory of existing social reality will it be mature.' This nonsense is marvellous for the precision with which it reverses sense. Faith – in an objective science of constants – has blinded observation. As if standing in the eighteenth century's last decades of natural necessity and slow-changing social regularity, the new men face fearlessly backwards, while E. H. Carr is merely one, most perceptive and lucid, of the moralizing old historians who notice the new condition of mankind:

It was not till the turn of the [twentieth] century that we complete the transition to the contemporary period of history, in which the primary function of reason is no longer to understand objective laws governing the behaviour of man in society, but rather to re-shape society and the individuals who compose it by conscious action.[7]

This is a truth for all parties, whether they wish, tomorrow, to replace or to preserve or to restore the social qualities and values of now or yesterday.

6. *Unthinkable alternatives*

Some realities look so attractive or unalterable that there seems no point in imagining radical alternatives to them. Some people, nevertheless, imagine alternatives so impractical or absurd that there seems no point in putting such wild dreams to scientific use. But it is worth while doubting both these homely thoughts, now and then.

One way to approach this topic is to reflect upon a certain curious European experience of America.

No library of social criticism is quite as vivid, funny, irreverent, penetrating, and downright accurate and businesslike as the American criticism of American society. The targets are the same as Europeans attack in America – the almighty dollar, the rough and smooth brutalities of competition for it, the going price of public officials, crime as a business and business as a crime and politics as both, the dealings and feelings of northern and southern WASPS with

Negroes and Jews at home and with the old banana republics and the new CIA dependencies abroad; split-level religion and obsessive plumbing and the DAR and many other mums; jungles, from abattoir to Madison Avenue; rootlessness and loneliness and other-direction. Of all these, the native critics are incomparably the best. They know more, detect better, understand more subtly, and enrich the styles of ridicule and anger. Their morals are often more puritan than any European's, but what from Europeans is merely sour disapproval, Americans sweeten and sharpen with compassion, self-recognition, and an Irish readiness to be entertained by villainous originality.

And yet (it seems to European radicals) these critics tolerate what they expose. Brilliant attention to the symptoms keeps everybody's mind off the diseases. It seems as if the superstructure of criticism lacks foundation because somehow the superstructure of corruption stands safe on holy ground. Critics of social evils refuse to explore their causes, or at least stop short of their more profound and sacred causes. At what ought to be the causal heart of American radical thought (Europeans feel) there is only confusion, uncertainty, vacancy. Causal chains are short, and unpatterned by theory. They will continue to be, while nobody wants to find causes which make America differ from anything very different. For some, nothing very different would be desirable. For others, nothing very different would be practicable – in America the foundations, like the winners, are too well entrenched.

There is the usual relation between the depth of causal analysis and the depth of change desired. To the same Europeans, it seems that modern American radicals have programs but no Program, revolts but no Revolution, a sure nose for evil but no Vision of Good. Or any visions they do have are ridiculous, visions of frontier self-reliance or town-meeting democracy which are consistent with the per capita production of, perhaps, 1840. What might be the world's most potent alliance of moral imagination and constructive technique, instead of reconstructing American society, nourishes its Community Funds. Even the efforts to extend the American Creed to racial minorities are efforts to make more of America like most of America already is; except in detail, nothing better than America is conceivable. So American radicalism is a social science without imagined alternatives. Because it imagines no serious alternatives, it discovers no serious causes.* European radicals have usually imagined that European societies would *improve* in direct proportion to the removal of *their* sacred institutions. German radicals rejoiced in the thought of a Germany without junkers or the private manufacture of steel. French radicals dreamed of France without army, church or urban capitalism. British radicals, though rarely bothering to dream away the monarchy, wished away their class structure and all its profound economic and social supports. All, often rightly, have thought fundamental change a real possibility, and deep causal inquiry therefore a useful activity. But even when Americans don't approve the foundations of their society, they do see them as predictably unshakeable. Both parties are right about their own, though the thought of both may have some self-fulfilling effects. As one result, the junkers and Krupps and the army and the church and capitalism and class structure have their causal activities thoroughly explored and their effects (perhaps) exaggerated. But what radical American wants to contemplate such alternatives as a British America, an aristocratic or proletarian America, an agrarian America, a poor America, or even a socialist America or an America of one instead of fifty states, or fifty instead of three auto-makers? Americans have both political and technical reasons for dealing in more proximate social explanations than Europeans deal in. They have less use for revolutionary plotting in life; and for the same reason, less use for Marx in social science.

This essay is fanciful, and exaggerates. But the European feelings are facts, and they do arise from the very different alternatives which, on opposite sides of the Atlantic, seem worth imagining. As two among many examples, Charles Beard in *An Economic Interpretation of the Constitution of the United States* and C. Wright Mills in *The Power Elite* seemed to suffer acutely from these frustrations. Marxist criticism concentrates upon particular qualities of capitalist society. Beard and Wright Mills attacked those same qualities – but not from

* For radicals, this is a frustration. For some others it has become a program – the productive, discovering divisions of social science (as distinct from its 'applied science' consumers) should now expel *all* dealings with unreality, or morals, or desire. A purely causal science of what *is* will be built without valuing nor imagining any alternatives whatever. In spite of such declarations, the declarers do use pasts, neighbors, abstract models and disintegration models, so the ban in practice is only on overt program-models. See, for example, the first and last Parts of David Easton, *A Systems Analysis of Political Life* (N.Y., John Wiley and Company, 1965).

the same base of theory, purpose or expectation. A consistent Marxist does not condemn the class role of the Founding Fathers. He sees it as an inevitable and progressive role, a step on the way to a very radical alternative. But Beard obviously disapproved of it. Avarice and the entrenchment of inequality are wrong. However historically determined, they are still sin. Beard was also a gloomier, better prophet than Marx. His more accurate prediction of America's future left him to thunder at the immoralities of capitalism without imagining any but slight ameliorations of it, and even those evoked a simpler past rather than an inventive future.

It is just as hard to infer from C. Wright Mills' *The Power Elite*[8] any very clear and workable vision of good. Who *ought* to run America, how *should* they run it, how *might* they be made to run it so? The social-democratic vision of a mighty central power used sensitively and well by officials under the vigilant control of a civilized, generous and peaceful electorate looked (for America) half-true already, and for the other half fundamentally unlikely, even to Wright Mills. When he tried to Americanize the vision, to adapt it practicably to real American resources and potentialities and states' rights, it became easy to condemn in his own implications the vagueness and romance which he himself condemned in others – nostalgia for town-meetings, and a Pentagon PTA. Frustrated by the insoluble problems of power, *The Power Elite* selects the evil features of power, the lateral interconnections between evil powers, and as many other causes and effects of those features as seem also to be evil in themselves. This gives the book a sort of order, though not perhaps the best order for examinations of intractable situations. A Marxist or a high conservative explanation of the same effects, if truthful, might have more unity and depth in its causal analysis. Wright Mills hunted about at the middle levels at which he was *generally* eager for intervention and reform, but at those levels he found few workable opportunities. So he could not give his book the good order of a program or an engineering explanation and had to give it, instead, the comparative disorder of a helpless warning. Except for the many goods achieved already, most good programs seemed impractical, most probabilities seemed dangerous or immoral.

But he had no such difficulty in selecting orderly engineering explanations for the unlovely facts of American sociology. Though

Wright Mills probably knew as much about American power as he knew about American sociologists, in my own opinion he wrote a better book about the sociologists. *The Sociological Imagination*[9] is work like Carr's and Myrdal's, to which this present array of examples is meant to contribute respectful support. If it is indeed a better book than *The Power Elite*, that is partly because its problem seems simpler, and curable – where other elites' situations are intractable, sociologists have no such excuses. As often as exposition gives way to explanation in *The Sociological Imagination*, the explanations are selected by a clear program-model.

In this program, sociologists should select, measure and explain whatever seem good, bad or important social facts in people's experience of them. To make the bad better, to imagine better still, and to judge (and enhance) the viability of good alternatives, should generally be the purpose by which causal analysis is organized. Properly understood, this program need not be the enemy of general, abstract or indirect science, whenever such methods honestly promise a useful yield, whether of engineering knowledge or educationally valuable understandings of society. But it is the enemy of abstraction, indirectness and generality as axiomatic principles of selection, as ends in themselves or methods without destination.

Wright Mills found it difficult to imagine good, viable alternatives to the misuse of power and maldistribution of wealth in American society. He proposed that social science should organize itself to develop such alternatives – and that did seem to be, for the profession of social science, one perfectly viable alternative to one current misuse of influence and wealth.

'Science without alternatives' may be contrasted with what many condemn as a science of unspeakable alternatives. Whatever its present shortcomings, Marxists' thought about 'post-Marxist' industrial societies could well be very fertile. Instead of urging them to give up their ridiculous communist visions and join instead in the open-minded search for scientific law, it might be better to offer the opposite advice, on both counts. Their present over-addiction to social law inhibits many of the good things which their radical vision of alternatives might otherwise achieve.

Marxist thought about noncommunist societies is organized by thought of very radical alternatives to them: a different historical process of change, toward a different structure and condition of society. These can organize a search of actual historical processes and real-and-present social systems, for the forces which have caused them to differ from the Marxian models which they 'ought' to resemble. Inquiries which go thus to 'Marxist depths' in economic and social structure, made insistent by Marxist indignation, can be as fruitful as any other radical research. One of the more reliable-looking noncommunist 'laws', for example, records similar patterns of inequality in most advanced industrial societies whatever their structures and ideologies. The necessities, choices and mechanisms which produce this effect deserve persistent study. Psychologically, indignant people who hate the inequalities are the likeliest to study their causes most ruthlessly. Technically, they will usually do best to look for whatever causes the facts to differ from some appropriate equality-model. Models of equalizing processes or mechanisms will often be more useful than models of, merely, 'equal conditions' in equal but unchanging social systems. Marx's model of the unequalizing processes which were to produce the crisis of capitalism provoked others to discover its many equalizing processes. It requires an 'equalizing model' to organize inquiry into the unequalizing aspects of the system. The searchlight should be turned on communist as well as capitalist societies. Oddly, those who defend capitalist inequalities as productive necessities are sometimes prone to explain communist inequalities as the effects of political tyranny alone. There have been all too few Marxist analyses of modern Russia since Trotsky died, and his could be improved on.

Of course, too many Marxists wear blinkers – as eagerly as any law-seeking sociologist, they select facts to fit laws or frames of reference already committed. A few manage to reconcile honest research with Marxist formalities. Others, shedding their blinkers, often shed their Marxist membership as well. It does not follow that they should give up the scientific use of Marxist models. Marxist models have great fertility still, rightly used, in questioning interesting ranges of the 'causal structures' of both capitalist and communist societies. So do Marxist morals, which can be as humane and stimulating as any other radical disapproval of existing arrangements; many of us would do well to follow Marx's example of harnessing that diffuse indignation to hard-headed research and theoretical illumination of the offensive social facts.

7. Facts without alternatives

There remains plenty of social science which has little to do with any imagination of alternatives, because it is not directed to discovering new knowledge about causes and effects.

There is work of observation and measurement, which finds out more certainly how people live, what they earn and spend and think and feel, where they sleep, eat, work, travel – and above all, in what precise numbers and places and circumstances such experience is distributed. From the census which counts people to the sociogram which maps their communications, this work may avoid causal analysis altogether, or concentrate on quantifying things whose causal structures are obvious. For all the great modern 'causal' discoveries, it may still be true that even greater contributions to social welfare have been made by improved methods of measurement, and their massive product of social self-knowledge. Knowledge of the quantities involved is often the most important but elusive requirement for effective social engineering.

There are also social problems, especially in rich societies, for whose amelioration causal knowledge is not wanting; what is required, is that people be persuaded to use it. (How to persuade them may of course be a 'causal' problem – not much helped if social scientists refuse to persuade.) One method of persuasion is simply to tell people the facts – facts about the distributions, pains and costs of social problems. Often the social scientists themselves can most vividly tell the rich what it is like to be poor, the white what it is like to be Negro, the Londoner what it is like in the Hong Kong – or the London – slums. Such work may select 'for value only'. It may do without any imagination of alternatives. Its only purpose may be moral, to persuade people to social action or to some different valuation of social facts. It is still too important, and its technical parts often too difficult, to be left to lay preachers.

Part 3 - Truth in Use

No dozen books could fairly represent social science. The dozen discussed in the next three chapters include none of the practical, planning science of communist societies, nor any of the spectacular modern improvements in methods of social measurement. The latter should not be mistaken for techniques of causal discovery by inference from correlation, which most of them are not, whatever some of them pretend. They have nevertheless allowed immense improvements in social life. The regulation of advanced economies waits less on new theory than on quicker measurement. Some types of social policy which have long been understood in principle become practicable with precise knowledge of the quantities involved. Many social problems have responded to old theory (or common sense) fortified at last by measurement (and changes of heart). In these improvements, many new methods have been technical and value-free, as befits most measurement, but their services to theory are few or indirect. Computers make more information manageable and new theoretical directions practicable, but even at their brilliant pattern-shuffling best, it is seldom the machines that solve the new theoretical problems. There are causal assumptions, sometimes new, in the development of reliable population and opinion sampling; but most of them improve measurement – the sampling, rather than knowledge of the causal relations of the things sampled. Such measurement of objects which have obvious quantities can often allow divisions of labor, leaving theory to theorists and sometimes, valuations to clients. By contrast, the following examples are best known for their theoretical contents. The best also include plenty of observation, including discerning discoveries of causal mechanisms.

Unlike some of the explainers of imperialism, these are too complicated for summary and too good to deserve it. The reader must read them for himself. If that seems absurd as a condition of understanding a few chapters of criticism, it can still be recommended for its own sake – if Marx and Weber and some up-to-date games theory were added, here would be a good reading list for a first course in social theory:

Elie Halévy	*England in 1815* (1913) which is vol. 1 of *A History of the English People in the Nineteenth Century*, tr. E. I. Watkin and D. A. Barker, second (revised) edition, 6 v., London: Ernest Benn and N.Y.: Barnes and Noble, 1949.
Talcott Parsons	Publications to 1963 are listed in his *Social Structure and Personality*, N.Y.: The Free Press, 1964. See especially 'General Theory in Sociology' in Robert K. Merton, Leonard Broom and Leonard S. Cottrell (eds.) *Sociology Today*, N.Y.: Basic Books, 1959.
Edward Hallett Carr	*A History of Soviet Russia*, comprising *The Bolshevik Revolution 1917–1923*, 3 v., 1950–3; *The Interregnum 1923*, 1954; *Socialism in one Country 1924–1926*, 3 v., 1958–61; unfinished and continuing; London: Macmillan.
Lewis A. Coser	*The Functions of Social Conflict*, N.Y.: The Free Press; London: Routledge and Kegan Paul, 1956.
Ralf Dahrendorf	*Class and Class Conflict in Industrial Society*, revised English edition, Stanford University Press; London: Routledge and Kegan Paul, 1959.
John Maynard Keynes	*The General Theory of Employment, Interest and Money*, London: Macmillan, 1936.
Paul Samuelson	*Economics, An Introductory Analysis*, N.Y.: McGraw-Hill, sixth edition, 1964.

W. Arthur Lewis	*The Theory of Economic Growth*, London: Allen and Unwin, 1955.
David Riesman	with Reuel Denney and Nathan Glazer, *The Lonely Crowd, A Study of the Changing American Character*, Yale, 1950; and with Nathan Glazer, *Faces in the Crowd, Individual Studies in Character and Politics*, Yale, 1952.
Oscar Lewis	*The Children of Sanchez*, N.Y.: Random House, 1961.
Gunnar Myrdal	*An American Dilemma, The Negro Problem and Modern Democracy* (with Richard Sterner and Arnold Rose), N.Y.: Harper, 1944; also *Value in Social Theory*, ed. Paul Streeten, London: Routledge and Kegan Paul, 1958.
David Easton	*A Systems Analysis of Political Life*, N.Y.: Wiley, 1965.

Of each of these it may be asked, how does he relate observation, understanding and valuation? What values and technics seem to guide his choices of classes and identities, and his imagination of alternatives, with what effects on his analysis of causes? How does he decide what needs explanation, and choose and know his explanations?

Most of these writers are paired for comparison, and most of the comparing is left to the reader. Does Halévy or Parsons deal best with social cohesion? Coser or Dahrendorf with conflict? Dahrendorf or Carr with change? Does Keynes or Samuelson, Easton or Myrdal give the best advice about the functions of theorists' values?

10

Social Cohesion, Conflict and Change

1. Elie Halévy

A History of the English People in the Nineteenth Century, un-finished at Halévy's death, begins with the volume *England in 1815* published in 1913. Although its title may suggest static analysis its contents reach backward and onward from 1815 to elucidate the forces then at work, and the processes and directions of change. This volume explores more of social structure, and explains change more generally, than do its narrative successors. It may be seen as a complex and impressive structural-functional analysis of a whole society. From it, functional analysts might learn much about the functions of valuation and the uses of models – especially, that a functional analysis of social integration may be organized better by systematic valuation of the system's detailed potentialities, than by the *general* model of disintegration which otherwise, consciously or not, has to organize any functional explanation of integration.

Halévy was not directly interested in either the integration (merely) or the persistence of the English social system; he was interested in the growth within it of some specific valuable qualities. It was those deliberately valued qualities whose causes he would seek in English society. Many of the qualities thus chosen as effects-to-be-explained were qualities of processes of change. From all the conditions necessary for them, he chose those which warded off particular alternatives – alternatives chosen as likely-and-dangerous for the English system. But sometimes he took these alternatives from recent French history, choosing what he valued as the most dangerous causes of its most destructive conflicts. He then looked for the English 'functional substitutes' for these French disintegra-tors. Just as its virtues do, the work's shortcomings (by which I mean its failure to relate the facts to his own values as well as it might have done) owe a good deal to these French choices. On the one hand French contrasts prompted fertile questions which had not occurred to native English historians. On the other hand the French alternatives were not always the most likely or valuable alternatives to 'imagine for England'. Alternatives bound less to French facts, deliberately imagined rather than borrowed or remembered, might have served Halévy's purpose better.

But if some details were ill-chosen, the general method was right. A functional analysis of the causes of social cohesion can only be as good as its imagined alternatives of disintegration are well judged for 'viability' and well ranked by intelligent valuation. The causes of a cohesion ward off an incohesion. Until you decide which breakdowns are worth watching for – a jointly technical and valuational judgment – it is difficult to select the significant causes of the cohesion. Since societies may be integrated by force, not every quest for the causes of integration need be organized by a conflict model of the alternatives to integration. But a conflict model is one promising organizer of a search for patterns of voluntary cooperation – for patterns of consent rather than coercion.

It would scarcely have occurred to Halévy that either pattern could represent a static equilibrium. Most of the problems of order and anarchy *are* problems of change; many conflicts to be contained by social institutions (including those generated by them) are conflicts about changes. So he looked for the causes of the peaceful modes and liberal directions of change. He often expected to find the causes in institutionalized methods of contriving and controlling change, but he expected these methods too to be changing, if more slowly. To find these things he systematically imagined their 'opposites' and asked himself what causes would have to be present to produce those opposites. By England's difference from his answers, he identified the causes of, and measured their effects on, English liberty and order. Except that, sometimes, he omitted to *imagine* what causes would be required to produce the illiberal alternatives in England, because he already *knew* what produced the illiberal alternatives in France. But I do not mean to exaggerate Halévy's shortcomings. Sometimes each model was apt for the other, and when it was not he often did put his outstandingly intelligent and well-disciplined imagination to work.

It may be best to begin by watching this imagination at work on a small scale, since 'imagination' and 'using a model' are in some respects misleading descriptions of it. In a broad sense the modelled or imaginary possibilities are always present, but in some of his detailed operations Halévy may be better described as understanding, selecting, extrapolating. Of every institution or group or idea that he investigates, he selects the disintegrative potentialities; then explains how these were balanced or contained (if they were) whether by impersonal forces, luck or contrivance. On the most local scale, see him do it to one group within one profession, citing both foreign models and his understanding of native propensities:

Active, wealthy, intelligent, but without social standing the solicitors had every inducement to become a discontented class in revolt against a system which condemned them to a position of social inferiority. John Frost, one of the leading 'Jacobin' agitators in 1794, was a solicitor. About the same period Burke made it a reproach against the new democracies of France and America that they were governed by solicitors. It would, nevertheless, be a mistake to suppose that the established order of society was ever in any danger from the grievances of the English solicitors; for they were comforted by the knowledge that it was in their power to win for their children the standing they could never obtain for themselves. A solicitor's son, called to the Bar, possessed the most favourable opening for a brilliant career . . . Changes caused by wars rendered access to the Bar even easier than before. And the moment a solicitor's son began to practise at the Bar he felt himself a member of the governing class and shared its snobbery. (22–3)

The passage is preceded, followed and footnoted by reports of facts that support it; but it goes beyond report, to imagination. Halévy cannot report any 'facts' of solicitors advancing to the brink of revolt, then remembering their sons' futures and retreating again. The disruptive potentiality has to be imagined as going to work *in fact* if different facts about the recruitment and reward of barristers are *imagined*. When Halévy turns from this imagination of the disruptive potentiality of a group, to put the same questions to the structure of an institution, he makes his imagination of disintegrative alternatives even more explicit:

A body of officials, drawn from the middle or lower classes and poorly paid, would be animated by feelings of jealousy towards the aristocracy. On such officials a monarch, greedy of power, could rely for support in a struggle against the arrogant pretensions of the heads of the great families. But it was to satisfy the claims of this aristocracy that those offices of wealth and influence in the Civil Service had been instituted. And these high officials, securely entrenched in their bureaus, bid the Crown defiance . . . In many respects the bureaucracy of London presented the characteristics of an hereditary feudalism.

'It is our purpose', contended the Opposition speakers, 'by a reform of the administration, to prevent the establishment in our midst of a powerful bureaucracy under the control of a despotic monarch.' 'Your contention is absurd', replied the supporters of the Government. 'These very abuses, at which you exclaim, effectively limit the royal prerogative and protect the aristocracy against the Crown.' We cannot be surprised that public opinion watched with an ever-increasing scepticism a dispute in which both parties were obviously fighting for their own interests. (15–16)

What that particular Civil Service caused depends on what monarch and aristocrats would be doing without it. But one cannot imagine them without any civil service, so Halévy poses a likely and dangerous alternative.

These samples fairly represent Halévy's approach to each of the groups, professions, classes, institutions, ideas and systems of thought and belief that he so methodically surveys. For a most intricate example the reader should follow Halévy's selection of the disruptive potentialities (not facts: dangerous possibilities) of Utilitarian thought, on pages 571–583, and his explanation of their peaceful accommodation, on pages 583–587 (almost all of which passages would be banned by many 'scientistic' rules of search). His more general, synthesizing explanations have the same pattern. So does the structure of his book.

Did English political institutions contain or resolve more conflicts than they generated? Did they sufficiently contain or resolve whatever conflicts might arise in society from other causes? Halévy concludes his Part One (Political Institutions) by answering 'no' to both questions.

The Government was systematically weakened, always a prey to internal strife, and deprived by the Constitution itself of the necessary means to repress economic or religious disorders, the war of classes and creeds. Nevertheless . . . What actually took place in England was this. The elements of disorder and anarchy inherent in the political tradition of the country lost their character and submitted insensibly to a discipline freely accepted. Though sects multiplied, sectarian animosities died down. Riot was softened into peaceable demonstration, and civil war became a party strife, waged in accordance with rules freely admitted on either side. We must, therefore, seek elsewhere, in the economic organization or the religious life of the nation, the secret of this progressive regulation of liberty. (200)

One effect of Halévy's method, of his detailed imagination of the disruption latent in each part of the political system, is that a critic of the above summary conclusion can usually base his critique on the very chapters it summarizes. For example, one assumption which underlies the summary, though often absent from the detailed explanations, is the notion that government contributes to social peace chiefly by repressing disorders. A strong government could keep the peace. But England combines social peace with weak government. Halévy deduces that there must be nothing to repress, that the causes of social peace must be elsewhere, not in the relations between government and governed. Yet it is easy to show (and many of his detailed explanations show it) that English governments sometimes did face, and more often feared, disorders. They often responded with legislative concessions in which they themselves saw little intrinsic merit. Strong among their reasons for giving way so weakly was their awareness of their own weakness. There followed some harmony for its own sake, and some of precisely the limited, deliberate, harmonious change that Halévy most admired. What this criticism alleges is that Halévy's summary explanation omitted an important class of facts (the extensive concessions which government made to what might otherwise have developed into rebellious forces) and an important cause of those facts (government's knowledge of its weakness). Of all people why should Halévy, composing a peroration with style and care, forget such factors?

His later explanations logically required this rejection of 'political solutions'. But his model and method may also have helped. Within his own plus one lifetime at least seven revolutions had overthrown French governments whose central civil and military powers extended to every corner of the country and to every level of local administration. Halévy noticed how weak, by contrast, English governments were; how much less they could do than even those fallen French governments could do, to defend themselves and public order. Some of the French conflicts could moreover be understood as conflicts between government and governed, conflicts which those strong Executives were still too weak to win. What Halévy perhaps noticed less, was the sense in which some of those Executives thought themselves too strong to lose. Charles X, Louis Philippe and the conservative republican regime of 1850 might well have conceded enough to their moderate opponents to avert revolution, if their apparent executive power had not blinded them to some of the dangers in which they stood. For a time the kings respectively defied and controlled their legislatures, and the republican legislators defied a good many of both revolutionary and anti-revolutionary opinions. Each might well have preserved his power by underestimating it and making concessions accordingly. Halévy's comparative method could easily have suggested this to him and with it, a contrasting English relation between prudent Executive cowardice and peaceful social progress. Neither Wellington nor Peel 'believed in' emancipating Irish Catholics. Neither William IV nor Grey 'believed in' enfranchising English shopkeepers. With French executive and military powers and budgets they might well have resisted both to the death. But all four justified their compromises by claiming that they might have been unable otherwise to prevent – even perhaps to win – civil wars.

Similar things can be said of Part Two in which Halévy asks what the economic system contributed to war or peace in the social processes of economic growth. His answer: powerful tendencies to conflict and disorder, tendencies uncompensated within the economic system.

Once again one can allege failures of discernment, and wonder whether they arose from the French education of Halévy's expectations, or from the religious and social interests that led him to *wish* for religious and social explanations; and to avoid, therefore, economic solutions for his problem. Most of the facts made his task easy, though his use of them did some unnoticed damage to the conclusions of his political Part One. In Part One he had emphasized the weakness of the Executive in any conflict with the other branches of government, or with the social classes whose power was entrenched in those other branches. He tended to generalize this as a weakness of 'government' against 'people'. But Part Two ascribes a good deal of the revolutionary temper of the poor to the brutal effectiveness with which almost all branches of central and local government combined to reinforce the efforts of the classes they represented to exploit the classes they did not represent. Even if this alters the picture of 'weak' government, it still strengthens the picture of 'net disruptive' government. But that is weakened in its turn, by Halévy's account of the extravagant and charitable response of many Poor Law administrators to the troubles of war and industrial growth; but even this introduced new conflicts between and among industrial employers and landowning ratepayers, and eventually, savage reprisals by both upon the poor.

Generally he presents an unoriginal picture of conflict between the economic classes and interest groups, and a more original picture of the disunity, confusion and conflict within each. In this whole section, models from economic theory or (implicitly) the English future are present more often than memories of French history. Only in one case, perhaps, do the latter do much damage to the argument. Halévy took pains to show that the new entrepreneurs, though apparently buoyant optimists, took many beatings from each other, from wild economic conditions and wilder economic theories, from the crazy arrangement of credit institutions, from a landowning government and from their own individual and collective inexperience. He is not content to ascribe revolutionary potential merely to the 'external relations' of a solid manufacturing class-interest, in its conflicts with governments, farmers and proletarians. He sees worse sources of disorder in the conflict and confusion within the business world itself. He does not explicitly compare the English with the more slow-growing and stable manufacturing enterprises in France, but once again it is possible that a French comparison misled where it might have enlightened him. French factories engaged a smaller group of entrepreneurs and preserved their capital more reliably; by this, the numbers and risks and ruinations and general confusion of English manufacturing may have been dramatized, and also perhaps its disorderly possibilities.

But more imagination was required: suppose there *had* been a French Manchester, *which* Frenchmen would have gathered to cut each others' economic throats in it? And what were these imaginary entrepreneurs doing instead, in the fact of a France without much of a Manchester? Not, perhaps, peacefully tilling the soil and supporting the government. The (merely relative) stabilities of French industry and agriculture may be joined with the central control of the vast French public service, to suggest another contrast – between French and English patterns of individual opportunity. That pattern may have mattered less to the more static French population. But still, for any able, under-graded French youth, business offered *comparatively* few and unexciting opportunities. There were *comparatively* less mercantile and colonial opportunities. There were many more public offices, but a great many of them were under a single political master – *personae non gratae* might grow actively ungrateful when one enemy could bar them from more than a million public employments, while an English youth retained as many chances as he had uncles, or his country had colonies. If the risks in English business were tremendous so were the rewards, and most of both seemed to most of the contenders to be more intrinsic to the game than curable by either government or revolution. Partly because of its conflicts, English society must have had a very high capacity to employ insubordinate talent, talent whose French equivalent may have found its opportunities more closely limited to the literary-revolutionary culture of Paris.

If there is any force in this point, there was nothing in Halévy's French comparison to obscure it from him. Unless, perhaps, a valued intention of that comparison. To argue as in the paragraph above is to see French and English responding differently *because* to different problems and circumstances. That *because* is only justified if we assume French and English to be similar people who would have responded in similar ways if they had found themselves in similar circumstances. But perhaps Halévy was using his French conflict-model, and gambling his greatest project, to discover *different* responses to *similar* problems. In his lifetime French industrial growth promised all the social disruption that English institutions had already, somehow, moderated. Sharing his contemporary Durkheim's anxious concern for a harmonious voluntary social discipline, he was searching the social history of England's industrial revolution for better-than-French solutions for the universal problems of industrializing societies. The circumstances and problems promised to be much the same in the two countries, but neither Halévy's social values nor his scientific expectations would tempt him to look for universally similar social responses to those problems. If quite distinct French problems caused the

French disorders, the disorders might prove incurable. Insofar as British behavior brought order out of *the same* problems, the French might hope to learn to behave better.

If not in politics or the economy, where else could Halévy search for the British secret?

E. H. Carr's history of Soviet Russia (to be noticed later) seems to be organized by a valuation of a certain sort of social liberty which has to be exercised collectively. In Halévy's work it is possible to see a milder operation of Carr's valuation of rational deliberation; and of the special causal importance which those who value it, ascribe to it. But although Halévy certainly searched for social choices, his regard for self-disciplined individual liberty continued to be the principal source of his social valuations. He might well have dissented from Carr's comparative valuations of the individual slaveries under Stalin, and the social choices which may open to the slaves' grandchildren. Carr's and Halévy's methods have other similarities. Carr brought all sorts of past-based predictions to converge on the 'necessity' of a Russian Thermidor, in order to measure and value the Bolshevik defiance of necessity. So did Halévy bring together well-based predictions of English conflict and disorder, in order to identify and value the liberating choices of 'voluntary order'. The Russian choices were made chiefly by a few tyrants; Halévy's England had no such minority in command, and he had somehow to search for the choices in the ill-documented lives of millions. He turned from politics and economics to 'another category of social phenomena – to beliefs, emotions, and opinions, as well as to the institutions and sects in which these beliefs, emotions and opinions take a form suitable for scientific inquiry.' (383)

In Part Three, as elsewhere, there is minor discord between Halévy's prologue, his conclusions, and the wealth of detailed explanations which lie between. The prologue announces the explanation for which he is most famous: Methodist religion explains the good order of English society. This, the least convincing of his larger explanations, might be crudely summarized (not by Halévy) thus:

The likeliest sources of revolutionary disorder were the industrial working and middle classes, and perhaps the farm laborers. The workers, town or country, would only be dangerous if led. But their self-selected best individuals, the natural leaders whose efforts raised them individually out of the class, registered their success by joining the Methodist church. There, they found an ascetic ethic which agreed with the requirements for business success in those days of self-financing (and slave-driving) entrepreneurs. They also heard a quietist, anti-political message; devoted themselves to self-improvement; and learned self-government in voluntary religious and charitable associations. So the natural leaders of the working class repudiated it, or lent their influence to reforming it, rather than to reforming society on its behalf. Any reforming energy left over from saving souls went to such wholesome causes as governmental honesty and thrift, religious equality, Sunday observance, evangelical charity and universal education.

Even with the best of evidence this argument is usually defenceless against the converse of it. If secular ambition took men into the church it may also have determined the message they should hear there. Even Halévy has them both joining and (a generation later) leaving the church for exclusively social reasons. While they were members, the causal link between the church's message and their conduct has to be inferred (as Halévy gently reproved Max Weber for inferring it) chiefly from juxtaposing the two, and discerning their logical relations. Halévy is no better than others who have failed to prove the influence of preachers on congregations or of congregations on preachers; or the influence upon each other of business, social and religious thoughts within any parishioner's mind. He might have done better to have discerned affinities (like Southern) rather than alleging causes (like Weber); though to some extent (like both) he does see the affinities themselves as giving coherence, and energy in all directions, to minds in which the religious and social and other thoughts agreed so well with each other. He might still have done better to use the method he used so well elsewhere. He might have imagined more directly and fictitiously what the rising individuals might have done without Methodism, and what Methodists might have preached if their congregations had been confined to unrising Welsh miners.

Perhaps the Methodists impressed Halévy in the crudest way, as one fair-sized English cause which was undeniably absent from France. Perhaps he was bemused by the scientistic dream of his friend Durkheim, that for any social effect it ought to be possible to find just *one* 'efficient' cause. Perhaps art – in this symmetrically constructed book – required a decisive conclusion, a resolution of the plot. Whatever his social, scientific or artistic strain to find a single cause, he did at least surround his choice of it by a very thorough understanding of a vast and intricate network of other causes at work upon the same effect. As a result, the rest of his explanations survive well enough without their Methodist connections.

Halévy examined the structure and activities of the network of English voluntary associations. Institution by institution and idea by idea, he continued his search for disruptive possibilities. Did its poorer yield (in Part Three) reflect the facts, or the diminished energy of Halévy's imagination? Strangely, he did not see the grass-roots as important causes or effects of weak central government, except that they explained how weak government could survive. Not only in the churches, but also in the institutions and ideas of utilitarian atheism and of science, art, literature, education and unofficial political debate, he discovered the springs of orderly continuous change and the schools for its orderly self-government which at last satisfied his curiosity by causing England's difference from his danger-model.

But 'model' remains a misleading word for Halévy's vision of alternatives. He did not use any single, simple model. He could not (as Carr could for Russia) survey all English society through the eyes of governors who analysed all and controlled most of it. Nor can the many valuations (which help the choice of the many detailed alternatives) be deduced from a single value. (Some moderns try to reconcile valuation with a strict deductive type of social theory by trying to make the valuations axiomatic, too.) Halévy's valuations cohere by affinity; they don't all derive from some simple value put upon the social system, or its integration, or its containment of conflict. He did value those things but he valued others too. He neither was, nor imagined any historical character to be, that simple dummy of scientistic fable, whose uncomplicated thoughts (though seldom called thoughts) can be distributed without scientific remainder as 'goals', 'instrumental means' to goals, and 'attitudes' to anything else. His valuations were as complicated and mutually sensitive as his technical judgments. His work was not faultless, morally or technically. (The objections are not always distinct – some objections to his estimations of effects depend on objections to his choice of effect-measuring alternatives.) But in the sixty years since he began it, there has perhaps still been no better short analysis of a national society, no more elegant application of what were probably, more than any other single author's, Tocqueville's methods. Its excellence was achieved by the goodness and coherence of Halévy's valuations, by the disciplined fertility of his imagination, and by the skilled relation of both to his patient and expert fact-gathering.

Historians may usefully look for the valuing selections on almost every page. Sociologists might glean new questions to ask (as Halévy could do, with profit, from modern sociology) and various means of mixing functional and sequential analysis, to the advantage of both. To scientistic imitators, different exercises are suggested: Delete from Halévy's functional analysis all causal statements which offend Durkheim's rule that causal relations may only be inferred from associations. Alternatively, permit the method of discerning but apply some other prohibitions: subtract all the effects of Halévy's valuations; replace all his selections by others derivable from value-free principles; subtract all fictions and their effects, except those derived from neighbors and neutral models – from France and the economic theory of 1913.

Or, as a more interesting exercise, compare Halévy's achievements with the principles proposed, and the achievements promised, by Talcott Parsons.

2. *Talcott Parsons*

In the first paper in Max Black (ed.) *The Social Theories of Talcott Parsons* (Prentice-Hall, 1961) Edward C. Devereux compresses what he can of Parsons' social theory[1] into sixty-three pages. There follow eight good examples of the criticism which Parsons' work attracts. Both the work and the critique are well known. This section is only to remind readers of them, and to put its own questions to them.

Questions about Parsons' knowledge of causes can be answered briskly. His search for repetitious patterns, though obviously aimed at establishing some general causal networks, does not appear to aim at the laws which would be required to strengthen 'impressionistic' knowledge of the more obvious, detailed, 'visible' causes of action. For these, *verstehen* will do; indeed, he is accused of 'understanding' the goals of systems as if they were just like the motives of individuals.

He understands action as thoughtful interaction, unintelligible apart from its situation; he understands situations as complicated inclusions of everything from the actor's physique to the normative patterns of his society; he understands how much of 'situation' is expectation of others' actions, including their expectations of one's own. The knowledge of causes which he usually recommends is mixed, direct, discerning, uninhibited; none of the workable holds on them is methodologically barred, though some are applied carelessly. Effects are measured by imagining, systematically and explicitly, what alternative effects would arise from alternative (often imaginary rather than compared) causes. Once Parsons decides what people should look for, there are thus many fashionable restrictions of knowledge of which his advice leaves them admirably free – especially behaviorist and disciplinary limitations and (curiously, in such a grand law-seeker) any inhibitions about discerning lawless causes in single cases. I can applaud these liberties more wholeheartedly than some more scientific critics feel free to do.

But what is the work for? We may ask, in turn, what use it is for deductive or generalizing, interrogatory, ideological or educational purposes. The last three are this book's business but not (by his own account) Parsons'. So we should glance, first, at his higher claims.

Parsons proposes classifications for use in attempting laws – perhaps 'strict' theories, perhaps empirical generalizations. There are many reasons for expecting the attempt to fail. Among the briefest and best are Max Black's reasons on pp. 268–288 of the volume cited above. Parsons' classifications presumably guess at identities whose relations will turn out to be regular. These classes and identities, however abstract, are at a familiar social level, where Black would not expect a 'social physics' to operate, if any operates at all. At the same time, many are socially unrecognized identities. They obliterate distinctions which people commonly make, between things to which people give different values and respond differently. This seems an unpromising guess at the subjects of whatever behavior may prove regular at this social level. It seems odd, too, to elaborate such artificial identities for thirty years without *finding* any regular relations between them. But in Parsons' picture of nesting systems in hierarchies *that* seems to be the hopeful purpose of his classifications for all systems' external relations, and his categories for the comparative analysis of all systems' internal structures. Regular relations are presumably not expected between social classes, between types of government and types of liberties, between stages and rates of growth, between rich and poor countries – these are not Parsons' classifications. Regularities must be expected instead in the structural patterns through which systems, or classes of them, comply with their functional imperatives, and in the classified (as opposed to any other) qualities of systems' relations with each other. For example, systems must regularly 'have goals' and any regular consequences must follow from their having them, not varying according to what the goals are. 'Collectivity-orientation' must be a quality regularly related in nominated circumstances to some other social facts, even though 'collectivity-orientation' includes anything from a martyr's devotion to mankind to an ego's consideration of a single interest of a single alter somewhere in the collectivity. Hate and love are not expected to have either distinct or regular social relations; it is their common element of 'affectivity' which is expected to have regular relations. To many critics these identities seem difficult to be sure of operationally, and unlikely to have regular relations anyway.

Other misgivings arise, not from the distance of Parsons' system from life, but from its reference to life. Too much of that reference seems to be ambiguous or false. For example, many classifications of orientations by the pattern variables seem to imply some untruth, either about the facts of behavior or about its functional effects, whether each pair of variables is meant to be dichotomous or polar. Many roles require 'friendly service' – a point of specificity within a penumbra of diffuseness – so that specificity and diffuseness do not exclude each other; nor can a dot within a circle be represented as a point on a line between dot and circle. Critics have noticed similar lack of fit in more important regions of the system, arising from Parsons' strain to relate concepts to each other rather than to the world they refer to. It seems to Andrew Hacker 'that Parsons, for the symmetry of his larger social system, wants to set up a wealth-power analogy in order to underpin an economics-politics model. The scheme dictates that if wealth must be created before it is distributed, so must power.' Hacker prefers 'men like Machiavelli and Hobbes who find the production and distribution of power an identical process.'[2]

Logical relations within Parsons' system lead to allegations of real controls in the social system. 'Superordinate' sometimes means at a higher, more inclusive level of generality; it also refers, at times, to a hierarchy of social control. '. . . the concept of the institutionalization and/or internalization of the structure of superordinate systems – in the specific sense of the hierarchy of control of action systems – is one crucial common feature of the relation of every system or subsystem of action to its environment.' More elaborately –

. . . for any given lower-level system in a system-subsystem hierarchy, the next higher order system is the most important part of the situation in which *it* must function . . . the lower order system is in certain respects "controlled" by the higher order system . . .
. . . the most general values of the highest level are articulated at successively lower levels so that norms governing specific actions at the lowest level may be spelled out . . . Thus the first respect in which the order under consideration may be said to constitute a hierarchy is that of levels of generality of the normative patterns . . .
The second respect in which our series of levels constitutes a hierarchy is that the "decisions" which bind larger and larger sectors of the social structure are made at progressively higher levels in the organizational system . . .
With respect to level of cultural generality and range of solidarity, one may say that the hierarchy is one of system and subsystem as directly structural entities. With respect to decision making and the control of facilities, it is one of levels of "operative" control of behavior.[3]

Here are both hierarchies, a logical hierarchy of generality and inclusiveness, and a hierarchy of controls alleged (though the quotation marks may indicate some unease about them) to operate in society. Parsons' examples, omitted from the quotation, make clear the latter reference to society. If alleged as universal all the allegations are false, i.e., most societies contain exceptions to them all. If they are alleged not to be always present but always to be functionally helpful whenever present, then the exceptions still cannot all be written off as dysfunctional, unless by definition for an unreal (and politically oppressive) system in Parsons' imagination. One simple method of showing this is to introduce Morton Kaplan's distinction[4] between system-dominance and subsystem-dominance. Kaplan designed it to distinguish international politics, which Parsons might fairly claim to be so unstable as to constitute no system at all. But many elements of subsystem-dominance exist in (and probably help to stabilize!) systems which Parsons does nominate as boundary-maintaining systems. A degree of subsystem-dominance is required by some of the most general norms of American society, and not merely in the negative form of entrenched liberties. In other works, Parsons allows for conflict between general norms and the local norms generated by the internal needs of subsystems. Some of the conflicts are accommodated by mechanisms like 'contextual segregation'. Some continue simply as dysfunctional strains. Some are now to be over-come by the subsystem's 'spelling out' the reference of general norms to its local problems of action. But what if the subsystem won't? I mean, contumaceously refuses? Any notion that the general will sometimes bow to the particular, be bossed by entrenched subordin-ates, against the functional interest of the superordinate system, seems to have been excluded by the passages quoted above. I do not only mean, as many critics have in mind, 'What is good for General Motors is good for America'. Many governments, like many general social norms, do what they are told or have their orders healthily disobeyed by labor unions or veterans' organizations or farmers or churches or student minorities; the local norms of these sometimes defy, some-times succeed in changing, the more general requirements of super-ordinate systems. Parsons says that the goals of subsystems include the provision of outputs required as intakes by superordinate systems. But in life, subsystems' goals often include self-determining their outputs, or otherwise asserting their own powers against the powers of superordinates. If Parsons' interpenetration of systems means that selection and control are always exercised by superordinate over sub-systems, then it is false. If he means that this relation would always be functional for both super- and subordinate systems, this too seems false on almost any plausible understanding of 'functional'. If it were true, most societies would be very different; many would probably be more strained, less stable, quicker-changing; and regardless of that, worse – illiberal and inflexible.

It is hard to see how any re-entry into the argument of power as a distributable commodity, or of over-riding general norms, can save this hierarchy of systems from the objection that logical relations between concepts have been allowed to double as false statements either of fact, or of functional necessity. This leaves the model little promise either as empirical hypothesis or as foundation for any effective predictive theory. I suppose (Parsons did not) that it might sometimes be useful as a danger model. But Parsons persists in the faith, whose alternative is not an open theory of uncertain systems, but despair: 'the concept of system is so fundamental to science that, at levels of high theoretical generality, there can be no science without it. If there are no uniformities involved in the interdependence of components there is no scientific theory.'[5]

More modest claims may still be made for Parsons' work. Does it prompt investigators to notice problems and to ask good questions? Not 'good questions for discovering universal regularities' which would merely return to the more ambitious claims of the theory; but perhaps good questions for understanding particular societies, for research into social problems, or for uncovering knowledge valuable for contemplation or for the education of the young.

How will the theory help researchers into particular social systems? In one way it limits the search more clearly and severely than do the simpler functional theories discussed earlier. Research and explanation should apparently run to the present internal relations of systems, or to their boundaries, where they may follow the trade of outputs and intakes with surrounding systems. This rules out the system's past, its directions of change, and any finer specification of its internal facts than the 'frame of reference' classifications allow. It is likely also to encourage much discussion, not obviously helpful, of which congeries of activities to define as systems and where exactly to draw their boundaries. (Which links in causal chains are internal, which mark – and cross – boundaries?) Parsons insists on the importance of the intersystem trade. His most valuable efforts have been in the direction of grasping (instead of treating as random invaders) systems' and disciplines' intakes from their environments. This is a good aspiration but often unhelpful in practice; omitting only time and change, it looks like another plea for completeness; and in default of the complete understanding of whole systems, standards of importance (valued) would still have to select and terminate explanations. But perhaps it is these standards of importance which are to be established by the theory's classifications. Perhaps the researcher should be satisfied when a fact is well enough identified to be located in its correct classification box. An equilibrium or disequilibrium is presumably explained or predicted by comparing the weight of social facts in the functional boxes with the counterweight of facts in the twin, dysfunctional shadow-boxes. These would be rational procedures, and useful selectors and limiters of explanations, if the theory were successful – if explanations were sought only for equilibria, if there were predictably reliable relations between the theory's classified identities, and if it stated truly what those relations were. But there are not, and it doesn't.

If investigators nevertheless forsake the classifications and choices suggested by plain language and by their engineering interests, and recognize only Parsons' identities, what will they lose? His classification seldom distinguishes types of social sanctions. It does not insist on distinguishing the equilibrating force of consent from the equilibrating force of coercion, or invite inquiry into the relations between consent and coercion. Once a rule or a role is established, sanctioned by a norm and not in practice resisted, we are not encouraged to ask how it got there or whose interest (except the system's) it serves there. Parsons might perhaps agree with Hobbes that people sometimes consent to be coerced and are often coerced into consenting, so that both words have ambiguous margins; but for whatever reasons, the distinction between them eludes many of his classifications. Scientifically this looks like a bad guess at their indifference as integrators. Politically, if consent and coercion are given different values, it means that the classifications will not help anybody who wants to value social systems as wholes, or the functional alternatives debatable within them.

When Parsons says that his methods allow dynamic analysis he does not usually mean that they allow the analysis of processes of change. He means that they allow the analysis of equilibria maintained by active pressures. But on inspection, his classifications do not appear to include many such distinctions between 'tense' and 'inertial' (or in his terms, dynamic and static) equilibria. They include no Lewin-like means of measuring or ordering the strength of the forces whose balanced opposition maintains a 'dynamic' equilibrium.

There are unequal bargains, when one party puts in more force or skill and takes out more profit. But besides varying thus between equal and unequal, bargains also vary between easy and hard – at one extreme a bargain is easy because the bargainers' interests are identical or perfectly complementary, and at the other extreme the bargain is hard because all the parties' interests (except their interest in a bargain) are opposed, so that each, if equally strong, must surrender half. Parsons' classifications allow only two alternatives – bargain or no bargain; and only one consequence of either – more system-equilibrium or less. Thus they do not encourage investigators to compare equal with unequal bargains or easy with hard bargains. Scientifically, this discourages investigators from expecting degrees of 'equality' or 'hardness' to have regular relations with other social facts. Politically, it discourages them from valuing bargains (institutionalized role-relations, for example, or intersystem exchanges) according to their equality or hardness, just as it discourages them from valuing the substance of bargains, or their good or bad effects (other than their equilibrating or change-resisting effects) upon the interests and values of the bargainers or anybody else.

Do Parsons' theories import any deliberate political or moral values into the work of research?

As theorist, he himself is not in business as a valuer and, believing in the more ambitious justifications of his work, he cannot be expected to be patient with these discussions of whatever residual values it may have. I do not agree with his view that 'The differentiation between scientific theorizing and the formulation of political attitudes seems . . . to be fundamental to the development of science, and particularly important in the social fields.' But I do dissent from other critics, and agree with Parsons, that 'the basis of social order is inherently problematical and, in the nature of the case, had to form one of the major foci of preoccupation for social theory'; and also 'To interpret this concern for order, as a theoretical problem, as justifying the allegation of a bias in favor either of static problems over dynamic, or of conformity over originality or creativity is, as I have stated, a gross distortion.'[6] That criticism may apply to the use that can be made of Parsons' work; but surely not to his motives for doing it. Nothing seems more obvious in his work than the primacy (however misdirected) of professional and scientific over any other motives. He gambles for general truths by the method of insisting on the generality, then seeing what truths can be found there. If sufficiently useful truths were found there, they might indeed be more powerful than anybody else's. The gamble is consistent with personal ambition, of a kind generally recognized as nobly scientific. But the work shows no sign of control by any political or social values whatever. It seems to be controlled by different, by methodological values: by an order of preference for generality, then cumulation, then truth, then (if at all) social value. Such valuations are still consistent with an expectation that the most general knowledge will have, in the end, the greatest social use; but the physical scientists who made such values famous did always reverse the order of the first three: truth must qualify generality and when it does, cumulation comes naturally. I do not personally expect any good yield to justify Parsons' order of preference, nor think it a faithful copy of its scientific original; but his work can surely be acquitted of any intentional social bias.

In his reference, quoted above, to the theoretical problem of order, the controlling valuations are not so much expressed in the choice of that problem (though it may have been chosen for its generalizing possibilities) as in the singularity of 'the *basis* of social order *is* . . .' The bases of social orders appear to vary from time to time and from society to society; but in none, does order look like a system independent of the distribution of power, independent of the 'goals' of the system's stronger members, independent of the *substance* of the 'patterns of normative culture', or independent of the speed, mode and direction of change. The varieties of order do indeed have things in common. But what they have in common – what can be stated generally as true of them all – does not appear to command the rest, to amount in itself to a system independent of the rest; will not, presumably, support a sufficient or predictive general theory of order. But those common characteristics may of course support a *selective* general theory of order. This will enjoin investigators of order in particular societies to seek and report only the insufficient few of its causes which (being present in most societies) are reported in the general theory.

There may not, on the other hand, have to be as many theories as there are societies (though even if there were, their predicting powers might still be very limited). But it does seem likely that each theory for each type of social order will have to refer to distributions of wealth and other forms of power, and to the substance as well as the forms of norms, programs, bargains and sanctions. These vary from system to system, limiting the useful generality of theory. They happen also to be politically interesting – the types and terms and costs and distributed benefits of order are central concerns of politics, precisely because so variable; and in different systems varying proportions of the causes of order are accordingly to be found in politics. Merely by being limited by truth, theory might well acquire a good deal of political interest; or by a politic effort to be useful, it might acquire a bias toward truths likely to survive test.

In a discussion of program-models in an earlier chapter, some other reasons were suggested for distinguishing Parsons' work from any intentionally conservative or liberal science. Even if this sort of equilibrium analysis is useless to radicals, it does not follow that it is the best science for conservatives. Disorder is low among social dangers at many times and places, and not alone among them ever. According to circumstances conservatives may fear disorder more than change (as Halévy's English conservatives did in 1832) or change more than disorder (as Halévy says they did in 1913). But liberals and conservatives may also fear other things: tyrannies by few or many, the orderly institution of barbarism, unlovely or unjust (but still coherent and efficient) social norms and authorities. They should always, perhaps, remember the limitations imposed by the functional imperatives; but the important questions of politics, as of social science, rarely ask *whether* these imperatives will be met, but how, by which of many alternatives.

As noticed earlier, one elegant feature of Parsons' theory is the way in which its complex classifications locate – and purport to exhaust – dangerous alternatives to the causes of his equilibrium. At the top (and identically for each subsystem) there are the four functional imperatives – and a single danger in all possible modes of non-compliance with each. Down among the details, any role requires its functionally appropriate pattern of five (or four, or six) characteristics – five (etc.) dangerous alternatives are thus indicated. At each level, for each system, the causes of equilibrium are (briskly) the presence of the required fact and the absence of its dangerous alternative; or (more elaborately) whichever causes of the one ward off the other. The objections to this procedure are both scientific and political. Scientifically this is no help to selecting the most predictably-likely alternatives, nor to finding what causes ward off those alternatives. Politically, this is no help to selecting the most dangerous or valuable among the viable alternatives, nor to sorting out the more manipulable from the less manipulable causes which produce or prevent them. It is not the way to find opportunities for choice or intervention, for it is only a small part of any inquiry into the causes and possibilities of change.

These objections apply, even if scientist and politician are prepared to limit the search strictly to the causes of equilibrium. Though Parsons does so, others rarely remember this limit consistently. The simpler functional analysts discussed in earlier chapters are frequent offenders, and their pupils seldom appreciate the limitation at all. It is absurd to propose that a structural-functional analysis of equilibrium can supply useful explanations of *anything* except that effect. It may answer questions like 'What does this thing contribute to the equilibrium of which system or subsystems?' or 'Which of the causes of this thing are also causes of the system's resistance to change?' Both answers must still depend on the answerer's selective identification of 'systems' and on his choice of effect-measuring alternatives, which may often be more usefully imagined for the system under study, than deduced from a general model. Altogether the model and its classifications bear such strict (though I believe not always helpful) relation to its solitary (arbitrarily indexed) effect-to-be-explained, and therefore leave such a wide range of questions unasked and unanswerable, that it is painful to hear the scheme called, sometimes, a frame of reference for inquiry into all sorts of questions, or a language and method for sociology as a whole. Consider this modest claim by a friendly critic of Parsons: 'equilibrium serves as an heuristically useful dependent variable or criterion of effect, in terms of which the manifold processes of system functioning may be analysed. It supplies an insistent standard of relevance . . .' If 'system functioning' means the same as 'maintaining equilibrium' that sentence says that explanations of an effect will explain that effect if they are relevant to that effect. But if system functioning means anything else, then this sentence is typical of the bad advice which issues from many schools of structural-functional sociology, for it says that theories and explanations of *other* effects should select only those among their causes which also contribute to the effect of equilibrium. Language devised to classify some formal (but no substantial) and some normative (but few coercive) supports of whatever effects are chosen as indexing an equilibrium, should limit what can be found and said about any other social problems – should be the vernacular of sociology. This advice will certainly limit the work conveniently and select and terminate the explanations, but it is scientifically and socially irrational.

We often misjudge the relative importance of the modes of social action open to social scientists. General social theory does not at present equip social engineers with predictive devices. It does, however, offer general images and valuations of society to society's members, especially to those who take college courses in the social sciences. What effects has the educational use of Parsons' theories? Four may be noticed.

First, there can be great educational value in Parsons' emphasis upon the complex responsive interaction of social systems and their parts, and in his emphasis upon normative patterns as 'systems and parts'. There are, of course, other and clearer ways of seeing and communicating most of these complexities. But however communicated, the emphasis warns against deception by apparently-closed systems, disciplinary boundaries, monocausal obsessions; it should therefore also enlighten, complicate and caution students' social valuations.

Second, however, it has its own monocausal tendencies, which arise partly from its choice of a single effect-to-be-explained, and partly from its scientific strain towards generality. Successful generalization allows one to dismiss a great deal of superficial variation from uniform underlying systems. If weak, unstable systems are all that underlie the apparent variety of many social orders and processes, then an obstinate faith in the presence of strong systems will simply breed more monocausal mistakes. Strength and independence will be attributed to whatever factors turn up most often, or to whatever qualities can, by elastic concept-making, be ascribed to all the members of irregular miscellanies. In Parsons' work the variable substance of social norms is neglected and their more regular presence emphasized. The eccentric facts of coercion and conflict are neglected and their undifferentiated 'danger' emphasized. Consent is there whatever the consenter consents to, under whatever duress. Some environmental and problem-solving causes of change are emphasized while its other causes are not. It would be unjust to call Parsons' system monocausal, but it does make simple selections of facts and their qualities and then disguise selection as 'ascent to a higher order of abstraction' or 'level of analysis'. Wherever any underlying systems are weak enough to be disturbed by the irregular company they find in every causal 'mix' they contribute to, then it may be misleading to relate all effects to the frequent attenders alone, and to pretend a fictitious independence for them.

Of nature this would merely be misleading. Of human society or personality it can also be persuasive. Parsons is not such a bad sinner in this way; but others do try to work with crude models of personality because science would prosper if regular relations *could* be found for some simple packet of drives and reflexes whose superficially various purposes could all be assimilated to a simple index of 'satisfaction'. As for personalities, so for social systems: you choose an effect; you find some regular attenders among its conditions; you come to believe (or your students do) that this relation is the system's *real* principle. Before long, in your students' minds if not in yours, it becomes the system's 'goal' and perhaps, even, a sufficient goal for systems.

This may merely be a misuse of his work by others, but for a third educational effect Parsons does share the responsibility. Social scientists are dreadfully prone to clean up the problems of ethics by simple declaration. Devereux, for example, purports to report Parsons: 'And what is morality, he reasoned, but the claim of some superordinate collectivity upon the individual or sub-collectivity.' Parsons cannot possibly be accused of neglecting morality, whose social manifestations are his chief concern. But his program for a value-free sociology does imply that the moralities manufactured elsewhere in society must be excluded from the study of society, to be replaced there by a new morality manufactured solely by the system-needs of the society of scientists.

Such manifestoes shut students' minds the more effectively by doubling as explanations of non-scientific moralities and also as academic rules for their exclusion from scientific thought. Neither the service which complex functional analysis might do for the student's valuing skill, nor the service which that skill might do for functional analysis, will be done at all if students are instructed ('persuaded' would often be too soft a word) that their own values are insidious and subtle enemies of their science. They should by all means learn to recognize when guesswork, moral or otherwise wishful, is a wrong substitute for observation and measurement, the activities to which the notion 'objective' has useful relation. But they should be introduced to more than one side of the debate about the scientific uses of valuation, and to the subjective, gambling or faith-healing basis of most of the alternatives to valuation in the tasks of selection which play as large a part as observation does in most social scientists' work.

I began as most critics of Parsons' work begin, by paying tribute to its virtues. Most critics proceed next to damn briskly, but then to dismiss, Parsons' prose. The dismissal is appropriate as long as none but the 'high' claims of the theory are in question. But without any hard discovery to its credit, the largest social effect of Parsonian sociology is the deposit its language leaves in many undergraduate (and not a few graduate) minds. Even this might be a social cost worth paying for a high scientific yield. But not believing in the yield, it is reasonable to protest against the cost. The cost can include the corruption, not only of students' capacities for clear thought and effective and good-mannered communication, but of their ideas of science as well. To encourage blind endeavor without yield, to sustain faith in more garden-level social uniformities than have been proven to exist, it is necessary to abandon the inconvenient precisions of English for a language specially capable of blur, obscurity and ambiguity. With enough difficulties of reference, theory is hard to *dis*prove. Meanwhile the jargon is defended as scientific terminology on the curious ground that the terminology of physics is *more* precise, distinctive and unambiguous than English. Whatever may be true of Parsons, acquaintance with some of his followers makes it very clear that their love for the jargon *is* love, and their reasons for it sometimes unlovely: it camouflages the failures of failing methods, and attracts scientific status without scientific performance. Language defended as morally and emotionally neutral is chosen for quite emotional and immoral reasons.

3. *Edward Hallett Carr*

The subject of *A History of Soviet Russia* is 'the history not of the events of the revolution . . ., but of the political, social and economic order which emerged from it.' From the many volumes of this still-unfinished work, and the manifesto which its author paused to write in 1961, a representative sample (because it includes every level of generality) is offered by the last three chapters of *What is History?* and by the first volume of *Socialism in One Country 1924–1926*, especially Chapter 1 'The Legacy of History' and Chapter 3 'Class and Party'.

Few historians are as systematic as Carr, either in relating many levels of general and particular explanation, or in making explicit the principles by which these explanations are selected, and related to one another. Does he choose causes in practice according to his professed principles? Since those require valuations, what are some of his valuations, and what do they do to his explanations? What models or alternatives tell him what needs to be explained? Do the same, or different, alternatives measure the effects of whatever causes he chooses? How does he know the causal links themselves?

. . . we distinguish between rational and accidental causes. The former since they are potentially applicable to other countries, other periods and other conditions, lead to fruitful generalizations and lessons can be learned from them; they serve the end of broadening and deepening our under-standing . . . It is precisely this notion of an end in view which provides the key to our treatment of causation in history; and this necessarily involves value judgments. . . . Only the future can provide the key to the interpretation of the past . . . the historian's judgment cannot rest on some fixed and immovable standard of judgment existing here and now, but only on a standard which is laid up in the future and is evolved as the course of history advances. History acquires meaning and objectivity only when it establishes a coherent relation between past and future.

(*What is History?*, 101, 117, 124)

Causes should be selected for their value to a general wisdom, and for their fertility. Both principles have been alleged by some to be value-free, though never by Carr.

By fertility, he usually means 'with an important future'. Identities of many kinds can have futures – individuals, classes, programs, ideas, trends in population patterns or productive methods. Any of these can be understood as helping to cause one effect, then surviving to cause others. If Carr thinks those later effects important, he will choose the 'fertile' causes of the first event accordingly, perhaps neglecting others, whatever the 'weight' of their causal contributions, if their futures look less interesting. Not all 'futureless' causes are defeated people or programs. But some are, and Carr and his critics often agree that in choosing causes, he likes to choose winners.

This invites comparison with an aspect of Kurt Lewin's field theory. From any conflict, change may result from either an increase of force for change, or a reduction of resistance to it:

In the first case, the process on the new level would be accompanied by a state of relatively high tension; in the second case, by a state of relatively low tension. Since increase of tension above a certain degree is likely to be paralleled by higher aggressiveness, higher emotionality, and lower constructiveness, it is clear that as a rule the second method will be preferable to the high pressure method.[7]

Do both parties worship success, Carr applauding victory and Lewin applauding surrender to it? Carr has been accused of that valuation and Lewin has not; it is worth digressing to see how it seems to have been smuggled into Lewin's work for the sake of scientific appearances.

Lewin's remarks above are taken from an article which draws theoretical conclusions from various studies of efforts to get small groups to change their habits – for example, their eating habits. Lewin wanted to show that people could sometimes be persuaded more easily in groups than singly, one by one. In that context for that purpose his remarks may have been sensible – until he introduced them with the observation that 'certain general formal principles always have to be considered' and opened the above exposition of those principles with the words 'For any type of social management . . .' He thus took some sense about a very local problem and generalized it falsely to a very large number of other 'types of social management'. Change does not always issue from conflicts of two. In many conflicts 'no change' is nobody's program. With 'secular' changes the force may come from the resisters. Hard-fought victories sometimes bring more peace than premature surrenders do. Aggressiveness and emotionality are irregular allies, and both are often very constructive. And so on. Lewin may, as he professed, have valued nonaggression, unemotionality and constructiveness; but to set about serving them by such manifest untruths he must have put higher values upon other things – perhaps a desire to think his simplest discoveries regular and general, and a scientific refusal to report facts not found in his laboratory. Perhaps he loved his model more than life.

Carr's values and selections do not resemble Lewin's, either in the understanding of change or in the choice of its causes. In his selection of causes and effects Carr has been variously accused of valuing winners as such, power as such, or bolshevism as such. But these are hard to accommodate to his own biography and his other writings,[8] while easy to accommodate as cases of his selective principles of fertility and 'generalizability'. ('Generalizability', as we shall see, requires valuation and has little to do with inevitable regularity.) It was wrong to accuse Carr of nominating the Bolsheviks as privileged causes of the revolutionary events of 1917. The book is not intended to explain those events. Before and for a short time after 1917, Carr has the Bolsheviks causing chiefly the formation of their own party and program, a party and program required for the explanation of a different revolution in the nineteen-twenties.

In the explanation of the events of the twenties their future (in several senses) may well be one reason why they get such attention. But they still share the causal honors with many other survivors of 1917, survivors who include other people and also more abstract social facts, both positive and negative: the legacy of encounters between native and imported cultures; the 'internalization' of Russian-Western conflicts in many of the minds and institutions within Russian Society; the remembered experience, structural results and ready expectation of revolutions-from-above; the destruction of bourgeois structures but survival of bourgeois individuals; the falling proletarian numbers but survival of proletarian structures; the absence of a productively-based western middle class; the presence of a rootless intelligentsia; and – most persistent, least flexible survivors of all events, an historical constant with constant causal fertility – the mind and power of the peasantry. The Tsar gets little credit for causing his own downfall in 1917; rather more, for his posthumous contributions to later events. He was above all the teacher of revolution from above. To heavy industry he contributed memories and methods of state direction, state financing and a state market. He helped industry to borrow western technology without many of the western relations of production – here Carr echoes Veblen's account of discriminate German borrowing. His constitutional experiments helped to damage whatever liberal hopes might otherwise have flourished.

The main subjects of Carr's explanations, the events of the nineteen-twenties, are indeed valued, and their causes selected, with an eye to futures; but that is not the only principle of selection. Many of the causes listed above get plenty of Carr's attention, though some still had futures and some were soon to expire. Stalin's personal future does not attract overdue attention to his early years. The imminent future of the peasantry may have led Carr to emphasize their causal importance through the twenties, though at every step there are abundant other reasons for that emphasis. The outstanding emphasis is on the causal activity of the ruling Bolshevik group. This might equally arise from knowledge of their local future in Russia; from a valued interest (for which Carr approved Collingwood's recommendation) in deliberate rational action; from a love of winners; from the conventions of political history and the accessibility of sources; or from broader, more abstract ideas of the general future of revolutionary government and of lessons to be learned from it. Before asking which of these selectors Carr seems to have valued and used most, or what he means in theory and practice by 'fruitful generalizations and lessons', it will be convenient first to look at his choice of models and his imagination of alternatives.

He uses one major model and a class of minor models. The major model is the Bolshevik program. The minor models are neighbors' pasts from the history of western Europe, especially from its French and industrial revolutions. Some hostile critics said he should have used two other differentiating models: a Russian liberal program, or a Russian Menshevik program.

The Bolshevik program-model begins as mostly prognosis, with minor adaptive elements of program: a prognosis of capitalist growth and breakdown, with some programmed revolutionary action to hurry it along. With every year of the twentieth century the model's content of deliberate program increases, as program increases its self-fulfilling command of prognosis. Carr's model itself thus changes as his history unfolds. It is a dynamic model in a double sense, and Carr can accordingly make it do complicated service. As an historical fact, it figures as cause or effect of innumerable other subjects of his study. At the same time it is made to organize a great deal of his study – more and more of it, to the progressive exclusion of the minor west-European models, as the Bolsheviks learn to get what they want.

The apparent reasons for this choice of model include some technical advantages and one exceedingly important valuation.

Technically the model is factual, discoverable and manageable. It is the usually-coherent program of a small but changing group of men who made their predictions and intentions incessantly explicit – so the sources for it are good. To know and understand it at each stage of its development is incidentally to discover much of what Carr must discover anyway, of Russian political history and its options and determinants. The model incorporates all the useful elements of conflict and consensus; it is fully functional and also fully dynamic. At any one time it models a future from tomorrow through several decades of development to 'pure' communism; structurally and functionally, it values, selects and defines the 'important' facts of the present and projected conditions of society, and it nominates what shall cause each stage to develop into the next. It is an admirably 'real' model, an historical fact of its own society; it does not derive its realism spuriously by true correspondence to some *other* society.

Only in one sense is the Bolshevik program a fictitious model: it is fictitious insofar as its analyses are false, its predictions are belied and its plans are unaccomplished. These margins of error (in Russia in the nineteen-twenties) define both a manageable and a peculiarly interesting body of effects for the historian to explain.

The model is thus, first, a selector of effects to be explained. Facts not mentioned in it can generally be ignored. For whatever facts resemble it, the explanations are usually contained within the model. For whatever facts contradict it, the explanations must be supplied by the historian. Even in this latter task, the model still helps: it nominates a specific 'imagined alternative' which may guide and limit the selection of causes for the deviant effects. When an event occurs to belie the program, the historian's tasks are narrowed to two. First, why did the programmers miscalculate? This requires retracing and criticizing their calculations. With his foresight of this need, the hind-sighted historian may well have included the necessary criticism in his original account of the calculations. Second, why did the errant event itself occur? The aforesaid criticism of miscalculations may often include a sufficiently satisfying forecast of the errant event. If not, the wide open selection of causes for the event is narrowed by the imagined (in this case, the planned or predicted) alternative supplied by the program-model. The open question 'why this fact?' is narrowed and specified: 'why this fact instead of that particular programmed alternative?' Why, for example, a short food supply this year? There is no need to explain the size of the food supply, which might require a very complicated explanation indeed. All that needs to be explained is the supply's difference from one alternative, a precise margin between model and performance. The explanation may lie in the (un-programmed, ill-predicted) weather, or in the few and particular respects in which peasants' or administrators' behavior deviated from Bolshevik expectations. All the innumerable other conditions necessary for the size or fluctuation of the food supply can be left asleep because the program already assumed or took account of them.

For events which thus deviate from the model, the model thus helps to select and limit explanations. It is worth emphasizing that this does not only apply to the historical explanation of once-occurring events. The model performs the same service for any developing or persisting facts of social structure or function which belie the program's social analysis or obstruct its planned changes or stabilities.

Another class of events which may belie the model, are changes in the program itself. In dealing with these the triple role of the program in Carr's book, as a fact and a cause and a discoverer's model, give it some queer and powerful fertility. At some particular date the Bolsheviks change a policy; the program changes that part of its content; the model changes that much of its form. The investigator asks why the Bolsheviks changed course. He usually limits his answer to understanding the Bolsheviks' new appreciation of some intractable facts which obstructed the former program. If the matter seems unusually important, he may trace some of the chains which converged to cause the intractable facts. In this task the model may not help him, unless he is content to limit his interest to such causes as figured in the programmers' calculations and miscalculations.

Meanwhile, for everything that does happen according to plan (including the persistence of the plan itself) the program-model provides a double explanation. It is itself a work of social science, containing the usual mixtures of logics and methods and explanations, claiming to be verified by its own success in action. In proportion as it does succeed and persist, it is itself an increasingly powerful cause, with increasingly pervasive effects which include its own persistence. Those parts of the program which merely analyse and predict the 'natural' or uncontrived parts of the social process can do the investigator's work for him; to the extent that he accepts this, he accepts Stalin's social science as his own. The increasingly important parts of the program which direct deliberate intervention and control of social processes are for the investigator both fact and science: they are causes which contain their own explanations. Thus the program-model partly selects, partly embodies, and conveniently limits the reportable causes of as much of social structure and social change as are specified within itself.

But is not this a pretentious gloss upon two familiar and simple sins? Is Carr merely reverting to a conventional political narrative of the policies and fortunes of governments? And in using the government's own program as model, is he not writing official government history, propagandist and worthless?

The first is true. Though it has never really been true that all historians limited themselves to narratives of government, the last hundred years have certainly seen great extensions of their interests beyond government, into the social and economic and intellectual and emotional history of society. Does Carr renounce all these extensions of interest, to revert to a narrow political history? On the contrary, he writes of the first modern government to catch up (for good or ill) with the modern historians. The social science on which Bolshevik government bases its calculations, the range of social and economic and intellectual structure and process which Bolshevik government comprehends within its power and its reconstructive intentions, are now so extensive that 'political history' comprehends most of the interesting history of society. From that same extension of power it also follows that more and more of the interesting history of society is now caused, not as it once was by impersonal or popular social and economic forces, but by combinations of those forces with the deliberate intent of government. If Carr 'reverts' to political history it is because so much of Russian history has become political. A history modelled by Mr Gladstone's or President McKinley's or even the Tsar's programs would omit a large majority of the important causes and effects in human history. It is right, instead, to study nineteenth-century history where its fertile causes were: in its social and economic structures, in its many independent sources of scientific and technological and social innovation. It seems to Carr to be equally right to study twentieth-century Russia where *its* fertile causes are manufactured: in the Politburo.

Does the model (which is the Politburo's program) control Carr, to produce official propagandist history? He might succumb by accepting either its values or its analyses. He does choose to accept many of its values, though as deductions from his own higher values rather than Stalin's. The model's analyses offer more dangerous traps, because of the model's technical service in organizing Carr's explanations. When the facts belie the model, there is obvious need for independent critical explanation. But when events occur as planned, there is always the possibility that the plan was more lucky than correct. The model, as selector for the investigator, is supposed to explain sufficiently whatever facts correspond to it; so the investigator may incorporate the model's lucky errors, plausible misunderstandings or wilful falsifications into his own assumptions and explanations. To detect any such mistakes in Carr's work would require a better knowledge of Russian history than his; I am not among the few who profess it. But if any such model-errors deceived him there were also many which did not. Throughout his history there is a running criticism of his model.

Some of the criticism is supplied by self-critical mechanisms within the (ever fertile) model itself. The Bolshevik program is a changing collection of analyses and policies subject to continuous disagreement and debate within the ruling group. Carr follows the debate and criticizes the criticisms. Sometimes he takes sides, entering the debate himself. At other times he stands apart and damns all parties, especially when their analyses seem to him to be technically disjointed from their own values. The chapter 'Class and Party' is one most critical of these occasions. At this point Carr flatly refuses to accept the model's own explanations, even of events which fulfil its plans and predictions and seem superficially, therefore, to validate its explanations.

Despite their Leninist education in political opportunism, the Bolsheviks are still explaining themselves as the superintendents of an economically-determined and class-structured process. They are leaving their own political will and power out of their analyses which are therefore false. Carr 'corrects' the error, and explains it. As the cause of the error he chooses a cause with a limited future: one of the few 'futures' to attract his severe disapproval, perhaps because in England and America it still has a future of anti-futurist anti-fertility. What deceives the Bolsheviks, and deprives their program and Carr's model of explanatory power, is a law-bound uninterfering science-of-the-past: a social science which, in proportion as it convinces as true of the past, will make its believers the captives of the past. Analytical methods which may have served to reveal the forces at work in nineteenth-century capitalist class systems will certainly not yield a reliable understanding either of social forces in revolutionary Russia, or of social possibilities. Nevertheless the model and its methods of analysis had a classical opportunity for self-verification. If the Bolsheviks had continued to believe themselves to be the mere creatures or expressions of social forces in an economically determined world, a world of durable regularities obeying durable Marxist laws, then they would have acted to perpetuate that world, which would then have conferred its retrospective blessing upon their analyses. By underestimating their own deliberate power they would have abolished it; and with it, their historic liberty of choice.

Carr's subsidiary models from European history are not unrelated to his principal program-model. Much of the modern history of Europe was built into the original Marxist model; the importation of Marxism into Russia added another to the many expectations already held by many Russians, of one or another 'western' future for Russia. But Marxism posed problems for Russian Marxists, one of which was 'what is the problem?' Was the problem to locate their present Russia correctly in an historical process already modelled in the west? Or was their problem to identify differences between a western and a Russian process, so that different programs might be devised to steer a different Russia by a different route to a common destination? Did Marx's blend of economic determinism and revolutionary deliberation apply equally to west and east, or did his economic determinism explain European facts while his political opportunism indicated some unique Russian possibilities? Besides these intellectual relations between the Marxist models of Russia and the west, might there also be more direct relations – must Russian political opportunities in practice wait upon prior developments in the west?

These debates, and the choices of organization and tactics which seemed to depend on them, are a main subject of the early chapters of *The Bolshevik Revolution*, in which Carr describes the formation, in Lenin and his party and program, of 'The Man and The Instrument'. *Within* this history of revolutionary preparation futures do appear to have been powerful selectors. Carr would agree with his critics that it is chiefly the parties' respective futures which distinguish Lenin's logic and realism from his opponents' mistakes and weaknesses. Crudely, history proved Lenin right: he proposed more action which succeeded. There is still room for critics to argue that the action succeeded from causes other than those alleged by Lenin at the time. Some think with Carr that Martov was ineffective because (among other reasons) he insisted that Russia had no option but to follow a western program, while Lenin more effectively altered the program to make it capable of altering Russia. This is to see the dispute as one between west and east, model and reality, passive science and active interference: between prognosis and program. But others see Martov opposing action whose consequences he rightly foresaw and rightly disliked; as working actively for a western future because, though harder to achieve, he preferred it to Lenin's future. Between such conflicting prognoses, if each were an uninterfering prediction, the future might be an acceptable judge. But when each is not an abstinent prediction but a self-imposing program, then the victory of one may foreclose the possibility of the other, without so conclusively proving that the other was intrinsically impossible. These latter judgments might be better based, not on the bald facts of victory or defeat, but on a detailed imagination of what conditions would have been required in order to fulfil the defeated program. In Carr's comparative neglect of non-Leninist revolutionaries in his first volume, the brisk facts of their failure are 'caused' by somewhat brusque characterizations of their weaknesses. Retrospectively these dismissals are better justified when in 'The Legacy of History' and 'Class and Party', chapters published eight years later, Carr explores some continuities and peculiarities of Russian history and society which do indeed make Plekhanov's and Martov's and Kerensky's programs appear unlikely to occur, difficult to impose.

309

There remain some cross purposes in the criticism. When in *What is History?* Carr scorned hypothetical questions, and seemed by implication to scorn any imagination of alternatives, any organization of explanations by failing rather than by prevailing programs, he did so in the context of an argument about free will and determinism and concepts of causation. Two independent propositions – 'everything has causes' and 'causes with fertile futures are valued as more interesting than others' – can be collapsed in careless theory (and in some critics' impressions of Carr's practice) into 'everything is caused inexorably by causes with fertile futures' – by winners.

If some historian valued the record of communism as wholly bad, and regarded alternatives to it, however unlikely, as the only 'possibilities' possessing any interest whatever, then Carr might agree that such a valuer would do well to organize his history of Russia simply to explain the failures of whatever programs failed. Such an historian might ask what caused reality to deviate from a monarchist or liberal or Menshevik model. (Some of the answers would still be found in Lenin's power and program; there and elsewhere this history would overlap with Carr's.) Carr himself acknowledges more interest in the losers of some other battles, for example in the unsuccessful revolutionaries of 1848. If they personally had little future, some of their revolutionary ideas had big futures. A modern critic may similarly argue that if moderate social-democracy had no local prospects in revolutionary Russia, it nevertheless has a future elsewhere, a future in which it must increasingly contend with revolutionary rather than with reactionary alternatives. The failures of Kerensky and Chicherin, Martov and Dan, deserve admission to Carr's class of pregnant failures, if only for the lessons they offer to later social democrats trying to do better. Perhaps the critics were wrong to make this demand of *The Bolshevik Revolution 1917–1923*, which professed to be preparing to explain events which only began after the conclusive extinction of liberal and Menshevik hopes. But they were right to insist, in general, that options closed by history may usefully be reopened in imagination, and their closure explained in detail. Some of them were also right to direct their attack chiefly at Carr's values. They should honestly (as many did) oppose their own values to his, rather than opposing (as some did) an imaginary but unspecified 'value-free' alternative to his 'distortions'. Writing before the appearance of *Socialism in One Country* or *What is History?*, and forgetting the moral parts of *The Twenty Years Crisis* (1939) and *The New Society* (1944), they may even have underestimated the more general and lovable implications of Carr's values – or mistaken the technical implications of their own. But Carr's own uses of models and imagined alternatives (though not under those names) can be reconciled with his condemnation of hypothetical questions only if the condemnation is charitably taken as merely insisting upon his right to his own values and imagination – why *should* he give a hundred pages to whatever facts closed the liberal or Menshevik options, or made the imagination of those options foolish in the first place? He prefers to imagine his own alternatives. Russian reality deviated less from Bolshevik than from liberal imagination. The difference between reality and Bolshevik imagination is more manageable and diminishes with time; it is a difference in whose study and explanation Carr sees more value. This choice of model, for immediate technical and somewhat abstract moral reasons, does not require that Carr adopt, in other contexts, Bolshevik rather than any other values.

Besides this debate between rival revolutionary models for Russia – a debate, and models, which mirror the real lives of the debate and the programs as facts of Russian history – Carr also uses models whose relation to Russia is more fictitious, western fact-models which merely compare, rather than connecting, with Russian history. Once again he has sometimes been criticized for using too few of them, for too seldom asking what caused the communist revolution to deviate from the liberal models of French or English history, even when those models did not acquire local factual status by becoming the programs of Russian politicians. Whether or not apt or valuable the criticism is true enough of *The Bolshevik Revolution 1917–1923*. It is less true of *Socialism in One Country 1924–1926*, in which there are ingenious uses of various western models. The culture and class structure which encrust western industry serve to differentiate some effects, especially upon the proletariat and upon the tradition of revolution-from-above, of importing technology ready-made into nineteenth-century Russian society. The western model of home-bred, class-based liberalism selects the differences to be noticed in the rootless imported liberalism of Russia. There are others, often justified by the need to make an exotic system intelligible to western curiosity, to differentiate Russian facts from the western images likely to be triggered by western words in the minds of western readers.

But the most interesting western model is the model of Thermidor, and its use resembles Halévy's use of the first explanation of Chamberlain quoted above at the beginning of Chapter 1. Carr uses the Thermidor model, among other devices, to set up a predictive explanation of something which never happened. Like Halévy, he does this in order to dramatize the alternative effects which *did* happen; but also to dramatize the incompetence of any past-based, law-based science (Marxist or other) to predict or explain what *did* happen.

For Soviet society five years after the first revolution, Carr 'predicts' a Russian Thermidor: 'the advance would not be resumed . . . the country would settled down into a modified form of bourgeois capitalism on a Russian national pattern.' Three types of argument converge upon this conclusion. First, a general model of revolutionary exhaustion, the French Thermidor repeated so often in so many other revolutions, bases the expectation of a Russian Thermidor upon a general social law. The second argument has been noted above – the Bolshevik prediction of revolutionary progress is belied by post-revolutionary facts; if there is to be any further revolutionary progress, it cannot possibly arise from the causes nominated in the revolutionary program, because those causes are weak or absent in Russian reality. Instead, other facts are present from which orthodox Marxist analysis must (by more deduction from general law) predict a Thermidor and adjust the program to surrender to it. In the course of criticizing this orthodoxy Carr himself supplies the third, and best, argument for Thermidor, in his own analysis of the forces of class, interest and economic necessity at work in the period of the New Economic Policy. Consistently with his own methodological inclinations, this analysis includes very little law and a great deal of understanding – much of it abstract and theoretical – of the unique pattern of pressures and potentialities within the Russian system at that date. It is not unmodelled, or unselective. It differentiates reality, when convenient, from details of western, Marxist and Bolshevik models. Its selection is organized partly by a fiction – it selects whatever indications pointed to a Thermidor which did not come. A stronger selective principle is

Carr's preference for 'rationality'. To Russian individuals, groups and classes he ascribes patterns of rational interest and purpose.

Thus the Russian Thermidor is predicted unanimously by two deductions from law and one exercise of understanding – by the methods of Marx, Crane Brinton and Dilthey. But obstinately, the revolution defies them all. Where the gentle equilibria of Thermidor should appear, there stand instead the brutal facts of heavy industry, forced collectivization, and Stalin's terror.

How was this paradox achieved – a paradox which falsified every current prediction and appeared to frustrate every attempt at rational analysis?

Carr answers his own question with a minor and a major explanation. The minor is corrective – a few contrary facts were overlooked in all three erroneous analyses. But these facts merely helped to enable, they by no means compelled, the resumption of revolutionary change.

The second reason for the apparent paradox is more profound, and relates to the altered balance of social relations in the modern period.

The Bolshevik leaders eventually *discerned* revolutionary possibilities, and *chose* to use their power to exploit those opportunities. For 'discerned' we may translate 'invented', which the fact of performance will distinguish from any fictional 'invention of knowledge'. Perhaps this is the Bolsheviks' future – their future as *inventive*, not merely strong and surviving, causes – which has earned them so much of Carr's attention in the earlier years during which they may have had less effect upon Russian affairs, but in themselves a spectacular and fertile cause was in preparation. This is not, except in an even broader sense, to be understood as a resurrection of a 'great man' theory of history. 'The initial verdict of those who failed to find in Stalin any notable distinguishing marks had some justification. Few great men have been so conspicuously as Stalin the product of the time and place in which they lived.' Nor do I offer any sort of summary of Carr's analysis of the Bolsheviks' acquisition and use of their coercive powers and historical liberties, which the reader must follow for himself in Carr's distinguished pages. But however impersonally 'determined' the forces which created the Bolsheviks' opportunity, however 'objectively' the opportunity may be known to have 'existed' before its discovery, Carr certainly declares that the

Bolsheviks *discerned* the opportunity and *chose* to use it to engineer a further fundamental revolution in Russian society.

Of that revolution, Carr thus selects deliberate Bolshevik action as a principal cause. How does he *know* the causal connection between action and effect? Not at all by 'associating' the two; chiefly by understanding their relation, in the minds of the actors and in the logic of the system; but partly also by imagining how the Bolsheviks would probably have acted if they had acted otherwise, and what effects would probably have followed from that other action. Is it the whole difference between Russia in 1923 and Russia in – say – 1933, which isolates and measures the effect of the deliberate or 'free' part of Bolshevik action? Certainly not. Innumerable other factors were at work together with the Bolshevik initiative, and would together have produced a good deal of the Russia of 1933 *without* the Bolshevik initiative. To be precise, Carr 'predicts' that they would have produced a Thermidor. The real Russia's difference from that imagined Thermidor is Carr's measurement of the effect of the Bolshevik initiative.

From the unfolding history of that deliberate revolutionary initiative, the values of other investigators will prompt them to select different abstractions: different things to be explained, different causes to explain them, different lessons to be drawn from them. One obvious selection, popular from Churchill to Kruschev, will be the tyranny: the Russian citizens' experience of some of the worst suffering, the most deliberate cruelty, the most capricious terror, the most wholesale slaughter of individual liberty, in modern times. The valuations which direct this selection would also gather support from another: from the same history one might select the blunders and inefficiencies, the gross failure of so much early planning and management, the dreadful performance which belied whatever good-looking reasons prompted the first collectivization, the human, moral, managerial, military and international costs of Stalin's purges. For these selections, Carr might not dissent from the attached valuations. So why doesn't he use them himself?

If a modern engineer should sneer at the weak, heavy, crude and occasionally disastrous inefficiencies of Telford's or Brunel's first iron bridges, do we agree 'Yes, of course', attribute Brunel's unlovely effects to the (undoubtedly necessary) cause that he used iron, and conclude only that *the use of novel methods and materials is dangerous?* Or do we shout 'Idiot! You are sneering at the largest single stride forward on the road from swimming, to the span of the Golden Gate. Instead of letting petty valuations of proximate effects direct your trivial history to its unimaginative conclusions, you should begin by valuing the Golden Gate. That may equip you technically to discern the significance of Brunel, even for your own values; and to know which causes of his successes had fertile futures, and which causes of his failures offered fertile lessons, even if all but one of his bridges had collapsed and killed their builders.' The same opinions are held about the short consequences of the early surgeons' bloody assaults on their patients. How many chapters on The Consequences of the War of Independence list only its corpses, and the sufferings of their dependents?

Carr first values his Golden Gate. He is a deductive scientist in this department only: his values seem unusually few, general and axiomatic, and from them his detailed valuations are derived with relentless consistency. He values human liberty. In a century which sees both high scientific sophistication and the continuing slavery of billions to necessity, he specially values T. H. Green's liberty: the social liberty of social choice, a liberty which has to be acquired and exercised collectively. This value leads him to abstract, from the history of Soviet Russia, its discovery of new possibilities of choice and its manufacture of an instrument strong enough to realize them.

The Russian is not the only modern increase of such liberty. Carr's is a 'high' abstraction which allows Stalin's enlargements of social choice to be identified with those contributed in the same decades by Hitler and Roosevelt powerful in their command posts, and by Keynes and Mayo and Myrdal 'powerless' in their academies. Slowly but surely the democratic and capitalist societies likewise take control of their historical fortunes and deliberate between multiplying alternatives. The choices need not all be taken by tyrants, or by central governments. One task of democratic social science is to educate larger populations to join in the deliberations. Nor are the new options equally valuable. But until their discovery, not only was social choice limited to that many options less; there was less confidence in choice itself, less courage to try, less defiance of necessity.

These seem to be the senses in which Carr chooses his Bolshevik

causes for their fertility, and because they 'lead to fruitful generalizations and lessons can be learned from them'. Are the lessons laws?
Carr's Bolshevik causes can be generalized – as he chooses to abstract
them, they are members of the class of twentieth-century additions
to the options and instruments of social choice, and more generally
still, to the social propensity to choose. But they support no 'law'
more precise than that choices will continue to multiply if men work
to multiply them.

A social law reports regular behavior. This may express (and
the social law report) the best calculations the people can yet make.
To try novel and better calculations (the revolutionary endeavor)
is always to risk mistakes (the conservative misgiving). One lover of
liberty may concentrate on this abstract of change, while another
remembers how many 'mistakes' have included the triumph of
villains and the enslavement or slaughter of innocents. Yet we all
live now by the lessons of past mistakes, enjoying the products of
past costs. In proportion as society is freed (not without mistakes and
costs) from its ignorant subjection to necessity, so will 'laws' and
'lessons' separate their meanings further, year by year. That is the
direction of liberty, and suggests its right relation to social science.

It does not merely suggest that the science should work as hard to
break laws, as to make them. It suggests also Carr's and Collingwood's chief principle for scientists' detailed search and selection.
Any element of choice in social action is action's most valuable cause,
because choice is good in itself; freedom is good. Freedom is the
margin between necessity and possibility. It is always an uncertain
margin – 'necessities' include the regular habits of people who can
sometimes think to change their habits; some possibilities are as
much invented as discovered. With this chronic unreliability, constraints and possibilities are still each other's limits. A literature of
'liberties only' is mere fantasy; so is a social science of constants
only. Depending on circumstances the constraints and possibilities
may sometimes be studied best by the method of understanding,
criticizing and valuing the choosers' reasoning. This was both the
technical and the moral point of Carr's choice of model. The Bolshevik program, as model, served Carr's valuation of deliberate rational
action as a privileged kind of cause; it contained the choosers'
reasoning, which offered for criticism its estimates of most of the
important constraints, freedoms, and opportunities for invention.

I understand and on most occasions join the outraged howl of anger which must greet any identification of Stalin as our century's champion of liberty. This is not the place to review the classical dilemmas of liberty. Most liberties include power against others, Stalin's the worst against the most. Collective freedom of action may have no greater value, but more dangerous power, than individual liberties. The two are sometimes each other's enemies (just as particular individual liberties are each other's enemies) but are often each other's necessary conditions. Many individual liberties are only as large as they are exclusive; collective discipline is often the only way for starving and oppressed majorities to create a choice between food, shelter, literacy, individual liberty, and their absence. But Carr needs no nice calculation of these present balances. Once more he gambles on futures, on humanity's likely application of its improving reason to its widening choices. If citizens of the already rich and individually free societies respond to communism by rejecting its inhuman destructions of liberty, their valuations are not at war with Carr's. This is precisely how his sense of the future *requires* them to behave. Will future societies as they grow rich select for use, from the inventions which history placed in Stalin's hands, only his contribution to the bloodier techniques of tyranny? Any lover of liberty who expects that, must denounce Carr as the enemy of all they both profess to stand for – and demand another history of Russia. But the future may prove that men will rather choose from Stalin's stock (as rich men do already, and even rich Russians perhaps begin to do) the new devices for wealth and growth and deliberate social choice. Just so, from the English industrial break-through others picked out the productive discoveries but rejected their associations with snobbery, class arrangements and uneducated management. Just so do many, including Americans, try to separate the American means to productivity and freedom from their associate levels of crime, competition and conformity. If in their turn the beneficiaries of Russian experience can break the 'laws' which associate collective action with collective slavery, and freely reject the whole illiberal range of Bolshevik brutalities, that will be an exercise of liberty, a reasoned defiance of experience. Not in detail perhaps, but in the general skill of the successful defiance of experience, Lenin and Stalin will have been among their best teachers. The lover of liberty who expects *this* future will greet Carr as a brother.

For my own part, a brother; but I admit, trembling somewhat, rather a Big brother. Besides his on the shelf there is room for that other history of Russia. When my children, with their more powerful Asian contemporaries, come to select their lessons from Bolshevism, their valuations will need to be well-informed. Besides the future in Carr's bones they should know something of the past in Russian graveyards – more than Carr's task left time to tell them, of the first experience of Bolshevism in a hundred million private lives.

In my opinion, other values should organize that other analysis. But what would it be like if they didn't? Could the job be done by some value-free 'frame of reference', or by a general theory of power, conflict and change?

4. *Lewis Coser and Ralf Dahrendorf*

'Social equilibrium is the thing to be explained; the social manufacture of consensus is the cause which explains it.' Of such integrationist theory, one can dissent from either part or both. One could – though few do – see consensus causing change. The other two possibilities are the subject of this section. Lewis A. Coser insists that conflict is among the causes of integration. Ralf Dahrendorf sees conflict causing change, and proposes another single cause as sufficiently completing explanations of both. At the same time Coser makes very modest claims for the power of such theory, while Dahrendorf's hopes for it are ambitious and strict. We may compare their views of society, their views of theory, and as far as possible the relation of both to their values.

Marx would explain Parsons' equilibrium as imposed by a ruling class. That class enforces rules which register, and norms which legitimize, the relations of production which arise from particular means and forces of production. Such an equilibrium must be temporary. If it lasts for a while, this may mean that the relations of production are still the most efficient for existing means of production; or it may mean that the ruling class is using its once-justified powers to defend outmoded relations against the changes now required to liberate new productive potentialities. Though the political superstructure does develop some such arresting power, this merely retards the date and increases the violence of the next revolution.

Thus change and equilibrium are not 'two faces of society', different effects to be explained by different causes; they are dialectical parts of a single process, and their common explanation lies in the secular growth of productive capacity. This theory has such unity and explanatory power that, while the non-interventionist majority of social theorists dream of a Newton, radical minorities dream of a new Marx. Why won't the old Marxism do? For a few, perhaps, because Marx already published it. As a stronger reason, it forecasts a revolution which many don't want. As a better reason, it was not all true when published and less of it is true now. For some, this merely shows that Marx was mistaken; for others (like Carr) it also shows how the unstable subject-matter limits the useful life of theories of this type. Ralf Dahrendorf draws neither of these conclusions; he thinks Marx's mistake was undue particularity, and makes Marx's view of the world a local nineteenth-century case of his own more general theory. In *The Functions of Social Conflict*[9] Lewis Coser does not explicitly join in this large argument; his aims are more modest, and chiefly corrective.

Coser's 'concern is mainly with the functions, rather than the dysfunctions, of social conflict, that is to say, with those consequences of social conflict which make for an increase rather than a decrease in the adaptation or adjustment of particular social relationships or groups . . . To focus on the functional aspects of social conflict is not to deny that certain forms of conflict are indeed destructive of group unity or that they lead to disintegration of specific social structures.' (8) If this seems to neglect the effect of conflict in causing structural social change, this is partly because Coser includes so much change in his concepts of 'adaptation or adjustment', and partly because he limits his task to refining the conflict theory of Georg Simmel, to fit it for service within structural-functional theory. His principles of selection can accordingly be simple. The effect to be explained is the persisting integration of groups. The causes to be chosen are whatever conflicts contribute to integration. Except for a few conflicts which people fabricate deliberately or unconsciously for integrative purposes, this is not an inquiry into the causes of conflict.

Causes are known and their effects estimated by uninhibited methods, including the explicit imagination (or more rarely, comparison) of alternatives. 'Would there be more or less integration if each particular type of conflict were absent?' Simmel sets the example:

Hostilities not only prevent boundaries within the group from gradually disappearing . . . often they provide classes and individuals with reciprocal positions which they would not find . . . if the causes of hostility were not accompanied by the feeling and the expression of hostility. (q. 33)

If we did not even have the power and the right to rebel against tyranny, arbitrariness, moodiness, tactlessness, we could not bear to have any relation to people from whose characters we thus suffer. (q. 39)

To Simmel's imagination these seem viable alternatives. Other alternatives, however desirable, are not imaginably viable:

Where [conflict] is exclusively determined by subjective feelings, where there are inner energies which *can* be satisfied only through fight, its substitution by other means is impossible; (q. 48)

Coser himself imagines alternatives, some viable and some not, for the same purpose of measuring actual effects:

If there were no antagonisms, status groups would dissolve since boundaries between them and the outside world would disappear; (36)

Without ways to vent hostility toward each other, and to express dissent, group members might feel completely crushed and might react by withdrawal. (47)

These safety-valve institutions help to maintain the system by preventing otherwise-probable conflict. (48)

Because the book is about the effects of conflict on integration, most of Coser's imagined alternatives are of the less integration which would follow if there were less conflict. But he also wants to distinguish integrative conflicts from other conflicts. So he sometimes imagines integrative alternatives in order to measure actual disintegrative effects. His discussion of scape-goating and other 'unrealistic' conflict offers examples. Scape-goating can release a group's tensions harmlessly upon irrelevant victims – harmlessly to the group, if not always to the victims. This may help the group to persist, if its original and real conflicts were such as might have disintegrated it; to this extent, scape-goating is functional. But if the real conflicts had been fought out, the real problems which occasioned them might sometimes have been resolved; the group's structure might thus have been adjusted better to accommodate real interests; to this extent, scape-goating allows structures to rigidify, pressures to mount, and perhaps worse disintegrations to occur more violently in the end. Coser can only determine what effects scape-goating *is* having, by first imagining which of the likely alternative consequences *would* occur *without* it.

This discussion of scape-goating is also Coser's nearest approach (in this book) to Marx, and to differentiating 'change' from 'disintegration'. He writes often of adaptation and adjustment, and often seems to see integration, his effect-to-be-explained, as a quality which may persist through, and be aided by, structural change. His interest in conflict makes sure that he does not forget that the citizens themselves have other aims than integration. Though integration remains the only effect to be explained, these other aims do interest Coser as causes, and what they aim to cause often is, or incidentally requires, structural change. Coser's problem is then to see how integration survives changes in structure – whatever 'integration' and 'structure' are.

The trouble is that without better definitions of both, 'how integration survives changes in structure' may mean exactly the same as 'how structures survive changes in other things'. But at least Coser's interest in conflict does bring him nearer than many functionalists to examining relations between change and equilibrium – between the things that change and the things that persist.

Since the outbreak of the conflict indicates a rejection of a previous accommodation between parties, once the respective power of the contenders has been ascertained through conflict, a new equilibrium can be established and the relationship can proceed on this new basis. Consequently, a social structure in which there is room for conflict disposes of an important means for avoiding or redressing conditions of disequilibrium by modifying the terms of power relations. (154–5)

It can scarcely be accident, but must rather be the influence of the non-valuing functional approach, which gives to this passage and others like it a vagueness and indeterminacy quite uncharacteristic of the rest of the book. 'Power relations' would seem to be a necessary part of almost any useful concept of social system or social structure.

Coser seems sometimes to distinguish power relations from both system and structure, but at other times to identify them. In the last sentence quoted, the undesirable 'conditions of disequilibrium' seem to mean strain between (non-structural) real powers, and power relations rigidified in structure. We think, perhaps, of a money-powerful middle class, or an organized-powerful working class, excluded from other (structural?) powers by an aristocracy entrenched behind an army and an outmoded constitution. This situation should be prevented by giving the 'real' powers early and open opportunities – to do what? To alter structures in their own interest, i.e., to use one power to acquire others? Or somehow to readjust power relations within an unchanged structure? What can it mean, to alter power-relations within an unchanged structure? Does it mean redistributing people among an unchanged pattern of roles? Does it mean redistributing legal rights without redistributing ownership or incomes? Does it mean redistributing rights to income or ownership without altering rights to other things? Or does it mean redistributing both, but without disturbing certain consensual values? These last must be unusual 'basic social values' if they say nothing about the distributions of income, ownership or constitutional rights. And yet, it is such patterns of 'basic values' which most functionalists seem to mean by 'system' and 'structure', however resolutely they refuse to nominate which values are 'basic' to which system.

If one sees social systems in this way, it does not seem sensible to distribute the values as some consensual, others not. No values, it is safe to say, are perfectly unanimous: there are even 'sane', purposeful murders and suicides in all societies. The societies most admired by functionalists are those in which there is the least superimposition, the most cross-cutting, of divisive issues. The stability arises out of the cross-cutting. Any faction united by one issue, knows that other issues divide it; knows that the enemy faction on one issue still contains allies on other issues. This is one useful way to see both the integrative effects of conflict, and the components (in the many shifting alliances) of consensus. The other useful way is to find which values, on which issues, have what power behind them: it may be the power of a tyrant or the power of a steady majority, but almost never is it the power of unanimous consensus.

Coser's argument is the one which underemphasizes power. He

depicts very vividly and well the good society 'sewn together' by the criss-crossing alliances created by criss-crossing conflicts. Why must he add a set of 'basic' values, standing like fortress walls around the arena within which the less important 'controversial' values may safely be fought over? Nobody names these fortress values except in words so general as to allow different factions to see different meanings in them. Perhaps Americans think of the liberties entrenched in their Constitution; but each of these is defended by a different majority, a different alliance, however overwhelmingly strong the alliance for some of them; and it would be hard to get unanimity for any one distinction of the 'basic' list from the rest. The good sense in Coser's conclusion seems to be that it is best if certain very valuable social structures are insulated from the rest, so that people who want to change the less valuable things will have no reason to attack the more valuable.

This would be valuing with a vengeance (and if thus done openly, it would not need to be a conservative vengeance). But if such valuation is to be avoided, what are the social scientist's alternatives? He may call 'basic' the values of big majorities, without asking whether the majorities got their values from a free or a dictated education. Or he may call 'basic' the values expressed in established institutions, without asking who established them or what tyrants or majorities support them now. But almost all such values are at one time or another subjects of conflict, and the rules regulating conflict are themselves on the list of values about which conflicts occur. Which values represent the system? Which others are free to change without requiring the investigator to say that the system has changed?

Coser distinguishes conflicts within the system from conflicts about the system:

Internal social conflicts which concern goals, values or interests that do not contradict the basic assumptions upon which the relationship is founded tend to be positively functional for the social structure . . .

Internal conflicts in which the contending parties no longer share the basic values upon which the legitimacy of the social system rests threaten to disrupt the structure.

One safeguard against conflict disrupting the consensual basis of the relationship, however, is contained in the social structure itself; it is provided by the institutionalization and tolerance of conflict. (151–2)

In the central organizing idea of functional analysis, confusion must continue until there are clear rules for distinguishing basic from other values, structure from whatever may 'adjust within' structure, and persistence from change. Coser could do it as easily as Halévy did it, merely by applying more consistently the values which are already clear enough between the lines. Though of course he does not say it, he *could* say: 'Bloodshed and other socially-caused sufferings (which could be detailed by detailed valuing) are evils worth avoiding. The causes that ward them off are therefore worth discovering. But it is wrong to suppose that all conflicts make for bloodshed and suffering. Personally, conflicts can be very satisfying. Socially, they can do much good (which could be detailed by detailed valuing). A society whose authorities regulate rather than resist attempts to force changes in any but its most precious institutions, will have a great many conflicts, but very little bloodshed or other social suffering. A society on the other hand whose authorities declare all institutions precious and defend them all, and declare all conflicts bad and repress them all, may eventually suffer such rebellious outbreaks as will cause terrible bloodshed and suffering. Such dangerous rigidities may sometimes be enforced by tyrants. But they may also be enforced by majorities, if the majorities judge unwisely which of their institutions are really precious, and which others are best left to be fought over by powerful factions.'

Among the values implied, might is perilously near to right and peace, at most prices, is well ahead of any notion of justice. But these are still coherent and viable recommendations – until the value-free idea of system-persistence enters to confuse them. This idea requires that *some* values be distinguished to index the system; so some must be declared basic, and the only alternative to *valuing* them as basic or *valuing* majorities as basic seems to be to imply, quite untruthfully, that they are unanimous. If Coser's argument had continued to be guided by his sensible values, it might have proceeded consistently:

'There had better *not* be basic values with the same majority for all of them, because this would consolidate and antagonise an equally permanent minority. It is better if each precious institution has its unique majority, so that majorities, their opposite minorities, and the conflicts between each pair, may all criss-cross. Then everybody should be able to support some precious institutions but attack others. Nobody need feel entirely complacent, entirely beleaguered, or entirely alienated. Individually, each should find his own happiest mixture of conformity and dissent. Socially, there should be no homogeneous party for full rigidity and no compact party for full rebellion . . .'

These terms seem to represent the marriage of Coser's intelligent values with his intelligent observations, whose full union is inhibited only by some unintelligent rules of his profession. These terms can of course be attacked, by proposing different values or estimates of causes and consequences, or both. But the work can only be *confused* by the confusing rule that all social analysis must relate to an equilibrium which can never be specified because valuing is banned.

Coser's more general notions of theory, and of the uses of generality, seem very sensible indeed.

There is one approach to social theory which has the advantage that it does not require the prior solution of presently insoluble problems. It may be that the uncertainties of social science arise partly from an intrinsically unstable element in social action, and partly from the unmanageable complexity of its more regular tendencies. But it would be absurd to assert either too confidently. It is even very difficult to decide whether a belief in free-willed variations is one whose justification *ought* to lie somewhere in the objective facts, or ought rather to lie in the scientific achievement (with other facts) of people who make the belief an assumption of their scientific activity. Science cannot stand still while these problems are solved. Meanwhile, to gamble for a strict deductive theory of strict regularities is to gamble on several unknowns, and the odds against each multiply into a long price indeed. For the most ambitious theorists, it is still victory or death. But there would be obvious advantages if theory could be kept consistent with all possibilities. Coser's approach (in practice: he makes no declarations about it) represents one common and workable variety of such 'open' theory.

In social structures providing a substantial amount of mobility, attraction of the lower strata by the higher, as well as mutual hostility between the strata, is likely to occur. Hostile feelings of the lower strata in this case frequently take the form of *ressentiment* in which hostility is mingled with attraction. Such structures will tend to provide many occasions for conflict since, as will be discussed later, frequency of occasions for conflict varies positively with the closeness of relations. (38)

This is part of one of a battery of sixteen propositions, derived from Simmel and improved for modern service. Like most of the rest, it is 'strictly' useless. 'Is likely', 'frequently', 'is mingled', 'will tend' make it, at best, an unquantified and probably unquantifiable statistic. If its last clause has a stricter look, it is only for 'occasions for' conflict (which is anyway included in the definition of 'close-ness'), not for the frequency with which people will seize upon the occasions. This passage was chosen as the most uncertain-sounding, but the more confidently-worded propositions have to be taken with the same grain of salt. 'Conflict with other groups contributes to the establishment and reaffirmation of the identity of the group and main-tains its boundaries against the surrounding social world.' (38) As Coser's text makes clear, this is neither strict nor sufficient; it describes what happens sometimes, not at other times, depending for example on the structure of the group and the particular values and interests at issue in each conflict. What use are these uncertain propositions? If they are seen as strict hypotheses, then to be fitted for test they will have to be made exceedingly complex by the nomin-ation of very large numbers of 'circumstances in which' they seem to hold. Or they may be seen as statistical hypotheses; testers will not then try to nominate the circumstances in which they are always true, but will attempt a statistical count of their truth for all circum-stances; but there will be plenty of complex problems in the selection of a representative sample of, simply, 'groups' and 'conflicts'. But if the propositions were worthless until tested in either of these ways, most of history and social science and social experience would be worthless too. (Some, of course, think it is.) The great value that it has, is as a battery of possibilities: things often present, but sometimes not.

Social clinicians can rarely approach real situations hoping to say: this is an A, and its outcome will therefore automatically be a B. They can more often say: of the different processes we are accustom-ed to finding in these A-type circumstances, these people seem to be choosing and acting out a D-type process, whose outcome has usually been E. The people know this, and are trying to avoid E, but we doubt if they will succeed; nobody has yet. Or, we think they will get half way; they seem exceptionally skilful and determined.

Theory may thus be seen as an organization of possibilities. It may be generalized as far as the facts allow it, but not beyond the possibility of identifying cases; not by resort to ambiguity. It may be strengthened, strictly or statistically, as far as the facts allow it. But of strictness they usually allow so little that it would seem obscurantist to limit theory to candidates fit for strict or statistical verification, while its other uses continue to be so fruitful. There may be philosophical weaknesses in Scriven's notion of 'normic statements' (p. 215 above) but it still expresses some practical wisdom; it describes the sort of theory which leaves open the question whether people are doing what people would invariably do in these uniquely complicated circumstances, or are doing one of the comparatively few things which people (usually, freely) choose to do in such circumstances. The investigator is, perhaps, trying to use statistical knowledge for the inappropriate purpose of identifying and predicting single cases; but it is still better knowledge than none, and he may still, if well educated, be able to triangulate his case by methods of different kinds, including asking the people what they think they are up to.

Simmel and Coser unpack the general idea that conflict may help to integrate societies into sixteen propositions which are scarcely 'testable' but make useful additions to the questions an investigator may systematically ask in appropriate cases. According to the answers he finds, time and experience may sort out the questions as less or more fertile. If the investigator's business is to keep a fruitful set of questions in his head, the theorist's business is to keep those questions up to date, add to them, order them, simplify them by subsuming several into one, clarify them by expanding one into several, economize them by relating them more strictly to particular purposes of inquiry. This is compatible with a continuing search for uniformities, but in many practical ways it will affect the direction of social science if it is to regard its task as improving the equipment of investigators, rather than *only* accumulating and winnowing a stock of reliable law.

Ralf Dahrendorf's social values seem more radical than Coser's. His scientific aspirations are certainly more radical. Are the two programs helpful to each other?

At least logically, physics, physiology, and sociology are subject to the same laws – whatever may render one or the other of these disciplines empirically preferable in terms of exactness. I cannot see why it should not be at least desirable to try to free sociology of the double fetters of an idiographic historical and a meta-empirical philosophical orientation and weld it into an exact social science with precisely – ideally, of course, mathematically – formulated postulates, theoretical models, and testable laws. The attempt must be made; and although the present study remains far removed from its satisfactory completion, I want it to be understood in terms of such an attempt. (*Class and Class Conflict in Industrial Society,* ix.)[10]

The attempt must fail if there are no strict, invariable uniformities in the facts. Dahrendorf seeks some few and simple axioms from which an extensive range of social behavior can be successfully deduced, and so predicted. The skeleton of the attempt is on pages 237–240 of *Class and Class Conflict in Industrial Society*. He modestly insists that this is by no means a theory, yet; but we are entitled to remember page ix – 'I want it to be understood in terms of such an attempt.' In my own summary (not his) this seems to be its theoretical backbone:

'If we ignore the elements of consensus and voluntary integration in society, it can be considered as if held together by its pattern of imperatively coordinated associations. In such associations, some members have authority and the rest have not. Those who have it strive to keep it, and thus to preserve the structure represented by their having it. Those who lack it strive to get it, and thus to alter the structure which deprives them of it. This conflict causes all structural change. How intense and violent the conflicts are, who wins them, and how the structure thus changes, depend on certain other variables – five for the intensity of conflict and three for its violence. Since one is the same for both, that makes seven altogether. The theory does not predict these other variables, which however are all conditions affecting conflicts about authority – i.e., none is an independent by-passing cause of structural change.'

To keep the theory clean, Dahrendorf reserves the word 'class' for possessors of authority who act together to preserve it, or for people without it who act together to get it. He appears – though less consistently – to define structure as the distribution of authority, and structural change as change in that distribution caused by conflicts about it between classes defined by it.

It would seem to follow from this, that explanations of structural change should identify the relevant imperatively coordinated association and its two contending parties, note the (in principle quantifiable) state of the other variables – and there, sufficiently, terminate. Similarly one who identifies an association and its classes, and measures the other variables, should be able to predict at least the general speed and magnitude of structural change.

What might be the uses of such theory? Five may be considered. The theory might point to things to look for, in analysing any particular society. It might be a valuable or persuasive ideology. It might be useful for differential description of actual societies and processes. It might (as Dahrendorf intends) become predictive. Or if not predictive, it might supply a convenient value-free selector for *ad hoc* explanations of change.

First it might modestly represent – like Coser's work – an addition to a catalogue of questions worth asking, about things worth looking for. For this purpose Dahrendorf insists it is only an addition, a supplement but not a replacement for the catalogue of integrationist questions.

People do sometimes divide sharply into governors and governed and contest the amount and distribution of the governors' authority. Sometimes they appear superficially to be fighting about other issues when 'really' they are fighting about this; sometimes their real interest in other things can be served only if they first acquire authority, so they are fighting about both, though perhaps only instrumentally about authority. These are certainly useful though scarcely original items in any catalogue of the important things that happen often enough to be always worth looking for, in any investigation of the causes of particular conflicts and changes. But for that purpose, is it useful to obliterate the distinction between conflicts about the use of authority, and conflicts about its distribution? Dahrendorf's theory requires us to see every dispute about the exercise of authority solely as a dispute about its possession. When I try to get somebody else to use his authority in one way rather than another, I may indeed be seen as trying to take some of his authority for myself; but not all cases are so simple. Seekers of authority may regard it as anywhere between a sufficient goal, and something wholly instrumental to other goals; Dahrendorf's heuristic assumption that such distinctions do not matter may perhaps do more harm than good to the investigator's systematic curiosity.

Second, the theory might have ideological value, as a persuasive addition to the citizens' valued images of social facts and possibilities, and indirectly to their programs. It can certainly, like Coser's work, correct unduly consensual images of society and unduly fearful valuations of conflict. While Coser, without often committing himself, seems obviously to value some conflicts because they knit society together, Dahrendorf values others because they change society. But this exaggerates the writers' differences, just as Dahrendorf sometimes exaggerates them when he refers to Coser's work. Many of Coser's 'adjustments' are what Dahrendorf would call changes, and Dahrendorf values most highly the pluralist societies whose many criss-crossing conflicts make changes come 'little and often' very much in the manner of Coser's 'adjustments'. However imperfectly specified, Coser's effect-to-be-explained is a constant: the persistence of some qualities of society most intelligible (in my opinion) if understood as Coser's choice of its most valuable qualities. While these persist, other changes figure not as changes at all, but as the adjustments and adaptations which allow the valuable qualities to persist. Dahrendorf's effect-to-be-explained is change (in the distribution of authority); as the effect which organizes the analysis, it is ubiquitously present. These different definitions of change mask very similar valuations of it, and of the little-and-often ways of achieving it. (Aristotle and Edmund Burke and Karl Popper are among the many who would concur.) When, instead of change, the two discuss 'creativity', their meanings and their valuations are more plainly alike and Dahrendorf cites Coser with approval.

Coser's values are not obscure, but he does not parade them. His corrective purpose, to redress the imbalance of consensual theory, often serves as his selector, and his selection might be described as 'other-directed by others' errors', though doubtless his values help to select the errors worth correcting. Dahrendorf, a distinguished exception to the usual coincidence of deductive and value-free aspirations, announces his social values quite confidently. But if his theory were simply meant to recommend them as good and viable values, it would have serious shortcomings. Its level and selection deny it any but some partial, corrective promise for ideological purposes. It does suggest technical objections to undervaluing conflict as such. But conflict *as such*, like change *as such*, has too little of the specificity which the public rightly wants in its ideologies. The public wants to consider what to change into what, or in what direction; which changes are worth fighting for or against, and which are not. Its interest in change and conflict is chiefly a dependent, instrumental interest. In other words, for ideological purposes Dahrendorf's is a theory about too few of the objects of value and desire, just as integration theory is.

Even Dahrendorf's attractive vision of 'the justice and the creativity of diversity, difference, and conflict' is consistent with a wide variety of social conditions, and not in its abstract self more valuable than some of them. This – in the last line of the book – is the first mention of its author's own notion of justice. Diversity may well be thought a more valuable quality of work, education and art than of wages, medical care or civil liberties. I personally value creativity in some relation to the things created – the novelties envisaged in *Brave New World* and *1984* would indeed be new creations, as were once Trial by Ordeal, the Inquisition, Murder Incorporated, and Auschwitz. This is only to make the point that an ideology should seek the level of generality at which it can generalize about generally valuable qualities, rather than the level at which it can generalize about uniformities whose social value may vary wildly with circumstances. But Dahrendorf did not intend his theory for ideological service. Certainly his own declared values would be imperfectly expressed in any ideology which invited the citizens to see and value nothing in society except its distribution of authority, conflicts about authority, and consequent redistributions of authority, while ignoring all other uses of authority, and all other objects of desire, and all other conflicts about them.

As a reference model to help the description of particular societies and processes, the theory is open to objections which also apply to its predictive promise. Either it is relevant only to changes in distributions of authority, leaving all other changes to be explained by some altogether different theory; or changes in authority so often command other changes, or are necessary parts or conditions or effects of so many other changes, that this authority-theory can somehow organize explanations of what appear to be 'other' changes. Dahrendorf's formal theoretical statement is strictly limited to the former meaning; but the two following chapters strain to give it as much as possible of the latter fertility. The narrow meaning would make the theory only as useful as changes in authority, caused by conflicts about authority between two parties only, are important and independent. The larger claim would make it important in proportion as the same causes and effects command other processes, or serve as reliable indexes of them.

These different theoretical claims are the more difficult to separate, because of two different 'superimpositions' which may occur. If one minority has authority in several associations at once, then many small conflicts about their authority may be superimposed into one big conflict. But there are also other conflicts, ignored altogether by this theory, which have nothing to do with authority. These also may be superimposed upon conflicts about authority. In this latter case the theorist may be tempted to ascribe all the superimposed conflicts to the single cause which his theory does comprehend. We saw E. H. Carr resisting a similar temptation, refusing to accept programmed causes as sufficiently explaining everything which appeared to coincide with programmed effects. A hostile critic can see much of Dahrendorf's last two chapters as an eager surrender to the same temptation. The nature of the temptation is made clearer, perhaps, in the words of an old fable:

Once upon a time a wizard gave a good boy a magic stone which had the power to make very rich and nourishing soup. "Put the stone" said the wizard "into a pot of boiling water. Throw in a lot of bones, and any meat you don't want, and turnips and onions, and cabbage and potatoes, and salt and peppercorns; and if you boil it long enough to let the stone work its magic, it will make wonderful soup for you." It always did, just as the wizard said it would. It was a wonderfully powerful stone.

To some conflicts, Dahrendorf's model fits well enough; for others, it may serve the investigator's confidence much as the wizard's stone served the cook's; but its vital shortcoming for deductive purposes appears to be that it does not include any means of telling (except by empirical investigations so thorough as to make the model unnecessary) which situation is which. If people seek authority in order to redistribute something else, how does one know whether independent conflicts are superimposed, or one (which one?) generated the other? Dahrendorf apparently rests his case on the ubiquity of authority, the variability of other objects of desire. (Meats and vegetables vary from season to season; sometimes there are turnips in the soup, sometimes leeks; but the stone is *always* there.)

There are two senses in which men might 'always' want power. Perhaps they want it for itself. But perhaps whatever else they want, authority is the only means of getting it; this was Viner's point. It does not seem to be Dahrendorf's. If it were, changing competitions for other prizes would cause inscrutable fluctuations in the competition for authority. Only once does Dahrendorf allow them to do so:

Property, economic status, and social status are no determinants of class, but they do belong to the factors influencing the empirical course of clashes of interest between conflict groups. (216)

Accordingly, the formal theory includes a clause based either on a meaningless distinction or on a spectacular historical untruth:

The violence of class conflict decreases if absolute deprivation of rewards and facilities on the part of a subjected class gives way to relative deprivation. (239)

If the competition for authority were a dependent open system it would obviously be an unsafe foundation for a closed deductive theory; so with the above exception Dahrendorf has authority-conflicts command the rest:

One of the central theses of this study consists in the assumption that this differential distribution of authority invariably becomes the determining factor of systematic social conflicts of a type that is germane to class conflicts in the traditional (Marxian) sense of this term . . . (165)

Whether descriptive or heuristic, this seems to claim that conflicts about authority are never controlled by, or sacrificed in favor of, superimposed conflicts about other things. I don't find this true of life, or promising as a theoretical assumption. But testing it is complicated by Dahrendorf's hypothesis that the intensity and violence and outcome of any class–conflict will depend on seven variables. There is usually room for argument, in historical cases, about the identification of the variables. In any case Dahrendorf is hesitant about them, and merely suggests that they stand until empirically refuted. In cooperative spirit, here are some candidates:

Theory (239–40)	Cases
4.1.1.1. The intensity of class conflict decreases to the extent that the conditions of class organization are present.	Russia, 1880–1917: intensity increased as conditions allowed organization. Russia, 1919–50: intensity decreased as organization became less possible. Likewise Germany, 1929–32 and 1933–9.
4.1.1.2 and 3. The intensity of class conflict decreases to the extent that class conflicts in different associations (and group conflicts in the same society) are dissociated (and not superimposed).	U.S.A., 1929–39. There appears to have been more class conflict with less superimposition, 1929–33, and more superimposition but less class conflicts 1934–9. Variations in Negro-White conflict, 1860–1967, have no apparently *regular* relation to varying superimpositions. Negro-White alliances sometimes reduce, sometimes increase intensity.
4.1.1.4. The intensity of class conflict decreases to the extent that the distribution of authority and the distribution of rewards and facilities in an association are dissociated (and not superimposed).	In the national political association of Britain, 1800–1900, class conflict increased while wealth and authority were dissociated, and was then reduced by superimposing them. This is a case of a common historians' generalization (since Aristotle) that there will be conflict for political authority whenever it is dissociated from the distribution of wealth and facilities. Rich classes want power; powerful classes use power to get a commensurate share of wealth. But still not 'always' – remember the rich Jews, and the authoritative Savonarola and Calvin.
4.1.1.5. The intensity of class conflict decreases to the extent that classes are open (and not closed).	Opening hitherto closed classes often increases conflict by encouraging militant expectations of mobility where previously there were none: Russia 1861, France 1789, the slave states of the U.S. after 1863.

4.1.2.1. The violence of class conflict decreases to the extent that the conditions of class organization are present.

Whenever classes *do* wish to fight, the violence will usually increase to the extent that the conditions of class organization are present, up to the limit of civil war. There are more free-labor rebellions than slave rebellions, and sometimes more violent free-labor rebellions in proportion as conditions (not necessarily laws) make rebellious organization possible. St. Petersburg, 1880–1917.

4.1.2.2. The violence of class conflict decreases if absolute deprivation of rewards and facilities on the part of a subjected class gives way to relative deprivation.

Contradicted by another well-grounded historians' generalization; as the most famous case among very many, see Tocqueville, *L'Ancien Regime*.

4.1.2.3. The violence of class conflict decreases to the extent that class conflict is effectively regulated.

True but trivial if 'regulated' means 'prevented'. If 'regulated' includes any meaning of 'institutionalized' or 'permitted within limits', the exceptions include: Australian industry 1904–66, with constant regulatory institutions, fluctuating conflicts, and both parties changing sides from time to time about the question of regulation. More spectacular contradictions of the theory may be found in the last colonial decade of almost any twentieth century colony achieving national independence; by such colonial cases, 4.1.1.1, 4 and 5, and 4.1.2.1, 2 and 3 are all flatly contradicted: and these are specially clear cases of imperatively coordinated associations within the terms of the theory.

In each case it might of course be argued that some of the other variables combined to counteract the effect of the one in question, which was nevertheless in itself operating as required by the theory.

The reader may explore these possibilities. They do not, in my opinion, help to support the theory; neither does my understanding of the causal mechanisms which, for each variable, the theory seems to call for. But these cases are not meant to correct the theory's arrangement of variables; they are meant to attack its notion of a constant. The constant is only a 'heuristic assumption'. Certainly, it may not matter whether heuristic assumptions are true; but there is likely to be trouble if this particular one is variable (unlike the wizard's stone, which truly was a constant). Though an element of 'imperative coordination' be present in all associations, it seems to be present in varying degrees, with varying effect. It does not always divide people into two parties only, one with and the other without authority; even 'analytically', this makes no sense of line authority or reciprocal authority, which between them exhaust the authority and sometimes even include all the members of a great many associations. However authority is distributed, the importance which the members attach to its distribution varies from case to case, and the variations are not explicable in terms (only) of the seven variables nominated by the theory. One whole class of invading variables, acknowledged in the preamble to the theory, must in themselves render the Constant inconstant. This theory abstracts class conflict from a causal network acknowledged to contain, also, elements of common interest, consensus and voluntary cooperation. Conflict and consensus are 'analytically separable', but are not alleged to be independent systems, nor yet to be in any *constant* relation to each other. At best, therefore, conflict theory could supply some analytic ingredients for synthetic predictions. Meanwhile the ubiquitous variable of consensus implies ubiquitous (and for this theory, random) variation in the 'constant' competition for authority.

Three points may be elaborated in conclusion. The theory neglects some facts of power; it dichotomizes authority unhelpfully; and it fails to determine one of its own internal problems.

Having accused 'integration theorists' of neglecting power, Dahrendorf seems to neglect some himself. Association creates a latent conflict between those with authority and the rest. Most of the conditions which will enable the parties to organize are then said to reduce the intensity or violence of the battle. This is sometimes true, of the cases Dahrendorf (and Coser) had in mind. But a lot depends on the parties' actual fighting power, of which the theory takes no notice. In life, the subjected are sometimes so strong that the authorities scarcely dare to use their authority at all, and while they don't, the subjected may suspend any pressure for structural change. The theory allows this condition to arise from dissociation of conflicts, but not from the simple strength of parties. Societies do include such situations, described internationally as 'balances of deterrence'. Yet the same equality of strength, in different circumstances which however this theory could not distinguish, may encourage each side into battles bloodier than would ever have happened if they had been 'equally weak' instead of 'equally strong', or if they had been obviously unequal.

Having thus incorporated some of Parsons' neglect of power, the theory next incorporates the dichotomy of classes which Dahrendorf criticized in Marxist theory.

In any imperatively coordinated association, two, and only two, aggregates of positions may be distinguished, i.e., positions of domination and positions of subjection. (238)

The author is careful to allow that many conflicts and all consensus will resist analysis based on this distinction, which is merely an analytical distinction; but he still strains to apply it to as many conflicts as he can. Some of the applications are curious. Bureaucrats, though dominated, are in the dominant camp, but do not dominate, except passively. In order to maintain this unusual conclusion it is necessary, throughout Dahrendorf's final empirical chapters, to avoid mentioning armies. Few associations agree as well as armies do with the definition of an imperatively coordinated association, and few have such uniform pattern in all societies. Are they, in terms of the theory, branches of authority, so always on its side? Are they bureaucracies, so always dominant but neutral? Or are the soldiers, most dominated of citizens, therefore always rebellious? It does not matter. Whatever the theory expects of them, it ought to be the same for all societies. But on a rough count of the armies of U.N. members over the last decade, more than half have been quiet (either loyal or neutral, but 'passively'); a few have been actively neutral, refusing help to either side as civilian factions overthrew one another; a few have been actively loyal, defending their masters vigorously against other contenders for authority; the rest have rebelled, seizing power for their officers or for civilian revolutionaries. Meanwhile most have not, but a few have, been internally troubled by those two-party competitions for authority which the theory says must be always latent within imperatively coordinated associations; but always absent from associations coordinated by line authority; except industrial enterprises coordinated by line authority, in which the competition is always present. The theory would have difficulty in predicting Kemal's or any colonial governor's efforts to dismantle his dictatorship. It has even stranger applications to democratic political systems. As politicians shuffle their supporting alliances, they are apparently creating and undoing imperatively coordinated associations, or shuffling blocs and interests in and out of the ruling class of the national association, as often as they trade an appointment for a vote.

A third problem is created by the theory itself, noticed here and there in the book, but not resolved. In any association the dispossessed, by definition a quasi-class, may proceed to form a class to strive for some authority. In practice this usually requires that they organize, thus forming a new association and within it, therefore, a new conflict. Two dispossessions are thus superimposed, though the corresponding ruling classes are not. But the two conflicts are not merely semi-superimposed; they are integrally related. As a rank-and-file labor unionist, I usually accept subjection to the union leaders' authority as the most effective means of disputing my subjection to the employers' authority. But sometimes I desire the employers to win the battle (if temporarily) because I believe in their case, or in order that I may more easily wrest authority from my union leaders. This latter may happen because I want to instal better union leaders who will lead the war on the employers more effectively; or it may happen because as a contender for union office I stand to gain more from winning the battle within the union than I stand to gain from the union's winning the battle with the employers. The theory leaves quite indeterminate, which pursuit of which authority will predominate. It does touch on the problem, in claiming that conditions which enable the dispossessed to organize will moderate the conflict, but even then it does not nominate as moderator any *regular*, always-predictable transfer of the dispossessed's hostility from the greater ruling class to the lesser. But this difficulty is co-extensive with the theory: wherever the dispossessed organize, they may (as the theory says) be moderated by various links with the enemy which arise from organizing against him; but they may also be strengthened to fight him more effectively, weakened by hostility to their own organizers, and free to choose which enemy they hate most, which authority they most want to reconstruct. In life, as in eclectic explanations of it, the problem is usually resolved by looking at the issues – i.e., at issues other than the distribution of authority. How do the parties value whatever is at stake in the two conflicts? Neither these other issues, nor the parties' valuations of them, are constant from case to case; but nor are they cared for by the theory's seven variables. Until they are, it is hard to see how the assumption of a competition for authority constant in *all* associations can promise any determinate prediction at all.

Related objections may be raised to the theory as a selector of *ad hoc* explanations after the event. Any investigator is entitled to study, selectively, the element of conflict-about-authority which is present in varying forms and degrees in most social conflicts. But of the three principles of selection he may adopt, this theory does seem to propose the worst.

He may say: 'I will define structure as the distribution of authority, then I will look for the causes which change it or stabilize it.' In this case he will not restrict his search to causes which are themselves conflicts about authority.

Alternatively he may say: 'I will look for conflicts about authority, and will then explore their important effects', which effects will usually include the distribution of many other things besides authority – indeed, those other distributions will usually distinguish the important from the unimportant effects.

But neither of these is the approach which the present theory recommends. At whichever end the investigator starts, he is encouraged to look for links between causes of one type and effects of that same type: between distributions of authority, and their self-generating redistributions of it. Even as moderated by the seven variables, this particular pair of cause and effect seem rarely, in real life, to enjoy much joint independence, or allow satisfying explanations of each other. Even their connection with each other may be hard to estimate unless other variables (more than seven) are grasped as well. Dahrendorf did not intend his theory as a guide to *ad hoc* explanations, though without exception his own explanations have that character. But in practice (including his own practice) that is what it is likeliest to be used for. Its principle of selection will replace the principles which explainers would otherwise derive from their particular purposes in explaining particular cases. Soon, by dismissing other causes from its explanations, the selector will claim to have proved its familiar and false assumption that 'all men want is power'.

Deductive theory requires that life be simple and preferably that one or a few factors reliably control it. If life is not like that, explanations can still be clipped like that. When ideological obsessions used to prompt single-cause theories, they did at least arise from desires to reform society. The same mistakes are less excusable when they spring from self-centred desires for the forms of science. But the use of unsuccessful theories to preselect eclectic explanations deserves a section to itself, in Chapter 13.

11

Political Economy

1. The best social science

By comparison with general history or general sociology, the more practical and better-agreed purposes of economics seem to allow clearer principles of selection. The subjects behave more monotonously. Regularity is a more fruitful selector. Some laws are possible – however local, they work, in a useful approximate way, for clinicians sufficiently skilled in recognizing limitations, interferences and exceptions. But as economists move from short-run analysis of established systems to study the change and growth of systems, so does their work resume much of the selective, incomplete form of historical explanation.

These pages can add nothing to the economists' expert discussions of the relations between their science and their values. The purpose of this section is merely to echo some simpler parts of that discussion, in an effort to show that the themes of this book can survive encounter with economics. Even if other disciplines succeed one day in approaching the power and self-knowledge of this best social science, similar problems of selection and valuation will still confront them, strains between the fit and generality of theory will still trouble them, the same choice and imagination of alternatives will be required of them.

Indeed, if others looked less enviously to natural science and more attentively to economics, they would notice that economics has abandoned some of the directions to which sociology and political science are now fashionably turning. Economics has prospered as it forsook generality, deduction from simple psychological axioms, symmetrically unified theory, and the search for sufficient explanation, for more practical attention to the facts of life and more specialization of diverse models and theories to the diverse particulars of relations in life. Nor are all the regularities of economic systems passively discovered. Economists, like the advertisers and employers and governments they advise, often teach regular behavior to people who are eager, or paid or made, to learn it.

People's dealings with money, and with the goods and services to which they are willing to ascribe money values, have high average reliability in advanced societies. Using the values of the economizing people who are their subject, economists identify many specialized problems. It would strain the definitions to pretend that many of these are other than technical, or that the theorists' social values contribute much to the work or could be inferred from its results. Much of economics can be value-free in the sense that 'given goals' and comparatively simple instructions from comparatively single-minded clients supply all the values it needs.

But even for specialized and short-run problems, this is not always true. The judgment and imagination required in model-building are mostly technical, but no sharp line divides them from the judgments of social utility which sometimes also guide the work. Some models' fixed and moving parts can be chosen purely for fit and predictive performance, or to simulate interventions desired by client rather than scientist. But other models are built with an eye to the social implications of different analyses. Which volumes to model, or how far to break them down to which components, may be a technical question, but it may also be affected by the business or social prospects of operating on particular components. There is dialogue between general model-builders and (whether in their own or in other persons) engineers. At the very least, general theory is affected by broad judgments of effects worth modelling, and of the components and identities whose isolation would (if technically possible) have the most valuable engineering uses.

Meanwhile the discipline has not forsaken its more general concerns. Only a few of the relations in long-range economic change and growth will support much strict or sufficient theory. A value-structured welfare economics continues as a busy division. Valuations of social needs, and of changing scientific styles and fashions, affect the curricula of education and training. If different schools adjust different proportions of the curriculum to general theory, political debate, and the local market for skills, these are social as well as professional choices.

The authors of general text-books and the theorists of welfare and of growth are no less scientifically 'mature' than the most mathematical model-builders; often they are the same people. It must be the nature of the subject-matter, not the 'maturity' of the scientists, that differentiates their performances. The objective purity of some specialized activities gives way to familiar uncertainties, and tasks for the theorists' values, when they consider whole economies, useful educational images of them, their output of well-being, alternative engineering holds upon them, and the processes of their growth.

This study could profit from examinations of many and various economic examples. All would be copied straight from the economists' own methodological writings, and they are better left there to be read in the originals. The two that follow are meant to emphasize some ambiguities of technical and social judgment which can arise, first, in discovery, and second, in education.

2. John Maynard Keynes

To purists it must seem improper that Keynes' most famous advance in 'high and pure' theory should have been made by such an uninhibited persuader, in the heat of controversy about urgent social issues, and should have gained acceptance by decades of persuasion and hesitant engineering rather than by anything very clearly resembling 'verification'.

It would be a difficult problem, in psychology rather than economics, to judge how important Keynes' social valuations were to some of the technical originalities in *The General Theory of Employment Interest and Money* (London: Macmillan, 1936). Its 'Concluding Notes' are 'on the Social Philosophy towards which the General Theory might lead'; they do not assert that the social philosophy led to the general theory. Some concern for the sufferings of his fellow men may have driven Keynes to work hard at economics, choose problems, and revolt against some orthodoxies; but it would need a more perceptive critic to disentangle that from the other concerns of such a complex and ambitious character. The technical conclusions of the theory are adaptable, neutrally, to a variety of political purposes. But did Keynes reason his way to those conclusions quite independently of his own opinion of how they might best be used?

First, it could be a neutral task to the degree that it was narrowly corrective, though even that was a choice. In an established body of theory he replaced only as much as was necessary to complete the fit of the theory to its own purposes and facts – facts and abstracts of behavior long ago selected for analysis, prediction and control.

Second, the corrections included some new conceptual arrangements to accommodate new observations – direct, understanding observations of savers' and investors' behavior. Keynes' 'new' causes were as visible in that behavior as they were crucial in his theory. What had obscured them from three generations of skilful searchers was seldom the searchers' social values but was rather the hypnotic attraction of axiomatic theory, of scientific ideas which had inhibited Keynes himself for thirty years *despite* his social values and desires, which they frustrated. When at last he escaped from habit and saw something new and clear, this was not merely by 'wishing it so'; but nor was he unhelped by wishing with increasing desperation.

Finally, it did not seem to Keynes himself to be either a value-free or a predominantly deductive job. He knew, somewhat practically and simply, what needed doing, and could have put his reasons into a few pages. A great deal of the deductive apparatus was propagandist, to persuade others to shed not their social values but their scientific convictions. The book has indeed a great deal of deductive theory, including backward speculation as to what psychological assumptions would allow observed events to be predicted; but its use of deduction is sophisticated, instrumental and not preferential – clean theory has no snobbish priority over messy pragmatism:

Thus the position of equilibrium will be influenced by these repercussions; and there are other repercussions also. Moreover, there is not one of the above factors which is not liable to change without much warning, and sometimes substantially. Hence the extreme complexity of the actual course of events. Nevertheless, these seem to be the factors which it is useful and convenient to isolate. If we examine any actual problem along the lines of the above schematism, we shall find it more manageable; and our practical intuition (which can take account of a more detailed complex of facts than can be treated on general principles) will be offered a less intractable material upon which to work. (249)

Perhaps 'useful and convenient' are respectively social and technical selectors. Perhaps not; both might be technical; but that latter interpretation requires that Keynes misunderstood what he was doing:

The division of the determinants of the economic system into the two groups of given factors and independent variables is, of course, quite arbitrary from any absolute standpoint. The division must be made entirely on the basis of experience . . . Our present object is to discover what determines at any time the national income of a given economic system and (which is almost the same thing) the amount of its employment; which means in a study so complex as economics, in which we cannot hope to make completely accurate generalizations, the factors whose changes *mainly* determine our *quaesitum*. Our final task might be to select those variables which can be deliberately controlled or managed by central authority in the kind of system in which we actually live. (247)

Keynes' ambitious 'strain to originality' coincided, so well that one cannot now disentangle them, with his feelings about the unemployment which no contemporary theory could explain or control. That was not the only coincidence. He wanted to maximize employment, and somewhat reduce the unearned extremes of inequality, by minimal intervention. The least would also be the most possible intervention, politically. He valued highly the consequence, that so much of the economic and social life of liberal capitalist society would thus be conserved. This desire for an economy of intervention agreed happily with the desire for elegant economy of theory. Work which was at first thought by many to attack classical theory is now understood (as the General Theory proposed) to complete and validate it; what was first feared by many as dangerous to capitalist liberties and inequalities is now accepted (as it asked to be) as an important aid both to securing those objects, and to bringing more of them into the range of free choice.

To select only the scientific ones from this happy agreement of Keynes' principles, is to forget by how many less economical methods unemployment might have been attacked. Those who want to cure other ills as well, may couple them with unemployment as theory's Effect-to-be-explained; or may select larger causes of unemployment for the sake of the other effects which they also cause. Keynes' final chapter depicts one alternative condition, from which his real world of 1936 was made to differ by the causes nominated, sparsely and precisely, in his theory. Or that chapter may be read as an account of the by-products of his explanation of unemployment: the other social facts which might be caused to change if one changed these chosen few only, of the innumerable conditions necessary for unemployment.

If Keynes' principles of selection seem thus to be explicable either as parsimonious, corrective principles of theory-building or as precise expressions of his social values, then they support no case for a value-structured science; but none for a value-free one either. But if urged in support of the latter, then they were in surprising coincidence time and again with Keynes' persistent search, in the *General Theory* and in much else that he wrote, for minimal means to force the rich and allow the poor to be productive – to contrive full employment and 'the euthanasia of the rentier' with the least other disturbance of what seemed to him a fragile but valuable structure of society.

3. Paul Samuelson

Professional debate about the objectivity of welfare economics reached its climax in the nineteen-fifties. Then it subsided, perhaps with the end of serious hopes that valuations of welfare could be derived from facts, and perhaps with the perception that this did not matter much. The debate had, perhaps, one faintly unfortunate effect on some readers – they tend to think of social valuations as characteristic of what is now conventionally labelled 'welfare economics', as if the discipline's other branches were, by contrast, 'value-free'.

Paul Samuelson is trebly and justly distinguished, as a contributor to that welfare debate, as a mathematical economist, and as the author of a best-selling beginner's introduction to economics. I offer no criticism whatever of the technical contents of the intro-ductory text, nor of any of the contents of his advanced work. But – enlightened by some of both – there does seem to be room for criticism of the advice about science, ethics and valuations which so many recruits to social science receive from his *Economics, An*

Introductory Analysis. (1948; references are to the sixth edition, N.Y.: McGraw-Hill, 1964).

What are the problems of valuation to which beginners need introduction? Perhaps valuations and facts are integral, each part of the structure of the other; or if separable, they are as necessary to each other in social theory as are the wood and the nails in holding up a house; or valuations are separable preliminaries, foundations on which the house can be built of facts alone. Economics is a partly-normative science; or is science, and should be called economics, only insofar as not normative. Economists have special skill in valuing the social effects of economic processes; or the selection and valuation of those effects can be left to laymen. Efficiency and equilibrium are partly normative or wholly technical ideas, or perhaps it depends on their use and context. What does Samuelson's *Economics* say about these problems of *is* and *ought*?

For the most part in any science, scholars discuss what *is* and what will be under this or that situation. The task of positive description should be kept as free as is humanly possible from the taint of wishful thinking and ethical concern about what ought to be. Why? Because scientists are cold-blooded robots? No, merely because a more accurate job of positive description, experience shows again and again, will be achieved if one tries to be objective. (Experience also shows that, try as we may, we humans never succeed in separating completely the objective and subjective aspects of a discipline. Indeed, the very choice of what scientists choose to measure, and the perspective from which they observe and measure it, and the reactions the observer produces in that which is observed – all these factors make the distinction between *is* and *ought*, between objective and subjective issues, at bottom a matter of degree rather than of kind.) (620)

This, with the page that follows it, is not such a bad simplification. It could be improved by clearer distinctions between observation and the many and various tasks of scientific selection; but as it stands, for its purpose, it is reasonable. Such simplifications for an elementary text are always difficult, and allowances should be made for them. The trouble is that this one is the only reasonable treatment of the general problem in the book, it comes near the end, and earlier references do not so much further simplify as, simply, contradict this later one. Elsewhere, objective and subjective are different in kind, not degree. Most *selections* are forgotten in some undistributed middle as scientific choices are brutally distributed as objective observations of facts, or subjective choices of 'goals':

> . . . there is only one valid reality in a given economic situation, however hard it may be to recognize and isolate it. There is not one theory of economics for Republicans and one for Democrats, not one for workers and one for employers . . .
> This statement does not mean that economists always agree in the *policy* field . . . Basic questions concerning right and wrong goals to be pursued cannot be settled by science as such. (8)

Two pages later the undistributed middle gets attention in an intelligent passage of good simplification – except that neither in it nor around it is there any hint that social values may, sometimes usefully, take part in these scientific selections. Republicans and Democrats, disagreeing about goals, are nevertheless expected to value identically as required by 'right', 'good', 'outweighed' and 'usefulness' in the following:

> Even if we had more and better data, it would still be necessary – as in every science – to *simplify*, to *abstract* from the infinite mass of detail. No mind can apprehend a bundle of unrelated facts. All analysis involves abstraction. It is always necessary to *idealize*, to omit detail, to set up simple hypotheses and patterns by which the facts can be related, to set up the right questions before going out to look at the world as it is. Every theory, whether in the physical or biological or social sciences, distorts reality in that it oversimplifies. But if it is good theory, what is omitted is outweighed by the beam of illumination and understanding that is thrown over the diverse empirical data . . . The test of a theory's validity is its usefulness in illuminating observed reality. (10)

Having emphasized that values cannot be derived from facts, and that observations of facts should be as free as possible of valuations, the text seems to extend this rule of objectivity, without argument, to all selections; though except for statistical sampling it nowhere suggests what objective selection might be, nor how Republican and Democrat will derive (from the facts, presumably) identical tests of what should be theory's right questions, useful identities and valuable illuminations.

Along with these there are some verbal emphases, perhaps haphazard but suspiciously consistent. If somebody's 'goal' is the production of marketable goods to maximize satisfactions for an existing distribution of dollar votes, the ethical status of this goal is rarely mentioned. But whenever any other goal is mentioned, its 'ethical, a-scientific' status is heavily emphasized. For an individual to prefer more dollars to less (or to anything else) and to bargain for them in a free market, is matter for scientific report; but his ethics are reported the moment he prefers anything else to dollars, or tries to get more dollars from a legislature.

Samuelson permits no illusions about the ability of market mechanisms to preserve their own freedoms or to optimize competition, employment, the national product, or anything else. In the main line of his exposition and in many 'applied' digressions, he attacks a great variety of whiskied-Republican and whiskered-Democratic dogma on this subject. He makes it very clear that purely competitive models are purely imaginary, while imperfect competition and deliberate welfare policies are hard facts. But still, the imaginary workings of pure models are often described in indicative mood, while deliberate redistributions are more often described in conditionals to indicate what *would* happen (scientifically) *if* societies (a-scientifically) were to *choose* (ethically) goals. If free competition produces short of the production-possibility frontier, this is recorded as a scientific fact, an imperfection which, it is often implied, quite a-ethically *ought* to be corrected. But if a welfare policy leaves the same production-possibility similarly unfulfilled, this always figures as an ethical choice with a scientific warning of its economic cost. As one example, these paragraphs follow each other on pp. 630-1:

1. In a pure unmixed competitive society, the economic problems of WHAT shall be produced, HOW, and FOR WHOM are solved in an interdependent manner by the impersonal workings of profit-and-loss markets. Each variable depends upon every other, but all tend to be simultaneously determined at their general equilibrium values by a process of successive approximations and readjustments.

2. [In a utopian economy] the final determination of the distribution of income would involve an outright social dividend or tax, in various lump-sum amounts to people as determined by explicit a-scientific ethical decision of government and society.

All economists, led by Samuelson himself, are familiar with the objections to the implied distinctions. But for young readers a few may be spelled out. At least since economics came of age, distributions became controllable, and deliberate distributions became small or large facts of every economy, the social choice of a competitive mechanism of distribution has been as ethical as the social choice of any other, including legislative, mechanisms. My desire for dollars is as ethical as my desire for anything else. My wish to maximize my gains in a market is as ethical as my vote for a redistribution. My encounter with another trader in a profit-and-loss market is as personal as my encounter with ward-heeler, tax-collector or pension office. To maximize production whatever its distributive effect is as ethical as to optimize distribution whatever its productive effect; and for various reasons, production cannot be judged to be maximized without some welfare valuations. Most of this, Samuelson asserts explicitly; but much of it, his text denies by emphasis, omission and implication.

It even appears, from some of the patterns of emphasis and omission, that some concepts, laws and other scientific selections may possess objectivity when cited to illuminate the service of some 'goals', but become ethical if put to the service of other goals: methods are ethical-by-association with their uses. The most remarkable chameleon is the Law of Diminishing Marginal Utility.

The existing distribution of property, income, education and economic opportunity is the result of past history and does not necessarily represent an optimum condition according to the ethical philosophies of Christianity, Buddhism, paganism, the American creed or other ideologies. (630)

Merely to record such distributions we do first have to value and index some concepts of property, education, opportunity, etc.; but we need not cavil at the working distinction between what is, and how people value it. What is interesting is the status of one particular law for, respectively, insurers and Buddhists:

pp. 421–2	pp. 624–5
We are now in a position to see why insurance, which appears to be just another form of gambling, actually has exactly opposite effects. For the same reasons that gambling is bad, insurance is economically advantageous. [A footnote identifies 'gambling is bad' as ultimately	Many people profess to hold the ethical and philosophical belief that different individuals' wants and needs are very much alike, and that the present market mechanism works inadequately because the rich are given so many more votes in the control of production than

ethical – but not 'insurance is good'] . . . Economic theory shows that the difference between these two cases is that the latter stabilizes income while the former destabilizes it . . .

Obviously, the law of diminishing marginal utility – which makes the satisfaction from wins less important than the privation from losses – is one way of justifying the above reasoning. *This law of diminishing marginal utility tells us that a steady income, equitably divided among individuals instead of arbitrarily apportioned between the lucky and unlucky people whose house did or did not burn down, is economically advantageous.*

the poor – which makes the market demand for goods a poor indication of their true social worth. Such people with a relatively equalitarian philosophy will welcome a great reduction in the spread of incomes . . . They may argue that taking away $1,000 from a man with an income of $100,000 and giving it to a man with an income of $2,000 will add to social well-being (by taking dollars from a place deemed low in marginal social utility to a place deemed higher). After the distribution of income between families has been determined correctly, according to society's fundamental (a-scientific) value judgments, then and only then will it be true that the dollars coming on the market will be valid indicators of the value of goods and services.

These inconsistencies, each trifling but all of similar tendency, seem to reflect a strain between two purposes. The critic of 'welfare functions' is rightly concerned to declare that distribution is a matter of ethical social choice; none can be justified entirely by reference to productive efficiencies. But this is crossed by another purpose, to draw the boundary of economic science along the line between *is* and *ought*. In practice this line is, as Samuelson says, 'at bottom a matter of degree rather than kind'. *Ought*, and the various morals and desires it stands for in this discussion, intrudes everywhere. Some of it, however, intrudes in factual form, in reports of present interests and desires. The boundary of economic science (an unmentioned *ought*) also divides the economic system from other systems, so we must add another limitation, and read 'reports of present interests and desires within the economic system, as expressed in present dollar votes'. It is thus that present distributions (and winners) acquire, indirectly, scientific privileges which would be withheld from them in explicit debate about the justice of distributions.

Efficiencies and economies and equilibria can seldom be assessed without reference to given distributions. To observe a present distribution is science, whatever the surrounding warnings that its presence does not make it just. To propose a different distribution is ethics. It may be proper for an economist to imagine the technical consequences of imaginary distributions, but whenever he does, there must be systematic disclosure of the hypothetical nature of his thought and the ethical nature of his choice of client. Meanwhile his harder-headed colleagues' choice of client – the winners from present distributions – escape such Buddhist identification. Present distributions and winners *exist*, and it is the purest science to report their existence, understand their operations, and offer helpful criticism of their economies and efficiencies. Present losers, dissenters and revolutionaries also exist, of course; but their wishes are not fed into an economic system by dollar vote, so they are for study by the disciplines of history, politics or ethics.

Another trick from Samuelson's text is quoted in the next section. They still amount to a small, one-sided and unfair selection from the text. But Samuelson writes with deserved authority for an important audience. His *Economics* introduces hundreds of thousands of the very ablest young people to its subject and often, if economics is the first they attempt, to the social sciences generally. He tells them firmly what relations they should establish (and which they should avoid) between their values and their science, and he tells them just as firmly that the latter is the payable part of their education. For all its wit and sophistication about the particular class of welfare judgments, much of the advice is still, in my opinion, loaded in aid of winners, while pretending neutrality. It is fair to add that it is better advice than students sometimes got from earlier texts. It is much better advice than they get, still, from many of their first teachers and texts in sociology and political science. But it would damage neither the technical excellence nor the liberal persuasions of Samuelson's text, if its few deceptive fragments were replaced by simplifications, instead of contradictions, of the good advice on pp. 620–1; and if the different relations of values to observations and to selections were made clear. Economists' selections, from technical concept to general curriculum, have their double relation, to their subject and to the purposes of studying it.

4. *General Equilibrium and Arthur Lewis*

General equilibrium, efficiency, and system-maintenance are among the effects for which explanations may be sought. By substituting them for more local, obvious or value-laden effects, some scientists have sought to isolate the economic system more decisively, and to make their work more general or more objective. Such ideas are rarely abused in modern economics. One view of 'general economic equilibrium' is nevertheless summarized below in double parody – in parody of radical objections which themselves parody the idea objected to. The aim of this nonsense should not be misunderstood. It does not represent any current economic theory. It is a straw-man, an Aunt Sally, with two uses. Its first use is to caution imitators from other disciplines, lest their new notions of system and equilibrium imitate those which economists have learned to do without. Its second use is as a foil, to introduce by exaggerated contrast the very different sort of theoretical unity achieved in Arthur Lewis' theory of economic growth.

'Equilibrium' may refer usefully to the dependence of chosen effects upon the interactions of chosen causes. But the idea has sometimes been overworked to confer privilege upon the unwilled or 'self-equilibrating' ones among such causes, to imply more closure and independence than most economic systems really have, and to dignify the disciplinary boundary of economic science as more 'natural' than it really is. These latter uses may be guyed as follows:

Economic activities are never 'left alone'. If men did not make laws to regulate property, contract, currency, etc., there would scarcely *be* an economic system. Such political regulations can rarely be to everybody's equal advantage, and are usually imposed upon majorities by minorities. Two centuries ago, many such laws already existed to preserve the grossly unequal distribution of wealth which had been achieved by the strong and the lucky.

At that date it appeared to some academic economists that everyman's pursuit of his own advantage, if limited by law to bargaining in free markets, would have the effect of maximizing everybody's rewards in a system of stable prices, stable full employment and steady growth.

Two things were wrong with this dream. Either it failed to account for the distribution of wealth and income, or (sometimes) it pretended that the market distributed them, whereas they were really distributed more by plunder, inheritance, unequal bargaining and rich men's law-making. Second, the theory was untrue of what it did describe. Everyman's pursuit of his own interest did not always produce free competitive markets; even when it did, the markets did not always stabilize prices or employment or rates of growth. Neither in practice nor in theory is there sufficient good reason why they *should* always do so.

As economists discerned these flaws, they shifted target. They accepted the grossly unequal distribution of wealth, and looked for ways to secure it by making full employment accompany it, and by making its income steadier. This program was attractive to the rich. Between them, the rich and the economists discovered one by one the 'causes of disequilibrium' – that is to say, the things which caused life to differ from the particular equilibrium they imagined as desirable. As each cause was discovered, it was if possible replaced by deliberate contrivance to cause the real economy to behave more like the imagined one. Once the false prognosis of the original theory was treated thus as a program, it became a better prognosis. Ways were found, for example, to contrive effective demand for goods, to control rates of investment, and to use national power for the advantage of national economies, or at least of some national interests and minorities. These steps inevitably included some redistribution of wealth, and more of income. Technical improvements altered the pattern of jobs, skills, education, and wages. The poor, for many reasons, improved their political influence. Intentionally or not, most of the redistribution went in the direction of greater equality.

Gradually, thus, the rich countries made their economies into nearer copies of the chosen model, though not usually by the methods or for the reasons which the original model had at first proposed. Experts learned how to manipulate all sorts of levers in the new system, to contrive all sorts of desired effects. But since there is now a wide choice of effects that can be contrived, and since contriving them requires much skilled, complex, deliberate and controversial activity, what is the point of calling any particular effect 'the general equilibrium'?

Besides the bad reasons for calling it that, there is some good reason. The manipulators could not and do not control every transaction. Their skill lies in using a manageable battery of strategic controls in such a way that the unmanageably vast remainder of economic activity *will* involuntarily equilibrate itself to join in producing the chosen effects. Thus a particular equilibrium is chosen, and contrived.

But involuntary and unaided self-equilibration was the original economists' model, and the rich do well to retain it as a propaganda model still. So as a first step, it is justified as a heuristic model. Textbooks have smooth circular-flow diagrams of the whole system, every exchange in the flow simulating a market – instead of truthfully eccentric representations, with snakes and ladders, stiles and water-jumps, and notes that 'Here be markets', 'Here be contrivers', and 'Here be Big Guns that guard Ye Old Distribution'. Instead, these heterogeneous realities are described by differentiation from the pure self-equilibrating model; and soon, the word for a difference from the model is 'imperfection'. Or rather, distortions of the model by private power are imperfections; distortions of it against private interests by public powers are not economic at all, but are ethical-Buddhist inefficiencies. After all, if the pure model worked, would it not be the cheapest, most natural, least contentious model? Are not interventions always expensive, value-ridden, and subject to error? The good physician helps nature, he does not seek to replace her natural wisdom. So, contrivance is justified when it helps economic life to resemble the pure competitive self-equilibrating model, and unjustified when it wrenches life away from the model.

This distinction is reinforced by the distinction between science and politics. Science is about what *is*. Of all the possible distributions of wealth, only one (here and now) *is*. Science is about that one. Talk about any other ones is politics. Economics is the science which explains, and helps nature to contrive, the natural equilibrium of the factual economic system. The content of that natural equilibrium now reads: optimal service of interests as now distributed. Interests are defined as economic, as members of the system, when they have a dollar—not when they merely want one. Economics is about their dollar votes, not their pasts, their futures, or their other votes. Recruits will learn in school that this is the boundary, and that there are no marks or grades for transgressing it. Besides its healthy share of the money, the winning alliance now has a monopoly of the skill.

This is indeed an intelligible goal for some winners in an economic system to propose for the system and for its experts. But in no practical system could it be the rationally self-interested goal of everybody. To some extent it is simply imposed by the power and skill of the rich and expert. To some extent it may appeal rationally to losers. They may value rich chances as an attractive gamble against the poor man's probabilities. They may embrace the deal as the best they are likely to get from the dangerously powerful rich. But the winners are more secure if they can convince the losers that this deal represents not a compromise of interests but their full reconciliation – that it represents the only viable economic system, the only natural system, the only rich system, the only free system – or the only scientific (as opposed to inefficient, ethical-Buddhist) system.

Thus with a little sleight of hand, the idea of a system in equilibrium can achieve a great deal. Politically, it registers a working compromise:

the poor can have as much as doesn't have to be taken from the rich. Professionally, it allows an important distinction between two classes of economic interventions: (1) Changes required to maintain employment and growth with minimal redistribution. These are first-class changes, deserve consensual support, are uncontroversially scientific, and may be proposed professionally by economists *as economists*. (2) Changes which would re-distribute wealth or chances for any other reason. These are second-class, controversial, ethical and a-scientific. Though economists may be consulted about their technical effects, they may not *as economists* propose such changes. Economists may however measure such changes for economy and efficiency and rationality, which they will usually be found to lack now that the ideas of *the* general equilibrium of *the* system have at last allowed 'inefficient, uneconomic and a-rational' to include the meaning 'redistribut-ing more dollar votes than is minimally necessary for the full employment of resources to maximize satisfactions for the dollar votes as already dis-tributed now'.

Can one equilibrium be more efficient than another? Yes, the one which, with given resources, produces most goods. But 'most goods' depends on their valuation which depends on the distribution of the dollars to the valuers. Can one equilibrium be more efficient for a given distribution? To some extent it can, thus linking the notion of efficiency (usefully for winners) to held distribution. But every fuller employment for the more efficient service of one distribution will include some redistribution, and change some dollar-voters' marginal utilities. So even these limited rankings of equilibria must include an element of valuation by whoever does the ranking. If he wants to be value-free the economist, like the sociologist, will have to pretend that his values did not choose his ranking rule. Sociolo-gists choose 'basic institutions' or 'basic values' ('basic' undefined in theory, valued in practice); economists can choose basic distribu-tions, or some basic right of the rich – for example, that they should never lose.

Despite Samuelson's own warnings about it, the textbook discussed in the previous section still pretends, here and there, that neutral judgments of efficiency can rest on present distributions. This is what it says about dinner-times and the peak-load pricing of electricity:

Ideally, efficiency would call for a flexible price pattern during the day. Varying how? Varying so as to be at the intersection of each hour's *DD* curve with the horizontally summed *SS* curve of generators' equated

*MC*s. Then, and only then, would people be encouraged to make the substitutions between peak-load and low-load periods that would result in *maximizing their own well-being.* (*Economics*, 467; his italics).

Speaking for my own well-being, it inelastically demands that I feed children a hot meal at sunset. A change from an averaged price to a higher peak-load price will transfer dollars from me to some lucky midnight eater. Provided that his demand is more elastic as to time of day, so that the new prices turn him into a Dagwood that he never was before, then there is an economy for someone in cheaper generating. There may also be diffuse advantages in rational accounting, and public knowledge of costs and subsidies. But my share of both may be less than I lose to the peak-load price, and less than Dagwood's share. The general economies of marginal cost pricing include no guarantee that those economies will be distributed with no losers. They are unlikely to maximize everybody's well-being. Quite apart from dollar gains and losses, the reconstruction of options – with agonizing dinner-time dilemmas – may worsen as many well-beings as it enhances. On the whole, those who want to draw the boundary of economic science between is and ought should probably avoid 'well-being' altogether; they will drive themselves to absurd distinctions between my pursuits of dollars from the market, dollars from the legislature, and dinner when I'm hungry. The equation 'Dollars × intelligent spending = well-being' is sometimes true, sometimes not. Envy, comparison, notions of justice, and the upward or downward trend of income have as much effect as those two factors, even upon the proportion of well-being that does depend on dollars. What the equation does often represent, is the interest of winners; if they can convince losers of it, their gains are secure.

The ideas responsible for this systematic political bias are not the ideas of system, equilibrium and efficiency; but these are put into political service when censored by the overriding ideas of disciplinary boundary and value-freedom. These, with a good deal of inert convention, provide that most non-Marxist introductions to economics define a science of man-economizing-scarce-resources, then neglect the large fraction of his economizing activity which consists in battling for shares of the resources *outside* the market. This boundary does indeed enclose many relations which are locally reliable and sufficiently predictable, whether because they are independent or because their environment is for the time being stable. The boundary still serves the interest of winners, withholds skilled representation from losers (or would, if all economists accepted it) and deserves none of the natural or scientific privilege it sometimes claims.

The idea of general equilibrium was sometimes valued for the theoretical unity it seemed to allow. The simplest and (historically, in the social sciences) the least fruitful conception of theoretical unity has envisaged a general theory of a whole system, reproduced in miniature in the detailed theory of each of the system's parts. Economics has learned to do without such symmetries. Once, it tried to see each economic relation as a market, with few, simple and uniform properties; just as Talcott Parsons now tries to see all social relations as alike to each other, each understandable by a simple classificatory theory which holds as well for interpersonal as for international relations, and as well for each subordinate-super-ordinate relation in the hierarchy between them. Followers of Parsons think their science promising in proportion as it approaches this elegant symmetry of theory. Economics has fulfilled its promises in proportion as it deserted elegance for fit. The particular mechanisms of economic relations vary so much, from markets to exercises of private power and public contrivance, that diverse theories have to be specialized to the diverse realities of the relations.

In their consultant and engineering capacities, no economists are seriously bothered by the boundaries of is and ought, of science and politics. But many still defend the boundaries in the education of economists. Winners are not without influence upon academies – these boundaries of economics prepare skills for winning service, and at the same time pretend a value-free neutrality which should exempt the schools from criticism or interference. It is also in school that pragmatic tests of theory matter least, and are mostly easily replaced by aesthetic tests. But for practical reasons there do have to be boundaries, and theoretical unity is attractive. Could they be achieved in other ways, without privilege for whatever *is*, and without persuasion towards equilibrating everything else, through competitive markets wherever possible, to the service of present distributions? What other boundaries and organizers might a different ideologist write into text and curriculum?

Among suggestions of varying frivolity, (1) he might differentiate each economic relation, both descriptively and causally, from whatever he valued as its ideal model in some viable-programmatic sense – perhaps this is what Samuelson did. (2) He might do without any single system or single, organizing Effect-to-be-explained, and let economic science be a battery of special theories and skills to explain (and teach how to defend, avert or contrive) a wide variety of effects selected as valuable and accessible to science. There would be some different economics for Republicans and Democrats, but only to the minor extent that their interests and values differ, and each could well learn the other's as well as his own. The neutrality of the school would be judged by its political fairness, not its abstinence. This is how most texts and teachers do behave, whatever their prefaces and protestations sometimes say. (3) He might replace the system's general equilibrium by some other single organizing Effect – for example, Growth, or for another example, (4) he might organize the discipline to explain Distribution, defining 'economic' as 'affecting distribution' so that a lot of history and politics would get in. (He might define as a-scientific any ethical decision to accept distribution as given.) He might impart the skill to discover, for any system, its dilemmas of productivity and distribution – of growth and inequality – and its best mode of growth for different values of each. Economists have unrivalled skills in tracing the ramifications of actions in complex social systems. It is against every interest (except those of a few winners) that these skills should be limited by the arbitrary boundary of discipline or the illusory boundary of value-freedom. Happily, more and more cross both boundaries these days. Particularly in the study of growth, and in modern cost-benefit analysis, they apply their skills to ever-widening ranges of the social implications of economic alternatives. The health of society and the subtlety of education must both gain much, to the degree that the accounting of economic *and* social values can be comprehended within one discipline. Of course as 'political economy' thus recovers its unity, the gains will not include unanimity, or a quiet life, for economists – but they have little of either as it is.

Most of these liberties are taken in the book reviewed below. Its subject is so very general as scarcely to qualify as 'economics'; but the same liberties are available in many specialized economic tasks, though genuinely irrelevant, of course, to many others.

Arthur Lewis' *The Theory of Economic Growth* (London: Allen and Unwin, 1955) could not be called 'The economic theory of growth'. Its subject, says its first sentence, 'is the growth of output per head of population'. For that economic effect, causes will be sought wherever they lie, or with only the restriction that it must be socially useful to know them.

Any theoretical unity must be that of a sufficient engineering knowledge for the understanding of an engineering task. It will not consist in any likeness of all theoretical parts to each other or to a prototype general theory.

> The factors which determine growth are very numerous, and each has its own set of theories. There is not much in common between the theories which one uses in studying land tenure, or the diffusion of new ideas, or the trade cycle, the growth of population, or the government's budgets. (5)

As Lewis insists, the book does not *contain* all the theories an explainer or an engineer may need. It merely lists them, indicating roughly what each can do, in the course of listing the conditions necessary for growth. (If structural engineers had had on their list 'Stability against turbulence: use aerodynamic theory', then the famous Tacoma bridge would not have blown down.) But Lewis' is more than a list; it is also a book about the relations of the things listed. If we imagine society as a mass (often, a mess) of interacting mechanisms, none independent, with no discipline theorizing about more than a few of them; if we therefore understand most social explanation or prediction or contrivance as requiring some synthesizing or mixing of the differently-disciplined understandings of the divers mechanisms at work – then Lewis' book is a manual for mixers. Social complexity and scientific uncertainty dictate that the advice shall be insufficient; but at least, for 'mixing' the single effect of growth, this is the most general account yet of what to mix, what not to forget, what mistakes of omission or ill-mixture to avoid.

Lewis values some things above economic growth, but science is never one of them. He obviously values science for what it can do, but loves no theory for its beauty or its proprietor, and allows no unproven promise to excuse any real non-performance. He would scarcely applaud the cumulation, convergence or codification of theory that was useless in the first place. Yet his own example of a *general* social theory seems as good an example as any yet written, of the limited but genuine services which 'cumulation, convergence and codification' can perform. Their useful services do *not* include wrenching diverse theories out of fit with their own facts into better fit with each other, by rationing to them a common jargon, or principle of selection, or disciplinary boundary, or monocausal faith. Rather, Lewis relates them to each other by relating them to a common engineering task; his interrelation of them has the form (but much more than the usual systematic care) of a complex historical explanation. That form can be generalized just as usefully as historians (often) localize it.

The author believes that it is good to have more goods and services, but the analysis of the book does not in any way depend upon this belief. In order to emphasize the fact that the book is about the growth and not about the desirability of output, he has relegated what he has to say about desirability to an Appendix at the end of the book. (10)

In so general a book, many simplifications must be half-truths; the above half-truths are among the very few whose other half is positively false. 'The analysis of the book does not . . . depend upon this belief' in one sense, that what it says is equally true for diverse believers. But what it chooses to say is not a selection of equal use to all, and is not what all would have chosen; and this includes both its selection of the causes of what *is*, and its selection of the causes which might produce its selection of future possibilities. Specifically, it includes (1) the conditions which, without deliberate contrivance *for that purpose*, make for growth; (2) all known or proposed *contrivances for that purpose* which may make for growth; (3) all constants, accidents or *contrivances for other purposes* which hinder growth. Its significant omission is (4) any attempt to organize, exhaust or add to *contrivances for the purposes of hindering growth*. A better handbook than this could be written for engineers of stagnation or decline. Lewis notices, often enough, how the interests of groups and the values of believers may lead them to oppose changes; sometimes, even, deliberately to oppose growth as such. When this happens, Lewis notices what weapons they may use. But these notices go as far as to warn the engineers of growth, and to warn all parties of some social costs of growth; they do not extend to sharpening, coordinating or augmenting theory for use by stagnators. The point is limited; engineers of stagnation could indeed learn a good deal from the book. But just as Lewis' valuation of growth must have helped him to want to write the book, so did it help him to select its causal structure. These are the causes and hindrances of growth, stagnation and decline which protagonists of growth should know about. It might be argued that there are no engineers of stagnation-as-such; so stagnation-engineering would never happen; so the causes which it might mobilize are mythical. But it must be among Lewis' hopes, that his book may add or improve at least one engineer of growth; while a *Theory of Economic Arrest* might attract, convert or re-arm at least one decadent ruling class, or half-exhausted oil sheik, or Portuguese colonial governor. To that extent at least, even if its structural values are not Lewis' own, his own must still select whose values should organize his book.

It is another half-truth, that 'he has relegated what he has to say about desirability to an Appendix'. That appendix should certainly be read, if only to demonstrate how largely technical, how far removed from a sermon or imperative declaration, the exercise of a 'valuing skill' can be. It could of course be analytically distributed between 'scientific' explorations of consequences, and valuations of these consequences. But it was not merely 'the facts', nor only factual reports of the subjects' valuations, which selected which consequences should be explored and exposed for valuation. In any case, the broad values of the Appendix are predictable from the text, because they helped to construct the text and are visible in its construction; though some are only visible in proportion as the reader is technically equipped to recognize selections and imagine alternatives to them.

Apart from its selection and structure, the book includes a running commentary on various values of the facts it expounds. Many of the facts *are* the subjects' values and valuing habits – their valuations of work, leisure and consumption are only the most obvious. There is much discussion of the social values and costs (including many by-products) of the various conditions of growth – partly because the subjects' valuations of them are themselves conditions of growth; partly because uninstructed, unskilled valuers will be incompetent engineers even of their own aims; but partly also because Lewis values the social accompaniments of growth or stagnation as important. Nor are Lewis' valuations distributed as that sentence of the preface implies – valuations of growth-as-such to the Appendix, and of its detailed modes and conditions to their appropriate places in the text. The text's running commentary exhibits everywhere the skill, coherence and interdependence of Lewis' valuations of growth-as-such, including his fair reporting and appreciation of others' valuations of it; while the Appendix on the value of growth-as-such is mostly about the values and costs of its detailed 'means' and by-products, and similarly includes more reports of others' values than declarations of Lewis' own.

In a simpler sense the book could no doubt be accused of bias (though of which, would largely depend on the accuser's own). Lewis is more charitable to the stagnant poor than to the stagnant rich. The useful and necessary services of coercion to growth are not neglected; but perhaps they are explored less thoroughly and enthusiastically than are the contributions to growth of a great many freedoms. He still does not pretend that individualism can accomplish what it probably can't, or that coercion cannot accomplish what it historically has; such wishful illusions would hurt, not help, the service of his values. If the values import a bias, it is into the more inventive parts of the work. Lewis strains to be clear, encouraging and original about the potentialities of free institutions, while his predictions of the coercive necessities of growth are honest, but unimaginative. There is no chapter, for example, on the rich output which obviously awaits the first growth-directed genocide. Indian cows, yes; human abortion, yes; infanticide, scarcely; but elderly peasants, you must theorize for yourself.

I make this fuss about two sentences from the Introduction only in order to attack any notion that this is, or could be or should be, a 'value-free' book. But even those introductory sentences scarcely claim it is that. 'The analysis of the book does not . . . depend upon this belief' for the truth of what it asserts. What do depend partly upon belief are other qualities of the analysis – its structure and its selections. These are among its best qualities. At every point (since it is not a strictly sufficient explanation) the relevance of its parts depends jointly upon their true or imagined relation to each other, and upon the use of knowing those relations; half the book's unity is in its valuations. Of these the most general is indifferently a 'scientific', a 'methodological', a 'social' or a moral value: the book is strikingly honest, about science, method, and society. If Lewis' Appendix shows how far removed a valuation may be from a sermon, his whole text shows how a deeply-felt social purpose, far from clouding the observer's vision, may just as well clear it. Lewis has all the courage needed to face unpleasant facts and impossibilities, measure them accurately, and distinguish them from wishful illusions. When the same purposes affect his selections of useful observations and manipulable relations, their effect upon 'science' is to economize it rationally. So will most men take more care to see clearly, underestimate no dangers, and order knowledge instrumentally rather than aesthetically, if they know that the futures of people they care for may be affected by their work. 'We know' Samuelson writes 'that a doctor passionately interested in stamping out disease must first train himself to observe things as they are. His bacteriology cannot be different from that of a mad scientist out to destroy mankind by plague.' Some of it is likely to be distinctly different: concerned more carefully with more qualities of more bacteria. Neither in his bacteriology nor in his use of it will his selections be improved if he makes it a professional rule never to notice any difference between health and disease which would require a valuation of his own. Samuelson might have added a third motive: to advance science for its own sake, or for fame or promotion. In its effects of honesty, clear sight and rational selection this lies somewhere between the other two; but how near to which, depends on the values of the others who judge the science and allot the rewards.

12

Values in Practice and Theory

Here are four best-sellers. In the first pair, values direct selections with spectacular effect, choosing causal networks for Riesman and quite different things for Lewis. The second pair offer opposite understandings and advice about the function of values in social theory.

1. David Riesman and Oscar Lewis

It would be easy to arrange for Myrdal's and the Lewises' values to confront and disgrace David Riesman's.

What should be the rich white minority's program in a hungry world? Besides distributing its goods more equitably among its own members, Myrdal would have the rich white minority produce for the international poor, and help them to produce more for themselves. So would Arthur Lewis. Both programs require some persuasion of the rich. Oscar Lewis' program to persuade the rich is announced less explicitly in *The Children of Sanchez* than it was in *King Lear* –

> Poor naked wretches, wheresoe'er you are,
> That bide the pelting of this pitiless storm,
> How shall your houseless heads and unfed sides,
> Your loop'd and window'd raggedness, defend you
> From seasons such as these?
>   O, I have ta'en
> Too little care of this! Take physic, pomp;
> Expose thyself to feel what wretches feel,
> That thou mayst shake the superflux to them
> And show the heavens more just.

Meanwhile the Riesman of *The Lonely Crowd* appears to recommend that the rich white people should learn to work more playfully, play

365

more skilfully, and choose more freely from more various and subtle styles of self-indulgence, to the end of extracting richer pleasures from their unequal stack of wealth.

It is not only Riesman's later writings which would make this easy theme a silly one. The rich white minority is a fact. Its defences look impregnable. Its experience is worth exploring. Its condition may be the poor's destination if the poor progress. In Arthur Lewis' *Theory of Economic Growth* there are discussions of the social alternatives consistent with productivity. The lonely crowd is one, not only in America, not necessarily the worst – perhaps to be achieved or avoided or improved upon by other societies in degree as they understand and value it in good time as a partly compulsory, partly optional product of productivity. Since the lonely crowd has cornered most of the world's wealth and skill, even small improvements in its sensibility are better than none.

If any rich white reader has not, he should read David Riesman with Reuel Denney and Nathan Glazer, *The Lonely Crowd, A Study of the Changing American Character* (Yale, 1950) and David Riesman with Nathan Glazer, *Faces in the Crowd, Individual Studies in Character and Politics* (Yale, 1952). There is excellent criticism of both in S. M. Lipset and Leo Lowenthal (eds.) *Culture and Social Character, the work of David Riesman reviewed* (The Free Press, 1961). From it, and from Riesman's afterthoughts, and from the confessional commentary that interlaces everything he writes, only three points will be recapitulated here. *The Lonely Crowd's* weaknesses in causal analysis owe more to others' theories than to Riesman's values; its strengths owe more to a valuing discernment than to other scientific methods; and its most important causes had not happened yet when it was written – they were proposals, not discoveries.

The Lonely Crowd is weakest as a history book. It offers sequential explanations for changes through time. These have both scholarly and theoretical shortcomings. Even such diffuse qualitative changes could be a little better identified, measured and dated. Single causes are often selected for them, absurdly but still by no apparent principle – not always facts of physical environment, not always technological changes, not always choices, not always intrinsically valuable. The two most important seem almost to have been chosen by a preference for theory over discernment. It was bad luck, perhaps, to borrow demographic theory in the last year before its reconstruction. Though no such repentance has overcome psychiatric theory, Riesman's historical applications of it are really no more convincing than were his historical connections of culture to death-rates. Some economic and some child-rearing practices are his twin causes of inner-directed character – but without trying very hard to count the actual proportion of independent adaptable roles in early capitalist societies; or the number of independents who followed, rebelled against, or scarcely or never knew, their fathers; or the ages at which they or their fathers left home. It may be by sure instinct that so many readers refuse the distinction between inner-direction and autonomy, or understand autonomy as inner-direction better informed by better radar, or better directed to love its neighbor. As historical explanations (which they are) psychiatric explanations are as selective of insufficient causes as any others, and their selections are as value-structured, and as open to both technical and valuing dissent. Riesman's historical selections seem monocausal, careless and quaint – until the present day, when present causes can be exposed and valued and selected in those imaginative three-cornered conversations between Riesman, his subjects and his inter-viewers (subjects, all three).

Here and now, causation becomes complex and uncertain. The choices and simplifications are more wideawake, tentative, sophis-ticated and aware of their costs than any, perhaps, in the literature of social science – perhaps more aware of their costs than are the choices in most novels. The ideal types, surrounded already by warnings in *The Lonely Crowd*, are further uncertified in *Faces in the Crowd*, so that in the end they signify not types of people but tendencies uniquely mixed in each, to become for each who under-stands them the raw materials of character, and a map of some of its more dangerous and valuable possibilities. There is still some strain to generality in concentrating more on the directive relationships than on what the directions say. There are complications when the directive messages say, Do it yourself, or, Don't ask me. But this is part of Riesman's point – autonomy is to include a new interest in the directions of 'direction', another progress from servility to contract.

Meanwhile the reportable causes of experience are selected by the same ubiquitous, undeducible, poetically-communicated valuations as choose the qualities of experience whose causes should be sought. There are constants, especially the organizational requirements of productivity, and the veto-groups which hinder deliberate institutional improvement. Given these crude power-relations between man and man, and man and nature, there remain the variable, intricate, reciprocal relations of people to each other and to their culture. Partly, culture is a compendious word for their modes of relation with each other; partly it is a thing apart, the school of feeling and behavior, having like other schools its passing fads and its durable library, and no sharp distinctions between teachers and learners. From its delicate networks Riesman discerns and selects valuable facts that contribute to causing each other, and searches for those which are in themselves and in their effects the most valuable of all – the chances for choices. In this cobweb, of relations which may flinch and change shape at the touch of inquiry, Riesman's causal analysis is best, relies most on valuations as selectors, seems most moral and soft, and attracts most criticism.

In this context there are two usages of 'soft' and 'hard'. One contrasts soft discernment with hard science. Perhaps one or two more of Riesman's connections could be hardened by more operational rigor. But the more likely effect of operational rigor would merely be different selection. Relations and distinctions within intricate patterns of thought would give way to associations and dissociations of crude attitudes – to a drunkard's search for other relations between quite other things.

But soft and hard also have political meanings. Since the hard facts of money and power and their institutions are cited among the causes of other-direction, why does Riesman nevertheless select most of his interesting causes and see his room for manoeuvre in the softer territory of culture?

Partly, no doubt, because it was the neglected territory. Partly also from scientific difficulty – it is not easy to analyse simultaneously private experience and the institutional control of it. But however the understanding of culture and character may suffer from the separation, the study of institutions suffers more. The causal analysis of institutional life is selective, and attentive valuations of effects (and their alternatives) upon the citizens' experience could do much to improve the dreary principles of selection which are the usual conventions of this branch of science.

Or perhaps Riesman's softness is a conservatism. Why reshuffle money and power when it takes so long to learn to use them well? There is no presumption in favor of new owners, from whose slow learning the rest of us must suffer. Rich and poor may be better occupied learning the manners and refining the marginal utilities of their present shares, than in brutalizing each other as they change places.

But obviously Riesman regrets some present distributions, many of the present winners, and most of the distributing mechanisms. If conservative, it is chiefly from resigned realism. No direct attack will dislodge the veto groups. Together for once, the tender and the realists may as well retreat to whatever independent base the college teachers can maintain, thence to develop a slow, harmless-looking sapping operation against the future. Benjamin Jowett, a Victorian Master of Balliol, had the same program, though he was complacently surer of the future power of his pupils, and of the autonomy he recommended to them.

There was more guarantee of virtue in Jowett's autonomy than there is in Riesman's, which includes virtue merely among the open choices. If it seems specially easy for college teachers to choose virtue happily, there are still careerist peers and College Presidents and New York publishers and great Foundations willing, with the best intentions, to complicate the choice commercially. If not too many college teachers, who else are convertible to freedom? Chiefly, the young are. They have the advantage that they are bound to win in the end. But powerful inner directors will have to be installed in four short years, to survive the decades of tempting and punitive re-education between college and their inheritance of power. As every peer re-writes his signals to contract with every other for the autonomy of each, the imperatives of productivity and competitive cooperation and mutual promotion await them. But perhaps they go a little better-armed than before; certainly, better armed than by any curriculum or any teaching staff selected for value-freedom.

We might use general theorists, empiricists, and Riesman to represent three broad principles of selection. (1) One may choose a general shape of theory, then select the details of life and of theory to bring the two into whatever correspondence is possible without damage to the shape or generality of the theory. (2) One may select knowledge for a predetermined kind of certainty, whether descriptive or predictive; what is worth discovering about society will then be chosen for its 'knowability'. (3) One may decide what it would be most valuable to know, then give the name and resources of science to improving, as far as possible without changing target, the means of knowing it. Riesman neglects surprisingly few of the methods of hard science when they can tell him what he wants to know; he merely neglects them when they propose to tell him other things instead. He searches for the useful causes of valuable effects, present or potential, and knows each by the best method to hand, however uncertainly.

There are social goods and evils for whose control new knowledge is not what is chiefly needed. Poverty (except pockets in rich countries) is scarcely one of them. To enrich poor countries, new knowledge would certainly be useful. By technical necessity the discoverers are usually rich, and some tend to select for knowledge which would help the poor without the rich losing. There may be practical as well as moral reasons for that. But even to arrange for the rich to lose, would call for more knowledge than the poor have got now. Neither sort of knowledge is much use without goodwill as well. Almost any help for the poor requires some persuasion of the rich. Of course persuasion works best when it identifies their good natures with their interests, but often the two are unconnected or opposed.

Everyone allows that it is proper for social scientists, as such, to persuade the rich by improving their technical understanding of their own interests. It is even permissible to extend the same technical service to the poor, if it respects the 'no losers' rule. But when division of labor is possible, the labor of 'pure persuasion' is less unanimously defined as social science.

In *The Children of Sanchez* (N.Y.: Random House, 1961) a family of five from a Mexican slum speak for themselves through Oscar Lewis' tape-recorder, translation and editing. Any 'causal analysis' is proposed by the subjects or has to be supplied by the reader. A technically effective attack on Mexican poverty would require much other knowledge (mapped by Arthur Lewis) but should not neglect this social photography, in valuing and choosing its objectives. But mainly, the book addresses the conscience of the rich.

There may well have been even more art than meets the eye, and some causal theory, in the order of questions which prompted those monologues, and in the editing and the expressive English translation. But in the analytic sense that the scaffolding of valuations has gone and the 'object' speaks for itself, this is as near as social science is likely to come to an objective, value-free report. It is a delightful irony that the method works in proportion as its purpose is exclusively moral (or perhaps, entertaining).

Oscar Lewis persuades by informing, baiting the information artfully to see that it is taken. Riesman also persuades by informing, but the causal nature of much of the information requires that it be more obviously selected and valued. He also recommends directions and values and voluntary causes of change. These tasks have traditionally been done better by the arts than by the sciences; indeed, critics complain that Riesman and Lewis are really artists. But artists have often drawn more than they acknowledged from the sciences – how much would be left of many modern novels if all the effects of Marx and Freud and Dewey could be excised from them? But much of the work is now done best by the scientists themselves. Fact has become more persuasive than fiction, and social analysis designed to persuade those analysed, or others, may not always be reliably transmitted to them by intermediaries. Upon some important audiences, novels and plays and documentaries impress less truth, less forcefully, than do *The Lonely Crowd* and *The Children of Sanchez*. To them, as to Keynes' attack on unemployment or Myrdal's on discrimination or Whyte's on bureaucratic morals or the town-planners' on urban squalor, the subjects may listen responsively, and the 'engineering application' of the science may be, chiefly, persuasion.

There may be divisions of labor, as between Arthur and Oscar Lewis. But there would be no advantage to science in publishing *The Lonely Crowd* in jargon or *The Children of Sanchez* in Mexican Spanish, both to be re-selected and mistranslated by Vance Packard. No division of labor could consign to different laborers, or to scientist and client, the facts and the valuations whose relations constitute the causal structures of *The Lonely Crowd*. Nor could any division of labor separate its valuing principles of selection from their 'scientific' product; or its discoveries from its persuasions. If Riesman or Lewis had selected either effects or their causes merely for uniformity and generality, or if Riesman had selected for certainty, then both society and science – but especially science – would have been poorer.

2. *Gunnar Myrdal's advice*

Gunnar Myrdal was asked to direct some research into race relations in the U.S.A., and he wrote his own conclusions into *An American Dilemma, The Negro Problem and Modern Democracy* (N.Y.: Harper and Row, 1944; references to Twentieth Anniversary edition, 1962) because officers of the Carnegie Corporation of New York believed that the task required someone fresh and uncommitted, for example a Swede from 'a non-imperialistic country with no background of domination of one race over another' (ix). That background promised one important value, and Myrdal's earlier writings confirmed it. Nor was the new work, however fresh, the slightest bit value-free. It is all about values. It alleges that many white Americans' values distort their observations and understandings of reality, which in turn reinforce their values. The psychological and social mechanisms of distortion were Myrdal's central subject; yet his own values openly directed *his* efforts to see clearly how others' values prevented *them* from seeing clearly. Except perhaps Keynes', no single work of modern social science is more justly famous for its direct achievement; and none so clearly exemplifies the problem, paradox, and fertility of values in social science, nor discusses them with more self-knowledge.

Can subjective distortion be analysed out from objective truth, even after the work is done? Not entirely; at best, the objective parts remain valued selections of objective truths about selected identities. Can the values be distributed as (1) organizers, and (2) objects, of the study? Not entirely. Myrdal's own judgment, mixing valuations and technical considerations, chose for him *some* American values which he would use instrumentally to organize his study of *other* American values. Thus the former, the values of 'the American Creed', were at once selected and selectors, valued and valuers, objects and organizers of the work: Myrdal's program-model.

Myrdal's conclusions about this method were more revolutionary, but have been more neglected, than his conclusions about the Negro problem. As a program for the Negro problem he proposed that the bad values still predominant in the minds of a white minority should be overcome by mobilizing the good values already present in the minds of all Americans including that minority. He did not so explicitly propose (but I do) the same program for the reform of social science. Against the bad values of social scientists we can only try to mobilize the good values which they and most of their clients also believe in – not merely because the bad values are immoral and contradict the good ones and each other, but also because by any scientific test they damage the work and yield of science. Especially, the scientific love of truth must confront the obsessive valuations of scientific unanimity and formal imitation. So should the public's valuations of social good and solid scientific yield confront valuations of the self-serving relations of explanation to otherwise-sterile theories. Values can indeed distort observation and mislead selection, but there can still be little of either without them. The problem is not how to be rid of values, but is rather how to decide which are best, and how best to apply and employ them.

For the Negro problem Myrdal thought the American Creed was best. It served him in at least four ways: as a subject of study, as a differentiating and selective discoverer's model, as a program, and as one among the causes which might put more of the program into practice in the future.

The Creed first allows an immediate and radical limitation of the study. We need not ask why Negroes are poor, unequal, sick, powerless, imperfect, or imperfectly cared for by society. A large majority of the conditions necessary for these facts can be dismissed, to the degree that these facts are also true of white people in the same society. The effect-to-be-explained need only include any *difference* of Negro from white facts which has among its causes some that offend the Creed. The explanation need only contain the causes of that difference, though it cannot be limited to the offensive causes only. Causes thus qualified are still numerous, but they are fewer and more manageable than would be the causes required for any general explanation of the absolute social condition of Negroes in America. For example, '*There is nothing wrong with inequality by itself.* The mere fact that the Negro people are poorer than other population groups does not *per se* constitute a social problem.' It does not constitute a problem for inquiry either. Why not? 'It does not challenge the American Creed.' Only if Negroes are poorer by reason of discrimination which *does* contradict the American creed, will they be regarded as a social problem for America and a scientific problem for Myrdal. 'Discrimination is . . . the key term in such a study. This term is *defined in relation to the norm of equality of opportunity* in the American Creed. In this sense it is, naturally, a "value-loaded" term, and rightly so. But it lacks nothing in scientific preciseness and definiteness.' (214–5)

Why all this trouble? Why all the exploration and explanation of the American Creed, a collection of opinions partly recognized as 'Creed' by the subjects, but somewhat sharpened and selected by Myrdal himself? Why did he not simply say 'Discrimination by color is wrong' and organize his study by that simple value, with fifty pages saved?

One reason may well have been propagandist – though like the best propaganda it had a solid technical base. The simpler alternative would have a Swede preaching to Americans: 'Accept a study based on *my* values; reform your institutions as *I* tell you.' But the book would be more acceptable, and its proposals more achievable, if their guiding values were identified as American. To anchor them at home, as native values, is persuasive. If discrimination is to be reduced by reform, the reforms must be practicable by Americans.

So Myrdal's values decide which good American values shall organize the study, both to recommend it to the people studied, and to organize its results for use by the reformers among them. One important reforming activity, is simply to *inform*: to get people to understand themselves, and to see contradictions within their own values so that they will choose between them, instead of continuing to entertain such contradictions.

These are not merely logical contradictions, which are easy to go on entertaining. They are, rather, the pursuit of incompatible ends. People must learn that in defending one valued institution they endanger others which perhaps they value more, or *would* value more if they saw both more clearly. Put most simply, science should help people to get what they 'really' want – what they *would* want if they truly understood the choices. And yet, Myrdal's 'true' account – or the American Creed's organization – of the 'true' choices, itself incorporates the values which organized it. This, Myrdal elsewhere calls 'the crux of all science'.

Here it seems possible to see some strains within and between three of Myrdal's methodological themes; and to ascribe some of the strains, perhaps, to the peculiarity of his American experience. It is worth examining (1) his distinction between theoretical and practical research, (2) his uses for, and advice for choosing, alternative value premises, and (3) a real distinction (not exactly his) between the theoretical and practical uses of alternative value premises. (The reader should first re-read the first two Appendixes to *An American Dilemma*, pp. 1027–1064).

Our entire discussion is based upon a distinction between two aspects, or stages, of social science research: the "theoretical" and the "practical". By "theoretical" research we mean here all the research which is directed purely and exclusively toward ascertaining facts and causal relations between facts. By "practical" research we mean the logical procedure of relating value judgments to factual situations and to actual trends of change and, from their combination, deriving scientific plans for policies aimed at inducing alterations of the anticipated social trends ("social engineering"). (1059)

In my own opinion it is not true that his 'entire discussion' either is, or need be, based on this distinction. Even if the distinction is analytically feasible, it still does not in the practice of most research distinguish 'stages' – only, at best, 'aspects'. 'Ascertaining . . . causal relations between facts' has its technical aspect, certainly; but usually also has its value-structure, and cannot happen without it, as has been argued above, and often by Myrdal himself. Of the relations between his own conceptions of theory and practice, Myrdal writes:

Knowledge of facts is never enough for posing the practical problems concerning what is right, just, desirable and advisable. Practical conclusions are, by logical necessity, inferences from value premises as well as from factual premises. (1059)

Something is omitted, or wrongly implied, in that last sentence. Factual premises are the product of theory and observation. Value premises are required for their application in practical research. But what has become of the value premises of the *theory*? Myrdal acknowledges them insofar as 'the direction of theoretical research is determined by the practical purposes held in view', but seems always to entertain the possibility of theoretical research *without* practical purpose. Certainly, theoretical research may avoid direction by the sort of social values Myrdal has in mind; but then it will need other principles of selection in all of which (in most *social* sciences) there will be elements of other valuations, that is to say of choices incompletely described by words like 'technical' or 'objective', and incompletely validated by reference to facts alone. There may be theoretical aesthetics perhaps, or a strain to originality, or to consistency with already-existing theory; there may be arbitrary rules about the proximity of causes or the boundaries of disciplines; the generality and certainty and utility of knowledge may be valued in any of their six possible orders. But in the last sentence quoted above, 'facts' and 'values' are dichotomized as if knowledge of causes were exclusively factual; whereas however pure or applied its motives I think it is usually a *selection* of causal chains, terminated at *selected* points, including many causes *chosen* because they determine *selected* effects by warding off alternative effects which in turn are *chosen* because they are *imagined* as possible and often also *valued* as important.

The point may be illustrated by a very general causal analysis at whose conclusion Myrdal repeats the distinction between 'explaining', and 'evaluating' for practical purposes:

There is a cultural and institutional tradition that white people exploit Negroes. In the beginning the Negroes were owned as property. When slavery disappeared, caste remained. Within this framework of adverse tradition the average Negro in every generation has had a most disadvantageous start. Discrimination against Negroes is thus rooted in this tradition of economic exploitation. It is justified by the false racial beliefs we studied in Chapter 4. This depreciation of the Negro's potentialities is given a semblance of proof by the low standards of efficiency, reliability, ambition, and morals actually displayed by the average Negro. This is what the white man "sees" and he opportunistically exaggerates what he sees. He "knows" that the Negro is not "capable" of handling a machine, running a business or learning a profession. As we know that these deficiencies are not inborn in him – or, in any case, in no significant degree – we must conclude that they are caused, directly or indirectly, by the very poverty we are trying to explain, and by other discriminations in legal protection, public health, housing, education and in every other sphere of life.

This scheme of causal interrelation is as important in explaining why Negroes are so poor and in evaluating the wider social effects of Negro poverty, as it is in attempting practical planning to raise the economic level of the Negro people. (207–8)

The last paragraph does not say whether value premises are required for the 'explaining', or only for the 'practical planning'; but obviously, they are required by both. Every step of that causal analysis *selects*: selects effects, and selects which causes shall be reported as determining which aspects or limits of these effects, and as preventing selected alternatives to these effects. If one turns from such a general summary to the detailed chapters which support each of its parts, then the same selective and imaginative activity can be found at work at every level of causal analysis, down to the most detailed. If the distinction between fact and value is to be strict, then it must run analytically right through the texture of causal or 'theoretical' science, which it cannot distinguish from 'practical research' as if the latter alone required its value premises. Of course practical research for one purpose may often reorganize and use causal analysis organized by other premises. But in a world insufficiently determined by strictly unbreakable, already-proven laws, causes are always 'chosen' as well as 'known', and there are elements of choice even in the 'knowing'. Yet there can be no purely 'factual' selection, and 'objective' selection is intelligible only as the neutral application of a chosen rule.

If this is so, then Myrdal's distinction between theory and practice is unnecessary to the rest of his argument, which would cohere better without it. Simple facts may remain as objective as before – though even *their* purity is exaggerated, as Myrdal often points out. Perhaps for the philosophical distinction of facts from valuations, we should often substitute a practical classification: facts, causes, values – the causes being a texture of the other two.

One of Myrdal's rules needs adaptation to tasks and circumstances. He says, make your value premises explicit. He makes his own explicit. But although *An American Dilemma* distinguishes scores of them in italic type, valuation is still more detailed and ubiquitous than even this would suggest. Elsewhere, Myrdal sometimes writes formally of '*the* value premise' of theory, as if it were a single premise. As suggested above, every causal statement is likely to require some selection and (however trivial in many cases) valuation. The logical label 'the value premise' thus has misleading descriptive implications. Many processes of research and reporting are better described as continuously exercising a valuing skill, than as merely requiring some prior insertion of *one* value premise. Incessant, microscopic weighing and discriminating go on hour by hour as the researcher investigates and the author writes. It is true, as Myrdal claims, that his formal italicized value premises are logically necessary to his conclusions; but so are the innumerable detailed valuations required on page after page on which no italic type appears. These running valuations are usually consistent with the formal premises, which may be seen as useful public indicators of the general tendency and principle of all the valuations.

Besides its moral consistency, much of the scientific unity and coherence of Myrdal's work arises from the sensitive skill and consistency of its valuations. In this his only rivals in this present collection of examples are perhaps Halévy, Arthur and Oscar Lewis, and Riesman. Carr is a bit strict, though still more flexible than those who try to build whole systems of political analysis by deduction from some simple, single valuation of 'democracy', 'maximizing choices', or 'system survival'. Just as a practical, not-always-conscious skill can often predict facts better than can rigorous or over-general deduction from imperfect premises, so also do valuers often achieve more consistency by the affinities, diffuse goodwill and practical compromises of their valuations, than by deducing them all too ruthlessly from a few generalized axiomatic 'values'. In altruistic valuations for example there must usually be strain and compromise between the altruist's and the subject's opinions as to what is 'really' good for the subject. Carr is rigorous; Myrdal and Arthur Lewis are respectful and compassionate, though inversely to the subjects' wealth; Riesman is simply tender, to rich and poor alike. The value-free pretenders try not to be altruistic at all (and there is of course only one general alternative). Fortunately they seldom succeed (as witness the Buddhist rebellions of Samuelson's better nature) but in the attempt they may shed some skill and sensitivity which might otherwise have made their science cohere better, and correspond more usefully to its subject matter.

Myrdal also recommends that investigators should often employ more than one set of value-premises. The alternative sets should usually be chosen from among the subjects' values:

Relevance is determined by the interests and ideals of actual persons and groups of persons. There is thus no need of introducing value premises which are not actually held by anybody. [*Footnote:* This is a rule of economy. There are, of course, no logical reasons why we might not anticipate combinations, syntheses, mutual modifications of existing value premises or even conjure up new ones and thus enlarge still more our perspective . . .]

. . . *The aim of practical research . . . is*, in general terms, *to show precisely what should be the practical and political opinions and plans for action from the point of view of the various valuations if their holders also had the more correct and comprehensive factual knowledge which science provides.* (1060–1)

About this, Paul Streeten asked Myrdal a question:

Since the choice of value premises in social analysis is itself a moral and political decision, why are we told to confine ourselves to those of actual and powerful groups . . .?

We seem to be told so for four reasons. The first two are explicit. The third and fourth (alleged below) may misrepresent Myrdal's intentions. All four are open to question.

First, the investigator limits his work to practical possibilities, and these are often confined by the interests and values already present in society. But if research is to be inventive, for example by presenting new options which may change people's valuations of old ones, then some moral originality may prove persuasive, and attract majorities.

Second, the investigator is a democrat: he defers to the values of the people he studies, whose futures his work may affect. Especially when the values are of the kind called interests and wants, this may not be quite as helpful as it seems. Somebody said wisely that it makes as much sense to judge societies by the wants they generate, as by the wants they satisfy. It can be conservative to judge an economic system by its efficiency in satisfying an existing distribution of dollar votes; radicals want to investigate the distribution. So with other wants. To insist that theory should derive its values from 'actual' wants and values is like insisting that economic inquiry should accept actual distributions as given. Present values relate to present understandings of present options, and were instilled by educational arrangements controlled by present powers. It may not always be democratic to make present values sovereign.

This much is allowed in Myrdal's footnote, and elsewhere in his writings. But a third reason for deference to actual wants is – if it weighed with him at all – more complicated. Since actual wants are facts, perhaps they can strengthen the factual foundations of science. It is worth recalling those earlier distinctions between fact and value, and between theoretical and practical science.

Theory . . . must always be *a priori* to the empirical observations of the facts . . . [But] If theory is thus *a priori*, it is, on the other hand, a first principle of science that the facts are sovereign. Theory is, in other words, never more than a hypothesis . . .

In the moral sphere, the corresponding logical process is moral criticism . . . As the valuations refer to social reality, and as therefore their interrelations logically involve people's beliefs concerning this reality, the process of correcting their theories to fit the facts plays at the same time an important role in the attempts to give clarity, honesty and consistency to their moral ideas.

. . . This is the logical crux of all science: it assumes in all its endeavours an *a priori* but its ambitions must constantly be to find an empirical basis for that *a priori*. (*Economic Theory and Underdeveloped Regions*, 1957, 160–1, 163; U.S. title, *Rich Lands and Poor*.)

If the juxtaposition of these sentences, omitting what Myrdal put between them, is misleading and misrepresents his argument, then apologies are certainly due to him. If not, it would be better to expel *from this argument also* that earlier distinction and contrast between theoretical and practical science: between the merely voluntary or temporary presence of value premises in theoretical science, and their logical necessity to practical engineering. It is, above all, Myrdal's own perception which has shown how often the *a priori* of theory includes an element of valuation; and whether or not it has conscious valuing intentions, any theory has valuing implications. Valuation is of understood reality, and varies with the understanding – but not with that understanding only. As Myrdal insists, the values however much affected by the facts can never be derived entirely from the facts. So in the above-quoted sentences, there seems to be a false contrast and a deceptive analogy. For theory, the facts are said to be *sovereign* critics. But in the criticism of values, the facts are said merely to assist – they play an important role, they help to clarify – but that is all. *An element* of any value (its defining element) remains impervious to criticism or disproof by *any* facts.

But if the *a priori*, the selected assumptions and hypotheses of pure theory, include an element of valuation, then the service of fact to theory includes in principle (though often in different proportion) the same service as the service of fact to valuation. To the extent that values do thus inhabit theory, to that extent it is incomplete to say that 'its ambitions must constantly be to find an empirical basis for this *a priori*'. Its ambitions should rather be (1) to find an empirical basis for the appropriate factual three-quarters of the content of theory, but (2) to propose to people, to persuade people, that the other fraction is 'useful', 'valuable', 'right' or 'just'.

If the argument takes this step, then the last retreat of *sufficient and exclusive* objectivity is breached, and the profession of social science has lost its last pretext for irresponsibility. The rules of objectivity will still apply as strictly as ever to the tasks to which they always did apply – such as measuring, observing and representative sampling. But theory guides all these. It chooses questions and concepts and identities. It simplifies and selects relations. It censors imagined alternatives. All these include dealings with facts, which ought to be objective. But they all, also, include discriminations to which the notion of 'objectivity' is simply irrelevant, and for most of which 'valuation' is as good a collective word as any.

If the argument does take this step, I believe that Myrdal's theory of social science becomes more complete, coherent, and true. Why does Myrdal not always, or consistently, take this step? Perhaps it is a false step. But perhaps even *he* cannot quite contemplate *all* science as merely the technical branch of politics, some fraction of its validity depending always upon the value of its political choices. If this is so, it is certainly not from cowardice. No more consciously responsible social scientist exists, and the rebellion against spurious objectivity has no more bold or original leader. But perhaps those old 'objective facts', though never wholly sovereign over theory, have achieved another sovereignty as 'a first principle of science', a sovereignty over the scientists, imposed by bluff and education. This argument is meant to suggest, impiously,* that Myrdal's third reason for wanting investigators to use only their subjects' values may have been some lingering, unrecognized desire still *somehow* to anchor his valuations

* However correct or mistaken these pages may be, their great and generous subject will appreciate the spirit which they learned from the footnote on p. 130 of *Economic Theory and Underdeveloped Regions*. When even the Cromwell of the methodological revolution is found to baulk at regicide, Keynes should be allowed to retaliate in the *General Theory*'s words: 'The difficulty lies, not in the new ideas, but in escaping from the old ones, which ramify, for those brought up as most of us have been, into every corner of our minds.'

to the facts: not merely, to let the facts criticize the vision of reality to be valued; but somehow to ward off relativism and a disunity of science by making the scientist's values respectable-by-association with objective facts; almost to *borrow* them from the facts, and thus repair the fractured sovereignty of facts.

In his own use of alternative value systems in *An American Dilemma*, a fourth reason appears for using only the values of 'actual and powerful groups'. One example will suffice:

From a conservative point of view, this [political instability] is the more dangerous as respect for law is undoubtedly gaining ground in the South. Not only the legal, but also the political, security of the white primary will crumble, and this is well known to conservative whites . . .

Our conclusion is . . . that . . . *the Southern conservative position on Negro franchise is politically untenable for any length of time.* If this analysis is accepted, and if the value premise is agreed upon, that *changes should, if possible, not be made by sudden upheavals but in gradual steps,* we reach the further practical conclusion that it is an urgent interest and, actually, a truly conservative one, for the South *to start enfranchising its Negro citizens as soon as possible.* This is seen by a small group of Southern liberals. (518)

There is much more to the same effect. Intelligent conservatives everywhere are said to anticipate, pre-empt, lead and moderate as many changes as are really inevitable. They 'cannot afford to abstain from the tremendous strategic advantage of forming the party of "law and order".'

To be consistent, Myrdal ought to construct this conservative program in deference to conservative values, as part of his program of technical education for each of the major powers in a society in which values and interests conflict. But does he really give effect to these policies in his book? Does he arm each substantial dissenter from the Creed with the science most useful to the anti-Credal interests of each? Does he really minister to rival powers and value-systems as Sir Basil Zaharoff is said to have ministered to various South American and Balkan powers, arming each as efficiently as possible against the others? Never. Myrdal's explorations of anti-Credal values end with the selection of the least noxious, to be mobilized against the rest. He may argue that these least-noxious are also the most valuable to their owners, however obstinately their owners may persist in blindness and resist persuasion. But this choice of the subjects' 'real' or 'over-riding' values is transparently Myrdal's choice. In fact, in the minds of many conservatives on many historical occasions, *It will last our time* and *Apres-moi, le deluge* and *If I cannot stop it, at least I can die fighting it* have been valuations as well-informed and wide-awake and internally consistent as the clearest social science could have made them. Perhaps Myrdal found no such genuine Metternichs in the conservative South; but even if he had, I doubt if they would have been offered genuinely helpful technical assistance.

Nowadays the best practical social science of discrimination could probably be found in the internal discourse of the South African government – not in its public propaganda of Apartheid but in the pragmatic ingenuities of Baasskap. Those policies of domination cannot be written off as unprofitable, self-defeating or deluded, whatever they may import for the policy-makers' grandchildren. But Myrdal would never consent to help such clients, and he helped none in *An American Dilemma*. Its selections, in this respect, resemble Arthur Lewis' in *The Theory of Economic Growth*. Discriminators get no more active or inventive help from Myrdal than economic stagnators got from Lewis. What discriminators actually think and do is reported, in reports arranged for use by their opponents; what anti-discriminators might or could do, goes beyond report to inventive strategy. Any deployment of values alternative to those of the American Creed is still done strictly, if sometimes indirectly, for the service of the Creed. The best performance to be hoped for from Southern conservatives is some grudging, gradual leadership of partial concessions to the Creed. They may be led to this partly because the Creed is already among their own values, but partly also because some less-vicious components of their anti-Credal conservatism may possibly be mobilized against its more-vicious racial components. In these selections Myrdal is warning, persuading, offering reasons for alliances and compromises – but all in the same interest and to the same good purpose. Just so did J. A. Hobson suggest to most of the malefactors of imperialism, that their other interests and values were at war with their imperial interests, and that those anti-imperialist others were their 'true' interests, and 'ought' to prevail.

This principle of selection, for the subjects' alternative value-systems, may be quite consistent with limiting programs to viable possibilities. It is consistent with Myrdal's explicit, strategic recommendation that reform must come from the better mobilization, between and within Americans, of the good values against the bad ones. But it is not consistent with any deferential service to factions in proportion to their strengths and in obedience to their own real valuations – a principle whose perilous affinity to 'might is right' was remarked by Streeten. It was an accident of the American case that 'neutral' prognosis, and the most generally held values, and the predominant powers, were all three on the same side; and so was Myrdal but, we may suspect, more because he thought them right than because he found them mighty. How would a study of *The South African Dilemma* choose its program-model from among the warring values of the well-secured whites and the (better?) values of the powerless majority?

Thus just as Keynes did, Myrdal took advantage of some happy coincidences. They allowed him to give his book unusual unity and power. They did no harm to his own clear sight and methodological originality. But they do perhaps enable readers, if sufficiently wishful, to evade the more embarrassing implications of his methodological message. He *chose* some values to organize his study; yet, other paragraphs allow that this study is practical research and that the equivalent organizing choices of theoretical science may somehow be validated by reference to facts alone. He *chose* some values of some Americans; the escapist reader too easily translates 'derived them objectively from the subject-matter'. He *chose* the more generally-phrased values of the biggest majorities; the systemic analyst translates 'basic system-defining values, which identify and choose themselves objectively'. From the same choice of the big majorities, the value-free careerist may also infer: 'talent bows to the sovereign facts of present distributions, and realistically serves the numbers or the money or the guns; to use it otherwise is to compromise it, to defy objective facts, to surrender neutrality, to cease to be a scientist'. *None* of these is Myrdal's conclusion from his experience. But the coincidences in his American experience, and his persuasive pretence that his book merely mirrored the Americans persuading themselves, did sometimes combine to obscure the author's own responsibility, and to make it easier for others to believe that such responsibilities can be scientifically evaded. 'This' they can conclude 'is biased practical science. We need only leave out the bias and all its effects, to turn it into pure theoretical science.'

Keynes and Myrdal were discoverers, but each thought persuasion as important as discovery, social change the appropriate verification, and mere discovery no guarantee of either. It happened that Keynes' first task was to convince other economists, which required an elegant technical attack upon their scientific convictions. Myrdal's task was to persuade by informing Americans about themselves – it would be equally true to say 'inform by persuading'. If one separates discoveries by Myrdal's colleagues, and those already available in American libraries, it is not unreasonable to judge Myrdal's persuasions about the Negro problem as more important than his own discoveries about it. A great deal of social science has to be judged thus, by both the novelty and the value of the social action to which it contributes. In this, selection, valuation and persuasion may be simultaneously the science and the engineering – the discovery, and its application.

There has been less success for Myrdal's other program, to persuade-by-informing and inform-by-persuading social scientists to a better understanding of themselves. This program arises from more novel discoveries and less welcome values. It invites the scientists into conflict and responsibility – a somewhat lonely and protestant responsibility for each. Such persuasion is not easy. Myrdal's opinions about the Negro problem were, in general tendency, already acceptable to majorities. The responsibilities he proposed were not all unwelcome. Moreover, he proposed rather 'soft' responsibilities, underplaying what has since appeared to many to be a need for tougher measures as well. But whatever their opinions of it, all do allow that the Negro problem is a proper subject for 'opinion' and disagreement. For Myrdal's other program, there is not always the same tolerance. Not every scientist will grant controversial status to the structure, methods and values of scientific thought itself. Men who would never prescribe an authoritative opinion of the Negro problem to the students whom they teach and examine, will nevertheless believe in 'value-free' science as a fact and require its pretenses as matters of discipline.

There does have to be discipline. It is a liberal hypocrisy to condemn all rules as such – academies and examiners must have authority to define curricula, select students, and distinguish good work from bad. But if wrong and irresponsible methodological rules are reserved from the area of free thought to the area of authority, then the wrong and irresponsible authorities are well-placed to perpetuate their principles by moulding and selecting their successors. But there are always libraries, rebellious tendencies in youth, a minority of elders to encourage them, and therefore as Keynes observed, abundant hope for those still under twenty-five or thirty, and a future for their young convictions when they grow old and powerful.

Of course some few may still decide to bow to the sovereignty of those facts; to adjust to what *is*; to be strictly brought-up to a career without misgiving, freed to care more for a contrived unanimity of science than for the engaging conflicts of society. For those, a good example follows.

3. David Easton's advice

The substance of David Easton's work, of which *A Systems Analysis of Political Life* (N.Y.: Wiley, 1965) is the latest part and the source of the following quotations, is left to the reader to review for himself. If C. Wright Mills still lived, he might translate it: 'Politics is an exchange of services for support. People support politicians and systems who do most for them, and make the least (or the least resistable) demands upon them. If people demand too much service and supply too little support, systems are in trouble. Then politicians may increase the services, use the services to reorganize the support and change the system, or see it break down.' Like functional analysis, 'systems analysis' selects some qualities as its Effect. Unlike functional analysis, it does have a rule for choosing causes. (*Select conditions which share some common quality with the Effect, and which have reciprocal relations with it. Thus isolate a homogeneous circular pattern. Define other conditions necessary for the Effect as 'intakes across the system's boundaries'.* Conceal the values which helped to choose and classify the identities and to pick out this pattern from the 'seamless web'; and conceal the historian's logic which discerned the causal relations.) But here, I wish only to draw attention to the book's first and last Parts, which discuss the forms and uses of such 'value-free' theory.

Easton's way with other people's notions of theory is to acknowledge, generously, the useful role of them all; then to condescend to them just the same. Consider carefully the following, as presumably a description of the work of Aristotle, Machiavelli, Hobbes, Vico, Locke, Hume, Burke, Hamilton, Tocqueville, Comte, Mill, Marx, Bagehot, Ostrogorski, Mosca, Michels, Simmel, Weber, Pareto, Mannheim, Lasswell, Wright Mills, and all the other political scientists before 1950 who apparently had little interest in the *facts* of politics:

The aspect that has thus remained concealed and which now rises to shatter the old image of the nature and tasks of theory may be described as descriptive, empirically-oriented, behavioral, operational or causal theory. The variety and indeterminacy of terms used to identify this kind of theory indicate how recently it has appeared on the horizon of political research. But to all intents and purposes, the terms are synonymous and will be so used here.

Until recently, it has not at all been customary for political theorists to avow an interest in causal theory or to accept its development as one of their major responsibilities. Traditionally, political theory, interchangeable here with political philosophy, has held and propagated an image of itself as narrowly engaged in and committed to the quest for an understanding of the nature of the good life or at least an understanding of the way others have viewed it. Analysis of the moral rather than of the strictly empirical world has stood at the peak of theory's hierarchy of priorities.

In the last decade, however, for the first time this limiting image has begun to change decisively . . . (5)

Because social values may be discerned in most political theory, Easton apparently wishes to assert that nothing else is discernible there. Because the social values discernible in his own are trivial and concealed, he claims that it will be specially apt for causal discovery. This is not the only passage of its kind. On pp. 18–19, for example, there is discussion of the capacities of political systems to adapt themselves, by changing themselves, to changes in their social environment.

Few systems, other than social systems, have this potentiality . . . Nevertheless it is seldom built into a theoretical structure as a central component; certainly its implications for the internal behavior of political systems have never been set forth and explored: (19)

One may well argue that Aristotle and Machiavelli and Guizot and

Tocqueville and Marx and Bernstein and Trotsky and Mao Tse-Tung and Toynbee and Schumpeter and Burnham and Wright Mills explored it inadequately – but it takes an unusually-educated Professor of Political Science to assert that it has never, except by himself, been 'set forth'.

These views of others are apparently meant to establish the novelty of Easton's own proposal, which seems to be: that there be a general theory of politics which seeks 'to illuminate the functioning of political systems in their entirety' by analysing the way in which 'political structures and their interrelationships' perform 'the fundamental processes or activities without which no political life in society could continue'. It is also proposed that this be done without any valuation whatever, and (on unclear grounds) that it is different from the task which Hobbes set himself.

Above all, it is different from anybody else's work; and for anybody else's work this value-free scientist is a master of the diminutive metaphor and the value-laden phrase. He himself will avoid valuation or moral debate, he will select only such facts as are necessary for systems' survival, and even of those, he will select only those that are true for every political system whatsoever. Are not these rules somewhat limiting? If systems differ, will not these rules rule out sufficient explanation of the survival of any one? Will not the limitation to mere survival rule out explanation of most of the variable, valuable and interesting political activities? On the contrary, these draconian selectors will liberate and broaden. They will somehow 'prevent research from remaining exclusively and narrowly preoccupied, at least implicitly, with one type of system, namely, democracy as it has developed in the West'. (So much for Evans-Pritchard and Fortes, Florinski and Neumann, Dahrendorf and Wittfogel, Fairbanks and Lindsay and Fitzgerald, and a hundred hitherto-inhibited Kremlinologists.) The new theory will 'shatter the old image' which was a 'limiting image' for scientists 'narrowly engaged', but whose 'shackles' will now be 'escaped'. Political theory will 'broaden its horizons and enrich its value' (by shunning valuations like 'enrich', presumably). It need no more be 'a monolithic subject confined exclusively to moral and philosophical inquiry' – there go Machiavelli and Hobbes again, and Hamilton and Jefferson and Pareto and the Webbs and Lenin. There may of course be 'recurrent efforts to squeeze theory into a narrow intellectual mold' of 'moral concerns'. (Doubtless this book is one.) But normative theories (Easton appears to instance most of economics) offer 'a relatively narrow prospect'. The new theory will shatter the bonds and enlarge the prospect by asking 'the most comprehensive kind of question' of 'the most general kind of matter . . . [namely] How can any political system ever persist whether the world be one of stability or of change? It is comparable to asking with respect to biological life: How can human beings manage to exist?' It would indeed be interesting to read a non-eclectic, value-free, sufficient explanation of that last problem. It might help, too, to show how these questions about mere survival will 'break the constricting bonds that tradition has imposed on the theoretical perspectives of political research' – for example, 'the very hortatory nature of moral inquiry, of which traditional theory is largely composed . . .' 'It would be a poor ethical theorist who was not convinced of the exclusive wisdom of his moral objectives and who did not believe all others ultimately to be half-truths at best or utterly false. Ethical theorizing has emerged not so much to analyze and understand the sources of ethical judgments – although this is an important part of its task – as to make them, to persuade others of their merit, or to warrant them in some manner.' It is not clear whether this refers to ethical analysis from Descartes through Hume to Dewey and Ryle, or to political analysis by men who valued what they analysed, from Aristotle through Marx to MacIver; but all can now be forgotten by 'causal' theory, which may be judged by 'elegance of formulation, economy of expression, simplicity, internal logic and rigor, fertility of insights . . .'

In justice, Easton does here add: 'But the ultimate key, of course, is the adequacy of explanation and understanding offered by the theory.' This adequacy, however, must presumably be judged without valuing the things explained or understood, or the engineering or educative value of the explanations and understandings. Not valuation, *but the theory itself*, will one day establish criteria for the importance of political facts. Until that day, by some uncanny prevision of theory's future form and identifications, Easton's conceptual scheme can do the job. A 'conceptual structure', chosen not by valuation but by selecting, from the conditions necessary for simple political survival, those only which are found in all societies, can

indicate first, the part of reality to be included within a systematic study
of political life and second, those elements of this broad area that ought to
command our prior attention if we are to understand the major determinants of political behavior. If concept formation does nothing else, it at
least provides criteria of political relevance to guide us in the distribution
of our attention to matters of theoretical, and thereby, of explanatory and
ultimately, of practical importance. (12)

Except for its reference to practical importance, this passage at
least is true. It describes how time and resources are to be used,
standards of relevance and importance chosen, and explanations
selected, in any Eastonian school of political science.

All the above quotations are from the first two chapters and the
last chapter of *A Systems Analysis of Political Life*. The reader must
judge whether their selection and juxtaposition are fair. As he reads
those chapters in order to do so, he can also try another exercise. He
will find scores of sentences which have 'theory' in their subjects.
Verbs follow, often normative. The reader should collect the com-
plements. For example, this would be a sensible sentence:

The utility of a general theory for explaining the behavior of the empirical
system to which it applies increases directly with / its true identification of
objective uniformities in that system, and with the generality, causal importance and value of those uniformities.

But that is not how Easton ends the sentence. This is:

. . . /the degree of logical coherence and consistency that obtains among
its component concepts and generalizations.

When the count is complete, the reader may then compare the
number of such sentences which ascribe the power of theory to its
internal structure, with the number which ascribe its power to its
truth or 'fit', or to the social value of any explanations which it
would (if true) generate.

Of course it may sometimes be fruitful to discuss the internal
structure of theory, though scarcely if such few and unenthusiastic
references are made to its subject-matter or its truth. But perhaps
Easton merely assumes as obvious, that every mention of theory is of
course implicitly qualified as 'true and applicable'. I doubt it. The
reason for doubting it lies in a related omission. If true or heuristically useful, the structure of theory is never unrelated to the structure

of the thing it describes. The structure of the theory of physics has its twin foundations in the thinking methods of physicists, and the structure of the matter they study. Of that second foundation, there is not a single mention in Easton's three chapters about theory. These chapters could only make sense on the (unmentioned) assumption that political life does possess strict, universal and commanding uniformities; specifically, that the sufficient conditions for survival of one political system are always identical with the sufficient conditions for the survival of any other. Any preliminary choice of concepts and structure for a projected theory must express some such guess about the structure and likely uniformities of its subject-matter. But nowhere in these chapters does Easton discuss any possibility of there being objective limitations upon the generality of political theory. His principle of selecting only universal uniformities, if applied to a collection of dissimilar systems, will yield neither a 'comprehensive' theory sufficient for them all, nor a theory capable of embracing the special theories required by each. Instead, it will yield few, uninteresting and causally 'weak' similarities, if these should prove in fact to be the only characteristics which all systems have in common. Not a sentence in Easton's fifty pages refers to these possibilities, or attributes the present shortage of true universal theory to any other cause than the 'shackles' of all past theorists.

Ironically he is right enough. Valuing truth is a shackle, it hinders one's range. Meanwhile Easton's own advice can serve, as he intended, to exemplify the value and promise of a program of 'value-freedom'.

13

A Summary of Themes

1. Sterility

What are the scientific and social effects of comprehensive theories like Parsons', Dahrendorf's and Easton's? If they express neither admirable moralities nor true laws, nor improve for any valuable purpose the investigation of particular systems and problems, who does buy and read them, and what are they used for?

They are used chiefly in the general education of young people at universities. There they are learned and the learning examined, and they are made to pattern the ordinary selective explanations of social facts which students must read, and learn to write, in the course of their education. The theories thus replace older disciplinary conventions, some of which used to impose equally arbitrary limits and selective principles upon such explanations. But a privileged theory may have more drastic effects than had those older conventions, especially if it selects for universality and requires that social valuations be concealed.

To discover and order knowledge for social use (however indirectly) ceases to be the explainer's purpose, the purpose from which his principles and methods of selection are derived. His purpose becomes, instead, to show that social activity is explicable by a privileged theory. In practice, with 'conceptual schemes', 'frames of reference' and unproven theories, this means showing that some aspects or abstracts of social activity can be named and classified by the theory. Social explanations are selections of necessary conditions; necessary conditions are selected identities; the theory can now select both. To explain the peaceful functioning of an institution, one theorist may refer to its members' consensus of belief about its legitimacy; another may select the conditions which have discouraged its subjects from organizing against its governors; another may select the pattern of minor conflicts which criss-cross to prevent major ones; another may select the resources of force and indoctrination possessed by the ruling minority; and so on. One, because his theory classifies them, may refer to the substance of the people's norms; another, whose theory selects cruder or broader identities, may refer merely to the presence of norms (substance unspecified) or to the extent of unanimity about them. Any of these explanations will be constituted by selecting whatever causes (a) relate to the effect-to-be explained and also (b) happen to be classifiable by the theory.

This might be a suitable use of theory if the theory stated true laws sufficient to determine the event to be explained, and if those laws were the ground for knowing the causal relation itself, in the particular case. No general social theory does either, so this patterning of selective explanations does not test the truth or utility of theory, though it often pretends dishonestly to do so. Instead, it terminates explanations neither when effects are connected to causes as cases of laws, nor when necessary conditions are chosen which it is socially useful to know, but rather when a few causal chains are discerned which go in directions, and reach particular links or standing conditions, which the theory happens to classify. This simply misapplies to one type of explanation the selective principles which belong to another type altogether.

There is a further step. Theories designed to select the causes of one effect (say, the survival of a system) are next made to limit what may be selected to explain other effects (say, social inequalities within the system).

Thus both the normal purposes of research are abandoned. It neither builds, tests or applies law. Nor does it serve any useful educational or engineering purpose. Instead, *theory-building and eclectic explanation have simply been brought into a relation of mutual service*: they assist each other, and suffice for each other, without serving any reputable purpose whatever.

There are not even likely to be the valuable educational effects which arise from, for example, the self-perpetuation of classical studies. Those studies may cultivate accurate, imaginative scholarship, the criticism and appreciation of great works of art, and debate about important moral and social issues. By contrast, the uses of sterile theory prohibit moral or political debate, spurn art and curdle communication, and teach deceptive misapplications of scientific method. Most of the values they insinuate are nasty, some of the facts they allege are untrue. Insofar as they claim to be uninterfering general theories of social behavior, the appropriate tests for them are political criticism of their selections, and systematic searches for detailed historical cases to limit or refute them – but how often are these 'ideological', 'idiographic' and 'prescientific' exercises the tests which instructors in sociology encourage? As approaches to the useful explanation of effects which allow no complete deductive explanations because they are not sufficiently determined by already-known laws, the theories make selective explanation quite irrational. But they are the selectors used in many texts, and required of students in assignments and examinations, in many schools of sociology and a few of political science.

These exercises are not unlike the educational uses of Marx's general theory in communist countries. There also, the general theory defines the scope of the science, unifies its subject-matter, sanctifies a privileged type of cause, patterns eclectic explanations and pretends that this makes them sufficient. In communist states, as more gently in some western colleges, tests of truth and utility can be further weakened by authority, and skill with the jargon comes to signify allegiance. Ways are still found to discuss real problems – many practical thoughts and specialized theories can make ritual use of the general theory's jargon. But whatever value-freedom it pretends, the general theory asserts political imperatives (in the west, 'value-freedom') which the practical work must not appear to contradict.

One Marxist imperative demands a productive, problem-solving, action-oriented science. Not much of this appears in the application of Marxism to 'post-Marxist' social facts, but it ought to be a good base from which to attack the sterile general theories of western social science. But curiously, communist critics more often attack the idealist, 'understanding' and individualist tendencies of bourgeois inquiry, and its assertions of indeterminacy, uniqueness and 'possibilism' in the study of society. This may signify a sure instinct for their real enemies. It may be traditional – these are the battles Marx and Engels gave attention to. But it may also reflect their own commitments as the most rigid and ambitious social lawyers of all. They themselves deserve to be attacked for their untruthful suppression and dishonest valuation of many unpleasant facts of communist society, and many pleasant facts of capitalist society. But scarcely by western general theorists, more interested in the form of theory than its fit. Marxism's theoretical symmetry and generality and internal coherence, and its orderly organization of innumerable theory-serving explanations, are above reproach. Marx's excels Easton's theory by every one of Easton's tests, and the values it conceals are at least more edifying than his.

Are my complaints excessive? There are plenty of excellent, honest schools of sociology and political science which avoid these corruptions. In their libraries the pretentious are outnumbered by the intelligent books: books which explore and debate particular systems; theories which refine and extend the discipline's stock of expectations, questions and skills; reports which sum up and limit discovered uniformities with honest care; understandings of the quality of individual experience of social and political systems; measurements of the distribution of such experiences; mapped distributions of people and money and ideas and work and leisure; illuminating theories of communication and decision-making; useful methodologies of observation and measurement; selective, perceptive, imaginative, valuable and true studies of causal networks in the functioning and change of systems. With so much wealth to choose from, why give so many pages to disapproving of a few sterile theories? I can only answer, that work of this sort seems to grow popular as it grows worse. As 'high' theory it begins to infect the useful 'low' sciences. It has, says one of its successful practitioners, 'begun to take its first steps in earnest and as its experience accumulates, it promises an exponential rate of development.'

Why should this be so? Perhaps because such work seems to meet two urgent needs. The older liberal educations had their general, speculative, unifying components: Plato and theology and mathematics and literature and general history and style. These tend now to be disqualified as too hard, too irrelevant, too fictitious or too value-ridden. Educationally, there is a gap. Also, scientifically, there is a problem, well explored by Talcott Parsons in *The Structure of Social Action* (1937). All the social systems are open systems. None is independently regular. Perhaps a general theory of all social systems will so relate them to each other that each may know what disturbance to expect from the others, and the science of each become determinate. (This guesses that all uncertainties arise from a system's environment, and none from the thoughtful behavior of the people inside it). So to replace Plato in the new liberal education, and at the same time to tame each discipline's invading variables, general theories suggest themselves. The progressive unification which the nature of their subject-matter allows to the natural sciences then suggests what sort of theories the general social theories should be.

The moment of decision comes when social action is not found, in fact, to obey such universal laws. Then, the noblest ambitions and the worst temptations impersonate each other. One man may say, for this subject-matter laws are not the appropriate things to look for. Another may limit his generalizations to whatever local uniformities he can prove. Another may reasonably wonder, what if Newton had observed all the differences between apples and feathers, and given up? Another, unable to find laws true of all societies, may decide to publish allegations general to them all, however vague or false. Another may say, because the uniformities are not apparent, it follows that they cannot consist of uniform relations between any identities we so far recognize; so I will publish a set of new conceptual identities and hope that other people may discover uniform relations between them. A more genuine imitator of natural science may say: in any search for uniformities, conceptual identities are useful in exact proportion as there do prove to be regular relations – strict or statistical – between the objects they identify. In my private notes I will play about with many patterns. But until their fertility is shown authentically (i.e., not merely by a theory-serving set of eclectic explanations) I will not put whole infertile systems at the center of my students' education.

Some academics nowadays renounce that last and virtuous course of action. Perhaps commercially, perhaps under pressure to publish or perish, perhaps from high intellectual ambition, they publish infertile systems. These flourish in protected markets. Eclectic explanations are translated and shaped by them, and 'fertility' is re-defined to include this self-service. Here is a bandwaggon. Once on its way, it devises defences. It easily resists uncomprehending human-ist criticism of its jargon. It also resists empiricist criticism of its evasion of experimental test or historical verification. It establishes hostile stereotypes of both critics. The first are reactionary fuddy-duddies, non-cognitive moralizers who fear science because they fear life, the future, and their own educational obsolescence.* The second are pedestrian research-assistants incapable of theoretical imagination. There are also subjective programmatic radicals, who want to subvert science in order to subvert society too. They wish facts instead of observing them.

Meanwhile the bandwaggon broadcasts its own moral imperatives. 'Don't value, or try to reform, the society you study. Care nothing for it – this will help you to treasure scientific forms and reputations despite their lack of social yield. Don't select theory for social service, select facts to fit intrinsically lovable theories. Love science, and segregate it.' Devastating technical instructions follow. 'Select qualities for their quantifiability. Imagine no valuable alternatives – derive them all from neighbors or general models. Fit theories and explanations to each other, not to facts or social purposes. Don't regard valuing as a skill – i.e., do not learn how to select rationally wherever the subject-matter's uniformities are limited or unreliable.' All these, because of the objective nature of the subject-matter, require correspondingly low valuations of truth and utility, and a re-definition of scientific progress from 'understanding and control' to self-augmenting 'cumulation'.

It is, I know, a mistake to let criticism grow so shrill, to trade stereotype for stereotype. But such stereotypes are too often used to put students under improper social pressure. In the years of their emancipation from childhood and parents they are vulnerable to sneers at technical and moral 'immaturity', and very ready to fall in love with a tough science. But the science should indeed be tough and truthful; not self-serving; not another icon, set up by the icono-clasts. The new scientistic schools teach students to condescend to the highest achievements of history and social science as to pre-scientific trifles. They tell a new generation it can excel those old

---

* For disturbed Professors of English Literature, here is an empirical generalization which they can easily test. Seven out of ten structural-functional sociologists and four out of ten value-free political scientists, within sixty seconds of hearing a disturbed Professor of English Literature utter the word 'jargon', will mention the religious persecution of Galileo. The conceptual identification underlying this reflex is a fair example of those they publish professionally; so is the level of modesty; so is the propensity, when an unproven proposition is challenged, to defend some safer one. If the Professor of English Literature wants to cultivate a similar reflex, whenever he hears a social scientist mention Galileo he can refer to the scientists' persecution of Semmelweiss.

fumblings (from Tom Paine and Thomas Jefferson to Myrdal, Hansen and P. A. Sorokin, from Howard and Rowntree to Beveridge and Titmuss and Keynes) by ditching half their scientific faculties and running the other half on faith instead of observation. However ill-mannered, it seems right to rage against such massive displacements of truth and value from the curriculum, and from the standards by which students' work is judged. As Parsons has noticed, in about two thousand words under the subtitle 'The Socialization Process and Its Reference-Group Structure', these judgments of students' work are both forming and choosing the next elite; and often, consenting to be formed is a condition of being chosen.

2. Theory

Theory may debate the values of social and political systems. It may analyse causal relations selected for their importance or their general occurrence. It may warn of dangers, report valuable trends or opportunities, propose programs, debate strategies of change or conservation. Politicians want their knowledge reliable – none of these purposes need reduce a theorist's power to discover and understand. Nor his power to generalize, wherever the facts allow it.

Even so, 'selecting for generality' is usually a mistake. Sometimes behavior becomes general because scientists propose it and people learn to enact it. More often a scientist discerns, selects and understands an abstract or process from one case, models it, then looks to see where else the model fits. Social theory usually has to be generalized by the detailed understanding of case after case. This is different from making generality itself a principle of selection – to theorize relations between only those facts or sequences that occur identically in all systems, is often to assume the uniformities you hope for, and exclude contrary evidence before you start.

Theories attempt different tasks. Some explain social facts and processes. Some debate the values of those facts and processes. Some advise investigators – they list possibilities, propose questions and principles of selection, impart skills.

Clear lines are seldom justified between these three – for example between 'empirical' theory, 'normative' theory, and methodology. Methodologies say something of what the methods are expected to find. Normative theories explain the world they moralize about. Empirical theories assume or conceal their valuations, and often use identities whose defining similarities are invisible without elements of moral or valuing perception. In another classification, some exact sciences distinguish between empirical generalizations, hypotheses and theories. There is no harm in using the same language of social science where it fits, but it seldom does. Empirical generalizations about society often include explanatory elements – reasons and intentions for example. Hypotheses rarely become laws or theories by conclusive proof – rather, they gain or lose friends by experience.

I do not mean to underrate the value of the social theory which does perform in a comparatively natural-scientific way, nor the search for more of it. It has plenty of applications to the more mechanical or statistical effects of habitual behavior – for demographic and economic trends, the congestion of communication channels, the logistics of war, health, education and a lot besides. Often it merely puts quantities – most usefully – to causal processes already understood by common sense. But there remains a range of social behavior – as large and at least as valuable – which looks intrinsically unlikely to support much determinate prediction, or for which statistical prediction, however accurate, is not the most socially-useful knowledge. For this range, which includes much of the subject-matter of sociology, political science, law, history, educational theory, the theory of economic growth, and many branches of management studies and urban studies, the theory actually in use and in prospect is very mixed indeed. It includes various blends of selective explanation, catalogued possibilities and advice for recognizing or contriving them, empirical generalizations with varying explanatory content, values and moralities implied by selection or debated explicitly. There is little point in isolating the pure predictors as alone deserving the name of theory. In fields where few predictors yet exist, or seem likely ever to transcend common sense, theory takes forms more appropriate to useful tasks and particular subjects.

What follows is not a review of the forms of theory to be found in the various disciplines. It is merely a reminder of three general varieties which deserve more credit than they sometimes get: 'normative' theory, 'open' theory, and theory meant chiefly to impart skills.

The public wants theories as aids to action, which must always issue from a texture of knowledge and choice. Theory apt for such use need not be ashamed to have the same texture. The options are rarely so few and clear that theory can present them all, fully explored, without favor. Whether the valuations and choices can be left thus to the public and the knowledge to the theory is often an accident of the subject-matter which need not arouse the anxieties it often does. Nor does 'pure' theory differ in this respect from 'applied' or 'policy-oriented' work. The purest social theory still selects identities, and fertile alternatives to measure their relations by; its valuations are as integral as any in market-research.

The dialogue between prognoses and programs can be very complicated, and not all of it will be improved by being carried on between strangers, in writing. Scientists need be no less moral than publics. Because values respond to changing understandings of reality, the scientists should in theory be more capable than the public of moral adaptability and originality, of deferring judgment for a better view of ramifications, or suspending prejudices which discovery, if uninhibited, might revise. At the very least, those who think they can exclude valuations should feel able to use them without confusing them, as laymen might, with 'facts'. There is no reason why scientists should not contribute to both parts of what ought to be the most subtle, well-informed and inventive possible debate about – and between – social options and their values. Much excellent social theory is about the relations between the two. It ranges from classical political theory to modern theories of welfare, delinquency and crime, education, urban development, and much besides. There is no good reason to inhibit or dismember it; if it is 'social engineering', it is also the method of most pure discovery in these fields.

There is no logical reason why theories which expose their values should be less imperialistic than theories which conceal them. Explanations could be dragooned as easily by Riesman's or Wright Mills' theories as by Parsons' or Easton's or (by far the worst offender) Marx's. In practice the former more often add to the catalogue of things to look for, while the latter more often tell explainers what to say and when to stop. These differences may arise partly from the different quests – for valuables on the one hand, regulars on the other. They may arise partly because most moderns (contrary to the stereotype of 'moral imperatives') propose valued selections with more diffidence than they assert 'facts'. But the differences may owe something also to overriding valuations, of science as a social instrument, or of society as raw material for scientific constructions.

The values which may join with technical considerations in theorists' choices are very various. It has been one obvious bias of this present study to stick to conventional political and social-engineering purposes, to the neglect of many others. Social research may be simply *interesting*. The interest may be curious, entertaining, philosophical, moral, aesthetic. Or it may attempt moral rather than scientific generalization. Love or liberty or equality may have similar value in societies which would require dissimilar causal explanations of their class structures or political systems – or of their outputs of love or liberty. Of course this moralist's advantage is often spurious – the more general his values, the more wishful his identification of cases. There may still be point in trying, as poets or novelists do, to see through apparent differences to moral or aesthetic identities, or to see different qualities of social experience in superficially similar events or institutions. We tend to think of engineering purposes as intending the defence or change of social rules and procedures and institutions. But another sort of engineering operates on the individual experience of these social facts. Research may be reported and theory written to persuade the citizen to new understandings, so that outwardly-unchanged experience may have some different quality for him. Simply to know and understand is good, as the value-free often remind us. It still needs a principle of selection, and if its purpose is uninterfering, there is nothing holy about regularity.

In the commoner argument between 'engineering' selection and its value-free rivals, there is everything to be said for the open use (rather than the covert misuse) of theorists' values. If the distinction is useful at all, most social science is of the 'applied' sort and is not transformed by asking valueless rather than valuable questions, about unrecognized rather than socially-recognized phenomena. If the facts were all regular we would have to choose their useful regularities. Whenever they are not, we have to select their relations from the tangled networks of imperfectly regular systems. Either way there is work for valuations, which should respond in their turn to the facts found. To teach students that their morals are extra-curricular is to deny those morals the very service which education and research should give them – disciplined relation to scientific understandings of social facts and options. The selection and recognition of all sorts of identities, and many elements in the construction of theory and the direction and design of research, depend on the rational response to each other of valuation and observation. These skills should be improved, not banned.

Wherever social life seems imperfectly regular or reliable, theory does well to deal in alternatives and uncertainties. It may list possibilities, estimate probabilities where it can, and look for more predictive knowledge without (when it doesn't appear) glumly blaming its non-appearance on the scientists. One method was exemplified in different ways by the work of Lewis Coser and Arthur Lewis. What effects *may* conflict have on social cohesion? What conditions are usually needed before output-per-head *can* grow?

This is the sort of theory which historians have in their heads. It might sometimes be worth suspending their prejudices, and writing it down. Works like Crane Brinton's *Anatomy of Revolution* and S. M. Lipset's *Political Man* are more fertile, and better understood, as catalogues of possibilities than as searches for universal regularities (which they also, legitimately but less successfully, include). For the study of constitutions, parties, social structures and processes, wars, revolutions, religions and economic systems, historians might reasonably write similar manuals of their experienced expectations. The idea is rightly resisted if it seems to propose that deduction-from-theory should replace detailed research into cases.* But historians should not resist the different activity of ordering and enlarging the battery of questions worth asking of particular cases. But historians suspect that the things to look for are, even in their essences, subtle; only to be recognized at all, in context. Wide historical reading, rather than summaries of it, should educate the historian's expectations. For example, 'questions to ask in explaining

* An example comes to hand as this chapter is written. A sociological reviewer attacks K. S. Inglis, *Churches and the Working Classes in Victorian England*, for failing to explain an effect of social class on Catholic church membership which 'will surprise no sociologist who knows his Max Weber well'. Inglis knew his Max Weber unusually well, together with the library of case-studies done since to test some of Weber's hypotheses. Weber's models proved unhelpful to the facts of English custom and Irish solidarity, so Inglis left them out of his book. To the truths he did observe, the reviewer would apparently prefer falsehoods deduced from laws misread in Weber.

stability and peaceful change' are as generalizable from Halévy's *England in 1815* as from Talcott Parsons' works. But Halévy's method conveys more warnings of the local and dependent purpose of asking many of them. To read many such analyses of many societies may always be the best preparation for analysing the next one. But orderly collections of questions and expectations might still assist education and make for better research, as long as they were not misunderstood as predictors which made research less necessary. 'These' (one might write in great detail, but still within one book) 'are the characteristics which revolutions have always, often or sometimes had; the known ways of classifying their elements; the lengths and directions of causal chains to which analysts of different discipline and persuasion have attached them; the many principles of selection so far applied to their explanation.' From more explicitly-comparative research, to such very general manuals of experience and expectation, there is room for historical theory which might, in its turn, admonish the over-confident law-seekers of other disciplines.

The above is only one department of a more general variety of theory: contributions to clinical and interrogatory skills. These can only be distinguished from more formal theories *about* society by differences of emphasis and balance, but such differences may be considerable. In proportion as social scientists have to educate, explain, advise or plan for irregular or imperfectly predictable situations, 'arts and skills' become the appropriate knowledge. All arts and skills include plenty of hard knowledge of the other sort, but the balance shifts from law and information about society to 'batteries of its possibilities' and to adaptable skills for measuring and dealing with its less regular problems. Much of the skill may still be expressible in theory, which may include true generalizations about the skills, as well as about the problems. Like historians' theory, the theory of public opinion tells less about how opinion behaves than about how to discover it reliably at moments when you need to know it. Games theory illuminates the games, but also improves your play. International theory suggests what you can, rather than predicting what you will, do next. Clausewitz generalizes and predicts, but incidentally to advising. Urban theory is precise about traffic flow capacities, but aesthetic and admonitory about the aims and arts of planning. Theories of education range from objective laws about perception and learning to moralities about teaching; the latter, if prescriptive in teacher-training, may predict as well as the former. Both moral and indeterminate elements must mix with others in any theory of 'teaching people to think independently'.

Through these and the other varieties of social theory there run no steady relations between the generality of theory and its objectivity, valuing content, predictive power, sufficiency or selectivity, reference to social facts or to scientists' skills. There is no harm in distinguishing orders of abstraction or generality, though the substitution of 'higher and lower' for 'different' or 'more and less' is a minor triumph for one faction's propaganda. As often as not these merely distinguish artificial from socially-recognized identities, or one fact true of fifty systems (though useless for understanding any) from fifty facts of one system, usefully related. When these rankings distinguish high from low science, or theory from practice, there may be pressure to select the most talented recruits into what are not necessarily, in these fields, the most promising or difficult or valuable fields of work. The value, use and 'heuristic promise' of social theories cannot rationally be judged by their height, rigor, generality or ambition. There are better tests in fitness to purpose and subject-matter, useful originality, prompt and genuine performance, and the social importance of the performance. Like most of the theories, these tests require valuations; but so do preferences for height, rigor and abstraction.

3. Objectivity

For a subject to see an object, both have to be there. No observer can enslave himself perfectly to what he sees – the psychology and education of perception, and the selective element in all perception, can seldom be quite identical for all observers at all times. In practice we can educate most observers to make the same count of five beans; but not always to make the same selections, which are by definition subjective, though they may have such qualities as fitness-for-purpose, obedience-to-rule, consistency, unanimous support, or justice.

For science the distinction is too crude. Observation and selection include, inseparably, elements of each other; but they are also unlike enough to make it absurd to hope that rules for objective observation will somehow suffice to produce, also, something called 'objective selection'.

Observation and measurement should be as exact and reliable as possible. They can often be unanimous, for all practical purposes obedient to their objects. Strict rules can ensure this, whether rules for human observers' behavior or reliabilities built into machines. Revolutionary improvements in observing and measuring, and in the propensity to measure, are among the most important achievements of the modern social sciences. But it does not follow that the different business of perceiving qualities, or selecting *anything*, should be abused because 'subjective' or 'impressionist'.

In one of its meanings, 'impressionist' is a just word for guessing what could be watched, understood or counted; 'subjective', for guessing not only lazily, but wishfully. Impressionist, subjective guesswork should be replaced wherever possible. But careful observation does not always mean the mechanical measurement of quantities (though that is one very reliable kind of observation). It depends, obviously, on what has to be observed. The nearest-available quantity may not be the most objective indicator of a quality, or a passage of human thought and feeling, even though it produce the most unanimous observations. It may unhelpfully report something else where understanding or impression would report the true object more faithfully. Measuring a few quantities within or near the real object may be as bad as any other way of guessing about it. Inferring effects from neighbor-models or extrapolated pasts may be worse guesswork than imagining them for the particular case studied. Deduction from unproven or over-generalized theory is another way of guessing instead of observing. All these deserve to be damned as subjective impressionism.

In the business of observation, objectivity and subjectivity perhaps stand for the ends of a spectrum. But that whole spectrum of observation is one end of another, which extends to selection. Sometimes the rules for selection can be as reliable as the measuring rules, sometimes not. In proportion as difficulties arise in selecting or recognizing and identifying the items to be observed, degrees of unreliability and irrelevance may have to be weighed against each other. There are no methods axiomatic for all cases.

Above all, it is stupid to try to expel subjectivity from science.

What that principle of selection will expel from social science may well be nine-tenths of its valuable methods, questions and subject-matter. As one spectacular effect, it may begin by expelling much of its *regular* subject-matter, many of its uniformities. There is a temperamental tendency to expect observable quantities, and uniformities of behavior, to occur together. This is quite irrational – the most regular behavior may be the hardest to measure, or for observers to agree about. Economists have seldom been troubled by disputes between behaviorist and understanding methods. 'With better statistical surveys' says one, mathematically eminent, 'I expect economists will learn to predict the volume of next year's investment better. With better study of businessmen's psychology, we might further improve our prediction batting average.'[1] But some sociologists and social psychologists and a few political scientists still make a religious issue of the distinction between 'mathematical' relations (exact as to quantities or orders, obtuse as to mechanism) and thoughtful relations, known by nonunanimous understanding. Humans can be educated better than machines can be built, both to select and to measure things like affectivity, satisfaction, expectation, frustration, intolerance, rejection. To 'operationalize' such observations by reading them off a few quantitative indicators – hours spent in interaction, yes-no responses to attitude questionnaires, criminal convictions, suicides, resignations or expulsions from membership – is to assume some laws which only 'understanding' could verify. It may often make the recognition of identities less reliable and their observation less exact.

In any case old-style subjectivity, as damned in scientific prefaces, is scarcely a serious danger these days. It never was very true that anxiety for useful results bred careless technique – military intelligence, military and medical science and corporation accountancy are merely extreme cases of the more usual relation. Observe the behaviorist scientist in any real-life emergency of his own – he reactivates all those more versatile and subtle faculties that he is trying to abandon professionally, perhaps disclosing thus his comparative valuations of his own and his society's problems. Nor does this generation really peer at nature, or itself, through rosy moral mists and religious prisms. We take in rationality with our mothers' milk. If we have to fear prejudgment and distorted vision, they are no longer those of an older innocence but are rather those of cynic incredulity, selection-for-disenchantment, the competition of each to be harder-boiled than the next. Things pass for scientific attitudes – and serve as scientific selectors – which are really styles and affectations no more rational and no less fashion-conscious than were any of the elegant, moral, or pedantic styles of humanists. Plenty of equations look as good on the page as plenty of footnotes used to do.

Ironically, an anti-moral 'objectivity' sometimes introduces purely moral selectors. Concepts and identities are chosen *because* they define morally-indifferent phenomena or even (to show hard-boiled) morally repugnant phenomena. Observers develop selective perception – 'if it doesn't stink, it isn't real'. Self-interests are pre-selected as observable, altruisms as illusions (or pretenses, or pathologies). Compulsions are observable, 'free' choices are problems for further research. Methodological styles can select as madly as moral ones. Qualitative or delicate perceptions (though the 'impression' be as precise as a photograph) are unfashionably pre-scientific. The pleasures of quantification or roundabout inference or private language are preferred to rational efficiencies of method. The modern form of the rainmaking dance is not prayer, but irrelevant quantification.

Perhaps there deserve to be two new concepts: mechanized subjectivity, and (for the drilling of all observers to select unanimously) authoritarian objectivity. Whether by machine or by educating human perception, it is always possible to 'see' quantities or self-interests or regularities only. Science must always select; but selectors should be adjusted to purposes, rather than becoming restrictive theories of knowledge. It is often important to go about with all your senses sensitive, none atrophied, and no impressions banned. It is equally important to photograph, measure and count whatever your more poetic faculties might misreport. Many tasks in social science require the intricate relation of both types of observation. Quite apart from their different efficiencies as observers, the methods also have all sorts of selective effects. 'Objective selection' gets a meaning at last – it means selection for 'objective knowability'. Objectivity no longer means a general fidelity of observation to objects, but ranks the facts themselves according to their visibility. In school, fashion or authority may turn the ranking into a rule. Obedience to such a rule may well achieve, for both observation and selection, that unanimity or 'intersubjectivity' which many regard as the after-proof of objectivity. There is both a good and a simply monstrous sense in which observers can be educated to select and see alike; it is as well not to confuse the two, nor always to accept well-drilled unanimity as the 'operational definition' of objectivity.

Objectivity can become a specially diverting selector for those who believe inference from regular association to be the only objective knowledge of causes. To establish mathematical relations between discrete identities they need reliable, quantifiable indicators for those identities.

For example, some quantifiable aspects of group behavior can be known more unanimously than may some of its other qualities. We are more likely to agree about the number of members and the frequency of their meetings, than about their intentions or feelings for each other. Scientists who like quantities often like regularities too, and like to infer rather than to discern causal relations. But this is merely a temperamental fact about those scientists. There is no good reason to assume that the quantifiable aspects of group behavior will also be its regular aspects – that a search for uniformities must be limited to relations between quantifiable identities. The relation between regularity and quantifiability is (before you start) random. But it is easier to get general agreement about relations between obviously visible quantities than it is to prove relations between qualities whose isolation or quantification requires subjective elements of valuing judgment. Simple-minded investigators may therefore stick to behaviorist facts: the numbers in groups, their physical movements, the hours they spend together, rates of recruitment and drop-out. Recognizing that these rules exclude precisely the *sociology* of the group, others choose abstract identities to isolate real social qualities, then 'operationalize' them – they look for objectively visible indicators of these invisible qualities. Now two relations need to be regular: the relation between the social qualities, and the relation of each to its indicator.

Of the difficulties that follow, there are good illustrations in George C. Homans' *The Human Group*. With rare candor, it is not on reason that Homans founds his program to imitate some logical forms of physical science –

... it is an article of our faith that, correct or incorrect, sufficient or insufficient in number though they be, our hypotheses are of the kind that a developed social science will formulate, in that they are statements of uniformities underlying the superficial differences in the behavior of human groups.[2]

But Homans is no behaviorist. His work is distinguished by the care and honesty with which he faces the difficulties of representing qualities by quantities. Using others' observations and understandings of five different groups, Homans tries to discern some underlying uniformities and to state them as hypotheses about the covariation of pairs of qualities. The qualities are activity, interaction, sentiment, and agreement about norms. There is no logical conflict between this attempt and the most sensitive, discerning, subjective measurement of the identities in the first place. But the discerning observers have to make all sorts of judgments into which elements of valuation have to enter. When members of a group agree about some norms but not others – or when they agree on forms of words but seem to give them different meanings – or when they agree about many trifles but dispute a few essentials – then which are the 'important' norms and the 'significant' agreements? Which feelings, when several seem to be present in different degrees, shall indicate the kind or the intensity of 'sentiment'? Should there be some weighting of interactions according to how trivial, routine, deliberate or decisive they are? Nobody could complain of the patience and sophistication with which Homans explores scores of such difficulties. What seems surprising is that his faithful quest of mathematical relations should survive the exploration.

Abstract similarities, discerned in all five groups, could support one sort of regular science. Model relations or processes might be discerned, understood and identified as present in all groups. It would take similar discernment, including similar elements of choice and value-textured judgment, to establish contrary cases and so limit or disprove any generalizing hypotheses. Except where its values were unanimous, this science could not expect its results to be unanimous.

Homans' aim is different. He hopes that science may somehow operationalize and objectify his discrete, analytical qualities (or others of their kind) so that their relations may be known unanimously and expressed mathematically. He does not profess to have succeeded, but hopes that others will keep trying. They have done so, often with less scruple than his. The most common result is a steady shift of interest from the social qualities themselves to objective indicators of them; and then another shift of interest, from the relation between quality and indicator, to the relations between the indicators. Between the indicators (operational substitutes for less measurable identities) regular relations may be discovered. But whether these relations hold also between the original identities, between the social qualities themselves, is a question which could only be answered by a discerning and valuing judgment. It would often be as sensible to discern the qualities' relations with each other directly, as to discern their relations to their indicators then mathematize the mutual relations of the indicators. Most investigators candidly confine their claims, and increasingly their questions and interests, to the indicators. There is nothing wrong with such work as an ecology of physical movements, communications or responses to directive questionnaires, but much of it has slight or no relation to the study of *social* life.[3] This general diversion of interest from valuable to trivial questions is the largest effect of the use, as a selector, of the rule of objectivity. It directs the drunkard's search not even where the light is brightest, but wherever the searchers are least likely to squabble about the trifles they find.

4. Bias

Commonly this is one man's name for another's principles of selection. Three meanings might each be useful if they were not so likely to confuse each other: (1) technical, as in the bias of a bowling ball; (2) abusive, for selections to which (as for the bowling ball) a neutral alternative is agreed to be available; (3) general, as a short word for anybody's values, on the understanding that everybody has some. But the second and third are so confused in popular usage that it might be better to use the first meaning only.

A bias can be deliberate, reliable and appropriate. A population sample biased to double-represent housewives, quadruple child-rearers, and grossly magnify launderers and hotelkeepers may be just right to predict sales of soap. It may also be poor for forecasting elections, useless for estimating the community's ownership of firearms, and prejudicial for empanelling jurors. If the population is sufficiently poor or unequal, it may even misrepresent the market for soap.

The word's use could be extended to the element of sampling and representation in a wider range of scientific operations. Historians, choosing minorities as important, slide into treating them as representative. Public-school spirit is attributed to Victorian Englishmen instead of to every hundredth; constitutional rights to the people instead of to males, whites, property-owners; racialism or enterprise or scientific spirit to societies instead of to a few of their minorities; most books called *World History* are about rich white literates, who nevertheless laugh unselfconsciously at the one called *World History from a Malayan Point of View*. At the opposite end of the scientific spectrum, as noted above, some 'operational definitions' deserve to be scrutinized as samples. They seldom misrepresent numerical populations, whose sampling has become very good; but there may still be doubt about their sampling of the population's experience and behavior. Do the hours it spends together represent the intensity of a group's interaction, suicides represent anomie, convictions represent crime or delinquency? The principles of population sampling apply, but their application will require more discerning judgment than multiplication of indicator-readings.

It is not always easy to separate technical from moral representation. The sampling question may be mixed up with the question whether a population shares responsibility for a minority's acts. Or the things sampled may be identified, by society or the scientist, partly by moral characteristics. Scientists who want indicators for a quality like friendliness usually distrust the sort of discernment required to test the indication. So indicators are chosen for practical experimental reasons; whatever its early references to qualities like friendliness, science sets about investigating something else. Though many will resist it, political criticism of such conduct is quite appropriate – to publish misrepresentations of the valued qualities of social behavior is a social act inviting social criticism, because the misrepresentations may be persuasive.

Some of the worry about the ill effect of values upon science arises from the obvious opportunities – and the many glaring examples – of samples and representations chosen wishfully, or with intent to deceive. Often this worry is the correct one, just as objectivity is an appropriate ideal for most observation. But sometimes, complaints are misdirected at the presence of the values when they ought to be directed at the content of the values. There could be no 'objective' choice of the significant features of the behavior of Catholic or Protestant, white or Negro, rich or poor. A choice of 'objectively representable' features would be as political as any other. So with more abstract qualities of society – different indicators of anomie or social cohesion will represent different selections of experience or behavior. Most arguments will have to refer to differences of valuation. In extreme cases, a critic may reasonably turn from valuing the subjects' behavior to valuing the investigator's. What matters is to distinguish the two or three senses of 'wrong'. An investigator may be technically wrong, misrepresenting the purchasers of soap or the Republican voters. Or you may think his values wrong, and dissent from his identifications of friendliness, while conceding his honesty and his right to his own values. Or you may declare with full indignation that he himself acts wrongly, misrepresents wilfully, selects unfairly – that he is a dishonest skunk. (He may, of course, manage all three.) There is no way of 'objectifying' the second sort of representation, though technical criticism may improve it. The bias gets worse, not better, if the critic demands more objectivity; this simply requires the investigator to represent something more capable of objective representation. Objectivity becomes a silly selector, and wrenches his sample even further from the population it set out to represent. Examples are common in academic examining. The more historians or sociologists resort to objective tests, or to non-discretionary marking systems, the more they may achieve reliable assessment of some students' capacities which they do not want to sample – and misrepresent those they do. The students, responding, may go to work to replace the relevant capacities by the irrelevant ones. Political criticism is, once more, appropriate.

The ordinary unscientific usage of 'objectivity' and 'bias' is perhaps the sensible one, after all. It refers as often to justice and fair dealings as to the obedience of observer to objects. Social scientists need both these meanings – but for justice, fair dealing or the center position between opposing factions, those themselves are less misleading words.

5. Values

Hume's 'ought' would do for a definition; as would roughly, 'any part of an opinion about conduct which could not be justified by reference to facts only'. Many 'evaluations' are ascriptions of value by rule; they should be called statements of value or fact, I suppose, according to whether the rule requires reference to goodness or to weights and measures. The practical dependence of many 'cognitions' and valuations on each other is sometimes underrated, and the analytical distinction between them is assumed to be sharper and simpler than perhaps it is. But for present purposes it will do to accept the enemy's definition: values are what value-free scientists say they want to exclude from science.

Few disagree that social purposes should choose the broad directions and tasks of research. Some problems are chosen for their social importance. Others may be chosen to fit the researcher's situation, the time and equipment he has, his skill, his need to publish, and the size and methodology and style of result required by a particular patron, employer or journal. In all these choices there is an element of social interest or valuation. Only a strictly-justified economizing judgment of the method most likely to crack an already-given problem deserves to be called an exclusively methodological valuation, and even these may often import the social purposes of the work into its methodological choices.

After tasks are chosen, considerations of social value continue to guide methodological choices often and variously. It is in selecting his assumptions and 'givens' and variables, the identities whose natures and relations he will investigate, that the purist usually believes that he distinguishes himself from the *ad hoc* engineer. He is sometimes right. But whenever he persists unreasonably with pure schemes unjustified by results, with levels of abstraction and identities for which he continues to discover no genuinely hidden or genuinely important or genuinely regular relations, then his 'purism' does become a predominantly social choice, and invites the criticism appropriate to any other extrascientific, 'non-cognitive' valuation. As a social choice it gathers importance and responsibility in proportion as the work occupies resources, or the curriculum of education and training.

Very important decisions have often to be made about classes and identities. The identity 'delinquent' is quite a valuable one, socially speaking. There are things we would like to know and do about the whole class of delinquents. It may still be too blunt or inclusive an identification for many purposes: different delinquents deliquesce in different ways from different reasons and causes, call for different detections and corrections, attract different moral judgments, and would respond to different preventions. But 'delinquent' is still a useful identification. Much knowledge true indifferently of all delinquents, or true only of the whole number of delinquents, would be useful for social purposes.

But delinquents may be a sub-class of 'deviants'. Is it better to look for truths general to the class or identity 'delinquent', or (more) general to the class or identity 'deviant'? Deviant, as usually defined, includes a variety of departures from social norms and expectations, including (besides delinquency) much art, crime, invention, social criticism, and happy or miserable (but uncriminal) social withdrawal. For any valuer, these activities have wildly different values, which is one reason why 'deviance' is a concept invented by scientists rather than by society. Its identification is always 'subjective', relying on the scientist's choosing whose norms shall define it. Knowledge true for all deviants is unlikely to be socially useful – socially *usable* – in any simple immediate way, though it may help to reveal the cost in poetry of moving too blindly against burglars. Generally, it will have to be justified by worth-while discoveries which could not have been found more economically by investigating the relations of socially-recognized identities instead. What if the only fact true of all deviants and of no others should prove to be the one that defined them in the first place: that each of them was disapproved by a majority, a different majority for each deviation? In that event, whether the identity 'deviant' was chosen as a strategically indirect approach to delinquency, or as a guess at the likely focus of uniformities in a detached scientific search for uniformities, it will prove to have been a wrong guess. This particular identity, though not as bad as that, probably is a fairly infertile guess. It lumps together sufferers and sinners and saints and oddities. The slender affinity by which an identity is imposed upon such diversities *might*, of course, prove to be a quality in strong and regular relation to other social facts; but it looks unlikely.

This discussion is simply a reminder of one familiar form of the engineering-or-science dilemma. One set of identities may be socially valuable. We already think of them as, and are prepared to treat them as, wholes or morally homogeneous classes. The human individual is one perfect case, because we ascribe responsibilities to him, as we do to many groups and institutions – other 'valuable identities'. Any class may be a socially valuable identity if we think it right to treat its members, in at least one respect, all alike: all burglars, all negroes, all investors, all do-gooders, all the old or young or poor; all inequalities of income, all equalities of esteem, all hatreds, all charities, all murders, all reforms.

But artificial identities may be worth isolating because however morally mixed or unrecognized they nevertheless, in some hitherto unnoticed way, act alike, have regular relations with each other, or otherwise support useful generalizations. Most people are morally uninterested in an economic classification which lumps together the needy widow and the bloated capitalist (though laymen have supported plenty of racial and religious classifications which did so). But an economist who identifies the two by one fact about them, as investors, or as consumers, manages to discover generalities about investment and consumption which, besides their 'pure scientific' interest, can have engineering value for both widow and capitalist. 'Study widows' (even if benefits for widows were the only purpose of the study) would have been worse advice than 'study investment' or 'study the economy as a system'.

But in many social fields such indirectness, and such neglect of society's own identifications, has not quite as many presumptions in its favor (nor triumphs in its past) as it can claim in economics or physical science. Even in economics, the exotic identities are discovered more often in the figures people deal in and their aggregate consequences, than in the mysteries of the people's own behavior. As Winch and others argue, much of the subject-matter of social science *is*, precisely, society's own rules for recognizing likeness, unlikeness, and value. It does seem likely that any interesting regularities in social behavior will be related in one way or another to the identities which the people themselves recognize and value. It often happens that the scientific temperament which likes to abstract novel 'non-valuable' identities, also likes to look for regular behavior. These preferences can hinder each other in scientific work.

A good ideology should speak of valuable, rather than of politically indifferent, identities. So should any social theory, unless it can

show that 'unrecognized' identities behave in a manner whose discovery will eventually allow better understanding or control of
things to which people do ascribe values. The only way in which
this is likely to happen (and the only promise ever claimed for the
method) is by the discovery of hitherto-unknown causal mechanisms or regularities. *Some* of these, if not necessarily all their
ramifications, should be expected to justify almost any publication
of socially-valueless classifications. Valueless classifications which
discover nothing but themselves, and fertilize nothing but a reclassifying industry, should not be accepted as payable originalities.

In the extensive fields in which the facts dictate that most
scientific activity will continue to be the selective exploration of
causal relations, to the end of useful *ad hoc* explanation, it is usually
sensible to let valuations guide or join with technical thought in the
choice of identity and class.

This introduces the most important service of valuation to scientific selection: its part in the selection of causal explanations,
including the most general. But Chapters 3 and 9 above were about
little else, and need not be summarized again.

It is worth noticing – practically, not philosophically – some
relations between observations, values and valuations.

Some think that objects are first perceived; then the perceptions
selected and understood 'cognitively'; then at last, values ascribed to
them. Most psychologists would insist that the valuing and selecting
begin with the original perception, and this agrees better with the
practice of most research. Formal or mechanical procedures of
observation may indeed, sometimes usefully, segregate and publicize
the principles of selection and make the observations more reliable.
This is the best way to count money or heads or votes; sometimes
also delinquents; but rarely deviance, friendliness, aggression,
frustration, alienation, conformity, or the content and effect of most
communications. What is required to recognize and index these is,
in varying degrees, a distinctively human perception, including a moral
sense. However coldly the scientist may treat the subjects' valuations
and identifications as facts, it still requires moral among other
perceptions to recognize and index them.

Of the relation of values to valuations, some think that values are
what men 'have', from which they deduce their valuations; so, the

detailed valuations in observation or theory can be derived from its 'value premises'. Others understand values as inductions from valuations – as affinities between valuations, and consistencies in valuing habits, discerned afterwards more often than planned beforehand. The requirements vary with the work, certainly; but there are few problems of much interest or complexity for which a simple moral or political premise is sufficient without also, for its application, a sensitive valuing skill, inextricably mixed in mutual service with 'objective' perception, and sometimes easier described in terms of art, skill or personality than of formulable premises and principles.

Above all, the services of science and valuation are reciprocal. Values cannot be derived entirely from facts. It does not follow that they are unresponsive to facts. They are constantly adjusted, sometimes revolutionized, and often improved in response to clearer understandings, more useful selections and more exact observations of facts. The intricate relation of valuations to more instrumental, technical selectors, a relation required often for scientific as well as social reasons, does not mean that the values must command the rest. Indeed, valuers can respond more sensitively if they work within the science, where there ought to be the best view of options, implications and ramifications, both of action and of scientific choices in the study of action.

Values are often studied as objects. Sometimes they are better exposed when they help to organize research into other objects. Direct examinations of values as objects, and research or speculation about their practical implications, easily have their conclusions predetermined by their selections – recall rival choices of 'the important' social manifestations of individualism, of private liberties and properties and rights. One may speculate about the implications of T. H. Green's valuation of 'social liberty' – or one may reflect on the product, when it organizes Carr's history of Russia. One may reason from John Stuart Mill's idea of individual liberties, to the logically-likely contradictions between many of them; but a wider, less-expected range of implications is exposed when Mill's values dictate the selections in Halévy's analysis of English social processes. When values arrange the study of other substances, there may even be something akin to the psychologist's projective test: the valuer is more unwary, difficulties are harder to skirt, more is exposed than might be willingly declared. When values help to choose the imagined alternatives of causal analysis, their work is public. When other considerations guide the conscious psychology of choice, and investigators imagine no alternatives at all, or imagine that they imagine none, then the implications of their causal selections can be spelled out into the alternatives they logically require; both the values and the technics of choice come under useful scrutiny.

Scientists sometimes depict moralities as rigid, superstitious, authoritarian, impervious to reason. There have been some like that, often because their owners refused to study the realities they valued. Of the wrong segregations of moral from scientific thought, the worst effect of all may be to encourage more of such frightened, uncomprehending, sectarian moralities. They need their skills as much as science needs its values.

6. *Imagination*

'Imaginative' is used differently of children, liars, business men and scientists. At one end of its meaning are insanities, at the other the precise prediction of other people's unlikelier acts. Somewhere between lie the creative arts, novel perceptions of familiar objects, the invention of programs, and the guess that starts discovery. A much-loved word, but unspecific.

One of its meanings is familiar in social science. What may seem to be another, was made to do duty in 'the imagination of alternatives'. But these two meanings are much the same. Everyone agrees that imagination is the word for whatever opens new perspectives, makes novel hypotheses, conceives new methods. But most of these express the 'bold guessing' meaning of imagination; however inventive, it proposes no fantasies but guesses at effective holds on objective realities. In the popular image of him, the discoverer invents methods or concepts because he *guesses* that their use will help to discover some reality which he *guesses* may be there. This has plenty of affinity with the reasoning which nominates A as a cause of B because of a guess that without A, the effect would have been C instead. Like any discoverer's, this guess may sometimes be confirmed by other cases of B and C or by experiment. But in complex social life it must more often depend on whatever support it can get from the imaginative isolation of causal processes patiently discerned and traced through their confusing habitat. In such analysis, without much experiment, with complex cases imperfectly comparable, and with limited confidence in the repetitive reliability of many of the factors, imagination gets little of either censorship or reinforcement from any clinching 'proof'; and a good deal of what it sometimes claims, from experiment or comparison, is proof of a somewhat imaginary, or else self-verifying, kind.

In the service imagination does for causal analysis, there are sometimes useful functions for what it is not unreasonable to call moral imagination. Brand new values and moralities are seldom 'invented'. But just as political originality re-defines familiar facts and looks ahead to contrive novel effects, so do politicians – and preachers, and social scientists – propose new values for old facts, look ahead to imagine what would be the values of programs if achieved, and introduce occasional new ideas into the continuing debates about love and justice, rights and obligations and distributions. In various ways the technical or discovering imagination may owe something to such moral thought, which can recognize novel identities and prompt new classifications, new programs, and new causal analyses.

7. Art

This heading invites a book*; in default, mere reminders of truisms.

Neither the selective and constructive methods of art, nor its perceptions, should be as neglected as they are by some social scientists. Whenever scientific operations can be separated as observation, then scientific ordering and reasoning, then reporting, all three might sometimes be improved if the first and third were done by novelists. No scientist should refuse to notice perceptions more exact and distinctive than are many of his own. His factual observations may nowadays rival the novelists'; but novelists and poets might reform his moral senses radically, if he would only let them.

Whatever the value of this present study it needs to be done again with art instead of science as its differentiating model. Artists

---

* Arthur Lee Burns has written, but not yet published, distinguished work on 'history as art', on which I have tried not to let this section trespass.

perceive differently, select differently, construct and report differently. They have different methods for recognizing and distinguishing uniformities from local variations, and different methods of communicating the distinctions. It would be absurd to categorize the differences in a few sentences, but two very general ones may be noticed. Writers of plays and novels and poems have as strong a strain to universality as scientists have. But the writers (at their best) generalize from more thoroughly understood cases, understood in context – their contexts may give very different meaning and significance to social routines and individual experiences which look superficially alike. Imaginative literature praised for its universality has often been exactly perceptive of individuality and local detail. Second, the uniformities of experience are seldom (by the best writers) distinguished explicitly (in asides to the reader) from its individualities and eccentricities. Each reader is offered the author's perceptions and selections; each reader contributes his own recognitions; you don't quite know which, or how universal, the universals are, until the sales and the centuries of survival register the readers' recognitions. The scientist's 'case study' with appended comparisons and theoretical commentary is often a rudimentary essay in the writer's use of particulars not merely to 'support' or 'exemplify' generalizations, but to communicate the generalizations themselves with precise meanings, distinctions and safeguards. Art and science mix subtly, without harm to either, in the communication of general and theoretical suggestions in Southern's and Halévy's histories.

Histories are still shaped, more often than other works of social science, by some literary inheritances. Useful measurement and patient analysis often surrender to good prose and a moving narrative. Some explanations get more of their structure from artistic than from social or scientific purpose – from experienced conventions which recommend a beginning, a middle and an end; suspense; a counterpoint of light and dark, fast and slow, action and reflection, vignette and generalization. The effects of art cannot all be written off as distortions of truth or rational selection (though many can, of course). The patterns and identities perceived by art may have special value to sciences of human experience. As communicator, art hoards experience of readers' receptivities. Explanatory sufficiencies and artistic unities are sometimes at war, sometimes (by the best historians, or with appropriate subjects) made to discipline each other usefully.

It would not do to imitate writers' methods, any more than natural scientists' methods, uncritically. A detailed comparison of writers' and social scientists' approaches to their many common problems would certainly not reveal a balance of skill and success on one side only. What it *would* do, in contrast to any science-modelled study, would be to draw attention to different qualities of social science. Art and science offer very different neighbor-models for the study of social science, and would prompt different selections of its qualities-to-be-explained, and different explanations of its successes and short-comings. It would be worth comparing, not lightly but with serious patience, Sinclair Lewis and Robert Lynd; Durkheim's and Faulkner's and Nabokov's understandings of anomie; Donne and Gide and Sorokin upon love; Jane Austen's and David Riesman's judgments of social conformity; Hans Morgenthau's and John P. Marquand's and Andrew Marvell's reasons for believing, and ways of reporting, that 'The same arts that did gain/A power, must it maintain'. Not only the immediate purposes and methods, but also the diffuse social effects of social science would suffer a different comparison, and different illuminations. The proposal is not meant as frivolous, but someone else will have to carry it out.

A final reason why social science should recover its lost arts lies in its most important modes of action, which are informing and persuading its subjects. Social scientists should not forget how to communicate with their engineers as effectively as physical scientists communicate with theirs. For social science most of the engineers are also the subject-matter, and plain is the language they read.

This hoary truth deserves repeating as often as printers can be found to print it. It is not by reference to the persecution of Galileo or the precision of physics that jargon has to be justified. The wishes and capacities of the subjects of social science create a presumption in favor of plain language wherever it will do the work, which is almost everywhere in history, sociology and political science. There are still stronger reasons. Plain English does for most of sociology what mathematical expression does for a little of it: clarifies and criticizes it. The half of sociology which is in plain or numerical language is, with negligible exceptions, its better half. Of the rest, nine-tenths could have used plain language with unmixed advantage to the reputable majority of its purposes. Careful translations, plain or mathematical, usually shorten it. They clarify whatever meanings and confusions were present in the original. They seldom lose or blur a useful meaning, and for the few exceptions there is a short, justified vocabulary of structure and function, class and stratum, role and set, and (except for the special requirements of computer-programming) very few more, of which most were easy adaptations of words in general service already. Thus fortified, the experienced and versatile 'plain' language becomes, in its precisions and capacities, much fancier than any jargon. Whenever work in jargon can be translated without increase of length or loss of meaning, there was no respectable reason to think or write it in jargon in the first place. Most of the technical language of science was needed for useful identities and distinctions unknown to plain language. Most of the jargon of sociology is needed to assert useless or spurious identities and to obliterate distinctions about which plain language is less capable of prevaricating. It is corrupt, and corrupting, to require students to translate plain thought, without improvement, into the private languages in which too many of their teachers have now a conceited, careerist or commercial interest.

8. Education

As societies grow richer, more of their members stay longer at school. More jobs require more training and however technical it is, it means more hours of life at school and less elsewhere. In the dwindling hours out of school, there is more communication and more of the communicators have been longer at school. Of the man-hours at school, the social sciences steadily increase their share. If values and valuing skills are acquired during the hours at home, at play or at work, and if technical needs and value-free selections combine to expel them from the hours at school, then both their chances are diminishing – or would do, without their share of magazine space and television time.

One should not exaggerate the present effects of professional social science upon the public's ethics or its understandings of society; among other things, this decade's effects come largely from earlier decades' lesser exposure to the influence. But whatever that influence, the simple statistics of education suggest that it ought to be increasing rapidly, and some infectious successes of popular social science support the statistics. In this, Talcott Parsons' picture of social structure as chiefly a pattern of normative culture should admonish us: we contribute to that structure with every book and lecture and allocation of time and money to research, and perhaps more effectively or dangerously with every judgment we make of students' work. From the particular methods of thought in the heads of every social worker, town planner, school teacher, journalist, economist, administrator and all the rest, to the most general public images of society and understandings of its legitimacies and causal arrangements, social scientists contribute increasingly to the quality and development of the societies they inhabit, and of the poorer societies which depend on theirs for peace or war or aid or trade. Besides whatever behavior they prompt, many of the understandings are social goods – or evils – in themselves.

Many of the disciplines teach much more than they discover; some, in whatever disguise, teach more moralities of selection than methods of discovery. For some, research chiefly means the technical and political discussion of options unmysterious in themselves: the education of judgment. It may be socially bad, and technically it is certainly very biased, that most methodological attention is given to the comparatively few science-like discovering techniques, or to those modes of social engineering which put the engineer into a manager's relation to the people engineered. The morality of such managers is important, and ought to figure in their education. But however diffuse, the general educational and persuasive effects of social science may well be as important as the whole sum of its detailed engineering effects.

There is a special problem for educators in any science whose valuations are acknowledged to be ineradicable, and useful. For students who value diversely, what should be the curriculum? How can one take care that their values respond to new understandings of the facts, rather than of the teachers? How can their work be fairly or reliably examined?

Of all teachers, probably historians meet the problem most, are least anxious about it, and cope with it most skilfully. Half that skill is moral. Many historians babble of objectivity and mistake for 'neutral' any one of a confused variety of political, conventional and ritual selectors. But such methodological talk seems to do little harm to the teaching and examining practice of the intelligent majority of them. The popular pictures of tory examiner down-grading radical work, or proximate-explainer down-grading generalization, are rarely true; if anything, the really shrewd examinee attacks his examiner's work by name. Competent historians can usually distinguish stupid from intelligent Marxism, stale from original conservatism, useful from sterile precisions, coherent from wild or opportunist selections, thought from memory and slippery wits from either: good work from bad.

Besides perceiving such qualities, examiners have to weigh them against each other. In this, most will concede a good deal more to an examinee's choices than they might to an author's in reviewing his book. Such university-bred tenderness is rarer in mass examinations of high-school scripts; there, fact-counting is supposed to aid reliability, but more often reflects the poorer pay, education, intelligence or morals of the examiners. The judgments, like the work they judge, have to be both technical and moral. The valuations in the judgments are related both to the professional and to some personal values of the judges. Good examiners must be conscientious, and keep their faculties alert though fifty tedious minutes of every hour of marking demand no very subtle faculties at all. They must judge work as doing good or bad service to the student's own values and curiosities, yet draw the line at some of those, remembering what the examination is supposed to test. Independent double marking helps, producing the greatest single improvement in reliability less by its corrective after-effects than by the foreknowledge of confrontation which prompts each original marker to take care and play fair. Besides such devices, and well-educated intelligence, the best safeguard is some genuine respect and concern for students, and for their education. The examining problem is not to convert the history schools to objective tests. It is rather to infect the pseudo-objective schools with the morals of good historians.

It is here, perhaps, that the hostile stereotype of the 'moralist' as a monster of imperative unreason, does most harm. The morals of the best historians, as teachers and examiners, can be so righteous but compassionate, perceptive but indulgent, pliant but incorruptible, loving but uninterfering, as to be complex and subtle beyond the amputated understanding of many an operationalized scientist. Historians don't monopolize such morals; a great many scientists of social problems equal them; David Riesman excels them. These morals, though not unanimous, are not private or ineffable or mysterious. They respond to encounters with each other, and with facts. They can be understood, learned, improved. It is merely that these are unselfish, difficult, responsible and divisive tasks, and materially unrewarded wherever value-freedom is the cruder morality of the employers.

In teaching society how to understand itself, and its professions how to use their skills, there may always be a majority of social scientists whose most effective social action, for good or ill, will be their critical and examining judgments of students' work. Inescapably, whether they like it or not, these include judgments of students' valuations, and of their uses of valuation. They are often the most peremptory, *and the most carefully noticed and learned*, of all the teacher's communications to the whole society of which he is a member. In this field, selection for 'value-freedom', and the neglect or condemnation or concealment of the valuations technically required through most of social science, can be enforced by brutal sanctions. To enforce them so does not express an abstinent respect for others' values, whatever its good intentions may sometimes be. It represents vigorous, authoritarian and immoral social action.

So social scientists should communicate as clearly as they can, and be as good as they are able.

14

A Political Science of Society

In politicians' discourse we expect valuable arrangements of true information. That is the structure of any other knowledge of society; and that is the status of whoever discovers and publishes it.

The mixtures of fact, value, selection and reasoning will vary with the problems. But a non-valuing, laws-only program is simply mad. Social scientists who refused controversial work would be as useless as politicians who refused it. Unanimous social science would be as sinister as unanimous politics. Researchers might avoid responsibility by the public service method of silence under political control, but they would have to stop publishing and teaching. Scientists may well defer to the citizens' values, but like politicians they must choose which ones, and their work suffers technically if limited by the citizens' present visions and valuations of facts and options. Altogether a scientistic program, though as political as any other, is not as conservative as is sometimes thought. It cripples causal analysis, distorts selection unhelpfully to any party, and preaches an uncaring morality hostile to most.

Facts are still sovereign, observation objective. Scientists need not adopt the false reporting, the one-eyed short-run commitments or the disreputable persuasions of bad political oratory; nor the blinkered uncandid purposes of some of the science reviewed in this book. They may sometimes come nearer to the good politician's balancing and conciliation of interests. But generally their employments allow them to be honest, altruistic, far-sighted and fair, and the technical fertility of much of their work requires that their valuations be complicated, subtle and unstereotyped. And above all, *good*. They need only fear the spurious simplicities of orators' or salesmen's values if they themselves adopt programs to conceal valuations, or make them unanimous, or 'deduce' them all from agreed value-premises. Or of course, if they value things like height, rigor, abstraction and generality above useful truth.

Whatever the scientists intend, their activity is anyway made political by its subjects. Some social science is inventive or self-verifying. For some, social trial is a more appropriate test than 'proof'. The language of 'hypothesis', 'verification' and 'discovery' can report only a biased selection of the inescapable relations between scientists and the listening, choosing, disagreeing, self-changing subjects of their science. Nor can 'value-free' stand to 'value-structured' as pure to applied. Indeed the more abstract and general the social theory, the more its construction must usually depend on valuations, and the likelier it is to be taught to people under authority. The language of 'application' and 'engineering' has to include in its meaning informing, persuading, tempting and coercing the people engineered. It makes no difference if they, rather than scientists or administrators, do these things for themselves and to each other; they still use the social scientist's work, including whatever values are (whether or not he intended or concealed them) built into the structure of the work.

Of course the tasks of social science are very various. The division of labor will usually provide a quiet life, unembarrassed unanimity and predominantly technical tasks for those who prefer them. This may be just as well, to keep out of mischief a multitude already brain-washed with the values of scientific imitation, careerism, and the unconcerned acceptance of whatever is. Resignation from life is a personal matter. But now some of them want to make death the program for everybody.

The scientistic program seems to distinguish itself from science by the following principles, of which the second frustrates the first, the fourth contradicts the third, and the fifth forgets the third and any other respectable purposes of inquiry:

1. Limit scientific activity to causal explanation.
2. Omit or conceal the selective imagination and valuation required by most causal analysis of human society.
3. Attempt universal laws.
4. However systems differ in fact, speak only of classes of them; but do not limit your class to systems to which identical

explanations sufficiently apply; instead, keep your class large and select only the causes which occur in all the disparate systems in it; then assert that these few causes constitute an independent system, and a sufficient explanation of each system in the class.

5. When your scheme has discovered no new information and has finished reclassifying the old information, then let it pattern eclectic explanations wherever (as in higher education) you can protect a market for them.

In practice this program sometimes selects politically indifferent phenomena for investigation – small details, uninteresting abstracts, such vast but unendangered effects as mere political or social survival. It often requires that socially recognized and valued phenomena be fragmented or compounded, conceptually, into socially unrecognized and morally indifferent identities. This may serve good purposes in particular cases, but as a generalized principle it has no general justification by results. Nor have the other principles which often accompany it – generalized preferences for quantities over qualities, for regulars over locals, for inferred relations over understood mechanisms of relation, for laws over skills, for letting methods choose problems rather than problems choose methods.

In the end, having thus atrophied some scientific skills, the program usually achieves one of three effects. It limits work to problems of no social interest. Or it limits work to areas of (at least among the scientists) political consensus. Or it plugs its own new moralities.

The first effect is obvious. The second is even commoner. Most practical rules of objectivity simply require unanimous valuations. Conventional, trivial, diffuse and ambiguous values are the least likely to be criticized, the easiest to conceal, and the easiest to contrive by authority or fashion – dissent can be dismissed as 'value-structured', not science at all. The technical effects of this are terrible. It inhibits whole ranges of perceptive observation, useful selection, original imagination of alternatives and possibilities and programs, and original discovery of facts and their relations.

Or, worst, objectivity begets its own politics. For a last example of the price of purity, exaggerate a current purification in urban theory. How can cities be measured, compared, explained? Past comparisons have been subjective, measurements untheoretical, purposes *ad hoc* and programmatic. From such impurity, rescue seems urgent. Find a measurable, objective indicator of an abstract, general and commanding quality of 'urbanity', and *then* you will have the beginnings of a pure science to unify and direct the brawling inconsistencies of 'applied' city planning. What are cities, essentially? They are systems of intense, hyper-efficient interaction. Interaction is quintessentially the transmission, reception and exchange of information. The basic unit of information is the simple clause or image, the 'bit'. The basic unit of interaction is the transmission of one bit from one human to another. Call this basic transaction a 'hubit'. Private face-to-face hubits are not countable. But the public channels of communication are all metered, one way or another. Count the hubits they carry. Weight them for distance carried. Divide by time and population, and you have indexed the intensity of interaction. Indeed you are on the way to a universal, abstract and reliable measure of urbanity, and a general theory of it. You also have a political program: to maximize urbanity. That may not mean maximizing the intensity of interaction. Objective studies, of the precise intensity at which neurosis overtakes productivity, will discover the urbane optimum. (Pretend you selected interaction and communication, isolated bits, identified neurosis and defined productivity, and chose the word 'urbanity', without valuing anything. Alternatively, you derived the value of urbanity objectively from the citizens' observed propensity to overcrowd. But refuse to value the bits themselves – the nature of the interactions or the substance of the communications. The pure science would become impure and the applied science would continue quarrelsome if some bits were valued above others.) Now that you are quantized and objective, there is no further call for divisive and subjective impressions of quality and desirability. You can revise the curriculum to tell the next generation of college-educated researchers and planners and legislators that two lies are more urbane than one truth. Two messages of hatred are better than one of love. Two crimes are better than one arrest. A minute of talk is better than two of thought. Taped commercials enhance the urbanity of public transport. Up to the optimum, that is – above the optimum, any silence is better than any protest. Now cross-fertilize with other disciplines which have similarly purified, indexed and quantified 'demand' and 'liberty', to show that ten lousy options enlarge consumers' choices more than five good options could.

Now at last city planning can cease to be utopian–directive. Instead, it can become empirical–adaptive, democratically responsive to the demands of whoever already has (objectively) the dollars, the land and the skills. Science, purged of its subjective and divisive valuations, can give its whole and pure authority to legitimizing winners, and to asking and observing and contriving, neutrally, which victories the winners would like next.

Scientism prospers. It is preached by leaders in many disciplines, and by some of their ablest followers and likeliest supplanters. Not all of it is wilful sin, though I think some is. Its dangers will be under-estimated by anyone who forgets its element of noble ambition, of high scientific hope and good social intention.

The many who suspect its sterility, or its vicious fertility, find themselves on the defensive. Fashion disarms them, making fun of their outmoded politics, their grandmotherly morals and literacy, their primitive notions of truth-telling. Promoters neglect them for teaching so much – or worrying so honestly – that they publish so little. Uncertainties of their own inhibit them – science is a most emotive word and they cannot always distinguish, reliably, science from its imitations. Most concede something – commonly, value-freedom – to modernity. But their confidence and skill are now very important. So are their weapons. Their appropriate rearmament is not so much moral, but is rather the coldest understanding of the principles of scientistic selection, and the reasons for their lack of yield.

For two centuries after Locke and Newton were colleagues, there were more social than natural scientists at work. Then and since, those who valued (and persuaded) the people they studied have helped with social achievements – from the disgrace of some tyrants to the decencies of some democracies, from the loving care of children to the higher education of millions, from safe streets to the modern grace of Stockholm, from the old age pension to the conquest of unemployment and the billions of international aid. Meanwhile the 'immaturity' of social scientism spans a hundred of those years. In the last forty, more resources, more numbers and man-hours and equipment and intelligence, have tried to scientize society than it took to get physics from the astrolabe through Newton to Einstein. Their costs have been high. They include some arrest of honest science and some taming, or confusing, of the young. Their useful yield is trifling. Surely, their excuses have run out?

But social evils can survive without excuses, whether by apathy, honest mistake or selfish intent. Most social scientists sit comfortably high in the hierarchies of race, class, income and power. That need not stop any one of them supplying to other people the services which poorer classes and reforming movements have commonly received, for one reason or another, from individuals richer than themselves. But comfort is seductive, and so is scientism. Scientistic selection avoids the radical imagination or discovery of poor men's chances for social choice or change or conservation. Like other censors, it hedges science and education into the service of established winners. Scientistic values may prompt the 'value-free observation that this educational reinforcement is 'functional for the system'. But others' values should equip them to see in the methodological disputes about scientism a real social conflict: a competition for the talent, conscience, judgment and recruitment of scientists and students, the advisers and next inheritors of power.

In that conflict, the scientist is a citizen. His duty goes beyond discovering and understanding. It becomes his business to win.

Appendix to Chapter 9

Valuation and the relation of cause to effect

Does valuation (other than methodological valuation) merely select causes for report, or is it part of the thought which relates causes to effects?

I

We may begin by distinguishing valuation, at every step, as merely a selector, in order to see if there is any remaining sense in which it is necessary for actually *connecting* causes to effects.

A is a social fact which forces social fact B to change; but A's effect does not specify what B must change into. In fact B changes into E. The conditions necessary for B to turn into E are a very large number including A,P,Q,R,S,T,U, etc. P and Q did not force any change in B, and had no direct effect in producing E. P and Q are conditions which allow E but prevent another, otherwise-possible, effect F. Similarly R prevents G; S and T singly do nothing but if both present prevent H; etc. So if the question is *Why did B change at all?* the answer is A. If the question is *Why did B turn into E-but-not-F?* the answer is APQ. If the question is *Why did B turn into E-but-neither-G-nor-H?* the answer is ARST.

If the question is *What caused E?*, then in social science an exhaustive answer is not practicable. A true law of the type 'Whenever AB, then E' might satisfy the scientist, and remove the engineer's interest to the causes of A and B, to be searched for manipulables rather than regulars. But science has added few such univeral laws to common experience, and few social effects are as simply determined as by any AB, merely. So in practice the scientist, using his own or his client's values, always translates *What caused E* into *What caused E-but-not-FGH*, or *not-GHI*, etc.

The cause R need not be mentioned until somebody introduces the possibility of the alternative effect G. What can require the introduction of G? If G was predictably likely, as a usual or occasional outcome of any disturbance of a B by an A, this is a technical reason for introducing G into the question and therefore R into the answer. If G is valued as a specially good or bad outcome, valuation may introduce it (and R) more often than predictably likelier but less interesting alternatives. G is rarely introduced if predictably impossible in any circumstances; but there may still be reasons for introducing it in order to prove its impossibility. These may be very indirect. For example, suppose that belief in the possibility of G, however widespread, cannot cause G to occur; G remains impossible. I do not care about the pain and frustration suffered by those who nevertheless foolishly expect G. But their expecting G may cause to occur another effect, X, which I think dangerous. So whenever I am asked *What caused E?* I will translate *E-but-not-G*, introduce R among the causes which produce E by prohibiting G, and thus myself help to cause *not-X*. This was the pattern, for example, of Edmund Burke's general explanation of the French Revolution.

Throughout these operations valuations select questions and therefore answers. They still contribute nothing to knowing the causal relation between any A and any E etc. No facts are derived from values, nor values from facts.

2

But social scientists cannot conclude from these analytical separations that many of their own statements about causes and effects can be value-free.

Most questions reach social scientists, or are first posed by them, in the form *How does this system work? What stabilizes it? What is changing it? What causes E? What does A cause?* or *Why do Bs turn into Es?* Complete answers, including all the conditions which determine E by preventing all imaginable alternatives to E, are rarely possible. Limited laws of E's associations (if there are many or recurrent Es) have their limitations expressed in selective explanations, in which the above problems recur. *What caused E?* or *In what conditions will E's association with A occur?* introduce the ordinary scientific break-down into answerable questions; this is typically the scientist's task, and skill, not the client's. Thus the selection of questions and imagined alternatives admits valuation to almost all answers or statements about effects, even though a philosopher could still in principle separate the knowledge of causal links as value-free. There may still be a sense in which it is reasonable to say that the *fact* of R's part in causing E depends on the *valuation* which introduced G as an alternative effect worth considering.

All the symbols above stand for identities, often in practice complex collectives or refined isolations. Valuations often help to choose the concepts and recognize cases of them. It may be possible in principle, but is absurd in practice, to expect that they can all be selected, with unanimous approval, for nothing but the generality of their occurrence and the regularity of their relations; or that a more powerful science would result if they were.

Independently of these arguments, William Dray's argument (above, pp. 18–19) applies to as much work as distinguishes human actions as 'causes' or 'transmitters', or deals in alternatives thought viable because people are judged to have had opportunities to choose them. There is a normative element in many judgments that people 'had a real choice'; in the nomination of their choices as causes, therefore.

Common sense may object: to many questions about causes, there is one obvious answer, true and sufficient whatever the answerer's values may be. This is often so. Sometimes the reason lies in all answerers' agreement about the *relevant* values (whatever else they may disagree about). More often, the manipulative possibilities and the viable alternatives worth considering are clearly and technically limited by the question and by the facts of the case – facts which may well include some unanimous values of the people studied. But only a fraction of social scientists' problems have such simplicity.

References

References to Chapter 1

1 Elie Halévy, *A history of the English people in the nineteenth century*, tr. E. I. Watkin, London: Ernest Benn (also NY: Barnes and Noble) second (revised) ed., 1951, V, 233-6.
2 *Documents diplomatiques Français, 1871-1914*, 2, III, 37.
3 R. C. K. Ensor, *England 1870-1914*, Oxford, 1936, 389.
4 William H. Dray, *Laws and explanation in history*, Oxford, 1957, 150.
5 Dray discusses a good example in *Laws and explanation in history*, 148-9.
6 Bernhard Prince von Bülow, *Memoirs 1897-1903*, tr. F. A. Voigt, London: Putnam, 1931, 326.
7 Halévy, V, 236.
8 Edward Hallett Carr, *Socialism in one country 1924-1926*, London: Macmillan, 1958, I, 93.
9 R. G. Collingwood, *The Idea of History*, Oxford, 1946, 215.
10 *Daedalus*, 91, 3, 1962, 578-598.
11 Blanche E. C. Dugdale, *Arthur James Balfour*, London: Hutchinson, 1936, I, 213.
12 J. L. Garvin, *The Life of Joseph Chamberlain*, III, London: Macmillan, 1934, 158.
13 Lady Victoria Hicks Beach, *Life of Sir Michael Hicks Beach*, London: Macmillan, 1932, II, 109-110.
14 Hicks Beach, II, 153.
15 Garvin, III, 627-8.

References to Chapter 2

1 Elie Halévy, *A history of the English people in the nineteenth century*, tr. E. I. Watkin, London: Ernest Benn (also NY: Barnes and Noble) second (revised) ed., 1951, V, 236.
2 London: Allen & Unwin, 1938.
3 L. B. Namier, *The structure of politics at the accession of George III*, London: Macmillan, 1929;
England in the age of the American revolution, London: Macmillan, 1930.
4 J. L. Garvin, *The Life of Joseph Chamberlain*, III, London: Macmillan, 1934, 627.
5 Julian Amery, *The Life of Joseph Chamberlain*, IV, London: Macmillan, 1951, 390-1, 393-4, 399-400.
6 Amery, 393.

References to Chapter 4

1 tr. Marie A. Lewenz, London: Cassell, 1914.

[2] Spring-Rice to Chirol; Stephen Gwynn (ed.), *The Letters and Friendships of Sir Cecil Spring-Rice, A Record*, London: Constable, 1929, I, 437. The remainder of this section is drawn from Henry Pringle's biography of Roosevelt, and Roosevelt's *The Winning of the West*.

[3] 1893; reprinted in Frederick Jackson Turner, *The Frontier in American History*, NY: Holt, 1920.

[4] page references in the text refer to the third (revised) ed., London: Allen and Unwin, 1938.

[5] D. K. Fieldhouse, ' 'Imperialism': An Historiographical Revision', *Economic History Review*, 2, XIV, 2, 1961, 188–9.

[6] page references are to *Collected Works*, Moscow and London: Lawrence and Wishart, 1964, 22.

[7] *Opportunism and the Collapse of the Second International*, 1916, *Collected Works*, 22, 119.

[8] the same, 110.

[9] Lenin's Preface to Bukharin's *Imperialism and the World Economy*, December 1915, *Collected Works*, 22, 105.

[10] Proposals by the R. S. D. L. P. to the Second Zimmerwald Conference, *Collected Works*, 22, 173.

[11] *Opportunism and the Collapse of the Second International*, *Collected Works*, 22, 111.

[12] page references are to J. A. Schumpeter, *Imperialism and Social Classes*, tr. H. Norden, ed. P. M. Sweezy, N.Y.: Kelley and Millman, and Oxford: Blackwell, 1951.

[13] A. K. Cairncross, *Home and Foreign Investment 1870–1913*, Cambridge, 1953; H. Feis, *Europe the World's Banker 1870–1914*, Yale, 1931; William L. Langer, *European Alliances and Alignments 1871–1890* and *The Diplomacy of Imperialism 1890–1902*, NY: Knopf, 1931 and 1935; Jacob Viner, 'International Finance and Balance of Power Diplomacy 1880–1914', *Southwestern Political and Social Science Quarterly*, IX, 1929, reprinted in Viner, *International Economics*, Glencoe: The Free Press, 1951; W. K. Hancock, *Survey of British Commonwealth Affairs*, Oxford, 1937–1942; J. Gallagher and R. E. Robinson, 'The Imperialism of Free Trade', *Economic History Review*, 2, VI, I, 1953, and *Africa and the Victorians*, London: Macmillan, 1961; Oliver MacDonagh, 'The Anti-Imperialism of Free Trade', *Economic History Review*, 2, XIV, 3, 1962.

[14] 1944; reprinted in Jacob Viner, *International Economics*, Glencoe: The Free Press, 1951, to which page references refer.

[15] 'Marxian, Liberal and Sociological Theories of Imperialism', *Journal of Political Economy*, 39, 1931; page references are to *The Pattern of Imperialism*, Columbia U.P., 1948.

[16] *Economic History Review*, 2, XIV, 2, 1961, 187–209.

[17] NY: Knopf, 1935; page references are to the second edition, 1951.

References to Chapter 5

[1] Dorwin Cartwright's Introduction to Kurt Lewin, *Field Theory in Social Science*, N.Y.: Harper, 1951, xiv.

[2] The drunkard's search is elaborated, and in some circumstances defended, by Abraham Kaplan in *The Conduct of Inquiry*, San Francisco: Chandler, 1964. See also the *Massachusetts Review*, Autumn 1961, where the footnote-checker will be rewarded by much of the argument of this present book, in seven pages.

References

References to Chapter 6

1 1952; reprinted in Patrick Gardiner (ed.) *Theories of History*, Glencoe: The Free Press, 1959, 363–384.
2 William H. Dray, *Philosophy of History*, N.J.: Prentice-Hall, 1964, 55–8; and in 'Some Causal Accounts of the American Civil War', *Daedalus*, 91, 3, 1962, 578–98.
3 E. Durkheim, *The Rules of Sociological Method* (1895), tr. S. A. Solovay and J. H. Mueller, Glencoe: The Free Press, 1938, 95.
4 Robert K. Merton, *Social Theory and Social Structure*, revised ed., Glencoe: The Free Press, 1957, 51.
5 for example Melvin Tumin, in papers cited in his article referred to on p. 181; and Howard Brotz, 'Functionalism and Dynamic Analysis', *European Journal of Sociology*, II, 1961, 170–9.
6 *Social Theory and Social Structure*, 40.

References to Chapter 7

1 Emile Durkheim, *The Rules of Sociological Method*, Glencoe: The Free Press, 1938, 125.
2 Maurice Duverger, *Introduction to the Social Sciences*, tr. Malcolm Anderson, London: Allen and Unwin, 1964, 15.
3 Werner J. Cahnman and Alvin Boskoff, 'Sociology and History: Reunion and Rapprochement' in their (ed.) *Sociology and History: Theory and Research*, N.Y.: The Free Press, 1964, 7.
4 H. Zetterberg, *On Theory and Verification in Sociology*, N.Y., 1953, Ch. I.
5 Ernest Greenwood, 'The Practice of Science and the Science of Practice' (1959) reprinted in Warren G. Bennis, Kenneth D. Benne and Robert Chin (eds.) *Theory and Practice of Planned Change: Readings in Human Relations*, N.Y.: Holt Rinehart and Winston, 1962. I thank Professor Greenwood for this reference.
6 Robert K. Merton, *Social Theory and Social Structure*, Glencoe: The Free Press, rev. ed. 1957, 48.
7 *Social Theory and Social Structure*, 49.
8 1929; reprinted in M. N. Srinivas (ed.) *Method in Social Anthropology, Selected Essays by A. R. Radcliffe-Brown*, Chicago, 1958.
9 1951; reprinted in *Method in Social Anthropology*, 128–9.
10 three real candidates, unacknowledged because cited out of context.
11 Albert K. Cohen and James F. Short, Jr., 'Juvenile Delinquency', in Robert K. Merton and Robert A. Nisbet (eds.) *Contemporary Social Problems, An Introduction to the Sociology of Deviant Behavior and Social Disorganization*, N.Y.: Harcourt Brace and World, 1961, 111–112.
12 Patrick Gardiner (ed.) *Theories of History*, Glencoe: The Free Press, 1959; Patrick Gardiner, *The Nature of Historical Explanation*, Oxford, 1952; William H. Dray, *Laws and Explanations in History*, Oxford, 1957, and *Philosophy of History*, Prentice-Hall, 1964; Morton White, *Foundations of Historical Knowledge*, N.Y.: Harper and Row, 1965.
13 see pp. 275–85, 299–318.
14 see for example many of the works cited in note 12, above; also Michael Scriven, 'New Issues in the Logic of Explanation' in Sydney Hook, (ed.) *Philosophy and History*, N.Y.U. Press, 1963; a review of the controversy in A. Danto, *Analytic Philosophy of History*, Columbia University Press, 196;

and of course, the works of Weber, Dilthey, Croce and Collingwood. In *Foundations of Historical Knowledge* Morton White argues that singular explanatory statements about necessary but insufficient causal conditions do imply that a certain type of deductive argument is available, but do not depend on its being known or stated, and do not require that the implied laws have any generality.

[15] in Gardiner, *Theories of History*, 466–7.

References to Chapter 8

[1] 1916; quoted in Patrick Gardiner (ed.) *Theories of History*, The Free Press, 1959, 240.
[2] *The Idea of History*, Oxford, 1946, 214.
[3] 'History and Theory – The Concept of Scientific History', *History and Theory*, I, 1961, from which all following quotations of Berlin are taken.
[4] London: Routledge and Kegan Paul; page references are to The Humanities Press edition, N.Y., 1958.
[5] quoted in Gardiner, *Theories of History*, 234.
[6] Abraham Kaplan, *The Conduct of Inquiry*, San Francisco: Chandler, 1964, 334–5.
[7] see Elton Mayo, *The Human Problems of an Industrial Civilization*, N.Y.: Macmillan, 1933.

References to Chapter 9

[1] John Maynard Keynes, *The General Theory of Employment, Interest and Money*, London: Macmillan, 1936, 50–1.
[2] N.Y.: Wiley, 1956; revised edition, Harper Torchbooks, 1963.
[3] 1915; page references are to the edition reprinted by A. M. Kelley, N.Y., 1964.
[4] Herbert Simon, *Models of Man*, N.Y.: Wiley, London: Chapman and Hall, 1957, 115–144.
[5] see above, pp. 180–3.
[6] *The Quarterly Journal of Economics*, LXVIII, 1954.
[7] *What is History?*, London: Macmillan, and N.Y.: Alfred Knopf, 1961, 132–3.
[8] N.Y.: Oxford University Press, 1956.
[9] N.Y.: Oxford University Press, 1959.

References to Chapter 10

[1] Begun in *The Structure of Social Action*, 1937, but most of the theory referred to here is in later works, especially *The Social System*, 1951; the third chapter of *Working Papers in the Theory of Action*, with collaborators, 1953; *Family, Socialization and Interaction Process*, with other collaborators, 1955; *Economy and Society*, with Neil J. Smelser, 1956; and 'General Theory in Sociology' in Robert K. Merton and others (ed.) *Sociology Today*, 1959. If criticism of Parsons' neglect of power is unjust, that ought to be evident from 'On the Concept of Political Power', *Proceedings of the American Philosophical Society*, 107, 3, 1963; 'Some Reflections on the Place of Force in Social Process' in H. Eckstein (ed.) *Internal War*, 1964; 'Cause and Effect in Sociology' in Daniel Lerner (ed.) *Cause and Effect*, 1965; and 'The Point of View of the Author' in Max Black (ed.) *The Social Theories of Talcott Parsons*, 1961. There is a full

list of Parsons' publications to 1963 in his *Social Structure and Personality* 1964.
2 in Max Black (ed.) *The Social Theories of Talcott Parsons*, N.J.: Prentice-Hall, 1961, 305.
3 Talcott Parsons in Merton, Broom and Cottrell, (ed.) *Sociology Today*, N.Y.: Basic Books, 1959, 5–9.
4 Morton A. Kaplan, *System and Process in International Politics*, N.Y.: Wiley, 1957.
5 'The Point of View of the Author', Black, *The Social Theories of Talcott Parsons*, 337.
6 the same, 349–50.
7 Kurt Lewin, 'Quasi-Stationary Social Equilibria and the Problem of Permanent Change', 1947, reprinted in Warren G. Bennis, Kenneth D. Benne and Robert Chin (ed.) *The Planning of Change*, N.Y.: Holt, Rinehart and Winston, 1962, 236.
8 especially his life of Michael Bakunin, his critique of realism in *The Twenty Years Crisis 1919–39*, and the aspirations expressed in *The New Society* and in chapters 5 and 6 of *What is History?* Nor does his own progress from public to newspaper to academic life look like a mad pursuit of power for himself.
9 page references are to the London edition, Routledge and Kegan Paul, 1956.
10 page references are to the London edition, Routledge and Kegan Paul, 1959; copyright Stanford University Press.

References to Chapter 13

1 Paul Samuelson, in Daniel Lerner (ed.) *Cause and Effect*, N.Y.: The Free Press, 1965, 125.
2 George C. Homans, *The Human Group*, N.Y., 1950; quotation from the English edition, Routledge and Kegan Paul, 1951, 443.
3 In 'Problems in Methodology' in Robert K. Merton, Leonard Broom and Leonard S. Cottrell (eds.) *Sociology Today*, N.Y.: Basic Books, 1959, Paul Lazarsfeld regrets that so little attention has been paid to the relations between concepts and their indicators; but he goes on to argue that it matters little, since any sensible choice of indicators will usually do as well as any other!

Index

Made in the USA
Middletown, DE
11 November 2023

42397192R00267